A TENDER VOYAGE

慈航

继秉真 著

A Tender Voyage

CHILDREN AND CHILDHOOD
IN LATE IMPERIAL CHINA

Ping-chen Hsiung

STANFORD UNIVERSITY PRESS

STANFORD, CALIFORNIA

Stanford University Press
Stanford, California

Cover image: "Children Playing with a Toad," by Su Tsuo (Sung
dynasty). A child holding a toad is a frequent image in pictures
of children. The picture vividly shows a child frightening another
with a toad, which a third finds amusing. This picture was said
to be printed by Su Tsuo, son of Su Han-Ch'ên. Courtesy of the
National Palace Museum, Taiwan, Republic of China.

Printed in the United States of America on acid-free, archival-
quality paper

Library of Congress Cataloging-in-Publication Data

Hsiung, Ping-chen, 1952-
    A tender voyage : children and childhood in late imperial
China / Ping-chen Hsiung.
        p.   cm.
    Includes bibliographical references and index.
    ISBN 0-8047-4164-6 (clothbound : alk. paper)
    ISBN 0-8047-5754-2 (pbk. : alk. paper)
        1. Children—China—History.   I. Title.
HQ792.C6X56 2004
305.23'0951—dc22   2004005497

Typeset by Integrated Composition Systems in 10/12.5 Sabon

Original Printing 2004

Last figure below indicates year of this printing:
12   11   10   09   08   07

Assistance for the publication of this book was provided by
the Chiang Ching-kuo Foundation for International Scholarly
Exchange.

For Yo-yo and Ch'ing-ch'ing from our never-never land.

Contents

Figures

Chronological Table of China's Dynasties

Dynasty	Period
Hsia (unsubstantiated)	2205–1766 B.C. or 1994–1523 B.C.
Shang	1766–1122 B.C. or 1523–1027 B.C.
Chou	1122 or 1027 B.C.–221 B.C.
Western Chou	1122 or 1027 B.C.–771 B.C.
Eastern Chou	771 B.C.–256 B.C.
(Spring and Autumn period)	(722 B.C.–481 B.C.)
(Warring States period)	(403 B.C.–221 B.C.)
Ch'in	221 B.C.–206 B.C.
Han	206 B.C.–220 C.E.
Western Han	206 B.C.–9 C.E.
Hsin (Wang Mang)	9 C.E.–23 C.E.
Eastern Han	23 C.E.–220 C.E.
Three Kingdoms Era	220 C.E.–280 C.E.
Chin	266 C.E.–420 C.E.
Western Chin	266 C.E.–316 C.E.
Eastern Chin	316 C.E.–420 C.E.
Northern and Southern Dynasties	420 C.E.–589 C.E.
Sui	589 C.E.–618 C.E.
T'ang	618 C.E.–907 C.E.
Five Dynasties Era	907 C.E.–960 C.E.
Sung	960 C.E.–1279 C.E.
Northern Sung	960 C.E.–1127 C.E.
Southern Sung	1127 C.E.–1279 C.E.
Yüan	1279 C.E.–1368 C.E.
Ming	1368 C.E.–1644 C.E.
Ch'ing	1644 C.E.–1912 C.E.
Republic of China	1912 C.E.–

Preface

This is a preliminary study of young children (from birth to age seven or eight) and early childhood in the late imperial period of Chinese history. History of children and history of childhood are not one and the same thing, although the former helps bring about a reconsideration for the latter. The understandings of children and childhood have been complicated by definitions. Unlike the Western-orientated and commonly held modern notion of a child in a biophysical sense (namely the youngest members of humanity experiencing the earliest stage of human life), the "child" in Chinese society could also be understood, and thus treated, as a social status (as junior members in a household) or a familiar role (the young as opposed to the old). The concept of adult children in relation to their parents, in modern sociological terms, suggests that this second category or layer of meaning of a child exists in other societies and culture as well. In their original contexts, the biophysical "child" in the first meaning and the social-cultural "juniors" in the second meaning are often (though not necessarily always) related. It is usually the younger members (*t'ung-tzu*) of society that are treated and expected to assume the "junior" (*pei-yu*) status or roles in that group; of course many people in this status or role tend to be at the beginning of their lives, in a dependent stage. The two, however, are not entirely overlapped in meaning or function, as quite a number of "junior" members in a family or social setting might no longer be in their physically young state at all. Servants, foreigners, or other "social misfits" in their adulthood continue to assume or be forced into "minor" or "inferior" statuses.

There is a third philosophical or abstract meaning of a child: the embodiment of the virtue or quality of innocence. This has many important effects in the development of Chinese culture and history. This aspect of human existence can be found in notions of a "child's heart" deliberated in left-wing Neo-Confucian thought; a childlike touch admired in Chinese brushwork calligraphy, painting, or poetry; and the infantile smile and childlike vigor envisioned in Taoist philosophy or alchemy. This definition originally may have been inspired by—but eventually works rhetorically against—the biophysical or sociocultural understandings of the infant and the child.

During my twenty plus years studying and researching in this field, much has happened in the scholarship of both historical studies and the humanities. The attempt to uncover children and childhood in the past not only fulfills a curiosity but also fills an academic gap. This unwittingly carries an implication to question some of the very propositions that history and modern historiography has for a long while assumed. When intellectuals like Philippe Ariès raised the question of "the discovery of childhood" (or the lack thereof) in history, he was participating in an intellectual and cultural terrain where the progression of time had been presupposed. He himself, however, as the complexity of his work aptly shows, harbored much ambivalence about the nature of that progress as it relates to a modern existence for the young and old. During the past few centuries, long before Ariès, enlightened intellectuals everywhere, including Hu Shih in early-twentieth-century China, consciously or unconsciously advocated the symbolic meaning of childhood and the treatment of children as a measurement of accomplishments of civilization and a universal yardstick for social progress. "A friend of mine told me," Hu once lectured with his old resolute flair, "that one but needs to look at three matters before he or she delivers a final verdict about a society: he or she can either look at the way people treat their children, the way they treat their women, or the way they spend their free time."[1] So the status of any society—be they civilized, civilizing, or uncivilized (or as he put it, barbaric)—is determined by the "state of evolution" in either the concept, the attitude, or actual treatment of infants and children. That is, the "emergence" of due care and concern for the very young has been deemed as both a revealing indication of people's ordinary decency in history and perhaps even more tellingly as a sign of professional elevation in conscience and consciousness in the scholarly pursuit of the humanities.

Venturing forth with such sweeping views and concerns, I fear the following can hardly stand as a monograph on Chinese children's history, although the opportunity to attempt a book of the kind, granted the time and vocational freedom, would be gratifying. In its place, here is a collection of essays to fill the void as a start on such an investigation. A stack of short stories can hardly be a novel, so these smaller works on issues or vignettes related to infant's and children's lives are a patchwork representation of Chinese history which may provide useful building blocks for varied narratives and more structured analyses. My work over the past twenty plus years in an Asian institution has not permitted an execution of a different project. These eight chapters grew out of speeches and papers I have been asked to deliver in English over this long period. They have since been revised, but some tones of the lecture remain. Some of the materials covered here were drawn from my studies more substantially presented in Chinese (Chapters 1, 2, 3, and 6), or German (the latter third of the Introduction) but none is a translation; all originated as works on the subject with an English audience in mind.[2] The rest of the chapters have no counterparts in any language. The three books I have published on children and childhoods in Chinese, and the fourth in the making, do give the topic a more structured treatment.[3] More room is obviously available here for minute enhancements, philosophical reflections, and an overall debate by comparison. I have explicitly and implicitly woven the Western experience and English language scholarship into the investigation, contemplation, and presentation of these materials.

My personal curiosity in the subject grew predominantly out of a childhood curiosity, long before history appeared on the horizon as an occupational or intellectual pursuit. To tell the story any other way would be making more of a vocational claim than was the case. The customary admission of singular responsibility for everything expressed can therefore be taken literally here. For an undertaking that has sprawled so long over time and space, mostly as a monologue, its pitfalls are easy to see. This considered, there are clear intellectual debts to be acknowledged as well as better visions to be dreamed of. For the latter, if I were the reader, I would like to see an elaboration of the economic and institutional aspects of children's and childhood history. Child labor at home and apprentices in the workshops of various trades also need further investigation. The status of the very young in state policies and law is another area with materials in need of treatment. In the works to come, I and others may be able to take on the question of children and childhood in religion, philosophy, aesthetics, and the arts. I have attempted a preliminary survey on children's literature, and I am uncovering the world of games and toys of the young.[4] Hopefully these may only create a hunger for more. As an author I cannot but hanker after the joining of kindred spirits from fields other than my own.

Still, since there are always ample ways to start something out of nothing, an anxiously fixed desire can turn the least relevant thing to the most stimulating. This all derives from the belief that the essence of knowledge is multidisciplinary and cross-cultural. For many decades, and in curious circumstances, professional and personal opportunities have led me to a number of authors and laborers on children and childhood in different lands and with varying viewpoints. The following, in many ways, is a field report from those experiences on an undeclared joint project, a tribute to an ongoing conversation with other fellow workers on a puzzle of an unrecognized kind.

Many gave their encouragement in good faith: Chang P'êng-yüan, Lawrence Gartner, Arthur Kleinman, Dorothy Ko, James Lee, Susan Mann, Marty Powers, William Rowe, Ann Waltner, Yü An-Pang, and Angela Zito. These colleagues and other friends far and near have generously cheered me on while seeing only the slightest sign of what finally appears here. Muriel Bell and her staff at Stanford University Press rewarded me with a professional experience in seeing this book through production.

For a project of this nature, the personal debt is easier to imagine: to my father, a children's story writer, who was happily surprised by his encounter with Rousseau in his later years and who glossed the frontispiece with his calligraphy; and to my mother, the primary school teacher for whom being an adult seems much more difficult than remaining a child. The link between their world and that of mine needs little explanation. As to my children, though kept in happy oblivion of my daytime activities, they poured forth infantlike smiles and childlike noises in such a disarming way that they filled in the imperative and creative voice and color of the project. To Yo-yo and Ching-ching, the best on-site representatives of the young lives inadequately uncovered and imagined here, this book is dedicated—in appreciation of the existence of similar children in times past, present, and future. My soul mate Mu-chou listened and lived with this book for as long as it was constructed, acting all the while as if that were the most delightful task. A small grower of a seedling could wish for no better company. Anyone who believes in the magic of air, water, and the sun to the bringing forth of life will need no further words from me.

Children and Childhood in Traditional China

Historical Studies of Children

Historical studies of children and childhood have not attracted major attention. The small number of scholars who venture into the field, with scattered efforts and seemingly random results, nevertheless labor with certain convictions. To them, history concerning children, or viewing the world from the vantage point of youth, is by no means a trivial matter. It is necessary, valuable, and imperative.

Among scholars, a certain necessity appeared the earliest: the challenge of the question of "the discovery of childhood in history." The artful and provocative work of Philippe Ariès took readers, historians, and others by surprise with his then novel idea that the notion of childhood in Western history was only a recent invention.[1] A number of industrious scholars, Europeanists especially, have since challenged this thesis, coming forth with evidence of early concepts of childhood as well as the evolving experience of children in history.[2] However, the premises that prompted historians of mentality like Ariès in their quest for a history of childhood remain valid. Namely, a better understanding of people's ideas and treatment of children must constitute an important part of the overall appraisal of that era. In fact, in Ariès's case, such an understanding was a means of accessing the core values of any given society. That notwithstanding, followers of the idea or the method remain few. For although manners and mentalities have drawn increasing attention from historians in the wake of the influence of the Annales school with its refreshing look at the humble and the obscure, the lives of infants and children have never claimed the interest of mainstream historians. This is the case despite the fact that Ariès and his critics have proven that children and childhood not only have a history, but also that the subject carries unique value as its own field of history. Their works judiciously demonstrate that the care of the young was never a fixed matter in time. Thus a society's evolving understanding of their youngest and most vulnerable members is in itself a story worth knowing and telling. Partly due to the vital nature of the endeavor, there has never been a lack of information, or of views, although the disconcerting abundance of material may overwhelm the conventional historical methodology.

While historians of mentality tackled the concept of childhood, family historians also felt compelled to look into the conditions of children in the past. Information pertaining to the experiences of the very young, though not the sole focus, became an important part of their narrative. The history of infants and children, for them, not only informs the study of families, it is also necessary to the familial story of society. A number of fine research in American and European history in the 1970s demonstrated the benefits that such a study of childhood could contribute to the general understanding of family and community. Philip Greven Jr., in his captivating reconstruction of four generations of family life in colonial Andover, shows how an appreciation for the experience of the young contributes to a better understanding of successive generations. He devotes particular discussion to the search for independence that developed out of the traditional mode of dependence among children of families in mid-eighteenth-century Massachusetts.[3] Readers as a result recognize the interdependence of all generations in their formulation of individuality as well as daily familial operations. John Demos's study of family life in Plymouth colony, entitled *A Little Commonwealth* (1970), shows that parent-child relations, as well as infant and childhood experiences, have become a regular concern for family historians.[4] Recognizing the "everyday routine" of "average people" in the fields of family and social history led scholars to the discovery of children and childhood. By the time Lawrence Stone produced his exhaustive observations on family, sex, and marriage in early modern England, therefore, adult-child relations constituted one of the cornerstones of his theory.[5]

Works on long-term changes in family history have also incorporated information on children. Steven Ozment's treatment of family life in Reformation Europe, Michael Mitterauer and Reinhard Sieder's explanation of the evolving function of families in central and Western Europe, Beatrice Gottlieb's analysis of the family in the West from the Black Death to the industrial age, and Ralph Houlbrooke's investigation of the English family from the mid-fifteenth to the late seventeenth centuries, all devote extensive attention to the questions of procreation, child rearing, parent-child relations, and the physical, social, and emotional conditions of children.[6] Studies of women's history and motherhood have also increased people's awareness of domestic conditions related to early-childhood experience.[7] The historical concept and the daily experience of the very young has become much more delineated than they were a mere few decades ago. In fact from the late 1970s and the early 1980s onward, discussions of children's lives have become integrated into standard Western family history, with parent-child experiences receiving special attention and unexpected discoveries.[8]

Scholars interested in changing prejudices and social welfare also turned their attention to issues regarding children, including such topics as infanticide, child desertion, and child labor. Selective elimination or active killing of newborn infants or young children, whether as habitual customs or as a way to limit family size, were thought to be found only in ancient and Asian societies. More recently, scholars have considered the existence of infanticide in the history of Western societies.[9] In addition to patterns and statistics, studies of infanticide in premodern times help reveal the socioeconomic circumstances for its occurrence. Since, in such considerations, the social and legal definitions of the "infant" were often broader than that of the neonatal, these studies invariably address human motivations as well as the cultural and historical environment.[10]

Desertion and neglect of children, a lasting and fairly widespread phenomenon, whether perceived from the viewpoint of the deserters or the deserted, have also been examined accordingly. Historical studies focusing on the fate of unwanted children in different eras and in various places have added to the understanding of the strength and quality of the social fabric.[11] Whatever the focus or concern, such studies have yielded a picture of abandonment, adoption, and foster care that had long been neglected as a vital aspect of social and institutional history.[12] The sudden surge of these studies in the 1980s and their shared outlook suggest, therefore, a new intellectual consciousness. The picture they present collectively extends beyond the discoveries of mere details in the lives of children to a wide host of issues on popular attitudes, social practices, family life, community networks, politics, urban and rural relations, economic developments, and demographic realities—a good example of the larger relevance and greater ramifications children's history can produce for the general knowledge of the past. A society's habitual "disposal" of at least a quarter of its newborns, or its witnessing three-fourths of its children perish before reaching their fifth year, obviously indicates a great deal about its inner workings and daily circumstances.

Child labor and the policy and laws it generates have also received recent historical attention. Along with scholars in other fields, social and demographic historians became increasingly aware of the fact that work was as much a part of children's routine experience as play. For a large number of children in premodern times, it represented a more significant activity than education or schooling. Although still lacking systematic analyses, historians of ancient Rome, early modern England, and colonial America have ingeniously pieced together data to depict the working life of youngsters.[13]

Those who study child labor in the early modern and modern era also unavoidably encounter the question of children's "rights and protection" as concepts that led the reforms in social legislation and welfare policies. Meanwhile, protoindustrialization presented new opportunities for employment of children, albeit under harsh conditions.[14] Just as infanticide and desertion bring up the questions of calculated cruelty and neglect, on the one hand, and foster care and philanthropy, on the other, the world of laboring children touches upon communal reliance, pauperism, and self-help. Scholars looking into the foundling hospitals, the poor laws, or workhouses often focus first on the administration of welfare. Inevitably, these discussions concern the development of civil liberty, social legislation, and state intervention, not just the lives of children. Similar was the issue of early education. Though not directly related to social welfare, it was concerned with the same kind of institutional construction of childhood as those mentioned in economic production and the labor force, or foster homes and adoption procedures. With varying degrees of success, employing different methods and teaching materials, and under all kinds of circumstances, an ever-increasing number of young children began to have access to pedagogical instruction in the early modern era. Historians of early education, though not necessarily with a sole interest in children, have uncovered much about the literary experience and the intellectual process pertaining to different learning activities.[15] A number of these studies contain information about vocational training, including that for nonelite children, even specific educational initiatives for girls, providing important glimpses into another significant, though previously blank, area.[16] Together, these studies demonstrate that for a fair understanding of any social change, a historical account that omits the experiences of the very young seems "incomplete at best and distorted at worst."

Historical demographers have also shown interest in children.[17] For them, coming to terms with the fate of the youngest group in the population is indispensable to a responsible grasp of their subject in the aggregate. Though mostly working with quantitative data and statistical models, they pose questions and present findings that are of vital value to historical studies of children. Historical demography not only reveals information about infanticide, but it also addresses the social implications of birth, death, average life expectancy, migration, and marriage. It thus creates new possibilities for structuring an understanding of children's lives as they move through time, space, and changing circumstances.[18] Historians have subsequently become aware of some of the fundamental forces under which the young coexist with the adults. The many discoveries in demographic history, minute or grand, often shatter old impressions or establish startling new assumptions in overall historical understanding. Furthermore, the demographer's emphasis on life cycles and the interconnections among personal time, group (or family) time, and historical time help to address the relations between individual lives and collective involvement, which suggests a linkage between microstudies and macrohistory. Historians of children and childhood everywhere, therefore, have a duty to make clear how such insights may relate their seemingly "insignificant" and marginal subject to the broader field of history or the study of children in other disciplines.[19]

This brief overview of recent inquiries into childhood history indicates the kind of directions and categories that may be pursued, whether from the angle of history of mentality, family, welfare, education, or demography. Many other important and potentially fruitful questions could of course be added to the list. At the end of which this study of childhood history and historical understanding of children, as those on women, the lower classes, ethnic or religious minorities, social misfits and other overlooked subjects can become legitimate intellectual pursuits. As a historical investigation, it begins by focusing on the experiences of the youngest section of the human population but soon mingles with those of the "mainstream." Together they also suggest the kind of intellectual curiosity and academic outlook such inquiries entail and further stimulate. One distinct sociocultural position for modern researchers to contemplate, both in the West and elsewhere, is the very modern definition of "children" and "childhood." Based primarily on biophysical understandings and the Freudian psychological scheme, the bottom line for all child studies, it is rarely treated as a hypothesis with specific cultural historical contexts.[20] In addition to the Enlightenment and its faith in rationality and linear progression, often found at the root of most studies on children and the history of childhood, modern investigations in psychology, cognitive development, and education remain powerful positivist forces behind most of the interest in children, including research into the childhood experience of the past.[21]

The Case of China

Interest in children and childhood thus far claims even less attention among historians of China than among those elsewhere. The history of mentality, the field that first spurred the history of childhood, has yet to attract significant attention from historians of China. The "concept of children and childhood" has hardly been an issue in Chinese history, as the main forces in modern Chinese historiography have thus far been preoccupied with quite different sets of problems. Any preliminary examination on children and childhood in Chinese history will also present findings at variance from similar undertakings in the West.

Amid this general oblivion, two works have recently dealt with the Chinese case at length. One is Jon Saari's study of the transitional nature of the lives of schoolboys growing up in the late nineteenth and early twentieth centuries, *Legacies of Childhood* (1990), and the other is Anne Behnke Kinney's edited volume *Chinese Views of Childhood* (1995).[22] Saari's study remains the only monographic treatment on childhood experience in Chinese history. As its title and many chapter headings suggest, Saari gives much of his attention to the problem of "growing up Chinese," especially to the particularities of that experience "in a time of crisis," that is, in the modern era. A richly nuanced study, it is a pioneering endeavor, shouldering many tasks and answering and raising a wide array of questions. Its primary purpose, however, is to show how a particular generation of elite schoolboys shaped their own views and self-management during social and political upheaval, applying Freudian and Ericksonian theses on character formation and personality development. The author succeeds in this to an appreciable degree. In his study of a mostly elite group of Chinese youths growing up at the very end of the Ch'ing dynasty (1644–1911) and the beginning of the Republic (1912–present) Saari reveals the sociopsychological theories of socialization, identity formation, and personal crisis, which, although useful, are ultimately limiting as intellectual tools. For the most part, Saari's sources are school-age youths (*shao-nien* or *ch'ing-nien*) seven to fourteen years old or even fifteen to their early twenties, rather than young children (*êrh-t'ung*). The questions he raises concerning the Chinese way of "learning to become human" (*hsüeh tso jên*) are therefore only partially resolved. The vital differences among infants, children, and young people with regard to the problem of growing up hardly receive adequate treatment. Even so, the work stands as a valuable groundbreaker.

Kinney's symposium volume, as its title suggests, is an overview of expressed "views of childhood" throughout China's long history. It explores the childhood question from a variety of angles (literature, art history, history, medicine, philosophy, and so forth) from early China to the twentieth century. Though not "a rounded history of childhood in China," as C. John Sommerville succinctly pointed out, the book focuses on "cultural and ideological aspects," presenting a good collective survey at an early stage in anticipation of "a social history of children."[23] Each essay contains merits of its own. Kinney's review of the philosophical, popular-mythical, and hagiographic origins of ideas related to children and Wu Hung's piece on the engraving of child images in early Chinese art are useful explorations inviting further elaboration.[24] For the late imperial period, Pei-yi Wu's fascinating introduction to the evolving parent-child bond brings a wealth of information. The essay addresses questions regarding the conditions of young children within the context of the inner world of Chinese familial relations and emotional life. It utilizes a wealth of the necrological literature (poems and burial inscriptions) to gain access to the experiential aspects of child-hood and the construction of emotional bonds in the formation of adult-child relations. Pei-yi Wu also points out that a general trend toward fo-cusing attention on children occurred from pre-Sung (roughly tenth cen-tury) times to the eighteenth century, with particular influence from the philosophy of the Wang Yang-ming school and the beginning of "the cult of the child." Pei-yi Wu's depiction of loving father-daughter ties and a poten-tially positive bias toward young girls, at least among educated Chinese families, also demands further examination.[25]

A few other essays in the volume discuss issues related to the lives of in-fants and children in the late imperial period. Charlotte Furth's analysis of the concept of the beginning of life and its origins in biomedical sources fa-miliarizes the reader with basic terminology and notions regarding birth, growth, and development.[26] Ann Waltner's provocative contemplation of the possible gender linkages among female infanticide, the dowry system, and the competitive marriage market in Ming society is a bold and imagi-native attempt that invites deeper exploration into the world of the "gen-dered status of children" in context to the political, economic, social, and cultural circumstances of this era.[27] Angela Ki Che Leung contrasts the new features of relief institutions for children in nineteenth-century China with their counterparts from earlier times as well as with those in the West. The emerging view of the child as a social being belonging to the community, she asserts, contrasts with the increasingly less protective treatment children were receiving from the state.[28]

As a whole, most essays in Kinney's edited anthology provide valuable clues to long neglected topics in Chinese studies. Many of the findings, in part due to the preliminary nature of the field, require further clarification and systematic investigation. These merits notwithstanding, this first fully fledged attempt to examine views of Chinese childhood fails on a few im-portant accounts. One, the conceptualization and treatment of the concept of children and childhood are imprecise. As the first work of its kind, it may be quite understandable to have included essays about gestation (Charlotte Furth) as well as about the adolescent in *Hong-lou Mêng* (*Dream of the Red Chamber*) (Lucien Miller) or rebellious youths in the People's Republic of China (Mark Lupher).[29] To prevent overly vague conclusions, working definitions are needed to distinguish traditional Chinese and/or general modern concepts of the stages of life, including infancy, childhood (early childhood, later childhood), adolescence, and youth. Second, scholars need to establish a clearer intellectual framework in order to produce a more sys-tematic and balanced analysis from these, at times, sparse, random, and seemingly anecdotal observations across massive periods of time and widely varying regions.

The very "Chinese-ness" of these cases, and their changing characters in time, need further explanation. Assorted views of children and childhood throughout Chinese history can leave readers with an unresolved curiosity about the familiar problem of "generality" versus "particularity" or theoretical concepts as opposed to everyday practice. Nor can the readers be certain as to the basic character of the kind of historical changes taking place around these views or the comparative significance of Chinese notions of childhoods in the past. Tentatively, one might ask whether the survey has whetted scholars' appetite for Chinese views on childhood. Does it tempt us to discover whether Chinese children's experience itself has changed and, if so, for better or for worse over these thousands of years? More importantly still, whose views or which children's childhood did such changes represent, during what period, in which places, under what circumstances, through what process, and for what reasons? Until such basic questions are confronted, our observations and concerns about things related to children and childhood will remain superficial, even superfluous, to the structural intellect.

Other related studies explore these issues in part: Ann Waltner's investigation of the practice of adoption and Hui-chen Wang Liu's and Charlotte Furth's analyses of clan rules and family instructions address key questions in Chinese family history.[30] Angela Ki Che Leung's study of relief agencies for orphans sheds light on the institutions and cultural environment in which the young lived; her work on early education in the Ch'ing reveals the extrafamilial forces impacting the "handling" of children.[31] The pioneering works by Liu Ts'ui-jung, James Lee, and Cameron Campbell and their associates in Chinese historical demography, furthermore, provide vital statistical data and answer key questions regarding the birth, death, and treatment of infants and children.[32] Even works in intellectual history and moral philosophy, rooted in the culture's peculiar approach to the ethics of neonatal life, can have much to say regarding historical "attitudes" toward, or "management" of, "the child." Joanna Handlin's insights into the concerns and labors of the sixteenth-century gentry-scholar Lü K'un (1536–1618) provide one such example.[33] All of these cry out for a more structured comprehension of the lives of children, one rooted in a substantiated conceptual framework.

Against this background, this study represents a collection of essays and lectures prepared under varying circumstances; it is not a preconceived and comprehensively executed monographic treatment. As such, the essays could hardly meet the requirement of an introduction to, or an organized presentation of, children and childhood in late imperial Chinese history. Yet, when examined with its intellectual siblings in Chinese academia, this study does suggest a set of thoughts and systematic inquiries. Although not a thorough treatment on the subject, this is a multifaceted, widely documented narrative on a few topics related to the subject of children and childhood in Chinese history. It asks broad historical questions, even though the answers may not be readily forthcoming.[34]

For instance, Have the lives of young children in China changed much? If so, In what ways, at what points of time, and how? As the rest of the population moved through China's long history, did children fare better or worse? Broadly and crudely speaking, between the establishment of a classical mode in pre-Han (221 B.C.–220 A.D.) times and the massive transformation after the mid-nineteenth century, two periods suggest themselves as time markers: the Southern Sung (1161–1279) and the mid-Ming (1368–1644) both ushered in mixed blessings for China's younger population. During the Southern Sung, or between the twelfth and thirteenth centuries, powerful social and cultural forces changed the lives of children in significant ways. Paramount among these was the maturing of Neo-Confucian philosophy and the establishment of pediatric medicine.[35] The former attempted to chart social, moral, and behavioral codes and to define the emotional and educational experiences of the young, thereby influencing domestic life.[36] Neo-Confucian philosophy also influenced clan organizations at the social level and character formation and daily attitudes on the individual level. The Ch'êng-Chu school's emphasis on the values of quietness (ching), respect (ching), and sincerity (ch'êng) redefined Chinese child-rearing culture and early-education training within families and in communal schools.[37] A certain emphasis on acquiescence, quietness, control in expression, and bodily gestures crept into the everyday experience of infants and children. Infants were more carefully bundled up and at times overly protected. Pets, outdoor boisterousness, and physical games (such as ball playing) became forbidden. Tacit, timid, inactive, shy and "girl-like" boys were openly praised and widely adored. Whether in the form of tightened family rules, or community reform efforts by such moralists as Lü K'un and his father Lü Tê-shêng with indoctrinating literature like the Words for Little Children (Hsiao-êrh yü) and Words for Little Girls (Nü Hsiao-êrh yü), or the trickling down of popular religious tracts and itinerant theater, the Neo-Confucian perspective formed a new baseline for mainstream concepts in human conduct, and thus also for the childhood environment during the second millennium of imperial China.[38] On the other hand, pediatrics brought "professional" care and "specialized" attention to this social group, resulting in a wide array of physical, material, and cultural reorientation. Furthermore, the artistic representation of young children in Sung paintings and other artwork points to a society in which many embraced an engagingly "focused" attitude toward younger lives. The provision of schooling and teaching materials is another important indication of renewed collective concern and cultural interest in children.[39] In the present work the essays in Part 1 and some in Part 2 allude to the dawning of this era in Chinese social and cultural history, including considerations from the angle of the children who lived through it.

The mid-Ming was another pivotal time of alteration and redirection in the lives of children and childhood. First of all, physical and health-related evidence suggests that pediatric medicine, which first established a foothold five centuries previously in the Sung, continued to mature and proliferate. By the mid-sixteenth century, premodern China came close to a society that provided special health care to a large number of the young. Better child-bearing practices, too, with pharmaceutical recipes and emergency self-aid procedures, were permeating into different regions, trickling down the social ladder, going from urban centers to towns and villages, following trade networks and other travel routes. Thanks to popularizing efforts by the elite, a booming printing industry, and the bustling commercialization of Ming society, the clinical work of pediatricians grew and debates occurred among them, helped by the relatively "open-ended" character of their knowledge, inescapably mingled with the suspicious conservatism of the society and endless gossip. Second, in the area of philosophy and education, the appearance of Wang Yang-ming (1472–1528) and his followers, and their optimistic view of human nature endowed with a peculiarly "liberating" air toward socialization and early education, marked another turning point. As a direct response to the Ch'êng-Chu school of thought, Wang Yang-ming's *hsin-hsüeh* (school of the mind) teaching brought forth an alternative view on humanity and early education as well as a revisionist view on the question of children's hearts (*t'ung-hsin*). It advocated some sort of a naturalist outlook, a more sympathetic attitude, and an overtly child-oriented emphasis. Wang, and his radical followers like Li Chih (1527–1602), spoke and wrote fervently on children's education and the innocent nature of the child, directing satirical criticism on the rigid discipline cooked up by what were to them polluting and hypocritical adults. This "emancipating" and iconoclastic spirit posed a subversive challenge to the old Ch'êng-Chu orthodoxy in child training and education. It also served as a major social and intellectual dialectic in late imperial Chinese discourse about children and childhood. As such it provided a vital inspiration from which later reform-minded educationalists and enlightened thinkers continued to draw upon for centuries in debate and renegotiation. How well either the restrictive Ch'êng-Chu or the liberal Yang-ming schools, or both, fared in formulating actual childhood experiences for different social groups and cultural-geographic regions is a subject begging further investigation.[40] Third, in the hardly touched field of children's entertainment and literature in this period, unmistakable signposts recommend themselves for further elucidation. Although literary productions for all sorts of pedagogical purposes had existed long before this period, and occasional mention has been made of special street entertainers catering to the amusement of young urban customers in Sung times, it was not until the late sixteenth and seventeenth century that we have direct evidence of the commercial "outpouring" of collections of stories explicitly intended for children.[41]

This crude "periodization" of Chinese children's history demands further substantiation, articulation, and revision. Both microlevel assessments and theoretical considerations on Chinese childhood and children's lives are needed. For example, improvements in the provision of children's health and health management seem to have been continuously on the rise since the Sung, though not without periodic setbacks or regional and class differentiation. Has the long-standing culture of ancestor worship and patriarchal clan organization finally coalesced with a philosophical emphasis on the onset of human life (birth)? Has such a new emphasis, together with growing commercialization and urbanization, brought about a supportive environment for the further spread of scientific-technological explorations that materialized into the medical specialization of pediatrics? Material provisions for the young based on daily accounts, biographies, and local history records appear to have improved for much of late imperial history. After the mid-sixteenth century, education and children's literature grew phenomenally.[42] Yet these very developments could be seen as signs indicating social pressure and institutional encroachment on the relatively carefree state of children's life up until then. Neo-Confucianism's intense interest in human nature and its "nourishment" and "cultivation" represented one such preeminent force behind people's concern and control over young children. Increased activities in early education, like the more elaborate ideas on the well-being of the very young in terms of family instruction and clan rules, marked not just intensified care but also greatly strengthened manipulation and refinement. The depictions of "children at play" in Sung paintings marked the last public appearance of the physically more carefree and indulgent older mode of childhood before it was "taken over" and "obliterated" from the social history scene. In its place came a child's life much reduced in scale, clarity, and centrality. (Note, for instance, the rarity of children's themes in Ming paintings as compared to those from the Sung and Yüan [1279–1368].)[43] Outdoor fun and physical activities were strongly discouraged until the Yang-ming school tried to engage the educated in an open debate so as to accommodate or even nurture them. After which came a protracted process of negotiation and exploration, both in people's minds and in social practices. The aftermath of this debate carries us right down to the modern era in the late nineteenth and early twentieth centuries.

A general "downturn" in the lives of children occurred when China's moral philosophy and social ethics developed an ambivalence about their interests and control of children's formative years. Over the last half-millennium, not unlike what had happened elsewhere, improved care, increased concern, enhanced management, and strengthened indoctrination were oftentimes merely different manifestations of exactly the same set of social and cultural forces.[44] Both positive and negative results regarding developments in compulsive schooling for increasingly younger children in Ming-Ch'ing China serve as a somewhat awkward concurrence to scholars like Ariès's pronouncements on the ambivalent implications of similar phenomena in European developments.[45]

From the Sung onward, the age for teaching basic knowledge and skills in small children appears to have decreased one year or so for every one or one and a half centuries. That is, whereas a highly privileged child in the eleventh century did not start learning arithmetic and writing until he (or very occasionally she) reached nine or ten, as recommended by Ssû-ma Kuang (1019–1086), some one hundred years later eight-year-olds received such instructions. The onset of primary education continued to lower until the Ming, when children at the average age of four or five were made to learn things that children double their age would not have managed a few centuries before. Significantly, this trend in training and the emphasis on early intelligence (*tsao-hui*) and child prodigies, though stressing cognitive abilities, was never limited to the social elites or confined to intellectual subjects.[46] Sketchy but discernible evidence from peasant, merchant, and artisan families indicates a similar pattern in competitive parenting and early apprenticeship for the middle and lower echelons of late imperial Chinese society. On the one hand, an increasing number of parents in farming, crafts, and various trades were anxious to send their children for a "functional literary" education. On the other, there were also signs that vocational initiation was administered to an ever younger age group as time passed. Under such factors as the entrenched civil-service examination and the growing commercialization in agriculture and industry, a growing awareness of the marketability of human capital helped integrate ever younger members of society into work units. As a traditionally utilitarian society was given increasing opportunities in profit making, a clear "reorientation" in values and everyday actions emerged quickly in social institutions. The nurturing of a "daughter-indulgence" culture in a primarily "son-favoring" society (as explained in chapter 7) provides another instance in a formation of great inner complexity.

What then can be gained from a history that includes children? How different is the intellectual terrain when childhood is put into proper perspective? For the former, the case of Chinese history in the late imperial period may serve as a good point of reference. Restoration of the experience of one-third to one-half of the population (an estimated portion of the young in any demographically pretransitional society) seems but belated redress for inexcusable negligence. The common inattentiveness becomes less bearable as other categories of neglect such as ethnicity, class, and gender begin to make their appearance in society and academia. Addressing the experiences of the young thus fills a void in our collective knowledge, even if such an endeavor scratches the mere surface of these issues as they were related to family structure, material life, health, medicine, education, social networks, economic development, politics, and philosophy. This kind of intellectual exploration, including a systematic consideration of the factors of age and phases of life, may produce a further understanding in a number of organizational concepts (for example, the achievement-measured and functional-oriented outlook in history) and operational methods (less reliance on textual evidence and more educated employment of informing objects) in research on the past.

Finally, this quest for a history of children and childhood is rewarding and challenging in two fundamental ways. First, it reminds us that history and human existence are not only made both of the collective and the individual, but each individual's life journey is made up of many different phases. A person's station and standing in any one of these various periods entails conditions and experiences that are not just culturally or historically specific but are also defined by his/her particular age in that society. Second, those living through the same period of time, in the same sections of population (in terms of region, class, and gender), constituted an "age group" whose historical dimension is hardly clear. This wrestling with a history of children and childhood thus raises conceptual and methodological questions unlike historical exercises of the familiar kind. For with "children and childhood" one is confronted with a social category that is both biologically and socially "transitory" and subjectively and objectively "tentative" in nature. This metamorphosing character of children and their social identity may be juxtaposed to other sociocultural categories such as ethnicity, regionality, class, or gender, which, granted degrees of fluidity, hybridity, and multiplicity, assume a mostly fixed and constant character. In looking at children and childhood, however, historians have to access lives in the form of social caterpillars or tadpoles to determine whether their particular state and stage in existence may generate interest or information of a lasting or mutating kind. This engages historical studies in ways potentially at odds with the older framework of social, political, economic, and cultural history, studied according to people's seemingly more lasting roles and statuses.

More than other "new frontiers" in the field of the humanities, the subject of infants' and children's lives requires scholars to move beyond conventional intellectual tools and training methods to try to employ (or

simply to imagine) ways that will perceive the basic picture in alternate fashions. Plenty of examples in the past have demonstrated that random studies introduced for the purpose of supplying additional information in a compensating or supplementary manner may turn out to herald the birth of entirely novel ideas, eventually leading to a new intellectual impasse. The study of children's and childhood history, if usefully exercised, requires a fundamental reexamination of historical outlook that will not only take the experience of the younger population into new consideration in a "mechanical," or "static" sense, but will identify social change and historical development by taking into account the interaction of generations of constantly evolving historical characters and social circumstances. Coming to terms with this need requires freshly conceived ideas and investigations. To address the subjective participation of young children and to elucidate "the voices" of infants requires scholars to mine hitherto unexplored sources and to get underneath or beyond accustomed ways of deciphering traces filtered through the literature of adults. In the unpacking of these nonverbal messages, body movement and physical gestures—the sights and sounds of weeping, kicking, smiling, screaming, or simply a restful sleep—are meaningful information for contextualization and systematic decoding. Toward this end, the chapters that follow have attempted a first step. In order to produce a better grasp of this subject, however, far more committed engagements are called for. In the end, we may discover that, with vigor and concern, the acts of the feeble and the sounds of the mute will not remain elusive or insignificant but powerful workings of life, much like the meanings of silence in music or speech or of empty space in a painting or architectural form. In history, as in the arts, the ability to take note of hidden existences and elusive presences is vital.[47]

Sources

Since the term "children" refers to the young section of a population, whereas "childhood" points to the experience of people and the philosophical, cultural, and social understandings of that phase of the human life cycle, the source materials that are pertinent in an investigation of the two subjects are related, though not identical. From a historical perspective,

FIG. 1. After "Royal Children," artist unknown. This picture is in imitation of Chou Fang's *Lin-chih t'u* by subsequent (probably Ming) painters. It depicts maids tenderly taking care of royal children bathing, dressing, sitting, crawling, and playing. Even though this picture does not illustrate infants from ordinary families, it shows the common hopes and aspirations of the public. Courtesy of the National Palace Museum, Taiwan, Republic of China.

both the conceptual and experiential aspects appear mostly as social and cultural constructs.[48] For China, as elsewhere, people's understanding and treatment of children and childhood in the past not only derived from words and ideas but were also revealed in deeds and gestures, as preserved, reflected, or suggested through textual and other evidence.

The multiplicity of the concepts of children and childhood in Chinese history are apparent in the various genres of primary sources. Such evidence challenges modern notions of these two subjects not only in society but also in the academics in humanities, social sciences, and science.

Materials in some way pertaining to the lives of children or a certain notion or treatment of childhood are scattered, though abundant, in Chinese history. Typologically, they belong to several categories. First is what one may call "prescriptive and didactic works." Among these one finds standard ritual texts, such as *The Book of Rites* (*Li-chi*) and the many family rituals (*chia-li*), which in their effort to codify social customs and daily behavior present passages devoted to child care and child education, usually from a normative perspective.[49] Philosophical treatises on ethics and education can also be viewed as a subsection under this category, as were discussions of human nature (*jên-hsing*), human heart (*jên-hsin*), rules for individual or group conduct, and materials for primary education. Different intellectual schools and changing times produced concepts and rules at a greater or lesser variance from one another. The differences often reflect larger philosophical, social, and political concerns. From these children- or childhood-related theories and opinions on education to the Neo-Confucian arguments on the "child's heart," we witness cultural forces large or small interplaying with social practices at the micro- or macrolevel.[50] Although never strictly or solely focused on children's issues, such forces were nevertheless intrinsic factors that shaped the world of the young conceptually and in everyday living.

Closely related to this last group of ritual texts and philosophical treatises were the numerous "family instructions" (*chia-hsün*) and "children's primers" (*yu-mêng*), produced with an aim toward molding the social character and intellectual development of the young. In terms of historical context, these two genres of literature did not come from the same background, thus they should not be taken as representing the same discourse. But in terms of social function and historical consideration, they were both formulated to produce properly minded, well-behaved offspring. Family instructions did so by telling parents and elders what to do. An example is the famous *Yen Family Instructions* (*Yen-shih chia-hsün*) from the sixth century or *Shih-lin Family Instructions* (*Shih-lin chia-hsün*) from the Sung dynasty.[51] Numerous Ming-Ch'ing writings of lesser status followed in terms of format and spirit; directly or indirectly they influenced people's treatment of children and the domestic experience of childhood, as borne out by large amounts of biographical data. Children's primers, on the other hand, appeared as a mirror reflection of family instruction. Instead of instructing the parents and elders with ways of handling the young they went directly to work on the youngsters' minds with well-prepared "soul food" for correct training. Over a thousand years, such popular items as *San-pai-ch'ien*, namely *The Three-Character Classic (San-tzû ching)*, *One-Hundred Surnames (Pai-chia hsing)*, and *One-Thousand Character Classic (Ch'ien-tzû wên)*, and things of the sort poured out, supplying children with their first characters and initiating them in basic knowledge of numerals, geography, history, and social norms. Other rhymed verses or illustrated manuals, such as *Words for Little Children (Hsiao-êrh yü)* and *A Collection of Valuable Stories for Elementary Learning (Yu-hsüeh ku-shih ch'iung-lin)*, also flooded the "children's market" in the late imperial period.[52] Ample evidence, therefore, of children and childhood can be derived from examining these instructive family tomes.

Individual descriptive and confessional voices, carefully elucidated, form a useful counterpoint to this formalistic general background. Biographical accounts like *nien-p'u* (chronological biography) and autobiographical records like *tzû-shu* (self-narration) or *tzû-ting* (self-compiled) *nien-p'u* provide evidence of a child's or a group of children's earliest years, with details of activities, incidents, and experiences encountered in a particular context.[53] Personal diaries, private notes, intimate letters, and poems exchanged among families and close friends yield records, through both flimsy memories and lucid accounts, of one's own or somebody else's childhood years. Recollections of joy or pain in the daily existence of youth memorial essays and poems remembering one's own children, by late imperial times, were no longer rare in the world of China's educated. Such genres may be checked against normative records to illustrate a certain kind of "children's culture" or "juvenile mentality." Family records, such as genealogies, *chia-p'u* or *tsu-p'u*, often containing meticulous household rules to be applied to the young, can reveal cases of specific children who were chastened or praised. For the study of children and childhood in Chinese history, in other words, the problem is not a lack of source materials but rather how one might approach, understand, and represent the wide array of this disjointed collection of materials that often bypasses or contradicts itself.

In contrast to the prescriptive and descriptive materials, there existed after the eleventh century what may be called technical or empirical data on children's physical conditions and notions of childhood in the context of people's knowledge and management of the young human body. Prominent in this category are the voluminous pediatric texts, a medical subspecialty that came increasingly into its own after the Sung period. Professional discussions on prevalent health problems (*i-lun*), therapeutic prescriptions enlisted for their improvement (*i-fang*), and clinical case records (*i-an*) reveal not merely disease and health patterns, but also the material conditions children lived through. Views on children and childhood and practices of childbearing are also found in these notes, presenting both the "expert's ideas" on the nature of human physiology and child care as well as actual strategies in ordinary familial handling of their young. Owing to the pragmatic and mundane nature of these sources, and owing to the large amount preserved, these medical records fill a vacuum in the appraisal of the material and physical aspects of Chinese children's experience. Any report on conceptions or treatment of children and childhood from this era cannot be complete without properly consulting these voluminous records in detail.[54] The pediatrician's understanding of the living child and infancy or childhood in the abstract is also of value to intellectual or cultural history as it constituted a particular historical force that, together with the more familiar social and cultural conventions, formed a varied and composite environment for the child. The qualitative details and the quantitative character of this pediatric archive, moreover, may be tapped to respond to typological questions such as the regional and class differences or the material conditions of this particular history.[55]

In a less substantial but still significant way, late imperial Chinese legal documents bear traces of people's recognition of the young. The act of granting amnesty demonstrates a certain appreciation for the special character of children as a legal entity. Records of prosecutions of actual lawsuits involving children (there were at least three homicide cases involving young children from Ch'ing legal documents) give concrete cases in which statutory regulations met with social reality on the question of young lives.

Other policies, institutions, codes, and regulations should also be sifted to gain a better idea of the conditions of children and childhood in politics and the public arena. Such information includes stipulations on taxation and the age of conscription, as well as evidence of actual child-soldiers participating in combat

Economic history materials address the childhood phase in regards to labor and productivity. To begin with, procreation could be a well-calculated act in family life. Fertility manipulation and infanticide are merely the tip of the iceberg in the reproductive strategies in historical China.[56] Child labor doubtlessly existed in the agrarian, commercial, and handicraft sectors, representing the connection of childhood from reproduction to production both in fact and in the abstract. This study addresses the contextualized understanding of this connection and the contrast between the need and welfare of living children and the understanding and changing notions of childhood.

Prescriptive, descriptive, and technical representations aside, artistic or imaginative works depicting children constitute yet an additional angle of appreciation and analysis. Illustrations of children at play (*ying-hsi t'u*), traveling toy venders (*huo-lang t'u*), and other auspicious social scenes focused on childlike activities—such as the symbolic picture of one hundred children (*pai-tzû t'u*), the humorous depiction of boisterous classrooms (*nao-hsüeh t'u*), the various joyful market scenes in *ch'un-shih t'u*, or idealized depictions of rural life in *kêng-chih t'u* (plowing and weaving)—flourished as special genres from the Sung onward. Similar children's themes appear in other traditional Chinese artworks, such as porcelain, lacquer ware, bamboo and woodcarving, woodblock printing, and paper cutting. With such bountiful presentations of happy life and communal prosperity there are obviously overt as well as hidden messages, not necessarily serious or realistic caricatures of children.[57] This notwithstanding, meaningful changes in the various "images" of children or childhood as depicted in, or reflected through, artistic means still invite educated interpretation. It is worth exploring whether they suggest any gradual evolution in the collective sentiment in attitude toward domestic life or young lives, or if they are simply a separate artistic realm of expression.

Two other kinds of material exist. One constitutes the various literary works created for, about, or by children; the other is the myriad of material objects surrounding the physical environments under which children lived. The former include stories produced directly or indirectly for the enjoyment of young audiences, and often developed around child protagonists, as well as the countless songs, rhymes, and verses accompanying children's everyday activities in bathing, playing, quarrelling, or simple distress.[58] Evidence of food and clothing, snacks and toys, furniture and architecture used by or designed for children tells much about the specific material conditions under which youthful days were spent and perceived by youngsters in different stations of life.

Childhood: A Multiplicity of Views

The discussion above reveals the complexity and multiplicity of views on the subject that are at once exhilarating and bewildering. Clearly, even in the same historical period, different concepts of children and childhood existed in different quarters and from different angles, each representing a wide array of complementary or conflicting forces.

Contemporary studies in sociology, psychology, and education that make a distinction between the adult-oriented and the child-centered position represent another set of polemics from which historians often formulate their investigations. The association with a cultural attitude or value system

that is considered "authoritative, disciplinary, and oppressive" as opposed
to "sympathetic, permissive, or indulgent" represents familiar rhetoric cast
in the "modern" intonation. This "modern" persuasion is characterized by
examinations of European and American family histories, including attitudes toward children, that equate traditional society with the former set of
values; the modern era is a time when people gradually moved closer to the
latter set of norms.[59] Evidence from late imperial China, on the other hand,
seemingly harder to fit into this latter set, may bring forth examples when
both strands of thought or practices existed side by side. Both practices involved negotiation, intermingling over centuries of social life and cultural
exercises, thus helping us to view critically any "evolutionary" or "enlightening" assumptions that deem society to be moving from the "authoritative" to the "sympathetic," or oscillating between the two. Whereas didactic and prescriptive materials in ritual texts and primers might be identified
as adult-oriented and carrying heavy disciplinary and oppressive weight, the
sources of personal reflection and biographical information, or the artistic
and imaginative depictions, may be thought of as relatively indulgent and
child centered. Technical records, such as the pediatric texts, belong to yet
another category of sources that could be argued as both firmly "progressive" and hopelessly "old-fashioned." Though not without their own cultural constraints, yet due to pragmatic and vocational concerns, practicing
physicians did not merely operate from within the normative moral culture;
they had to see, feel, and understand the situation from their young clients'
positions. Although this may not be the same thing as "permissiveness," it
does provide concrete examples and tangible evidence of views other than
the authoritative-versus-child-sensitive mode from the premodern context.
Artistic and literary depictions can suggest a similar outlook; even private
letters and memorials may be analyzed to show sentiments varying from
mainstream presumptions and authoritative "adult" views of the child. But
these are not the same as the child-centered or childlike representations that
somehow satisfy the modern inclination. All of these traces related to children and childhood, as a matter of fact, coexisted and intermingled in the
everyday life of the young and old in imperial China. A complex of the concepts of children and childhood in the past cannot be captured under any
monolithic mode of explanation. It certainly diminishes the usefulness of
any usual binary approach—the old "child versus adult," "positive versus
negative," or "progressive-versus-traditional" mode—whereby the concept
of a continuous social evolution or linear progression in history surfaces.
Elements of both not only coexisted for a long time, they probably also
shared some kind of a working relationship to form a world with views of
the young that are neither entirely "adult oppressive" nor "child indulgent." For those investigators looking carefully and skeptically into the so-

cial, cultural, and conceptual history of the child, reconstruction of the past cast in terms of the binary approach make clear nothing but the very domineering and almost inescapable character of historical studies, primarily grown out of, nurtured, then developed and executed under the peculiarly "modern mentality" long in the making in the mostly European-American cultural context (whose history is too complicated to be reviewed here, though whose implication is by no means insignificant to our present concern).

THE CHILD: THREE RELATED MEANINGS

Examining the multitude of sources, one might also realize that linguistically and conceptually the subject of the child (*tzû* or *t'ung* or *yu*) has meaning at three different levels, the first being the "social child" focusing on the "junior" (*pei-yu*) position it has vis-à-vis the "senior" (*tsun-chang*). Since this terminology and its compounds are used flexibly and interchangeably, it is important to denote their semantic implications so as not to misread or overinterpret them, while at the same time learning to appreciate the sociocultural interconnectedness of their various connotations. Broadly speaking, this notion of "child," a *tzû*, is understood here mostly as a social status relative to his or her elders. It denotes the subordinate, humble, and inferior status of a child in a subservient role to that of his or her elders, ancestors, and others in a hierarchically superior position. Thus it implies an identity that, though it often relates to youth, is not necessarily tied to it. In this sense, as long as one's parents were alive, or whenever speaking or acting vis-à-vis the elders in the house, any offspring at whatever age always assumes the position of a *tzû*. This was the "child" that most Chinese ritual texts, such as *Li-chi*, referred to when mentioning the word. It is also the meaning most of China's philosophical references, family instructions, and legal documents adopt in consideration. Socially speaking, that is how *tzû* was meant to be read in such important contexts as the *Twenty-Four Stories of Filial Piety* (*Êrh-shih-ssû hsiao*). The broad, social meaning of *tzû* as a relative status gave it a role with clear obligations and definite rules, regardless of age, a key point in the concept of the "child" in its premodern context. It is in this social, culturally immature, secondary, and legally unaccountable position that societies, including historical China, relate other nonkin categories of inferior people such as slaves, servants, and foreigners in the inferior, dependant status of a child. Most modern societies can also understand the notion of an "adult child," though this aspect had hardly been elucidated by historians, psychologists, or sociologists of children or childhood as an issue closely associated with their subject.

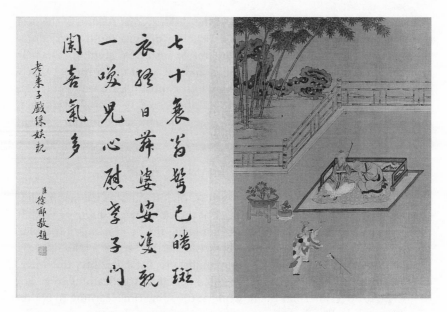

老萊子戲綵娛親

七十衰翁鬢已斑
衣經日弄婆娑復親
一噯兒心慰孝子門
閙春氣多

徐郡敬題

FIG. 2. "The Old Boy Lao-lei-tzû Entertaining His Parents" shows a child in the social role of a junior to parents, with no restriction by age. Reprinted from *Twenty-four Stories of Filial Piety* by Ch'iu Ying (Ming dynasty), courtesy of the National Palace Museum, Taiwan, Republic of China.

A second layer of meaning in the Chinese notion of child is one closer to the common modern understanding. It is perceived as a phase in a person's lifespan, the early period of human existence before adulthood. This narrower, more mechanical and biophysically defined notion of the *tzû* is seen in such technical literature as traditional Chinese pediatric texts, but also in such areas as early education (*mêng-hsün*), biographical, and autobiographical writings. By the Ming period, interestingly, important thinkers like Wang Yang-ming and Li Chih adopted this more specific meaning of *t'ung-tzû*, a young child in the narrower sense, to combat the more general definition of the child, creating a fresh, more liberating attitude toward children and child education.[60]

Finally, a third and more abstract meaning of "child" takes place when *t'ung* and *tzû* are used philosophically and aesthetically to highlight certain specific traits or qualities as a state in human nature, to refer to qualities as existentially "childlike" characteristics. Especially in discussing art and literature, but also in other cultural settings, people can speak of some inclination, artistic styles, or ethical values as representing or appearing close to "the spirit of a child." Many a Chinese proverb uses *t'ung* and *tzû* and their associated adjectives to stress this cultural appreciation of "child" as a state

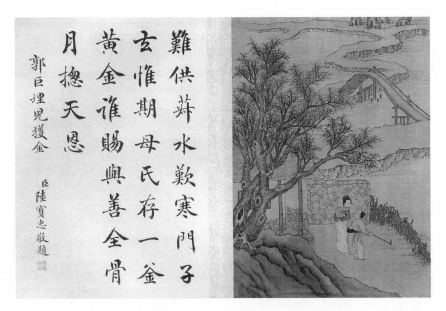

難供葑水歎寒門子
古惟期母氏存一釜
黃金谁賜與善全骨
月揔天恩

郭巨埋兒獲金

臣陸寶忠敬題

FIG. 3. "Kuo Chü Sacrificing His Child" (Kuo Chü mai-êrh), illustrates how the adult man Kuo Chü (shown here in the act of burying his own son) rather than the young baby was the real child in the Chinese cultural discourse. Reprint from Ch'iu Ying's *Albumn of Twenty-four Stories of Filial Piety* (Ming dynasty), courtesy of the National Palace Museum, Taiwan, Republic of China.

of mind: to describe a person as remaining "innocent" (*t'ien-chen*), to admire poets and painters as having "the sentiment and fun of a young child" (*chih-ch'ing chih-ch'ü*) in their artistic expressions, to praise a functional adult as someone who has "not lost his or her child's heart" (*t'ung-hsin wei-min*), or even to marvel at a person (usually a man) whose hair is "like the (old) crane's yet with the appearance of a child" (*ho-fa t'ung-yen*). These are the innocence, heart, sentiment, fun, and physique of a child that anyone may embody regardless of age or status. This enlarged, intellectualized, philosophically contemplative meaning of the child is seen operating actively in the Taoist philosophy and religion. In their convictions, pursuits, and practices it represented cultivation of a physical and mental state approaching that of an "eternal child," picturing "innate innocence" as something akin to immortality. This concept of a child in spirit and in body also exerted a powerful influence on Chinese medicine and health culture in its search for the healing exhibited by the body's natural ability to rejuvenate and regenerate. Though not entirely unknown to other societies or modern Western references, this understanding is particularly important to our appreciation of the Chinese concepts of childhood because it brings out a typical feature in the broad discourse about the child in China's multifaceted and interrelated contexts that carries deep theoretical and comparative implications.

The relatively autonomous yet mutually communicative character of these notions of a "child" in three different domains ensured that though a certain understanding of "childhood" may be the operating force when it comes to specific areas of activity or concern (for example, regarding problems in health, domestic life, or philosophical exercise), no singular view dominates the overall conception or treatment of children or childhood. First of all, the prevalent social value that sees children as indispensable junior members of the family obeying and serving the needs of their elders as well as transmitting and carrying on the familial line was a most powerful force that prompted the birth and maintained the growth of the old pediatric medicine. Second, this technical understanding of infants and children as humans in their biophysical initial and younger stage of life helped to protect and preserve the survival of people's offspring and thus rendered possible the practice of the social ethics required of the junior status of the young. On the other hand, this evolving biophysical appreciation of the human body in its constantly evolving state accepted, contributed to, and also revised people's changing consideration of innocence, naiveté, and youth, an area deserving separate treatment that is too complicated to deal with here. Third, the philosophical, religious, and aesthetic search for a permanent infantile child in the abstract as representing the nondegenerative, permanently elevating quality of one's "childlike nature" provided a much needed contrast and counterbalance to both the limitation of the biophysical law physicians recognized and the rigidly suffocating subservient status that younger and junior members were assigned in the late imperial Confucian social order. The liberating, rebellious, and subversive character of this philosophical, existential child as an eternal possibility at all stages of people's lives regardless of the familial roles or worldly obligations expected of them created a timely crack and precious breathing space in Ming-Ch'ing social hierarchy and politics. It also promised or suggested a spiritual transcendence outside of or beyond the visible and physical existence of humanity.

An assessment of the world of children and childhood in Chinese history, therefore, has more to offer than an opportunity to patch up lost chapters in human experience. It opens up new windows to appreciate the power of such categorical factors as age and biosocial phases at play in the organization and operation of human society. As an analytical tool, it also reminds people of the illumination history can bring to bear on the culturally specific character of many social sciences in the examination of questions pertaining to the "intrinsic state" of humanity. Such studies can be conceptually

FIG. 4. "Tending the Flocks in Autumn," by Liu Sung-nien (Sung dynasty). Boys herding cattle was a familiar farming activity. The image symbolizes freedom and a natural lifestyle. Courtesy of the National Palace Museum, Taiwan, Republic of China.

披髮偏蕭淨法身
手持經卷現童真
性門不二善言語
佛挽昆邪俟上人

太霊山比丘 志恩拜贊

FIG. 5 "Portrait of Wen Shu as the Epitome of Innocence." Children are often associated with innocence in religious or genre paintings. The picture shows the personification of innocence, a common motif in devotional art to show the humanity in its natural state as close to the admirable quality of the pure, original, and authentic Being. Courtesy of the National Palace Museum, Taiwan, Republic of China.

limited by the very "modern" outlook of disciplines like social psychology, early education, or sociology, and demography. On the other hand, these academic perceptions as products of modern sociocultural forces themselves have been powerful influences informing and formulating the attitudes and experiences of the subjects they are supposed to investigate. Historical evidence coming from a different era, constructed under different forces, by contrast, alerts people to common social science theoretical models as potentially self-fulfilling prophesies based on data their ideas in part helped to create. By the same token, evolutionary psychology appears too sweeping to satisfy our curiosity about the daily operation of different societies, whereas evolutionary biology when applied to human society is too crude an inspiration to illuminate the changing practices and circumstances of human customs.

The concept of *tz'u-hang*, originated in Chinese Buddhism and later used in Ming pediatric literature (known as the journey of compassion and loosely rendered here as tender voyage), reminds us of the existence of an outlook toward infants and children borne out of a different phase in human history.[61] In its slightly twisted English incarnation, usually translated as "a compassionate journey," it reintroduces a sociocultural ecology whereby life, at its early stage or not, is much more interconnected and thus requires more imaginative elucidation than historians might admit. The modern "discovery" of children and childhood, by society or scholars, therefore entails more than a recovery of the biophysical, material, and socioemotional conditions that dictate the survival and maturation of infants and children. It certainly cannot be any indicator or measurement of the linear progression of the collective, as a theory once posited by some historians and still circulated by others. Its presence in late imperial Chinese history points out that this very experience and its representation have never been, and thus should hardly become, traces of either particularity or universality. With it the ever changing multiplicity—in time, regionality, gender, ethnicity, and class—of this history of children and childhood has only begun to see the light. What we have learned so far alerts us to the generic, constant, biophysically defined children or childhood often (though not always) implied in such modern disciplines as pediatrics, early education, and child psychology, which together with sociology and demography can now finally benefit from some of the complications afforded by time and space.

The lives of young children and the experience of early childhood are projected here as a tender voyage in Chinese history.[62] This earliest phase in a long arduous journey through the human lifespan exemplifies the frailty of human existence, sustainable only with compassion. Though in late imperial China the roughly one hundred million infants and young children who existed at any given time represented different things to different people and certainly lived differently in different locations. The temporary, vulnerable, yet enchanting quality of that existence invites and requires attention, the significance of which goes beyond the Chinese political or cultural border. In the considerably altered material and cultural environment of modern times, much of the context to that struggling existence has been shifted, along with its accompanying economic, philosophical, and physical conditions. For an intellectual voyager, then, this present attempt hopes to inspire further understanding in the journeys ahead.

Part 1

PHYSICAL CONDITIONS

Physical survival is the first and most serious challenge a child faces at birth. The staggering mortality rate of infants and children in traditional societies, which increases dramatically the lower the age, is a reminder of the grave odds faced by all. The emergence of the subspecialty of pediatrics in the Sung (960–1279) certainly changed the approaches to physical care of infants and children. The following three chapters describe the maturation of this vocation and its involvement with the practical need of newborn care and nursing. As they show, change was not an outcome of singular reforming forces from the experts in the field. But pediatric records illuminate the physical conditions of young children in late imperial China. Information elucidated from these texts reveals changing patterns of childhood diseases and Chinese children's health; the economic, social, and cultural forces behind them; and China's evolving material conditions and biological environment.

1   *Treatment of Children*

In the seventh century, the famed medical author Ch'ao Yüan-fang (550–630) included six chapters and 255 items of deliberation on the health problems of children as part of his *opus medica, On the Origins and Symptoms of Diseases (Chu-ping yüan-hou lun)*. Less than a century later, the medical authority for medieval China, Sun Ssû-miao (581–682), had a separate list of "procedures for children and infants" in his *Prescriptions Worth a Thousand (Ch'ien-chin fang)*. At the time, physicians as a whole still regretted that effective medical assistance could hardly be expected for children under the age of six. For the very young who fell ill, often little could be done other than "to predict (whether the child) would survive or perish." Roughly three hundred years after that, Ch'ien I (1032–1113) based his medical reputation on caring solely for young children and won himself a professorial appointment at the Imperial College of Medicine during the Sung dynasty. Another three centuries or so later, early in the fourteenth century, one found, deep in China's interior, in Hupei province, a plaque hanging on a building: "The Wan Family Pediatrics." A thousand years after the T'ang physicians' prudent self-chastisement about their collective inability in treating the very young, the Ch'ing imperial compendium of the medical section in *The Complete Classics Collection of Ancient China (Ku-chin t'u-shu chi-ch'êng)* included no fewer than one hundred chapters (*chuan*) of treatises, prescriptions, and case histories under the category of "pediatrics" (*yu-k'o*). None of this tale squares easily with Philippe Ariès's assertion that the recognition of children as a special category of human beings is but a modern phenomenon.[1] The questions of how, why, or what had happened to the children and their health care over the ten centuries in between certainly need explanation.

Philippe Ariès's thesis has stimulated debate as well as soul-searching research. European and American historians have since looked further into the Western attitude toward children using materials covering a wide range of time and space.[2] Scholars concerned with non-Western cultures have also responded to Ariès's premise. A similar inquiry, when applied to Chinese history, uncovers a heretofore unnoticed world that had direct association

FIG. 6. "Pediatric Clinic on the Street." This picture is a detail from *Along the River During the Ch'ing-Ming Festival*. A Ch'ing imitation of a Sung painting, it shows a clinic that specialized in the treatment of younger children. The four characters at the bottom of the sign indicate that profit making will not be a sole concern. Courtesy of the National Palace Museum, Taiwan, Republic of China.

with children's lives, leaving behind rich archival materials, including the works and records of traditional Chinese pediatricians. Other than as direct documentation on the emergence and development of an important sub-specialty of Chinese medicine, these pediatric texts, prescriptions, and clinical case records provide an unusual entry into the world of children: the ills and well-being of their health, the knowledge and treatment of their bodies, the seasonal changes and contents of their daily diet, the habits and patterns of their ordinary activities, and the general material provisions and physical circumstances of their everyday existence. They also offer an array of concepts and treatment about children and childhood.[3] Due to the broad meanings under which Chinese pediatric medicine was conceived, and to the active role it played in the country's medical development and health practices, literary evidence, directly or indirectly resulting from health care activities, abounds. From elite professional pediatricians to the street peddlers carrying patent drugs, first-hand witnesses have testified to the way children were understood and managed physically and psychologically by physicians, the educated elite, and the state, as well as by their parents, kin, and other caretakers in the last millennium of Chinese history. Exploration of the growth of this special discipline within traditional Chinese medicine reveals how the young became a focus of professional attention in traditional China.

Providing Care for Children's Health

Compared with other civilizations, a concern for children's health developed relatively early in China. In addition to fragmented ancient medical texts whose titles allude to pediatric care, well-known existent documents in this area date back to at least the Sui dynasty (581–618 C.E.). Like other branches of traditional Chinese medicine, pediatrics at the time was crude and not wholly devoid of sorcery. *The Classic on the Soft [Spot of the] Skull* (*Lu-hsin ching*), said to have been written by a sorcerer named Fang (Wu Fang), provides one such example. The fact that it specified care of the "soft spot of the skull" (the fontanelle) shows the empirical inclination of the discipline.[4]

Medieval medical texts contain sections devoted especially to the subject of health care for children. In the seventh-century text *On the Origins and Symptoms of Diseases*, for example, Ch'ao Yüan-fang allocated a section for children's problems. "Recipes for Infants and Children" (Shao-hsiao ying-ju fang) in Sun Ssû-miao's eighth-century *Prescriptions Worth a Thousand* is another example of a section on children that was placed at the very beginning of the book. These two medieval medical texts cover, on the one hand, matters concerning newborn care such as cutting the umbilical cord, mouth wiping, bathing, feeding, and clothing. On the other hand, they express contemporary medical views on the common illnesses of children, their origins, symptoms, and treatments.[5] The eighty-six items in two chapters of Wang T'ao's *Medical Secrets of a Frontier Official* (*Wai-t'ai mi-yao fang*) also focused entirely on ailments of children.[6] Subsequently, most leading medical authors of the T'ang, Sung, and Yüan dynasties (the seventh through fourteenth centuries) devoted parts of their writings to children's health. Some of them, in addition, created separate entries at either the beginning or the end of the main texts, making it easier for the consultation of practitioners and general readers alike. This could be seen as a forerunner of the specialization of pediatrics as a separate discipline. Because of the fame of these authors, materials on children's health were widely circulated. Sun Ssû-miao's "procedures" were so well received that they soon appeared in a separate printing. Throughout the medieval and late imperial period people continued to make hand copies and reprints.

As a whole, however, due to a lack of focused physiological knowledge and clinical skills, the development of medicine for the young (yu-i) remained limited until the end of the T'ang dynasty (618–907). Medical texts of the time admitted that the handling of health problems of the very young was limited "to predicting [whether the victims] will survive or perish, and to distinguishing the cases of the living from those of the dying."[7] There was little assistance for the care of children under the age of six that made much practical sense. Whenever an infant or a young child contracted a serious ailment, there were few effective cures a practitioner could provide.

Despite this, medical experts strived to break new ground to meet the social needs for the health care of children. At which juncture, Ch'ien I's career and the medical legacy he left behind in the form of a three-chapter text entitled *Proven Formulae of Pediatric Medicine* (*Hsiao-êrh yao-chêng chih-chüeh*) was the long awaited breakthrough. According to the biography by his disciple Liu Ch'i, Ch'ien I was born into a medical family of the Ch'ien-t'ang district (today's Hang-chou area) of the lower Yangtze valley. Both his father (who soon abandoned his family) and his adopted father were medical men by vocation. As medicine in those times was a trade passed down from father to son or master to apprentice, Ch'ien I became a common practitioner by family trade. What is noteworthy, however, is the fact that he was said to have become increasingly known for "practicing children's medicine in the Shantung area."[8] By the middle of the eleventh century, the social need for practitioners specializing in children's health and the occupational skills for fulfilling such a need had converged to usher in a specialist career like that of Ch'ien I.

Due to Ch'ien I's performance in treating noble children, moreover, he was later summoned to the palace and appointed professor in the Imperial College of Medicine. "The nobility, gentry, and common folk flocked to the master's house; so much so that he was left with no leisure. When he addressed issues of medicine, not even experienced medical scholars could make a criticism."[9] With such acclaim, not only was Ch'ien I's authority as a pediatrician further established, the specialized profession of pediatrics also received wide respect among the practitioners. Ch'ien I's *Proven Formulae* defined the nature and direction of the profession, as he won for himself reverence as the founding father of Chinese pediatrics.

Beginning in Ch'ien I's time and slightly thereafter, other texts on

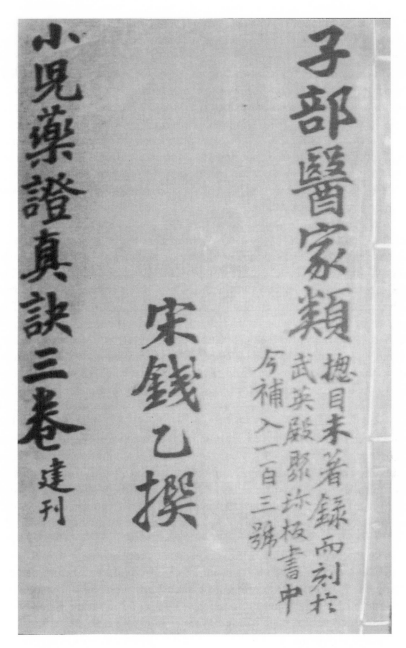

子部醫家類　　　　　總目未著錄而刊於
武英殿聚珍板書中
今補入一百三號

宋錢乙撰

小兒藥證真訣三卷　建刊

FIG. 7. The Cover of *Proven Formulae of Pediatric Medicine* (*Hsiao-êrh yao-chêng chih-chüeh*). It was a text attributed to the career of Ch'ien I, the first practitioner to take seriously the treatment of the very young. Courtesy of the National Central Library, Taiwan, Republic of China.

children's health appeared as well: Tung Chi's volume on pox and measles, *Emergency Treatments of Rashes and Measles of Small Children* (*Hsiao-êrh pan-chên pei-chi fang-lun*) in one chapter;[10] Liu Fang's *A New Text for Protection of Children* (*Yu-yu hsin-shu;* 1150) in forty chapters; Ch'ên Wên-chung's text *On Poxes and Measles of Small Children* (*Hsiao-êrh tou-chên fang-lun;* 1214); and the anonymous *A Thorough Discussion on Infant Hygiene* (*Hsiao-êrh wei-shêng tsung-wei lun-fang*) from the mid-twelfth century were some of the better known.[11] Pediatrics was becoming a specialized field, in part due to developments associated with Ch'ien I's bold theoretical approach, innovative pharmaceutical devices, and personal efficacy. There is little doubt, however, that Ch'ien I himself was a product of the long development of China's medical and health culture. His medical knowledge, theoretical deliberations, and pharmaceutical formulae all manifest direct influence from the early and medieval Chinese medical heritage. He agreed with the traditional opinion that pediatrics was a particularly difficult area, a challenge worth taking on intellectually and technically. He was accorded to have expressed the hope that other colleagues would rise to the occasion with him, gradually opening up this vocational frontier. The aim, as ascribed by him, was "so that the very young be spared the pain of premature death, and the elders freed from the sorrow of losing their offspring."[12] In terms of medical theory, Ch'ien I adapted earlier understanding on the functions of organs and circuits to the new field of pediatrics. His theory on "diagnosis and treatment according to [the symptoms of] the five organs" (*wu-tsang chêng-chih*) served as guidance and foundation for Chinese pediatrics until the nineteenth century. He claimed that children, "because their internal organs are weak and fragile and can be weakened or strengthened easily, thus suffer more easily from cold and fever."[13] The idea thereafter became the motto of Chinese pediatrics. His diagnostic skills of stressing the usefulness of reading "facial signs" (*mien-shang chêng*) and "signs from the eye" (*mu-nei chêng*) as opposed to the "pulsing" and "questioning" techniques commonly employed in adult medicine were widely implemented.

From the twelfth century onward, pediatrics took a steady turn toward maturation. A strong need for specialized care for children's health had evidently existed in China long before Ch'ien I appeared on the scene. The deep-rooted Chinese belief in ancestor worship and in family value could have provided a vital edge to the universal imperative to save the young. Further developments in family ethics and lineage organization brought this old attentiveness for the physical well-being of one's offspring to a new height in the eleventh and twelfth centuries, occasioning a historical figure like Ch'ien I and heralding his "unprecedented" vocational accomplishments. It was probably this same broad social context that continued to allow for the growth and expansion of pediatrics as a flourishing subspecialty within Chinese medicine. The specific physiological theories, pathological observations, clinical skills, and pharmaceutical inventions were but the "scientific" and technological achievements fortuitously meeting an existent demand, without which neither Ch'ien I nor generations of pediatric practitioners could have wielded much personal influence. This generally "attentive" attitude toward children, in other words, could be perceived as the background rather than the evidenced result of a "favorable" environment for childhood in late imperial Chinese society. Scholarly research and technical inventions broadened the influence and propagated it among the populace.

The significance of the emergence of Chinese pediatrics did not rest solely on its precocity. Recent inquiries only intensify the search for the broad historical circumstances in which Sung pediatric medicine dwelled. How did it come about and what did it signify? A few dates may be helpful to put things in perspective. In the case of Europe, the earliest medical treatises devoted to the discussion of disease and health needs related to children were written in the late fifteenth and sixteenth centuries.[14] In Colonial America, "right up to the eighteenth century, in fact, children and young infants were women's business. Physicians were not much help, nor were the apothecaries, barber-surgeons, or other male health care providers who accompanied the early settlers."[15] In Thomas Cone Jr.'s astute observation, it was not until medical practice fragmented into specialties late in the nineteenth century that children were released, reluctantly, from the internists to the pediatricians. Linear progression no longer exacts much hold on contemporary academics, thus it is worthwhile to investigate the emergence and development of professional pediatrics in imperial China compared to its latter budding, albeit under different circumstances, elsewhere. What were the forces behind such a scientific-technological growth and sociocultural phenomenon? In contrast, what took place or existed elsewhere that may have preempted similar developments? Answers to these questions will be illuminating, not only of a better understanding of the Chinese history of science and medicine, but of a comparative view on the historical conditions of childhood and children.

Propagation of a Specialized Knowledge

During the early sixteenth century, the secretary to the Department of Personnel, Hsü Tsan, presented to the Ming dynasty court a curious medical text published by Li-ch'üan-t'ang, a printing house in northwestern China. The ten-chapter book was called *One Hundred Questions on Infants and Children* (*Ying-t'ung pai-wên*). In his foreword, Hsü said that he had come upon the text while serving as an imperial editor; it was "writings of a famous person in the past," passed down in the form of an "anonymous" text. Under the title page of chapter 1 in the original, however, appeared the comments that such were the "Learning of Lu Po-ssû," which many take to be an indication of authorship.[16]

The value of this text rests as much in its content as in its special format. As its title suggests, it is a pediatric text composed in a question-and-answer format. The one hundred questions constitute a wide variety of health problems related to infants and children. Their answers drew on knowledge and skills available to contemporary pediatric practitioners. "For each question, the origin of the symptoms is examined before meticulous treatments are given. It passes judgments by close observation of the physical appearance and prescribes medication according to the ailment. All in all, it is quite comprehensive."[17]

The text consists of two major sections: "Infant and Child Care" and "Diseases and Treatments." The former refers to ideas learned from medieval medical authorities such as Sun Ssû-miao and Ch'ao Yüan-fang, the latter further developed and elaborated on ideas from Ch'ien I. Many of the topics concerning infant care read similar to chapters on the same subject from famed medieval medical books. The text first deals with newborn care, moves on to infant rearing and protection, and finally discusses infant diseases such as lockjaw, mouth grabbing, and umbilical tetanus. For the newborn it recommends immediately administering cinnabar-honey paste, coptis japonica, licorice, or the like as a first step to "cleanse their systems." People were advised against dressing infants too warmly; rather they should try to bring their babies outdoors for sunshine and air and observe moderation in nursing and feeding, "never to overfeed so as to cause indigestion from gorging." Special attention is also paid to proper techniques of breaking the umbilical cord to avoid infection and the resultant "umbilical wind" (ch'i-fêng; neonatal tetanus).[18]

Other chapters discuss questions related to infant growth and development as well as children's diseases. For example, in chapter 4, question 31 inquires into infantile diseases, and question 32 asks about the unclosed soft area (fontanelle) of the skull. In Chapter 5, question 41 asks about slowness of speech, and question 42 explores the problems of hunchback, crane-knee, and slowness in learning to walk. From these samples one might gather that the author of One Hundred Questions was familiar with previous pediatric texts. In the area of pediatric ailments, the text was clearly influenced by Ch'ien I's theories and treatments, especially on such topics as pulse taking, a child's complexion, conditions seen through the eyes, as well as the discourse on diagnosis and treatment of the five organs, fright, vomiting, diarrhea, colds, and fevers. There are of course sections in which the author enjoyed putting in his own opinions and contemporary medical judgments, some with views more precise and articulate than those known in the eleventh and twelfth centuries.

From a historical perspective, however, the structure of this text is of even greater significance than its content. As mentioned before, its question-and-answer format—posing hypothetical questions about the health of infants and children, followed by a general discussion, clinical analysis, and suggested practical treatment—was all formulated in plain, simple language. The discussions were fairly concise and easy to comprehend, the analyses precise and substantive, and the treatments uncomplicated. The author was among those who had an interest in popularizing specialized pediatric knowledge to make text like this one a convenient and useful tool for the vocational novice and ordinary people living in the technological "backwaters."

With the publication of One Hundred Questions, traditional Chinese pediatrics had certainly achieved a rich body of knowledge by the end of the fifteenth century. Furthermore, people acquainted with this "expert" knowledge had come to appreciate the need for popularization. The first printing of One Hundred Questions appeared in the Lan-t'ien district of Shensi province in the northwestern corner of the empire, where it was noticed and presented to the court by local officials. From then on it was disseminated with the authority and sponsorship of the imperial government. On the first pages of its early-sixteenth-century edition, still extant today, there is not only a foreword by the presenter Hsü Tsan, but also a preface by Grand Secretary Yen Sung (1481–1568). The author's idea in producing a "common edition" for general circulation had found its best espousal.

In propagating this sort of "technical" knowledge and skill, the question-and-answer format promised a simple structure and easy access. With the ten chapters and one hundred short questions, "key" achievements and abilities of contemporary Chinese pediatrics were given to the readers, expert or lay, as the format became a familiar style. Other medical fields had adopted the fashion in compilations like One Hundred Questions on Gynecology. Meanwhile, to spread knowledge about children's health, medical scholars experimented with other media, such as songs, rhymes, and verses. The idea was to promote oral transmission and to bring medical knowledge and techniques to a largely uneducated rural population.[19] Wang K'ên-t'ang's Standards of Treatments in Pediatrics (Yu-k'o chun-shêng) of the early seventeenth century contains sections in rhymed verse.[20] As a matter of fact, the various herbal prescriptions (t'ang-t'ou ko-chüeh) from the Ming-Ch'ing era can be viewed as components of this popularizing movement represented by the One Hundred Questions format. Methods of popularization, in important measure, compensated for low literacy and limited education in the circulation of technical information in traditional China. They enabled the spread of much needed medical and health knowledge to obscure places and to various social strata by way of simple colloquial language or rhymed verses. A fair amount of practiced and effective medicine became disseminated. The rapidly growing woodblock printing, a booming publishing industry, and the quickly expanding "book market" in this period no doubt facilitated the spurt in this popularization process.

A text such as *One Hundred Questions* reveals much, therefore, from more than one aspect. In addition to the general demand for health care of children, access and availability of medical service played an increasingly important role. By the fifteenth and sixteenth centuries, in the area of children's health, an energetic profession and its enterprising participants addressed this practical need. These were not limited to the vocational practitioners with specific knowledge and skills but included the informed and concerned who felt the need to connect with the popular demand. Vital channels were constructed, therefore, to render this "technical commodity" accessible to its more remote and underprivileged consumers. Improved delivery and innovative provision of the knowledge of children's health care could then be translated into changing living conditions for many of China's younger population, not just the privileged few.

The Consolidation of Children's Health Care

Despite various innovations, traditional medical practitioners continued to be viewed as technicians, relegated to the rank of craftsmen. During the late imperial period, few could lift up their heads with full self-respect when compared to scholars.[21] Until the Ch'ing dynasty, all medical texts were categorized as "miscellany" (*chi*) rather than "classics" (*ching*). In the official dynastic histories, biographies of physicians had been customarily placed under the category of "magicians and craftsmen" (*fang-chi*), along with alchemists and occultists. Such was the social status accorded to medicine and health providers. In this cultural context, the transmission of medical knowledge and the training of medical skills, as with astrologers and the like, mostly passed through kin from fathers to sons, or from masters to apprentices. Expertise and technology transferred through these particular channels, as did the accumulation of experience along with continuous "professionalization" of the trade.[22]

The professional growth of pediatric medicine after the Sung dynasty can be demonstrated by the example of the Wan family. The Wans began practicing medicine in the fourteenth century in Lo-t'ien district, Hupei province, in the mid-Yangtze valley. After a few generations, they gradually began specializing in children's health. Their first recorded ancestor, Hsing-ch'êng, is said to have been "renowned in pediatrics."[23] When he died at a young age, his surviving son Chü-hsüan vowed to "continue with his ambition and implement his will." "Near and far, Wan family pediatrics were heard of and talked about."[24] Their third generation inheritor, Wan Ch'üan (1499–1582), was the author of *Elaboration on Pediatrics* (*Yu-k'o fa-hui*). At the time of Wan Chü-hsüan's death, Wan Ch'üan, a grown-up son, had received some education and could presumably have availed himself of other career choices. He felt, however, "that pediatrics is presently neither understood nor well practiced. Had its predecessors not produced any writings, the profession would have remained obscure, even if effective. And if its followers did not elaborate on it, the trade could not spread out even though prosperous."[25] Thus Ch'üan became determined to record the accomplishments of his ancestors and to make known the experience of Wan family pediatrics. In his spare time he "sought out the threads of the family tradition, collected those [texts] that had been scattered and lost, supplemented those that had been missing, removed those that were redundant, and corrected those that were erroneous."[26] Through Wan Ch'üan's careful editing, generations of specialized knowledge and clinical experience were compiled into a concise text, *Family Secrets on Infant-Care* (*Yü-ying chia-mi*). As he put it, his purpose in writing the book was simply "to leave it for the consultation of our children and grandsons."[27]

Ironically, though Wan Ch'üan himself had no fewer than ten boys, not one of them was interested in continuing the family practice. Gaining in age, Wan Ch'üan said he was pleased, however, by an increasing reception of his work on pediatrics. *Family Secrets* was quickly distributed in the provinces of Hunan, Hupei, Fukien, Honan, Chekiang, and Kwangtung. It received widespread acclaim, as "no one denied that it represented the long-inherited Wan family pediatrics."[28] At the same time, Wan Ch'üan was distressed that not a single child of his would carry on the family business, leaving more than one hundred years of hard work to obscurity. This prompted him to take yet another action: He wanted to compose an additional book expounding further details of the Wan family trade, turning vocational treasure into public property. This was what later became known as the four-chapter text *Elaboration on Pediatrics*.

From "family secrets" to "open elaboration," pediatrics in late imperial China took steps toward "professionalization," as illustrated by the career of an accomplished practitioner like Wan Ch'üan. Wan Ch'üan himself described the process and his mentality in "An Account of the Origins of Wan Family Pediatrics" (Hsü wan-shih yu-k'o yüan-liu), printed as a preface to the *Elaboration*:

I often remind myself that what cures an ailment is the correct method, and what guides the treatment is a right idea. If the method has not been opted correctly, the treatment will be in vain. Had the ideas not been finely explained, they alone are useless. Thus treatments can grow complicated while ideas appear not at all beneficial. So much so that one might as well go without any texts. This is why I decided to write *Elaboration on Pediatrics*. It is to explicate the ideas and to make clear the theories behind *Family Secrets on Infant-Care*.[29]

When a discipline moved from considering technically "the methods of treatment" to striving for "the ideas behind the treatment," there appeared signs of erudition and specialization. In the process, a family of pediatric specialists made public its old secrets through publication about the "ideas behind abstract notions and theoretical implications."[30] From that point onward, intellectual property could be transferred from the hands of the offspring and apprentices of the Wan family to all "gentlemen of later generations," through the market mechanisms of vocational maturation and knowledge production. Furthermore, with the publication, circulation, and consumption of works such as this one, previous oral traditions first generated through father-son and master-apprentice transmission were converted into a literary heritage. A textual-based pediatric medicine and an argumentative health culture of child care was reproduced and facilitated.

As Wan Ch'üan put it:

That which I do not comprehend will be understood by gentlemen of later generations. If I do not hand [this] down to them, I fear that they may not be able to grasp it or practice it, and the benevolence of the Wan family will be cut short from reaching a fourth generation. If handed to disciples, suppose the situation were [as good] as when Duke Yin found Duke Yü, as in teaching a disciple one finds a worthy person to confer the knowledge, the chain of learning shall not deteriorate [be broken]. But if given a person like Ch'ên Hsiang, even the wisdom as good as that from the Duke of Chou or Confucius would be all but lost. This is the thought I would like to leave with the intelligent among my readers to dwell upon.[31]

A paragraph from his "Foreword to Elaboration on Pediatrics" (Yu-k'o fa-hui hsü) pronounced that:

The Wan family, it can be said, has accomplished something commendable in this profession. . . . If we were to hand it down only to disciples and consider it a family secret, I, when facing this great land of innocent children, will not have widely spread [the knowledge]. This is like concealing the great kindness of Heaven, so that those who cannot obtain [the benefit] from the Wan family are also deprived [of the blessings] from Heaven. Whereas for me, I can no longer consider [this knowledge] to be from the Wan family trade. I see it as [a blessing] bestowed from on high. Only thus should it be closer to the [Heaven's] idea of wishing to be protective to all.[32]

With these words came the emergence of a vocational ethic at a different level, elevated from concerns of self-gain to consideration for the need of social well-being.

The experience of the Wan family, though remarkable, was not an isolated case. The middle and lower Yangtze valley region at this time was China's cultural center as well as a key area for pharmaceutics distribution. The Wan family's popular practice had thus a much broader and deeper background. Similar examples can be found in other developed and developing regions. Famed pediatricians began pouring, in increasing number, from small town clinics. Books on pediatrics continued to supply the markets, with sons writing about their families' practice and disciples coming forth with their masters' trade. Important children's diseases like measles and smallpox became subdisciplines in the sixteenth and seventeenth centuries. Dissemination of technical know-how to the public through publication was but one method in the expansion and maturation of Chinese pediatrics in this period. It created an environment of intellectual interchange and vocational competition that stimulated further developments in health care for children.

This entire phenomenon, furthermore, can be viewed from a broader perspective on the historical experience of children and childhood. For in this "blooming" of pediatric medicine that the Wan family clinic represented, specialized children's health care continued to make strides qualitatively and quantitatively. By the time of Wan Ch'üan, some four and a half centuries after Ch'ien I, pediatricians were growing in numbers, practicing in small towns or larger cities, and confirming the need for and arresting the doubts about child experts. They were also passing their knowledge from generation to generation, transmitting acquired "secrets" or "expertise" from the private domain to a certain public arena. When medical authors such as Wan Ch'üan declared that caring for the young represented the great "kindness" or "blessing" of Heaven that "wishes to protect all," he was expressing a personal view yet also acting on behalf of a broader trend. That is, as pediatric medicine further matured, institutionalized, and professionalized, the historical force working in favor of child survival, child protection, and a certain "child centeredness" was also consolidated. Along with it, the old Chinese cosmological belief in a benign Heaven provided the fortuitous intellectual foundation for a vocational transformation and quiet social transition. People's private need to bring up one's offspring and the elite's or state's public interest in protecting the young converged to create an increasingly beneficial environment for the survival and support of the young.

The Role of the State

By premodern standards, and in comparison with situations elsewhere, the Chinese state had played an active and significant role in the development of medicine and health care. Throughout the imperial period, the government never ceased to show a strong interest in medical improvements or to bear responsibility for the provision of people's physical existence. It influenced the development of Chinese medicine in history, not the least of which included pediatrics.[33]

The publication of *Complete Writings on Infant Protection* (*Pao-ying ch'üan-shu*) by Hsüeh Chi (1488–1558) and his father Hsüeh K'ai, issued by the Ming imperial government in 1556, serves as a good example. Hsüeh Chi, a renowned pediatrician during the first half of the sixteenth century, was from the Su-chou district in the lower Yangtze valley. His father was also an accomplished physician. Records state that Hsüeh Chi was "exceptionally intelligent and capable of committing to memory anything that passed before his eyes, was learned in medical books, and familiar with many aspects of clinical practice."[34] In the early sixteenth century, after being selected as a court physician, he was later promoted to be the medical examiner in Nanking. During the Chia-ching reign (1522–66), he became a professor in the Imperial College of Medicine. As a result, his father, Hsüeh K'ai, was granted an honorific title. The professional reputation of this father-son pair had much to do with the publication of their medical works: *Sixteen Groups of Medical Case Records from the Hsüeh's* (*Hsüeh-shih i-an shih-liu-chung*; 1529), *The Essentials in the Protection of Infants* (*Pao-ying ts'o-yao*; 1556), and *Complete Writings on Infant Protection*. An appraisal of the composition and distribution of *Complete Writings* reveals the contributions the court and the Imperial College of Medicine made toward the development of medicine in general and children's health in particular.

The Chinese government's promotion of pediatrics can be examined from three perspectives: in its recognition of values, in institutional enhancement, and in the pooling of resources. First of all, under the sway of Confucianism, the Chinese imperial government liked to uphold the idea that in ruling its realm it needed to protect the people, as a parent would his or her own children. As the emperor and his officials had to nourish the people to retain their legitimacy, it follows that promoting medicine, publishing medical books, and dispensing remedies were legitimate state functions and indispensable public duties. The imperial censor Wang Ch'i explained this in his foreword to the original edition of Hsüeh's *Complete Writings on Infant Protection*:

The Book of Documents [*Shu*] says that the state should take care of the young, "just as one would protect one's own children." *The Art of War* also advises, "Treat soldiers as if they were your infants [so you] may have them with you while going into [the battle in] deep ditches." Now our sage emperor has great compassion [for the people], even at times when things appear calm as when there is not a single ripple in the sea. And our minister [Duke of Chao] also wants to protect the people, as he would treat small children, to foster soldiers as in keeping a baby. This is why our land appears peaceful in all directions, and the people have been spared untimely death. Similarly, in medicine, one brings forth useful remedies, as whenever tried, they show results. Such benevolence is enough to shield the whole world, it does not simply protect the infants.[35]

The passage reveals a conceptual root, of long tradition in Chinese philosophy, that connected politics and health provisions. Imperial governments since at least the T'ang period never shied away from sponsoring compilation and publication of medical books, making a considerable contribution to the propagation of technical knowledge and the provision of physical needs. Some of the most important works include *The Sage and Beneficial Recipes from the Great Peace* (*T'ai-p'ing shêng-hui fang*, 992 C.E.); *The Complete Book on Sage Remedies* (*Shêng-chi tsung-lu*, Sung dynasty); *Recipes for Aiding All* (*P'u-chi fang*); the medical section in *The Great Imperial Library of the Yüng-lo Emperor* (*Yüng-lo ta-tien*, 1408 C.E.); the 520 sections of *A Complete Collection on Medicine* printed in *The Complete Classics Collection of Ancient China* (*Ku-chin t'u-shu chi-ch'êng*, 1723 C.E.); and the category of medicine in *The Imperial Library of Four Treasures* (*Ssû-k'u ch'üan-shu*, 1787 C.E.). Besides editing and compiling, the court also facilitated limited medical education, gave medical examinations, and dispensed drugs free of charge.[36]

A second area of engagement concerns the establishment of medical institutions, especially that of the Imperial College of Medicine. The establishment of government offices for medical administration and medical education appeared early in Chinese history. The classical and Han periods (221 B.C.–220 C.E.) recorded names of related bureaus. The T'ang dynasty had an Imperial Office of Medicine (T'ai-i shu); the Sung, the Imperial Bureau of Medicine (T'ai-i chü); and for the Ming, the Imperial College of Medicine (T'ai-i yüan). In these late imperial institutions a special field dealing with "youth and child medicine" (*shao-hsiao k'o*) or "children's medicine" (*hsiao-fang mai*) began its existence. It provided medical education in the pediatric subdiscipline, promoting related policies and activities.

With such organized force, the state brought with it the advantages in mobilizing power inherent in a public agency. The Imperial College of Medicine, for instance, identified acclaimed recipes and recruited famed physicians. Wielding an imperial wand, it collected knowledge and expertise, making them available for the consultation of middle rank or lower echelon local practitioners. Under better conditions, the state could also encourage studies in medical practices, sponsor systematic medical education, and develop judicious health policies. In the vast empire of China, these could hardly have been initiated without the involvement of the state. For the most part, the court was mobilizing the financial and human resources at its disposal to propagate and distribute knowledge, to dispense free drugs, or provide accessible health services. Motivated medical practitioners benefited from gaining recognition from the court and from information flowing out of the Imperial College. The much-revered title of Medical Professor of the Imperial College (T'ai-i yüan shih) boosted status and morale. To the common people, the reputations of government physicians carried authority. Advances in pediatrics had, in various stages, benefited from government agencies, as in the case of Ch'ien I's prosperous career at the Sung court, demonstrated by the composition and circulation of the *Proven Formulae*.[37] Hsüeh Chi with his achievements in practicing, teaching, and writing for pediatrics is another illustrious example.

State government could enhance medicine through indirect channels as well, in promoting and propagating health care through the officiating networks of the gentry. Philosophically, the elite's concern for medicine and health care were founded on the same ground as that of the court. The emperor's responsibility and the official's compassion came from the same conceptual source and carried the same social message. Showing its good will through the functions of its bureaucracy and the activities of its gentry was a sensible way for the government to extend state compassion for popular well-being. This was the case in the publication *One Hundred Questions on Infants and Children* and the *Complete Writings on Infant Protection*. Numerous other examples resulted from the same scholar-official or central and local collaboration. Wang Ch'i, who wrote the foreword to the *Complete Writings on Infant Protection,* held the post of right deputy censor of the Imperial Court of Censors (*tu-ch'a yüan yu fu tu-yü-shih*). Shên Yu-lung, who helped edit and reprint its new edition in the early seventeenth century, came also from the ranks of the gentry-officialdom.[38] As a matter of fact, a large number of the extant texts of traditional Chinese pediatrics, as revealed in their forewords and postscripts, came into being because of the enterprising efforts of scholar-officials as devout agents in welfare activities. A fine printing of any sizable work, such as the twenty chapters of *Complete Writings on Infant Protection* by the Hsüeh family pediatricians mentioned above, with its considerable substance, could hardly be feasible unless the court was to underwrite its cost.

In modern times, the provision of medical service and care to the young is still regarded as an essential means of exhibiting a state's social responsibility and political power. The imperial Chinese government furnished with Confucian ideology performed a similar function in the past. The growth of Chinese pediatrics, along with other branches of medicine, benefited from this tradition. Qualified physicians became recognized and were brought under government patronage; effective recipes and treatments were gathered, compiled, publicized, and propagated to a wider population; and the

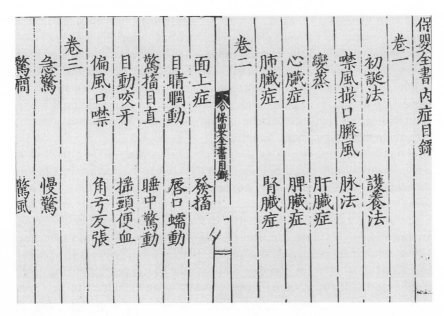

FIG. 8. Table of contents from *Complete Writings on Infant Protection (Pao-ying ch'üan-shu)* by Hsüeh K'ai (Ming dynasty). Reprinted in the Ming dynasty several times, the book was a key text for late imperial China pediatrics. Courtesy of the National Central Library, Taiwan, Republic of China.

needy and the poor were given medication and advice through philanthropic institutions. The educated were encouraged to work hand in hand with the officials in a common interest to enhance reproductive health and the well-being of the next generation. The effect on the fate and experience of children, in turn, can hardly be overlooked.

In the increasingly diversified social stratification during the late imperial period, religious orders, clan organizations, philanthropic groups, even able individuals contributed to the development of medicine and the welfare of children. But the institutional influence of the state never ceased to be a powerful factor in the enterprise.

Engagements of Confucian Scholars

As in other times and places, people pursuing medicine in late imperial China came from numerous sectors of society representing a variety of interests. In their ranks were scholars and professors in the Imperial College of Medicine, specialized physicians, common practitioners, and traveling drug vendors or "bell-ringing healers" (*ling-i*), each serving different func-

tions with their own clientele. Not all, however, entered with strictly "vocational" purposes. Among the nonprofessionals, Confucian scholars drawn
into medicine wielded the greatest influence. These were educated men of
gentry background who, later on in adulthood, out of personal interest or
family need, threw themselves into the study of medicine. Accustomed to
immersion in the classics, they were familiar with the rigors of study. Their
ability in conducting medical elucidation "on paper" transcended, therefore, their standing as mere "amateurs."

Standards of Treatments in Pediatrics (Yu-k'o chun-shêng), part of a
larger compendium called Standards of Treatments in Medicine (Chêng-
chih chun-shêng, also known as Standards for Six Disciplines, Liu-k'o chun-
shêng), serves as good testimony to this phenomenon. Its author, Wang
K'ên-t'ang (1549–1613), was a native of the Chin-t'an district of Chekiang
province in south China. He held the highest degree (chin-shih) from the
official examinations during the middle of the Wan-li reign (1573–1619)
and at one time served as grand secretary to the Ming court. Suffering a de-
motion and sent to be examination commissioner of Fukien province in
his later career, he gradually distinguished himself as a respected classical
scholar with a special expertise in medicine.

Wang's Standards of Treatments in Pediatrics was divided into six sections by subject: the newborn, liver, heart, spleen, lung, and kidney.[39] Such
structure indicates the author's adoption of his diagnostic treatment according to the theory of the five organs (wu-tsang chêng-chih). These six sections covered a wide range of discussions, drawing inspiration from pediatric texts dating back to the Sung period. It was intended to be a comprehensive and authoritative textbook, as its title suggests. Wang aimed at
providing a general guideline of diagnosis and treatment for all practitioners of children's health. As a scholarly doctor (ju-i), he had considerable advantage over the less "academic" practitioners in the field.

The book discussed such subjects as newborn care, infant pathology, the
feeding and raising of normal infants, abnormal growth, and nutritional
diseases of children. For every problem, it listed opinions of earlier experts
before adding Wang's own judgments.[40] Wang K'ên-t'ang had begun as a
nonprofessional medical scholar, entering medicine as an interested Confucian. He collected information, gathered data from a plethora of sources,
conducting at times both clinical and philological investigations. Soon after
the printing of Standards of Treatments in Pediatrics, it was received as the
"guide for all physicians." His biography in the Official Ming Dynasty History (Ming-shih) honored him as the most outstanding among "scholars
who achieved fame in medicine."[41]

Confucian scholars' endeavors in pediatrics, related to their concern for
practical social needs and physical well-being of families, were part of a

larger picture of health-related activities of the educated. The particular focus on pediatrics, with its concern for infants and children, gave additional ethical value and cultural meaning to their undertaking. Saving lives of the newborn and safeguarding the growth of young children matched well with the Confucian value of humanity (*jen*) and the social obligation that scholar-officials espoused. Their intellectual skills and social resources, along with the commitment to medical studies, in turn strengthened the understanding, appreciation, assistance, and support for young lives at a time when learning carried a broad implication and before medicine, as a clinical profession, closed against the curiosity of all amateurs.

Conclusion

Due to a steadfast Confucian concern for posterity and family preservation, Chinese society showed an intense commitment to the survival of children. Since medieval times, medical scholars devoted separate attention to the health of children. This soon fostered specialization and growing publications in the field. The knowledge gained then was spread through society, couched in rhymes and lyrics. The pediatric physician's ideas concerning the physiological and psychological states of the young thus gradually seeped into the popular mind. Pediatric medicine appeared not only as a specialized field but as a social and cultural force speaking to the populace about the character of young lives—about the nature of children and childhood. By the late imperial period, materials on child education reveal a sophisticated and meticulous appreciation for developmental stages of infancy that can be traced directly or indirectly back to this process of specialization. This vocational-medical world of ideas and practices may look different in its specifics from what Ariès and others would consider in their European terms or modern sense as "*the* concept of childhood." Yet it shows clearly that in a society rooted in family ethics, the state, its educated elite, and medical professionals could all converge to create an environment attentive to the special conditions of children.

Besides professional services, the development of pediatric medicine in the last millennium of Chinese history has much to reveal. In reintroducing the world of Chinese pediatrics, its ramification goes beyond tracing simply the history of a scientific development and its early origins. To have a Department of Youth Medicine dating back to the eighth century and a pediatric specialty since the eleventh century is remarkable, considering that specialized medical texts on these subjects began to pour out in noticeable numbers in Latin and German in the fifteenth and sixteenth centuries. In the United States, the development of the pediatric profession began under the leadership of Dr. Abraham Jacob and others, with the establishment of professional associations and journals, the building of children's hospitals, and further subspecialization after the mid-nineteenth century, ushering in of course an entirely different era in the health care of children. Yet in light of all these later developments in the West, the path the Chinese pediatric practitioners traveled merits a different kind of appreciation. For one, their very existence marked a collective recognition of the need for special care and focused attention on the very young. Second, developments in pediatrics in China or any other place almost always presuppose a view on the interest in the distinctiveness of young lives. The emergence and acceptance of a vocational discipline like pediatrics reveals a recognition of this special feature of a child and the childhood it entails. As newly established authorities on children's matters, traditional Chinese pediatricians capitalized on their biophysiological views of the first stage of human life, one quite unlike views derived from other socioculturally anchored perspectives. Third, the broader social need that occasioned the profession in the first place continued to sustain its growth and demanded the spread of its service. China's long tradition in learned medicine thereafter provided a historical background that nurtured its vocational development and the social environment that enabled it to flourish. Fourth, state institutions and government regulations that supported its development from the top down secured a basic supporting network from the public sector. Records of contact between pediatricians and the parents and children they were attending provide a rare glimpse of the activities of children in illness as in health and in pain as in gaiety.

2 *Newborn Care*

For any traveler moving through the medieval Chinese empire chancing upon a T'ang rural woman giving birth, the scene would have been revealing. First, as the baby emerged from the birth canal, a thick brownish paste was quickly pushed into the newborn's throat, as if the mother was fearful of anything else taking place beforehand. Second, the body was dipped in a prepared water basin by the mother for a quick wash; the umbilical cord and, at times, even the afterbirth may have still been attached to the body. After this, the umbilical cord was broken, either by the mother's own teeth or with a piece of earthenware tile. The infant was then wrapped in a quilt stitched from old garments and put to the breast to nurse. One millennium later, if a traveler were to visit the same scene, little would appear recognizable. A quick dry wiping had replaced the old wash in warm water. Immediately following the delivery drops of pig's milk or scallion juice would have been administered to the infant's mouth for stimulation, and the old habit of bringing down the "fetal excrement" was no longer a concern. Most surprisingly, cauterizing scissors or blades were used to cut the cord that had been tied with a red thread a few inches away from the body. Moxabustion and an "umbilical branding cake" were applied after the procedure to seal the wound before the stem was covered with medicinal powder and wrapped in new white linen squares. If questioned, these rural women would confess that they had learned the skill from other folks via rhymed verses on health care and medicine. These rhymes also contained instructions on emergency rescues for difficult births, premature deliveries, and for reviving " nonbreathing babies." The stories and novels of the day as well as elegant Sung poems depicted gatherings for the customary newborn "baby washing on the third day" (*hsi-san*). What had happened to the reception of Chinese babies over the years? More importantly, how are we to account for the history behind the everyday stories?

The history of medicine and health care in both the West (where it is better studied) and other societies (where it has only been observed) has enjoyed a surge in interest recently. It has been received with both exhilaration and a new ambivalence. The excitement comes from an intellectual relief that finally medicine and health, the epitome of modern science and technology, has been recognized as a measure of socioculturally constructed activity. A slight awkwardness remains, however, because the cultural studies approach may threaten to render any observation of familiar accomplishments or "objective" change in history problematic, thus the basis for critical reflection rather than simple recognition. Developments in medical knowledge and health care techniques, or accounts thereof, represent both cultural discourse and the practical struggle to confront death and suffering. Do they need to be debated as mutually exclusive aspects of the same story, at each other's expense? Or could there be an alternative way of historicizing the evolution of notions, concepts, and sociocultural acts?

The development of pediatrics (*yu-k'o*) or newborn care (*ch'u-shêng yang-hu*) in imperial China is as good an example as any to assess both the cultural discourse and pragmatic reality of medical knowledge. The cultural discourse approach links science, technology, and institutions with the larger picture and deeper currents of social mentality, personal attitudes, and cultural values. Its counterpart, factual reality, brings into consideration related observations on social history, economic developments, demographic structure, material life, and ecological factors to establish more than a fluid account of the progression of objective discoveries and technical progress. To history and historians, the development of Chinese pediatrics, and its wrestling with the problems of children's health, is a new subject with an unexpected significance. Newborn care as an entry into that vocational service highlights the interplay between expert intervention and popular needs, which may be understood in more than one perspective.

Despite its widely recognized accomplishments in the modern era, "Western medicine" was neither the most effective historically nor the more prevalent in practice. Specialized attention and medical care for children, for instance, did not emerge in Europe until relatively late in history. Partly under the influence of the Enlightenment and Rousseau's philosophy, and generally along the trend of further diversification and specialization, specialized medical treatises on the diseases and health problems of children began to accelerate in Europe after the eighteenth century.[1] Pediatric medicine as a branch of the medical profession, however, only gradually came into its own in the middle of the nineteenth century, first in Western Europe and then in the United States.[2] Before then, infant care, especially that of the newborn, had existed as part of obstetrics. In premodern times, midwives or family helpers cared for newborn infants in Europe and the United States. Although there are instances where pre-twentieth-century medical texts discuss children's health and illness, little can be found on infant care in particular. The shift in neonatal care from obstetrics to pediatrics in the West was a gradual process that began in the latter half of the twentieth century.[3] Neonatal medicine as a field of its own (called neonatology as a subspecialty under pediatrics) has developed only in the last few decades.[4]

In contrast, specialized medicine for children both as a coherent body of knowledge and as an active clinical profession appeared considerably earlier in China. Ch'ien I and his medical teachings (in the form of a small book called *Proven Formulae of Pediatric Medicine*) marked the beginning of practicing pediatrics, at least since the second half of the eleventh century. In addition to general medical writings on children, pediatric medicine had evolved into an active medical discipline, with its own theoretical ideas, empirical experience, and therapeutic devices.[5] Fostered in part by Confucian values, particular focus emerged in the area of infant care.[6] A historical sketch of the changes taking place over one thousand years may illustrate this evolution in knowledge and techniques developed out of concerted efforts to improve the chances of survival for the newborn.[7]

Documentation and Main Trends

The primary materials for this study are Chinese pediatric texts from the eleventh to the eighteenth centuries supplemented by a contrast provided by Sui-T'ang medicine. Traditional Chinese texts on pediatric medicine are numerous, some with meticulous details. While information on pediatrics could be found in texts on general medicine, gynecology, and pharmacology from the seventh century onward, numerous titles also specialized in the field. Tens of dozens of these exist for consultation. The more important of these often went through dozens of editions in various regions in this period. These texts deal with general pediatric health as well as children's diseases and their treatments. For each problem, they usually present discussion (*lun*), treatment (*fang*), and case histories (*an*), often resulting from generations of clinical experience. This set of primary sources on children's health and pediatric medicine provides rich material for understanding the health records of infants as well as the kind of care provided by medical experts and society at large.

The crude picture generated by these medical texts spanning over one thousand years is one of a conscious and continuous effort to secure a better chance of survival for the newborn, especially by professional pediatricians. In part due to the Confucian emphasis on posterity, later joined by the Buddhist compassion for life, special concern for infants and children appeared strong and early in Chinese medicine.[8] Well before pediatric medicine came into its own, from at least the seventh century onward, prominent medical authors devoted special attention to the needs of newborn infants.[9] Upon close examination of these medical texts, furthermore, it is clear that the term "newborn" (ch'u-shêng) in the texts refers to infants just delivered from the mother's womb. Chinese medical writers by then had in fact identified newborn care as a problem deserving special attention and concrete instructions.

By the eleventh century, as pediatrics branched off from general medicine into a field of its own, it greatly facilitated development in newborn care.[10] Between the tenth and fourteenth centuries, therefore, elaborations on "newborn care" not only appeared in almost all important medical texts, but special discussions on the newborn in pediatric manuals also became increasingly detailed and complex.[11] Medical authors sought improvements in key procedures immediately following birth such as the cutting of the umbilical cord and discharging the meconium. They also better appreciated the importance of such matters as body temperature, hygiene, and umbilical stump care.

During the fifteenth and sixteenth centuries, pediatric discussions on newborn care strengthened both in quantity and complexity. Infant rearing began to be treated in separate books.[12] Leading pediatric texts presented elaborate information on proper care and newborn protection, giving explanations and advice on particular needs.[13] From these discussions emerged a clearer recognition that preventive medicine provided by proper care was the most sensible answer to many of the fatal problems threatening the newborn at that time. A growth in the publication and dissemination of such specialized knowledge, moreover, revealed a conscious effort to popularize this pediatric expertise among practitioners and the educated elite, on the one hand, and a relatively receptive lay audience, on the other.

Important changes in newborn care began in the eleventh and twelfth centuries and reached their height in the sixteenth and seventeenth centuries with matured theory and practice. From the early seventeenth to the mid-eighteenth century, a separate subject called "Care of the Newborn Infant" (Hsiao-êrh ch'u-shêng hu-yang mên) appeared as a subsection under the category of pediatrics in The Complete Classics Collection of Ancient China (Ku-chin t'u-shu chi-ch'êng). This in fact began the opening chapters of the section on health care for the young.[14] Discussions at that time show awareness of the correlation between the age of the infant and its fragility and vulnerability. The care given during the first hours after birth thus appeared critical to the survival of the baby. At the end, considerations of emergency measures for difficult and premature births also surfaced.[15] With these developments, the premodern Chinese search for improved newborn care achieved its climax. As it evolved from concerns about normal healthy infants to emergency help for high-risk babies, it revealed a pattern shared by modern pediatrics centuries later.

The cumulative effect of this scientific discovery and customary practice can be identified in at least four areas. First, the long attention paid to the life-threatening crises of the newborn yielded important breakthroughs. The best example is the grappling with the pathology of neonatal tetanus and the subsequent development of better methods for breaking the cord and caring for the stump. The value and historical impact of this advance in knowledge and care can hardly be exaggerated. Second, practices in the handling of newborn infants evolved with better knowledge and improved techniques. Changes in mouth wiping, the first wash, and expulsion of the meconium represented a new appreciation in the physical hygiene of the new-born infants based on empirical observations. Third, pediatric practitioners not only continued to care for the healthy newborn but also began looking for ways to save those at risk from difficult birth, premature birth, or other birth defects. Significant investigations were made into the maintenance of body temperature and other rescue measures in an emergency. These represent important milestones in the overall development of newborn care. Fourth, and most important, attempts were made to spread knowledge of newborn care. Pediatric texts increased in the market, at times going through numerous reprints in different regions. Hand copies of popular pediatric works were also in circulation. These constituted a social force for improving the health of infants. In addition, pediatric practitioners and the educated elite rendered methods of infant care into rhymes and simple question-and-answer manuals with charts, drawings, and illustrations. Popularized forms did much to spread developing techniques. Qualitative changes in traditional newborn care thus made quantitative differences in history and historical demography.

Primary Procedures

The main procedures of newborn care appeared to take on common features throughout China, with minor regional and class variations. The first act performed on an infant by the birthing woman or other attendants was to "quickly wrap a piece of soft cotton around the figure and wipe the bad fluids [o-chih] from his mouth."[16] This custom of "mouth wiping" (shih-k'ou), or cleansing of the mouth, had been practiced well before the Middle Ages and has been documented in detail.[17] After the infant let out his first cry, the next step was to clean his body, referred to as the "first wash" (ch'u-yü).[18] This first wash could be done either with a full warm bath or with a simple, dry wiping.

Following the mouth wipe and the bath, the third procedure was to "break the umbilical cord" (tuan-ch'i)—a key task in childbirth. It could be completed by biting, severing, burning, or cutting.[19] Over the centuries, important changes took place in this area. Once the cord had been broken, the stump was carefully wrapped. This procedure, called "umbilical wrapping" (*kuo-ch'i*), was viewed with considerable concern. Fairly elaborate rules were devised.[20] The infant was then wrapped in "old clothes" or soft cotton—a step called "swaddling the infant" (*kuo-êrh*).[21] The idea was to keep the infant warm but not too hot. It was also thought to secure the baby's body so as to help reduce the chances of injury.[22]

In most societies, the first phase of newborn care was complete after the first cry, bathing, umbilical care, and swaddling. The next step was to give the infant back to his mother to nurse and rest. Medieval Chinese custom, however, required the administration of some medicinal compounds (such as cinnabar and honey paste, licorice drink, or *coptis japonica* juice) to clear the digestive and intestinal track before beginning breast-feeding.[23] This originally developed out of an ancient medical theory known as "fetal poison" (*t'ai-tu*), which later took on a new meaning in infant hygiene.[24] Therefore, some infants did not start breast-feeding until hours or even a day after birth.[25]

Regional and class variations existed with the above procedures. From available evidence, one can detect at least three kinds of variations: one, partial rearrangement of the order of the steps;[26] two, slightly altered handling of each step;[27] and three, overall simplification.[28] Whereas the general procedures of newborn care in late imperial China proper remained similar across geographic areas and social strata, continuous efforts were made to improve upon key principles and the steps of this shared pool of knowledge.

Breaking the Cord, Umbilical Tetanus, and Stump Care

The most serious threat to a healthy newborn before the advent of modern hygiene was neonatal tetanus caused by improper handling of the umbilical cord. The disease erupted within the first days of life, accounting for a large portion of infant mortality in the premodern era. Records in traditional Chinese medicine offer advice for the cutting of the umbilical cord, care of the stump, and treatment of the wound.[29] Revisions made by Chinese pediatrics from the eleventh to the seventeenth centuries led to significant breakthroughs in newborn care in the late imperial period.

From folk sources and traditional medical texts, two methods in breaking the umbilical cord in ancient China can be identified: severing it with a sharp instrument (a knife, pair of scissors, or simply a shard of pottery or ceramic) or biting it off, often by the mother (probably practiced widely among the rural population).[30]

There is much evidence that the Chinese population had long been trou-

bled by umbilical infection and that medical authorities had struggled with
what was essentially neonatal tetanus for some time. As early as the late
third century, for instance, the *Chia-i Classic* (*Chia-i-ching*) had mentioned
the work of the famous scholar Huang-fu Mi in conducting acupuncture
treatments on infants with "umbilical wind" (*ch'i-fêng*).[31] Umbilical wind
in early Chinese medical texts comprised assorted ailments in addition to
neonatal tetanus. In the eighth century, medical experts such as Sun Ssû-
miao advised: "Once the infant is born . . . first bathe it, then break the
umbilical cord. In so doing, one must not use a knife, but have a person bite
it off through a single layer of cloth. Then blow on it seven times and wrap
it up."[32]

By this time, Sun Ssû-miao and other medieval medical authorities such
as Ch'ao Yüan-fang and Wang T'ao all recognized that newborn infants suffered easily from umbilical wind.[33] The more astute among them had also
arrived at the conclusion that this disease, contrary to the previous notions
of fetal poison, indeed originated from a certain "contamination" of the
umbilical area. They believed it to be directly related to improper handling
of the cord and saw it as a vicious and usually fatal ailment that occurred
within the first week of birth.[34] Sun Ssû-miao's instruction was therefore
rooted in a cautious and experimental attitude. The earlier method of using
a knife to break the cord was suspected to be unsafe, thus the admonition
against metal blades. Direct contact between human teeth and the cord was
also thought to be unprotected, hence the advice about shielding the cord
with a layer of fabric.[35]

The real change in the understanding of neonatal tetanus, and conse-
quently of an improved method of cord cutting, appeared in the mid-twelfth
century when an incisive discovery was made on the characteristics of the
disease. The pediatric text *A Thorough Discussion of Infant Hygiene*
(*Hsiao-êrh wei-shêng tsung-wei lun-fang*), published by the Sung Imperial
College of Medicine in 1156, first made the following observation:

Around the seventh day after birth, the infant's face turns blue; he wants to cry but
has no voice. His mouth may become locked and lips tightly shut, and no longer is
he able to nurse. At this juncture the infant's lips turn blue and he spits out foamy
saliva. His limbs then turn cold and stiff. These are indeed symptoms of umbilical
wind and mouth grabbing [*ts'o-k'ou*].[36]

It vividly established the clinical symptoms of what appeared to be
neonatal tetanus. The text then offered the view that the origin of this disease came actually from outside the human body, not from fetal poison or
anything else intrinsic, as many believed.[37]

Following this, the text took a great leap in empirical observation and
made a bold statement: "This [umbilical wind] is similar to the tetanus

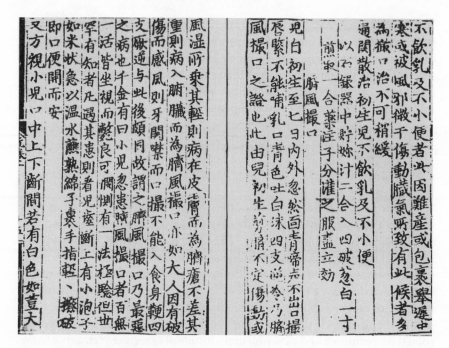

FIG. 9. "Umbilical Wind and Mouth Grabbing" (Ch'i-fêng ts'o-k'ou), in *A Thorough Discussion on Infant Hygiene* (*Hsiao-êrh wei-shêng tsung-wei lun-fang*), author unknown (Sung dynasty). This was a key passage in the long debate on cord-cutting practice, published by imperial medical scholars in 1156. Courtesy of the National Central Library, Taiwan, Republic of China.

adults contract after receiving an open wound [*yin-yu p'o-shang êrh kan-fêng*]; they are seen with their teeth tightly shut, their mouth locked and are unable to take in any food. Their bodies then stiffen like flagella and the limbs become unwieldy. All symptoms appear quite identical [to the ones observed for infants]."[38]

This seemingly inconspicuous paragraph in *A Thorough Discussion* cut through the ancient riddle of umbilical wind with uncommon shrewdness. It pointed out the novel idea that the progression of umbilical wind in the newborn and that of adult tetanus are one and the same—an act of astute observation and intellectual inference well before the arrival of modern microbiological theory and the discovery of tetanus bacilli. Once the connection between umbilical wind and the "receiving of an open wound" was suspected, ground was laid for an improved method of cutting the cord.

A Thorough Discussion, informed by the recognition of adult tetanus in general medicine and influenced probably by its handling of traditional Chinese surgery (*yang-k'o*) and acupuncture, then proposed a revolutionary

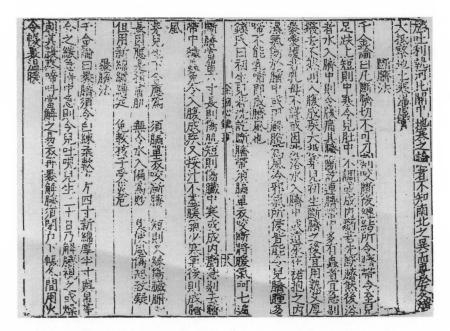

FIG. 10. "The Method of Cord-Cutting" (*Tuan-ch'i fa*) in *Precious Guide for Saving the Young* (*Ch'üan-yu hsin-chien*), by K'ou P'ing (Ming dynasty). Wound contamination through bad cord-cutting was a main cause of death of newborns before modern times. The National Palace Museum, Taiwan, Republic of China.

procedure. A sort of "umbilical branding cake" (*lo-ch'i ping-tzû*) was to be prepared along with moxa to cauterize the raw umbilical wound.[39] This form of cauterization gradually gained ground among pediatric experts and educated parents. Though umbilical tetanus was by no means eliminated, records show that high heat and cauterization was an important step in the right direction.

From the twelfth to the eighteenth centuries, changes were made in cord cutting and umbilical care, alongside the developments in pediatric medicine and the increase of pediatric practitioners. Equally important, this evolution took place amid much debate, deliberation, and exploration.[40] By 1742, in the Ch'ing imperial compendium, *The Golden Mirror for Medicine* (*I-tsung chin-chien*), a standard method of cord cutting and umbilical care was described. First, as the infant is born, one should tie the umbilical cord off at six or more *ch'un* (Chinese inch) from the infant's body to secure a safe cutting spot. One should then scorch the scissors and use them to cut the cord. After this, one should use a flame to cauterize (*lo*) the umbilical wound, completely sealing it off after it is cut. Finally, an umbilical branding cake and moxa should be applied to the stump. Medicinal drying

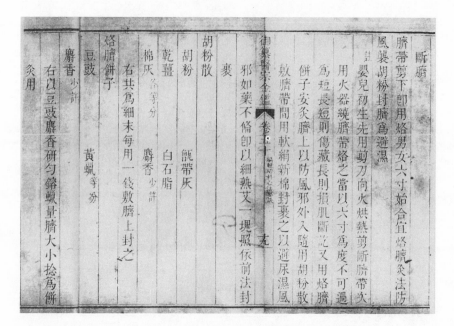

FIG. 11. "Recipe of Preparing the Umbilical Branding Cake" (*Lo-ch'i ping-tzû fang*) in *Key Methods for Various Diseases in Pediatrics* (*Yu-k'o tsa-ping hsin-fa yao-chüeh*), by Wu Ch'ien (Ching dynasty), collected in *I-tsung chin-chien*. People in the Sung dynasty recognized that bad handling in umbilical cutting could lead to lethal results. Inspired by traditional external medicine and acupuncture, this Ch'ing text spreads the advice on cauterization of the raw umbilical stump to lesson the chance of contamination. Microfilm in Fu Ssu-nien Library, Academia Sinica, Taiwan, Republic of China.

powder should then be applied to prevent moisture and enhance healing before the umbilical stump is wrapped. To disseminate this technique, the editors rendered the entire procedure into a rhymed quatrain.[41]

The changes that took place in the area of cord cutting and umbilical care in late imperial China were not accidental. A better clue on neonatal tetanus and the revised method of cord cutting are testimony to this process. By the sixteenth century, moreover, there were references not only to a certain medium of "pollution" believed to cause the umbilical wind but also to some kind of a nesting or "incubation " phenomenon before symptoms appeared. The experienced Ming pediatric practitioner Wan Ch'üan (1499-1582), for one, raised the novel notion that transmission could have been carried out by a physical agent—which he called some kind of "seed" (*p'ao-tzû*)—which passed through the umbilical wound and "fell upon the belly," causing the infant's ailment.[42] The author of *The Golden Needle of Pedi-*

atrics (*Yu-k'o chin-chên*), Ch'in Ching-ming, suggested that as the disease progressed from the wound, it moved through a stage of "evil sweltering" (*yün-hsieh*).[43] The suggestion of a sort of fermentation, nurturing, or "incubation" process fortuitously matched the long-standing recognition that the disease struck infants usually after the fourth day of birth.[44]

Gradually, by the sixteenth century, some astute pediatricians became alert to the possibility that ordinary umbilical infections and the lethal kind of umbilical tetanus might have represented two unrelated types of problem.[45] Common infections of the umbilical area such as "umbilical wetness" (*ch'i-shih*), "umbilical swelling" (*ch'i-chung*), and "umbilical boils" (*ch'i-ch'uang*) occurred mostly from wetness (from moisture or urine) that remained local, categorically different from the detrimental problem that umbilical wind (tetanus) represented. With this came, on the one hand, further consideration of stump care, under the name of "umbilical wrapping." On the other hand, general local umbilical infections were separated from the life-threatening signs of tetanus in prevention and treatments. Umbilical wrapping typically included the application of medicinal compounds to the area after the cord was severed, careful wrapping of the stump, regular inspection of it thereafter, cleaning and changing bandages, and avoidance of wetness and soiling. The concern was to keep the area dry and unspoiled.[46] As both the cutting and the wrapping of the umbilical cord improved, a birthing culture emerged, revised from its medieval antecedents. It advised birth attendants and family members to hold the cord with new fabric, tie it off a few inches from the abdomen, cut it with scissors previously fired, cauterize the wound, and carefully wrap the stump with a bandage.[47] Popularized renditions of these technical procedures enabled uneven but continuous dissemination of this information.[48]

Attendance to the Physical Cleanness of the Newborn

The understanding and practice of the physical cleanness of the newborn in traditional Chinese health culture primarily evolved around the three activities of mouth wiping, first bath, and cleansing the digestive tract. All three procedures underwent important changes during the late imperial period.

MOUTH WIPING

The long-practiced "mouth wiping" was an inherited custom.[49] Most medieval theorists, following the ancient notion of "fetal poison," argued that dirty fluids, if allowed to enter the system as the infant opened his mouth to let out his first cry, could cause assorted illnesses (especially fatal children's diseases such as pox and measles). Such thinking remained primarily unaltered from the eighth to the fifteenth century.[50] More progressively minded sixteenth-century pediatric authorities such as K'ou P'ing admitted that "methods for saving him [the newborn] must be stressed, though the reason behind these was understood by few."[51]

By the end of the sixteenth century, the physician Chang Chieh-pin (1563–1640), aided by his rich clinical experience, at last came forth with a more perceptive argument. First of all, he expressed doubt about an ancient theory of "fetal poison" (t'ai-tu). Nor did he believe that infants could develop ailments simply because they had upon birth swallowed foul matter from their mouths. To him:

All texts on pediatrics in the past have stated that at the time of birth, the infant held clots of blood in his mouth. With the first cry he may swallow them, causing poison to dwell in the vital vein, thus diseases such as fits, fever, pox, and measles may develop later as a result. At first this theory seemed reasonable. Yet, as I understand it, the infant's entire body is composed of blood. Since these clots are also blood, how is it that they can come to poison the body? Even if the infant does swallow them, they should be expelled right through the bowels. How can it be that holding them alone can cause further harm? All of that seems quite nonsensical.[52]

He asserted that the true reason for mouth wiping ought to be because the infant's "body has been newly formed, so one should cleanse it." It was thus oral hygiene, not the prevention of swallowing dirty matter, that may have justified the continuous practice of mouth wiping. He argued, furthermore, that in the event that matter in the mouth did enter the infant's body, it would not cause any serious problem because it would go right through the digestive tract and be expelled.

Chang's pragmatic attitude helped to demystify the medical reason behind the mouth-wiping custom. Medical scholars at the time appeared to be watching for two kinds of harm caused by the foul fluid in the newborn's mouth. First, the mucus or fluid in the infant's mouth could become a vehicle for an ailment of the mouth and tongue, which could then create feeding and health problems. The various newborn oral problems described in medieval medical texts, such as "heavy jaw" (chung-o), or "goose mouth boil" (o-k'ou-ch'uang), suggested related concerns and treatments.[53] To this day modern doctors and nurses continue to use gauze or suction instruments to clean a newborn's mouth and nose primarily for hygienic considerations. Second, breathing in fluid that has been contaminated by the meconium (called meconium aspiration in modern medicine) could lead to an infection of the respiratory tract.[54] In medieval and late imperial Chinese medical texts, diseases attributed to a lack of oral cleaning (such as high fever, sputum, and colds) could be hints of symptoms related to bronchitis or pneumonia, caused perhaps by accidental inhalation of contaminated fluid into the lungs. Ordinarily, no doubt, the first consideration formed the basic reason behind mouth wiping, which, as Chang Chieh-pin insightfully commented, "has really nothing to do with the fetal poison theory previously devised."[55]

By Chang's time, in the latter half of the sixteenth century, mouth wiping had become more varied and elaborate. Besides wiping the mouth with new, clean, soft cotton wrapped around a finger, people should also "prepare thin slices of licorice. As the time of delivery approaches, have ready cotton and boiled water with licorice steeping in it. Upon receiving the infant, wrap a finger with soft cotton, dip it in the licorice juice, and wipe his mouth."[56] Some wiped the infant's mouth with licorice juice, mild ginger soup or "silk soaked in salt water," while others wiped the infant's mouth, tongue, gums, and cheeks with tea leaves dipped in fragrant powder.[57] For many households in late imperial China, these customary practices achieved both ritualistic and practical purposes.

By the early nineteenth century, as the practicing physician Ch'êng Hsing-hsüan (1736–1820) composed his pediatric synopsis in *Medical Deliberations* (*I-shu*), there was no longer any doubt about the true value of mouth wiping. He recommended, along with others, that the practice be repeated a few times a day until the child's first birthday.[58] Others suggested that people also employ clean silk to wipe the eye, face, and head areas to prevent infection.[59] Customs rooted in old suspicion, such as mouth wiping and the ancient idea of "fetal poison" were adopted to become "sensible" practice founded on changed hygienic understanding. By the nineteenth century the practice had made the routine list of infantile care in China's more developed regions.

THE FIRST WASHING

Emerging from the birth canal, an infant's body is wet with blood and other fluids. That some sort of a wash is in order seems obvious enough, though there had always appeared different ways of doing so. As early as the T'ang dynasty a medical text mentioned the act of "first wash." Following delivery, as an infant's mouth was wiped, someone was supposed to "first wash the child, then break the umbilical cord." The reason given for this was that "if one breaks the umbilical cord first and then washes him, water may get to the umbilical stump." The text also stated that "when bathing the newborn, take the juice from a pig's gallbladder and add it to the hot water [*t'ang*]. [The child] thus will never suffer from scabies for life." Attendants were warned "not to use arbitrarily any water [*tsa-shui*] to wash him."[60] The word *t'ang* (hot water) referred to water previously boiled.

More elaborate instructions from the same period advised people explicitly to use boiled water (*shou-t'ang*) with medicinal ingredients in bathing the infant. When finished, "rub powder [*fên*] on his body."[61]

By the twelfth century, pediatric texts became more elaborate. There was a clearer notion about the importance of boiled water. Some asked people to boil water until it was reduced to seven-tenths of the original volume—sterilized no doubt in the process.[62] It had become common, moreover, not to allow a newborn to come into contact with unboiled "raw water" (*shêng-shui*). Concerned that people might not have enough time for on-the-spot boiling, they were instructed to prepare the bathing water beforehand and store it. While bathing the infant, people were reminded to be attentive to the temperature and to keep the umbilical stem dry.[63]

By the fifteenth and sixteenth centuries, there was increasing concern about keeping the infant dry and warm at this vulnerable stage.[64] This idea in turn drove some medical scholars to consider alternative methods of cleansing without using water. In order to keep the infant warm and to avoid danger caused by water, pediatric specialists of the Ming period suggested wiping instead of washing right after birth. They instructed parents to use either a towel slightly dampened with boiling water or a piece of dry cloth to wipe the infant's body quickly and then immediately swaddle him.[65] With this revised procedure, an infant could be cleaned without risking contamination or catching a cold from a wet bath. It was probably a method originating in the cold and dry regions of north China but by mid-Ming times had found its way into numerous pediatric texts and many regional customs.[66]

The first real washing of the infant was postponed often until the third day after birth. This gradually developed into a custom called "washing on the third" (*hsi-san*). By the Ming-Ch'ing period, "washing on the third" had evolved into a ritual widely practiced among commoners as the first formal washing of the infant. Many people selected an auspicious hour and date for the activity, inviting relatives and friends to attend the ceremony. Medical documents of the time bear abundant evidence of the practice.[67] Lively descriptions are also found in biographical accounts and contemporary literature.[68] The water used for *hsi-san* was either boiled water with juice of a pig's gallbladder (*chu-tan chih*), five-root soup (*wu-kên t'ang*) prepared with peach, apricot, and other roots, or fluid made with other medicinal ingredients.[69] With regard to *hsi-san*, thoughtful medical authors continued to council people not to practice it literally or be too rigid about it. The idea was to protect the infant from cold or infection. People need not fix the washing on any particularly divine, auspicious date. For the weaker babies, however, they did advise waiting for another ten or fifteen days, which would do no harm.[70]

FIG. 12. "Bathing a Newborn Child." Late imperial Chinese pediatrics were increasingly concerned about preserving the body heat of newborns. Hence the advice of waiting at least three days before bathing. This illustration shows a gap between the folk art (which continued to depict the dated custom of bathing upon birth) and the narrative of the novel (which described the custom of postponing the wash until a later date). From Hsiao-hsiao-shêng, "Wu Yüeh-niang Shih-ou Shêng-êrh," *The Plum in the Golden Vase* (*Chin-p'ing-mei*) (Ming Wan-li edition, 1617), chapter 79.

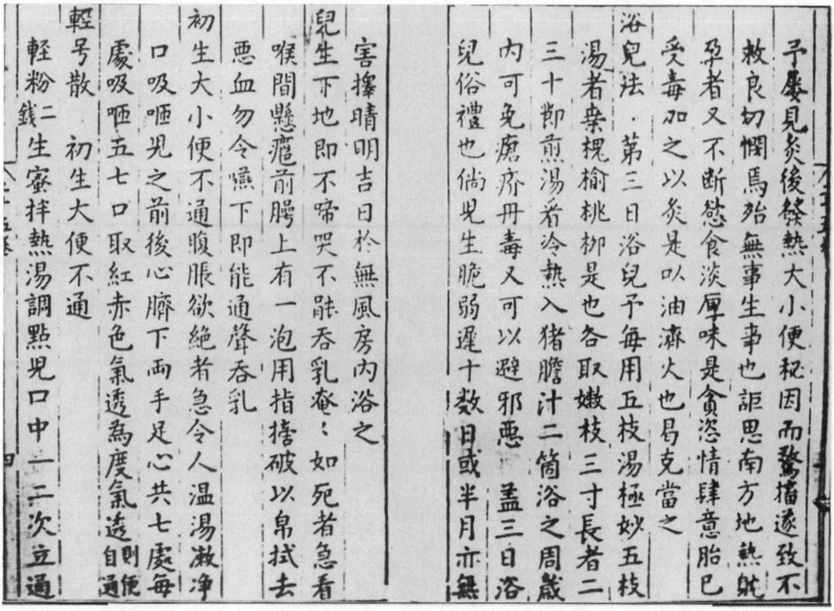

予每見灸後發熱大小便秘因而驚搐逐致不
救良切憫焉始無事生事也詎思南方地熱妊
孕者又不斷慾食辛厚味是貪恣情肆意胎已
灸毒加之以灸是以油潑火也易克當之
浴兒法・第三日浴兒予每用五枝湯極妙五枝
湯者要視榆桃柳是也各取嫩枝三寸長者二
三十節煎湯肴冷熱入猪膽汁二筒浴之周歳
内可免瘡疥丹毒又可以避邪惡　蓋三三日浴
兒俗禮也倘兒生脆弱遲十數日或半月亦無

害撩晴明吉日於無風房内浴之
兒生下地即不帯哭不啼呑乳奄；如死者急看
喉間懸癰前腭上有一泡用指撞破以帛拭去
惡血勿令嚥下即能通聲呑乳
初生大小便不通腹脹欲絶若急令人溫湯澈净
口吸唖兒之前後心臍下両手足心共七處每
慶吸唖色氣透為度氣透自即通
輕号散初生大便不通
輕粉錢二生蜜拌熱湯調默兒口中一二次立通

FIG. 13. "Methods of Bathing Infants" (*Yü-êrh fa*), in *Ch'ih-shui yüan-chu*, by Sun I-k'uei (Ming dynasty). Against the Sung practitioners, who advised that three days had to pass before bathing a newborn, this Ming text advocated an even more liberal view: The body could be kept clean for ten days or more before finally bathing it when the infant appeared strong. The National Central Library, Taiwan, Republic of China.

CLEANSING THE DIGESTIVE TRACT

Upon birth, a baby must start nursing. According to old Chinese custom, however, people were not to begin breast-feeding immediately, but rather to give licorice juice or other thin medicinal drinks to clear an infant's system. After the body had been rinsed out, the infant was then allowed to nurse. Before the Middle Ages, licorice juice or *coptis japonica* was often used for the procedure. Such medical texts as Ko Hung's *A Handbook of Prescription for Emergencies* (*Chou-hou fang*) indicate this was a practice from earlier times. Its popularity had been closely related to the then commonly held notion of "fetal poison."[71]

By the fifteenth and sixteenth centuries, two new trends developed with regard to traditional practice of newborn cleansing. First, milder devices were promoted to replace the at times pungent old recipes. Discussions such as K'ou P'ing's "Bring Down the Fetal Poison" (Hsia t'ai-tu) began to nurture new ideas.[72] K'ou disapproved of strong laxatives used in the past, such as cinnabar and *coptis japonica*, recommending a milder liquid made of lightly fermented soybeans (*tan tou-shih chih*)—an opinion shared by most pediatricians of the time.[73] Secondly, K'ou and others were of the opinion that the true reason for the practice was that the fermented soybeans with low salt had the effect of cleansing the digestive tract and helping "the digestion of milk and food to come."[74]

Thus, by the sixteenth century, Chinese pediatricians had devised a certain "pragmatic" reason for the long-followed but little-understood folk custom of "expelling the fetal excrement" (*hsia t'ai-fên*). The improved methods adopted by late imperial physicians, such as the juice of lightly fermented soybeans, chive juice, or pig's milk, could, on the one hand, clear the infant's digestive tract, just as diluted fructose water or plain water do in modern times. Both late imperial Chinese devices and their modern counterparts act to clean the stomach and intestines and induce sucking movements. Furthermore, lactation may not begin immediately following the birth. Pediatric texts from this period suggest that, under such circumstances, the infant could be given licorice juice, the juice of lightly fermented soybeans, and especially pig's milk as temporary substitute intake. With this, the custom of "bringing down the fetal poison" was renamed as the "mouth-opening method" (*k'ai-k'ou fa*). The general populace now carried on the traditional custom with newly "discovered" reasoning, quite unrelated to the old fetal poison theory first posited.[75]

Saving the Baby

Societies are known to deal with healthy infants before they spare any care for the critical or handicapped. Medieval Chinese documents devoted their discussions almost exclusively to the care of healthy and full-term babies. Hardly anything was mentioned about abnormal or vulnerable newborns. By the Sung dynasty, experts began to discuss rescue measures for infants suffering from complications or birth abnormalities. These efforts to save the newborn took primarily two forms: a growing concern for maintaining the infant's body warmth and searching for devices to rescue infants born under precarious conditions.

PRESERVING BODY WARMTH

In discussing the initial bath, breaking the cord, wrapping the stump, and swaddling, traditional Chinese pediatric texts invariably reminded attendants at a delivery to keep the infant warm and to protect him from wind, wetness, and cold. This could be accomplished by making sure that the doors and windows were shut for required activities, such as cord cutting, stump wrapping, and swaddling. On cold or wet days people should make a fire, or they should select a warm and dry day for activities such as the first washing.

From the Sung period onward pediatric specialists developed an even keener sense of the value of body temperature. This new awareness manifested itself in two ways. First, increasing stress was laid on the absolute value of maintaining the body warmth of healthy infants. Second, pediatric practitioners realized that upon difficult births, the ability to maintain body warmth was often decisive in saving the baby. A good example of the first is an article in Chang Kao's (1149–1227) *On Medicine (I-shuo)*, titled "Newborn Infants Are Afraid of Cold" (Hsiao-êrh ch'u-shêng wei-han), it recommended that:

While waiting for the bathing water, a newborn infant should be wrapped in cotton and held to the chest of an adult to keep him warm. This should also be done after the bath. Even during summer months, the quilt must not be suddenly removed. Instead, one may gradually remove the cotton lining from within. This is because when an infant suddenly comes out of the mother's womb, it cannot be exposed to cold air.[76]

In Chang's view, one ought to be careful to wrap up the infant while waiting for the bath. That is, as soon as the infant emerges, regardless of anything else, it should be immediately wrapped in a cotton quilt to keep it warm. The idea was that the body heat would not disperse rapidly to threaten the newborn with colds, an attitude shared by many pediatricians.[77]

The earliest documentation of the view that maintaining body temperature was vital to rescuing a vulnerable newborn was in *A Thorough Discussion*. In a discussion of emergency measures, it said:

If, when an infant is just born, it appears out of breath and cannot cry, it either experienced a difficult birth or is suffering from the cold. One should quickly wrap this infant in cotton cloth and immediately place it to the chest of an adult for warmth. If it is already swaddled, one should increase [quilts]. Also, never proceed to cut his umbilical cord right away, but place the placenta over hot charcoal and burn it. Light a big paper torch soaked in oil; then move the flame over the umbilical cord area back and forth. This is because, as the umbilical cord is attached to the belly, the effect of the fire will enter the body through the umbilical cord. Afterward, use hot vinegar to rub and wash the cord, at which moment the infant may come back to his senses and start crying. One may then proceed to bathe the infant and cut the cord as usual. This is an extremely useful measure, which has saved many lives.[78]

This is a clear emphasis on the importance of body warmth. Other medical texts of that time and later mentioned that in such critical situations all other procedures should be delayed. The infant should first be swaddled in cotton quilts already warmed over hot charcoal to help preserve body warmth. Methods of rescue by warming, such as that suggested in *A Thorough Discussion*, were widely circulated among Ming-Ch'ing pediatric authors.[79]

Owing to this stress on keeping warm, late imperial Chinese families were asked to pay special attention to matters such as avoiding wind, wetness, and cold. This reduced the chances of healthy infants catching cold, which may result in bronchitis and pneumonia, important causes of neonatal mortality. As for high-risk infants under less favorable conditions, maintaining body warmth also helped improve chances of survival.

ABNORMAL BIRTHS AND EMERGENCY CARE

Initial discussions of abnormal births and emergency measures began in the Sung period. Methods such as maintaining warmth, heating the umbilical cord, rubbing the cord with hot vinegar, and so forth, as described in *A Thorough Discussion*, formed the core of the opinion. What pediatricians claimed to labor over were infants with difficulty crying, namely "infants who, upon emerging from the mother's womb, appear late in letting out a cry." In addition to the method of maintaining warmth mentioned above, other measures included so-called ways of reviving newborn breath (*hsiao-êrh ch'u-shêng hui-ch'i fa*), and the more traditional "scallion whip method" (*ts'ung-pien fa*). The latter advised that upon receiving an infant crying or moving with difficulty, or who shows signs of breathing difficulty, one should "quickly use the white part of the scallions to whip his back gently." The idea was that to hit the child lightly on the back would provide stimulus from the pungent smell of the scallion and could help to incite the infant to cry so as to return to normal breathing. "Chanting the father's nickname" at the same time was also suggested.[80] The practice evidently combined folk beliefs with a practical purpose. However, these methods were intended to save full-term, healthy infants without other physiological impediments. Their critical conditions appear primarily due to trouble breathing and crying.

As time passed, pediatric experts showed an increased interest in the next level of newborn rescue.[81] They began to look into the "facilitating bowel method" (*t'ung-pien fa*) for "treating newborns who could not have bowel movements or urinate, and whose abdomen had become mortally swollen." Moreover, experts developed methods to help infants "whose noses are stuffed and breathing heavy," or those who "have no anal tract," or even those whose "entire body appears without skin."[82]

In the eighteenth century, a special chapter entitled "Newborn Emergency Care" (Ch'u-tan chiu-hu) devoted to abnormal neonatal conditions and rescue measures appeared in Ch'ên Fu-chêng's (1736–1795) *Complete*

Works on the Care of Children (Yu-yu chi-ch'êng). It discussed ten different kinds of abnormality, including problems raised by earlier physicians such as "inability to cry at birth," "no breath after difficult birth," and "revival of the dying." In addition, new topics were brought up, such as "kidney constriction after catching cold," "inability to cry due to a sealed umbilical cord," and "not urinating after birth." This chapter also offered revised methods for handling difficulties such as being born "with no anal tract," "no skin," and with the inability "to have bowel movements or to urinate."[83] Given the medical and social resources of the time, emergency measures such as Ch'ên's appeared to have the intention of saving a portion of premature, deformed, and mildly disabled infants.

From the eleventh century, focus was placed on the care of normal and healthy infants; by the eighteenth century, Chinese pediatrics had become curious and attentive toward procedures for complicated births and rescuing premature and deformed babies. This could not yet meet all the demands, obviously. But in comparison with conditions elsewhere at that time, Chinese pediatrics of the late imperial period was far from a static form of knowledge or art.[84]

The Popularization of a Specialized Knowledge

In late imperial China, there were many barriers to the effective delivery of medical care or the improvement of health conditions. A large population, the majority of whom were uneducated and widely spread out on the then mostly inaccessible Eurasian continent, was in itself a formidable handicap. Improved newborn care represented a fairly specialized kind of technical knowledge that demanded much explanation and propagation. The preventive nature of many of the procedures, on the other hand, rendered popularization absolutely critical. Little would result if new knowledge and skills remained only in the hands of experts. The kind of efforts made to convert important discoveries into accessible forms was thus crucial to the broader social implications of these evolving understandings.[85] Lu Po-ssû's *One Hundred Questions on Infants and Children (Ying-t'ung pai-wên)*, for example, was composed in a question-and-answer format to readily inform its readers of the achievements and abilities of contemporary pediatrics. Other medical authors experimented with songs. Plates and illustrations were added to short manuals to provide clear guidance to laymen and traveling healers. Even doggerel poems for temple divinations were not omitted as a tool for transmitting information. The promotion of oral transmission was mobilized to make "new" knowledge and useful techniques available to a poorly educated rural population.

In the area of newborn care, this popularization and distribution process took many forms. To propagate proper cord cutting and umbilical care, for instance, the Ch'ing government's official text, *The Golden Mirror for Medicine*, put the technique into quatrain form:

> Use a branding cake to burn, when the cord is cut,
> Six inches from the stem is your best bet,
> Moxa burning stops the wind [in boys and girls] but,
> Always powder well and keep the stump from the wet.[86]

To disseminate the basic skills in umbilical care, Lu Po-ssû explained the key steps in simple language in his question-and-answer book. Wan Ch'üan's *Family Secrets*, K'ou P'ing's *Precious Guide*, Ch'in Ching-ming's *The Golden Needles*, and Wu Ch'ien's *Key Methods for Various Diseases in Pediatrics* (*Yu-k'o tsa-ping hsin-fa yao-chüeh*) all put the method into rhyme.[87]

Attempts were also made to render newly understood medical notions or hygienic skills into easy to memorize verses. K'ou P'ing, for example, composed a rhyme to explain the importance of "mouth wiping":

> Don't let your newborn gasp
> For filth is in his mouth
> Keep cotton within your grasp
> And wipe it quick away
> Cinnabar and honey
> Should be quickly taken
> Lest measles and sores
> From the filth be maken
> This method is sovereign and true
> Though understood by a few.[88]

The "Mouth Wiping" chapter in *The Golden Mirror* summed up contemporary understanding in lyrical stanzas as well:

> To wipe the mouth, we powder fragrant [*yen-chih fa*],
> With no foul matter, no oral ailment,
> Our fathers said do this [*hui*] before he should cry,
> That's only because they didn't know why.[89]

Similar endeavors to propagate ideas and practices of newborn care continued throughout the late imperial period. Works by pediatric experts, supported by the state, Confucian elite, and religious organizations facilitated the distribution of inventive concepts and innovative skills. The overall market of commercialized consumption and cultural production, along with a lively publishing industry and widely circulating goods, was certainly an important part of this same picture in which simple—sometimes rhymed—descriptions given in such manuals as *Precious Guide*, *One Hundred Questions*, and *The Golden Mirror* from the fifteenth through the early eighteenth centuries popularized the importance of dry wiping and preservation of body temperature. Because of works such as these, "washing on the third" or "bathing the infant on the third day" (san-chao hsi-êrh) became a common practice—even to the point of being a ritualized custom—by Ming-Ch'ing times. A similar process gave new meaning to the old custom of intestine cleansing, as we see in the spread of the appetite induction "mouth-opening method." It was probably the successful endeavors in disseminating more sensible ways of newborn care that prompted pediatricians to be increasingly interested in rescuing babies from difficult births and infirmity from the sixteenth century onward.

Historical Implications

Presently, Chinese historical demography cannot supply sufficiently detailed data on the survival, morbidity, and mortality rates of the newborn to yield a meaningful evaluation in relation to the performance of pediatric medicine for this particular period.[90] But the development in the four areas stated above, in and of themselves, are significant. These implications can be appreciated in a number of ways. First of all, the identification of vital newborn health hazards such as umbilical tetanus and astute use of cauterization to reduce the risk of contamination and infection marked an important breakthrough in empirical medicine. Even without statistical data on neonatal mortality from this period, we may infer that this improved knowledge and procedure could have had important effects in reducing mortality. Similar observations can be made, though perhaps in a less dramatic way, regarding revised knowledge and practices in newborn hygiene, maintaining body warmth, and emergency care. Second, newborn care represented but a small fraction of the overall performance of Chinese pediatrics, and pediatrics in turn was but a part of the general development in Chinese medicine. This general picture, though by no means uniform, shows a perseverance in continuous exploration, observation, study, and debate. In the process, medical experts were at times able to correct errors of the past, break away from previous assumptions, and enhance the health and well-being of the population. Furthermore, these developments in newborn care were not medical achievements existing in isolation. Improved knowledge of the physiology of infants, growth and development, as well as nursing and infant feeding is evident in a wide range of technical handbooks and family history records.[91]

The health environment of a society is integral to the conditions of material life. Changes in Chinese material conditions (such as food and nutrition, clothing, housing, or transportation) were never one-dimensional, therefore, and still await further research. The relatively early specialization of pediatric medicine in China in the eleventh century was unique in world history. The progress made in the area of newborn care between then and the eighteenth century shows how specialized attention and vocational dedication may better meet vital health needs of a traditional society. The level of medical knowledge and techniques in improved newborn care remained unmatched elsewhere to the end of that period. It should be of value, therefore, for scholars to assess the differences such technical and social disparities may have made in demography and history, both in China and the world.

Conclusion

Newborn care in China underwent impressive developments in the late imperial period. This was especially pronounced in the areas of cord cutting and umbilical care, physical cleanliness, maintaining body warmth, and emergency care. Conscientious efforts to popularize such medical achievements, moreover, helped to instill specialized knowledge and skills into social practices. This process matured and made its cumulative impact in the two hundred years between 1550 and 1750, though it was rooted in a long-standing Confucian concern for the survival of one's offspring. Medieval medical texts reveal particular concern for the well-being of the very young, preceding the birth of pediatrics, and anticipated the changes in such areas as newborn infant care. Pioneering pediatricians in the Sung period, grounded in this earlier tradition but enhanced by specialized understanding and clinical experiences, made forceful breakthroughs in newborn care as well as other areas. It was after these initial groundbreaking steps that Ming-Ch'ing pediatric experts pressed forward with additional revisions and substantial improvements in key steps of infantile survival. Persistent endeavors to spread newly available information also turned changes in newborn care into a dynamic historical force.

Inadequate study has been done on the conditions of health and health care in traditional China. Our understanding of the broader physical and material aspects of Chinese history also remains limited. The present investigation, however, confirms that similar or related efforts may be made to fill in the empty areas in the map of historical China.

3   Nursing and Infant Feeding

Life, or a glimpse of life, often depends on where or how it is encountered. Sayings and records from different corners tell different stories regarding a matter as mundane as bodily needs. Information about nursing and infant feeding in biographies and family notes speaks of the deficiency of milk. The anti-T'aiping campaign leader Tso Tsung-t'ang (1812–1885), for instance, was but one of the countless babies born to a mother short of breast milk. His mother chewed rice to feed him the juice.[1] Better-off families looked for surrogates, but wet nurses, too, were difficult to come by. With Shao Hsing-chung (1648–1711), the family tested ten women before settling on an acceptable one.[2] Ts'ên Yü-ying (1829–1889), when less than one year old, refused to take breast milk from any other woman when his mother passed away, forcing the grandmother to feed him with congee as a substitute.[3] In medical history literature, however, one is confronted with the problem of overfeeding. As early as the twelfth century, Ch'ien I, the highly regarded founder of Chinese pediatrics, gave his views on how to handle infants "refusing to nurse" (pu-ju).[4] The fifteenth-century pediatrician Wan Ch'üan discussed the various kinds of nursing problems such as "throwing up or spitting out milk" (ou-ju) from overzealous mothers with a copious milk flow.[5] Pediatricians offered suggestions about wet nurses, food substitutes, overfeeding, and weaning, but there is an undeniable discrepancy in the pictures presented by the documentation, which goes beyond narrative positions and interpretative angles. Doctors and mothers reported differences in the problems they confronted and how they tried to solve them. Evidence pertaining to China's long heritage in constructed "motherhood" or the perceived understandings of the shifting management of nursing and infant feeding may be collected from both tangible traces and various subjective sources.

Some historical factors are no doubt more difficult to retain than others in the realm between the abstract and the practical. For many centuries, nursing or breast-feeding has represented one such area. What follows is an introduction to the world of instructions and practices on breast-feeding

FIG. 14. "Knick-knack Peddler and Children," by Li Sung (dated 1210, Sung dynasty). Pictures depicting ordinary woman breast-feeding in public were not unusual in China and probably reflected the social mores of the time. Courtesy of the National Palace Museum, Taiwan, Republic of China.

and infant feeding as contained in Chinese medical writings from the Sung period onward. This body of advice literature changed over time and varied as adaptations were made for economic or regional circumstances. Included were pediatric case records that practicing physicians kept for clinical reference or apprentice training. Biographical data, family records, personal letters and poems, and the usual social history documentation provide a kaleidoscopic array of voices to complement or compare against this technical literature.

People's concerns, customs, and rules for such "natural acts" reveal much about how society perceived life or how anyone new to these tasks managed the daily needs of children and the physical conditions of women. Studies on maternal diet and infant suckling also reflect the "scientific" interest in the phenomenon of lactation and the composition of breast milk.[6] Its bearing on female fertility and the resulting demographic implications have attracted analysis.[7] When comparing the records of breast-feeding and infant feeding in traditional Chinese medical and biographical literature with the available information elsewhere, reflections, concerns, and practices become of primary value in the construction and reconstruction of the experience of children and the world they lived in.[8]

Traditional Breast-Feeding Instructions

In the T'ang dynasty, before the development of pediatrics as a medical subspecialty, well-known medical texts already incorporated discussions on the proper feeding of food (*pu*) and milk (*ju*) to infants.[9] By the Sung dynasty, when emerging pediatrics increasingly addressed child rearing, the anonymous text *A Thorough Discussion on Infant Hygiene* (*Hsiao-êrh wei-shêng tsung-wei lun-fang*) offered an elaborate discussion on breast-feeding.

For all women with milk, it is blood and vitality (*hsüeh-ch'i*) that are transformed into milk. Therefore we say that good and bad are both born of blood and vitality. If a mother is unrestrained and uncontrolled, and nurses a child in such a state, the child will contract an illness. If, when [the mother is] tired because of activities of the bedchamber [that is, after sexual intercourse] and breastfeeds a child, this will make the child thin, fatigued, cross-legged, and unable to walk. If the child is nursed while [the mother is] drunk, it will cause the child's body to be hot and its belly full. If the child is nursed while [the mother is] suffused with heat, this will make the child turn yellow and be unable to eat. If the child is nursed while [the mother is] angry, then the child will be startled and gasp in a spasmodic manner. If the child is nursed when [the mother is] experiencing problems of vomiting, then the child will be made enervated, thin, and his vitality weakened. All of these must be avoided.

Whenever breast-feeding a child, the nursing mother should first press [her breasts] with her hand to dissipate heat and then give it to the child to suckle. If the breast is stimulated and the milk flows vigorously, for fear that the child will not be able to swallow quickly enough, and in order to avoid choking, [she should] temporarily pull it away. Make the child relax momentarily and give it to him again. It will be fine after several attempts. One should try to control and regulate according to the extent to which the child is hungry or full. Ascertain how many feedings a day are sufficient, and adopt this as the norm. Every morning, if there is overnight milk [in the breasts], it must be discarded by squeezing. If, in the summer, hot milk is not discarded, the child will throw up; if, in the winter, cold milk is not discarded, the child will cough. Also, after the child has been greatly excited, one should not nurse him immediately; this will make him spasmodic. After the child has cried heavily, one should not nurse him immediately, this will make him throw up or have diarrhea. Furthermore, the nursing woman must not overeat as to be too full, fearing that [the food will be] held up and cause indigestion. If the child becomes too full, give him/her an empty breast and it will be alleviated.[10]

Whenever nursing a child, the mother should place the child's head to rest on her arm, so that the child's mouth is at the same level with the breast, and then nurse him. Do not use the shoulder, for fear that it may be too high; this will cause the child to nurse uncomfortably, often resulting in choking. Also, if the nursing mother wants to go to bed, she should withdraw her breast, lest she fall asleep, and the breast fill the mouth and nose [of the child] unawares, causing other problems. Moreover, she would not know if the child were still hungry or already full.[11]

The above passage touches upon three important points: one, the proper method of breast-feeding (procedures, regularity, posture, and other things); two, requirements and restrictions placed upon the nursing woman; and three, suitable physiological and psychological conditions for the child in receiving milk.

THE PROPER WAY TO NURSE

Early modern Chinese pediatricians advising women on the subject of breast-feeding wanted to show the appropriate methods of nursing: the correct preparatory procedures, the right posture, the appropriate regularity and temperature of the milk, the rate of flow, freshness, and other details. Their goal was to help the nursing mother, or the wet nurse, to adopt a safe and comfortable approach. *A Thorough Discussion* made suggestions on such grounds. First, the woman is advised to use her hands to press the breast to dissipate the milk's heat before feeding. When the breast is first given to the child, the woman should make sure that the milk is not too copious or flowing too vigorously. The infant, unable to swallow quickly enough, may be choked. When such a thing occurs, the mother should immediately pull her nipple away, allow the child to breathe, and then give it back to him. Repeated a few times, the mother will find this a suitable way to nurse. Next, in order to establish a regular rhythm, she ought to observe the extent to which the child was hungry or full at any moment. Gradually she will figure out the proper amount per feeding and the appropriate number of feedings per day. Lacking a regulated schedule, a child's unstable eating habits may affect his health adversely.

The text then focuses its analysis on the milk itself. Each morning, if the breasts contain "overnight milk" (*su-ju*), the mother was asked to squeeze it out before letting the child suckle. Furthermore, she ought to discard the "hot milk" (*jê-ju*) from the summer and the "cold milk" (*han-ju*) from the winter before nursing. Such reasoning reflected a peculiar contemporary concern for "freshness" as suggested in the ever changing quality of the human milk, as indicated for instance in its "temperature," the expression and discarding of the so-called overnight milk, or the summer or winter milk.

In order to achieve a convenient, comfortable, and safe way of breast-feeding, furthermore, *A Thorough Discussion* instructs women to adopt an appropriate posture. Whenever nursing, a mother should support the child's head with her own arms, putting the child's mouth at the same comfortable level as her breasts. As the text indicates, since many women seemed to enjoy breast-feeding while lying down, they are particularly warned against using their shoulders to support the children's heads. The added height may cause the milk to be suckled too slowly or cause the child to choke. Here, safety seems a big concern at all times. Before going to bed, the mother was asked to withdraw her breast so it would not block the mouth and nose of the child if she fell asleep. Furthermore, nursing while sleeping made it difficult to control the amount fed.

A Thorough Discussion provides such a complete treatment for breast-feeding that later medical texts, though continuing to deliberate on the subject, hardly exceeded its scope for more than six centuries. The Sung dynasty pediatric author Ch'ên Tzû-ming, for instance, expressed similar views about regularity and amount but in a much simplified manner: "After starting to breastfeed, continue at appropriate intervals and with proper amounts. Do not make the child too full for fear that he will spit out or later get into the habit of throwing up. This would be difficult to control."[12]

Later physicians concurred with the principle that infants should be nursed at regular times and with the appropriate amounts. The famous Yüan dynasty (1279–1368) pediatrician Tsêng Shih-jung composed an essay on timely feeding, entitled "On Irregular Nursing and Uncontrolled Feeding" (I ju-shih-shih pu-pu-chieh). It stated that regular breast-feeding was extremely important for a child's health and development. The idea was to do it "according to a balanced medium." If an infant was not nursed regularly, not only would he not be able to "strengthen his tissues and flesh," his health could also be adversely affected, therefore "becoming weak without any obvious illness." Parents were also warned against depriving their children of breast-feeding too early and replacing it with other food, thus rendering their children vulnerable to ailments.[13]

Tsêng Shih-jung cautioned that a mother should nurse her child regularly and worried that some families did not pay enough attention to the serious task of breast-feeding. His opinion, practical and valuable as it seemed, represented in fact a rare voice at the time. Most late imperial Chinese pediatricians, while concerned about irregular nursing, feared still more that the mother's intense love for the child could cause her to overfeed him, not underfeed him, as Tsêng cautioned. The widely circulated Ming dynasty text *Advice for Safe Birth, Infant Rearing, and Maintaining Health (Pao-ch'an yü-ying yang-shêng lu*), quoted past exhortations "not to make children overly full . . . fullness surely leads to overflowing, thus causing vomiting."[14] Overnursing seemed to be a fairly common problem. Physicians' repeated urging of self-control indeed represented an enlightened and progressive view. Making the same argument were "On Nursing the Child" from *Precious Guide for Saving the Young (Ch'üan-yu hsin-chien)* by K'ou P'ing of the Ming dynasty; "On Nursing and Feeding (Infants)," from *The Essence of Pediatric Medicine (Yu-k'o lei-ts'ui)* by Wang Luan; and "Nursing and Feeding," in *Complete Collection of Medicine Past and Present (Ku-chin i-t'ung ta-ch'üan)* by Hsü Ch'un-fu.[15] *Precious Guide* in fact contains an essay entitled "Forced Nursing and Forced Feeding Make a Child Sick." It claims that a child's frequent ailments came not from the lack of cooperation from the child but from the obsessiveness of the parents. Quoting an old saying that "if a child is often sick, it is harmed by being [overly] full," the author asks parents to pay more attention to controlling the proper amount.[16] *The Essence of Pediatric Medicine* cites the same proverb, approving a child's "enduring a thirty-percent hunger and eating only until seventy-percent full," a seemingly radical advocacy that would be followed by physicians of later generations.[17]

The historical background to this evolving pediatric discourse merits special attention. Did the caution of overfeeding from the thirteenth century onward represent a stern reaction to a more lax attitude toward nursing and infant care? Or are we witnessing medical reflections on a popular custom in breast-feeding and maternal attendance that showed evidence of increased indulgence from the Yüan period onward? Careful comparison of medical texts and family records over an extended timeframe suggests an interesting combination of both. Compared with the early medieval period between the eleventh and thirteenth centuries, professional pediatric physicians indeed appeared to be developing an increasingly "serious" and particularistic attitude toward infant care and child attendance. These pediatricians and progressive authorities thus labored hard to establish themselves by giving detailed warnings. On the other hand, beginning with the period from the thirteenth to the sixteenth centuries, for the better situated, family practice in infant feeding and physical care of young children seemed to be slipping into laxity and overindulgence. Biographical information shows increasing material provision for ever younger members of the family, as even larger numbers of toys and reading materials were produced for the consumption and amusement of affluent children. Such evidence prompts one to ask whether the idyllic Sung depictions of happy and healthy "children at play" ceased after the Yüan dynasty simply because the ideal of the past had been realized, in some measure, thus losing its old image as a fantasy. In any event, pediatric scholars scolded Ming mothers for fanatically pressing their breasts upon full babies. They had at least in part replaced the T'ang or Sung parents who stirred up Tsêng and his colleagues because they were stopping the milk supply short of need and stuffing solid food into babies' mouths long before they were physically ready to receive and absorb it. Changing medical philosophies and evolving social practices together conjured up this composite picture of physicians loudly reprimanding mothers, first for depriving infants and then for excessive pampering in parenting and infant care.

Subsequent to *A Thorough Discussion*, other authors continued to debate the freshness, temperature, and quality of breast milk. Ch'ên Tzû-ming warned that a nursing mother should not consume "large amounts of either food and drink too sour or too salty" and should avoid "breast-feeding the child right after being exposed to cold or heat."[18] It was feared that the temperature of breast milk might have an impact on the child's acceptance and digestion. Furthermore, after *A Thorough Discussion*, both *Effective Recipes of Experienced Physicians (Shih-i tê-hsiao fang)*, by Wei I-lin of the Yüan, and *Precious Guide for Saving the Young,* by K'ou P'ing of the Ming, shared this vague concern for the freshness and temperature of the mother's milk.[19] Both insisted that the mother should squeeze out "overnight milk" from her breast before nursing.

After the publication of *Effective Recipes of Experienced Physicians*, medical authors had different ideas about the correct posture of breast-feeding. Ch'ên Tzû-ming, for example, suggested that the mother prepare a few beanbags as the child's pillow. These beanbags should be placed on both sides of the child's body, supporting the child and bringing him close to the mother. Ch'ên indicated that if the mother needed to breastfeed during the night, she should get out of bed and sit down while holding the infant, suggestions that showed concern about both comfort and safety.[20] K'ou P'ing continued to talk about the old style of supporting the child's head with the arm while lying down but agreed that when nursing at night one should get up and hold the child.[21]

For safety reasons, many physicians advised mothers to discontinue nursing before falling asleep. Wei I-lin, in *Effective Recipes of Experienced Physicians*, and K'ou P'ing, in *Precious Guide for Saving the Young,* both made this argument. Wei I-lin's reason was that "while asleep [the mother] may not ascertain [the child's] fullness."[22] K'ou P'ing's reason was that "she may not ascertain fullness, thus resulting in vomiting later."[23] Neither mentioned the danger of smothering the child, as stipulated in *A Thorough Discussion*.

Chinese medical authorities from the twelfth to the seventeenth centuries recommended sensible procedures for breast-feeding, many not in disagreement with modern ideas. On frequency and amount, however, there was no adjustment according to the age and development of the child. Strong emphasis was placed on the quality, temperature, and freshness of the breast milk; as with most concerns of physicians at the time, they were conceived in close relationship to the physical and emotional well-being of the child. Of course, from our contemporary understanding there could be excessive views, such as expressing overnight milk.[24] Moreover, some medical texts had taboos against throwing breast milk on the ground, where it could be eaten by ants, believing that this would cause the woman's milk to dry up.[25] Elements of folklore mingled liberally with the ideas and practices of medicine.

ADVICE FOR NURSING WOMEN

Traditional Chinese physicians believed that the character and composition of the breast milk was directly related to her physiology and psychology. For a nursing mother, therefore, a woman's diet, emotional state, body temperature, and changes in her health could all immediately affect the "content" of the breast milk and in turn influence the health and well-being of the child. As a result, there were extremely broad and rigid restrictions on the daily diet, activities, and emotions of a nursing woman. *A Thorough Discussion* asked that a nursing woman pay particular attention to dietary restrictions, avoid breast-feeding immediately after sexual activities, as well as when drunk, angry, suffused with heat, or vomiting. These cautions concerned the four areas of diet, emotion, temperature, and health that medical works addressed time and again. Ch'ên Tzû-ming, for instance, reminded women that, "when the yin and yang are joined [that is, during sexual intercourse], one must not breastfeed the child. For this is what is called copulatory milk, which is bound to cause swelling of the spleen." Furthermore, "nursing mothers must not drink alcohol often, lest the child contract the illnesses of coughing with phlegm, hot spasms, and dizziness with blurred vision."[26]

Warnings against nursing immediately after sex or while drunk are common. Christian culture in Europe used to prohibit breast-feeding following intercourse, considering it immoral and licentious. The instructions in the Ming text *Advice for Safe Birth* were broader. They cautioned against nursing after bathing, when pregnant, inflicted with a "wind illness," or sick from overeating.[27] Later on, *The Essence of Pediatric Medicine*, by Wang Luan, *Complete Collection of Medicine Past and Present*, by Hsü Ch'un-fu, and *The True Method of Caring for the Young* (*Tz'û-yu hsin-chuan*), by Chu Hui-min, made minor additions and revisions, without raising any new issues.[28]

For the same period, the most elaborate discussion on infant illness from breast milk was an essay entitled "The Milk That Makes Infants Sick" (Ju ling-êrh-ping chêng) in *Precious Guide for Saving the Young*. Ten kinds of undesirable breast milk were listed: exhilarated milk, angry milk, cold milk, hot milk, exasperated milk, ill milk, static milk, ghost milk, drunken milk, and licentious milk. The text explained the kind of illnesses "bad milk" might cause in a child, referring to comments of earlier medical scholars.[29] Of these, four (ill, static, ghost, and drunken milk) had to do with the mother's ill health, another four (exhilarated, angry, exasperated, and licentious milk) referred to her emotional state, while the remaining two (cold and hot milk) concerned the milk's changing character by season. This was the first time that the nature or quality of breast milk was considered as directly stemming from the conditions of the nursing mother, reflecting a common conviction among physicians that the physical and psychological states of the lactating woman directly influenced the make-up of her milk. Therefore a woman's activities or the condition she was in before or during breast-feeding would immediately influence her milk and affect the health of the child. At the beginning of Wang Luan's "On Nursing and Feeding," (Ju-pu lun) in *The Essence of Pediatric Medicine*, he stated:

When an infant is first born, it relies on milk to provide for its life. One cannot be careless concerning the method of nursing and feeding, for this milk is a transformation of vitality and blood. As to the nursing mother, she should be especially careful and restrained. For once drink and food is swallowed, the milk is produced. When moved by passion and desire, the milk responds. If ill *ch'i* [energy] reaches the milk, its liquid will be static. For the child who gets the milk, illness immediately arrives: if not vomiting then diarrhea, if not boils then heat, or a sore in the mouth, or convulsions, or crying at night, or pain in the abdomen. On the first arrival of illness, his urine will be scant. Then one must inquire [of the mother] and treat her according to the symptoms. If the mother is well then the child is well. It is thus possible to eliminate the source of calamity before it takes shape.[30]

Belief in certain connections between the milk that an infant takes in and the character he or she grows up to become is not unique to the Chinese. Ancient Western taboos against the use of animal's milk in feeding the infant or folklore and mythology that attributes personal strength or vulnerability to some special milk received in infancy testify to a similar assumption. From at least Roman times, Europeans were convinced that "the child sucks in the temperament and disposition of its nurse." Advice from thirteenth-century encyclopedias propagated the notion that "good milk produces good progeny, and bad milk bad progeny," which makes the choosing of wet nurses—the "professional breast-feeding women"—all the more important. Compilations such as *Practica Puerorum* recommended dripping breast milk upon a fingernail, a rock, a polished sword, or looking at it through a crystal to check on the quality of a nursing woman's lac-

tation.[31] Abiding by a similar principle, the Chinese practice of treating illness in suckling infants through the medication of the nursing women also
existed in Europe.[32] Modern medicine now accepts the importance of a
nursing woman's diet and its influence upon the condition and quality of
her milk. It is less certain that emotional state and body temperature can
also influence the milk and the child. Late imperial Chinese physicians certainly believed that milk minutely reflects the mother's physical as well as
mental or spiritual condition. Since the milk had a direct impact on the
health and well-being of the child, people preferred to create broad and severe restrictions on the woman rather than risk the life of her weak and vulnerable infant.

Selecting a Wet Nurse

Traditional Chinese medicine believed that breast milk from the
child's natural mother was his best choice. *A Thorough Discussion* said, "In
the event that a child is born and one nurses him oneself, all the rest [of the
problems] need not be discussed."[33] Nursing by the mother, it was believed,
prevented most common worries. However, if the mother was not able to
do so, neither society nor the medical community had much objection to the
hiring of a wet nurse as a substitute. The only document with reservations
about hiring wet nurses focused its concern on humanitarian considerations, not the health of the child. The Sung Confucian philosopher Ch'êng
Hao (1032–1085) thought that a woman employed as a wet nurse might
abandon her own child. Thus people who hired a wet nurse might deprive
someone else's child of milk and leave it destitute. Therefore, Ch'êng suggested, it would be better to hire "two women to nurse three children," that
is, to hire two women who would bring their own children each to be nursed
along with the child of the master.[34] Consideration from Chinese scholars
and physicians on wet-nursing was also formulated due to the way it was
conducted in host families who brought the hired women into their residence for the business. The host families not only were responsible for the
food and drink of the woman but also had an opportunity to supervise the
way she handled matters. This was unlike the early Western practice of sending the child out, which allowed the wet nurse to bring the infant to her
house and nurse him on her own, which accounted for a much higher mortality rate that later aroused concern and opposition.[35] Interestingly enough,
when early modern European reformists directed their attention toward improved wet-nursing, they too demanded bringing "farmed out" babies back
home and closer supervision.[36]

If one decided to hire a nurse, Chinese medical texts had plenty of advice
for their selection. In the T'ang era, "The Method of Selecting a Wet Nurse"

(Tsê-ju-mu fa), in *Recipes for Infants and Children* (*Shao-hsiao ying-ju fang*), by Sun Ssû-miao, said:

For any mother with milk, it is her blood and vitality that becomes milk. And since the five emotions and good and bad nature [of any human being] are all born of blood and vitality, those who nurse a child should be careful about their happiness and anger [that is, emotions]. There are many signs to look for in the appropriate appearance of a wet nurse. It is not possible to be perfect, just choose one who does not have smelly armpits, gland swelling in the neck, coughing, scabies sores, a hunchback, baldness, scrofulous wounds, watery lips, deafness, snotty nose, or epilepsy. Anyone who does not have these kinds of illnesses can nurse a child. Experienced men could examine her old acupuncture scars and be able to tell the source of her previous illnesses.[37]

Sun was concerned about character and appearance, but the most important thing was the woman's health. He enumerated eleven kinds of women who, for problems of skin, breathing, epilepsy, and so on, would not be fit to serve. Should the prospective wet nurse not volunteer her medical history, he cleverly indicated having an experienced person examine the scars on her body from previous acupuncture treatments as reliable, indirect information. From the locations of these scars, one could surmise the person's disease history. From the Sui-T'ang to the Sung dynasties, opinions on the selection of wet nurses appear similar (for example, *Medical Secrets of a Frontier Official* [*Wai-t'ai mi-yao fang*], by Wang T'ao, and *A Thorough Discussion on Infant Hygiene*).[38] They believed that although a woman's emotional state and appearance were of consequence, her health was of primary importance. In "On Caring and Protecting Infants" from his *All-Inclusive Good Prescriptions for Women* (*Fu-jên ta-ch'üan liang-fang*), Ch'ên Tzû-ming summed it up this way:

In selecting a wet nurse, one must look for a woman with good spirit and a healthy body, one whose emotions are peaceful and happy, whose flesh is firm and plump, and who has had few illnesses. She should know the appropriateness of cold and warmth, be able to regulate and control herself while nursing and feeding, and whose milk is thick and white. This is a person suitable for feeding a child.[39]

Ming dynasty medical works on women and children devised even more meticulous requirements for the selection of a wet nurse. One criterion was that she not be handicapped or ugly. A second had to do with the emotional and moral state of the woman. In "The Method of Selecting a Wet Nurse," in *Advice for Safe Birth*, women were described as either "one eyed, lame, turtle-chested, hunchbacked, ghostly, bad looking, or with any handicap" could not be hired. Furthermore, it points out that "after being together for a long time, the characters of wet nurse and child become assimilated. It is like the gradual transformation that happens to a grafted branch, the principle of which is very clear." There was serious apprehension, therefore, over the influence the wet nurse could have on the character of the child.[40] In "Selecting a Wet Nurse," from *Precious Guide for Saving the Young*, K'ou P'ing also said that those with "ugly appearances are not appropriate for nursing," to which those with "sores or leprosy" were added. He adopted the view that after a long and intimate relationship the child was likely to be influenced by the disposition of the wet nurse.[41] Beginning in the sixteenth century, pediatric works such as Wang Luan's *The Essence of Pediatric Medicine*, under the topic "Carefully Choosing a Wet Nurse," had surprisingly given up any concern for the medical history of the woman. This piece focused instead on a deliberation over her character, disposition, and emotions and on how a child might grow up to be like her. Hsü Ch'un-fu's *Complete Collection of Medicine Past and Present* expressed a similar view, and Chu Hui-min's *The True Method of Caring for the Young*, also stated that "for a wet nurse, one should select a woman who is clean, pure, sincere, and with thick milk. If she is handicapped, ugly, or her milk thin, it is not appropriate to employ her." It was agreed that the character of the wet nurse would have an influence on the child. Her personality, personal hygiene, and any crippling diseases were thus all worthy of circumspection. The essential point, of course, was that she should be able to supply good, thick milk.[42]

Seventeenth-century pediatricians, like Wang Ta-lun in his "On Selecting a Wet Nurse" (Tsê-ju-mu lun), in *Essentials in Looking After Infants and Children (Ying-t'ung lei-ts'ui)*, expressed similar views. Wang first described: "A child breathes along with the mother. If the mother is healthy then the child is healthy. This principle is inevitable. . . . The child, receiving the essence and blood from his father and mother, is created and born accordingly. When he first leaves the womb his blood and vitality is fragile and weak, relying on the milk of the mother to nourish and raise him."[43] Because of this, the wet nurse was very important. When selecting a wet nurse, it was important, on the one hand, to be concerned with her character. She "must be stable, calm, and lacking in desires." For when the child "becomes savage and violent, or calm and peaceful, he follows the character of the wet nurse. If she is slightly inappropriate, the child will be accordingly transformed. It is like the difference between the rivers of Ching and Wei, if the source is clear then the branch is clear, if the source is turbid, then the tributary becomes turbid." On the other hand, one could not neglect the importance of her physical health. She should be "without chronic illness, scabies, or sores." Furthermore, "if the wet nurse is plump and strong, then her milk will be thick; the child who suckles it will have a strong body. If the wet nurse is thin and weak, then her milk will be thin; the child who suckles it will also have a thin and weak body. Strong or thin,

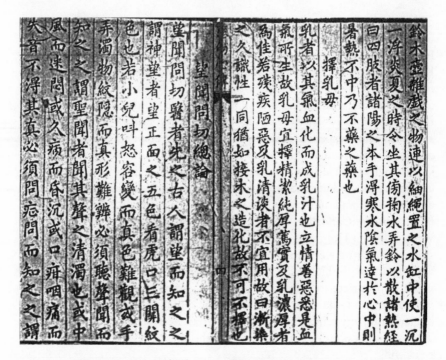

FIG. 15. "The Correct Way of Selecting a Wet Nurse" (Tsê-ju-mu), in *The True Method of Caring for the Young* (*Tz'u-yu hsin-ch'uan*), by Chu Hui-min (Ming dynasty). Traditional Chinese practitioners believed that as long as the surrogate was selected carefully as instructed in this text, a hired wet nurse could be quite acceptable. Courtesy of The National Central Library, Taiwan, Republic of China.

it will be the physique of the child for life. It is by no means a small matter." However, unlike previous authors, Wang did not list all the names of illnesses that disqualified a woman for wet nursing. Nor was he against the handicapped or the ugly. Instead he particularly mentioned that "for those who have had syphilis, if a child suckles this milk, he will develop the same disease. When such a child erupts in pox, not one out of ten stands a chance of survival." Wang also observed that "if a child suckles his milk from those with smelly bodies, he cannot avoid having smelly armpits," but he did not oppose taking such women.[44]

These suggestions for selecting a wet nurse pertained mostly with the contemporary understanding of the nature of human milk and of the responsibility of a wet nurse. The assumption that the constitution of the wet nurse and her medical record could influence the quantity and quality of her milk seemed significant, including both illnesses she had contracted in the past and those that presently afflicted her. Present illnesses could most possibly affect her breast milk, resulting in inappropriate "ill milk." As to the illnesses previously contracted, if these were chronic or contagious diseases, they could influence the health of the woman or be transmitted to the child, therefore rendering her service unsuitable. A chronic cough, infectious skin diseases, certain mental illnesses, and so forth were all taboo. Minor and temporary diseases, from which the woman could have completely recovered, and thus might not influence the secretion or the feeding of her milk, were of lesser concern.

That these medical scholars should have discriminated against the handicapped and the ugly represented a social stance not necessarily rooted in strictly medical or physiological considerations. On the other hand, the stress laid on the character and constitution of the nursing woman was probably founded on two related grounds. First, if the personality of the wet nurse was violent and unstable, it was thought to be possibly influencing her sense of responsibility as well as her judgment while feeding the child. Second, a wet nurse was believed to have also played a role as a surrogate mother responsible for the daily care of the child and often constituted the most intimate personal contact for the child during his infancy and early childhood. Her emotions and disposition, therefore, could have a direct bearing on the habits and inclination of the child. Included in the advice for the wet nurse were instructions for treating the child during sleep, while bathing, in movement, and at play. Discussions on the social and emotional implications of wet nursing, while outside the realm of specific medical principles, nevertheless carried implications of direct relevance to the pediatrician's concern.

Feeding of Other Foods

Of equal concern, but a separate subject in this advice literature, was the provision of foods other than milk. What we today call solid foods are crucial for infants because they either substitute or supplement human and animal milk. The questions of what, when, and how to give foods appropriate to the infant's needs under different circumstances thus became the focus of these discussions.

Sui-T'ang medical texts, speaking on "the methods of infant-feeding" (pu êrh fa), focus primarily on the right time to begin solid foods and the correct types. Wang T'ao's Medical Secrets of a Frontier Official for instance, gave the auspicious dates, respectively, for initiating either a boy or a girl on solid food (ch'u-pu). It also cautioned "not to feed them salty things."[45] The context suggests that Wang had in mind the question of beginning infants on foods other than milk, not simply using them as substitutes or supplements. Giving food to an infant was a subject of interest, though the author touched upon neither the appropriate age to start, nor the proper ways of preparing these foods.

After Sung times, the new pediatric writings were much more elaborate and specific about the problem of infant feeding. Their discussions evolved out of the four topics of the amount, the combination (with milk), the starting time, and the food items to be employed. On the proper amount of food, much advice from medical writings cited overfeeding as the greatest concern. Excessive or compulsory feedings might have indeed been a problem, both in terms of the practice of the upper echelon of society concerned here and in the eyes of medical experts. More plausibly, the prominence of such warnings could have arisen from the indulgent style of child rearing among elite families, thus the focus of attention of these pediatric texts. The section entitled "Nursing and Infant Feeding" (Pu-ju) in Tsêng Shih-jung's *Daily Deliberation on Saving the Young* (*Huo-yu k'ou-i*) serves as a good example whereby the author identified "unrestrained feeding of food" (*pu pu-chieh*) together, and in contrast with, "untimely [inadvertently] giving milk" (*ju shih-shih*) as the two most worrisome problems in nursing and infant feeding. Food provided in a timely and appropriate manner, Tsêng conceded, "can be nurturing." Yet people should be watchful that these feedings not be started too early, like those who "indulged [their young] on the rich and tasty as soon as [they reach] one month." "Uncontrolled feeding is especially bad," he continued, as it would result in "a child being weak though with no apparent aliments."[46] Similar remarks represented the first concern medical authors had for the feeding, in fact the overfeeding, of infant foods.

A second apprehension expressed by medical authors was the simultaneous feeding of milk and food. The following passage from "Methods of Nursing and Infant Feeding" (Ju-pu fa) in Wei I-lin's *Effective Recipes of Experienced Physicians* represented such a view:

Do not give food after nursing, and do not give milk after solid food feeding. [An infant's] spleen and stomach, being weak and fragile, can hardly receive and digest milk and solid food presented side by side. While young, a child [with such difficulties] may develop vomiting, and a knot may form in the belly that causes pains. As he/she grows up, it can cause swelling of the spleen [*p'i*], indigestion [*chi*], and problems in nourishments [*kan*]. These all derive from the present problem.[47]

Ming-Ch'ing pediatricians shared the idea that milk (mostly breast milk) should not be given at the same time as other foods so as to avoid causing digestive difficulties. Similar discussions from such texts as *Advice for Safe Birth, Infant Rearing, and Maintaining Health* and *Precious Guide for Saving the Young* in Ming times attest to this commonly held precaution.[48]

A third issue that concerned medical authors was the appropriate time to start an infant on solid food. There is a marked difference in views from ear-

lier times and those of the late imperial period. The following passage from
Ko Hung's (283–363) *A Handbook of Prescription for Emergencies* (*Chou-
hou fang*) represents the former: "Three days after a child is born, his stomach should be stimulated to help with the digestion. Take ground grains and
make them into a thick drink having the consistency of custard. Give him
an amount the size of a bean and make him swallow it."[49] The idea seems
to be to start a newborn on some kind of real food early so as to get his digestion moving.[50]

A T'ang medical authority was also quoted as having the view that "an
infant may be given a rice drink after the seventh day [of birth], in the
amount of three beans or so."[51] Such evidence suggests that until the T'ang
dynasty, people were interested in giving a slight amount of food (usually in
the form of ground-up cereal drinks) to an infant a mere few days after
birth. The idea seems to have been aimed at stimulating the digestive function, not providing additional food intake or nutritional value.

As early as the Sui period (581–618), there arose a different approach to
infant food feeding. Ch'ao Yüan-fang (550–630) was reported to have said
that:

Thirty days after a child is born, he should be given some food, in the amount of
two dates or so; after fifty days, that of a cherry; after a hundred days, that of a large
date. In the event that breast milk is insufficient, one may add [the amount] as
deemed appropriate. Do not give too much for fear that he may be unable to
take it.[52]

The focus is clearly on giving food as a supplement, providing it when an
infant becomes older and increasing it if the breast milk appears inadequate.
The Canon of Sagely Benefaction (*Shêng-chi ching*) from the Sung period
also advised that "after thirty days, food should be provided [to an infant],
but not in an excessive amount. If [the child] shows less desire to eat, do not
force him, as force-feeding may cause indigestion, which can bring on diseases."[53] K'ou P'ing's ideas on "infant feeding" (*pu êrh*) adopt a similar
line: "In the event that a nursing mother was found deficient in milk, the old
method [of infant-feeding] should not be followed. Rather, one should increase the amount as appropriate. Yet, do not feed [the infant] until too
full."[54] For this later period, discussions on infant feeding shifted from seeing it as stimulating an infant's digestion after birth to using it as a source
of nutrients to supplement breast milk.

The questions of when to start and how to give the child such food were
essential. Experienced pediatricians such as Ch'ien I had regretted that
"many children, because of the overindulgence thrown upon them, have
never touched any food even when they reach two or three years of age. This
weakens their digestion and physique [*p'i wei*], causing many illnesses."[55]
The right way accordingly was: "When [a child] is half-a-year old, cook a

thin congee with old rice, or make noodles, and give this to him from time to time. After he is ten months old, gradually give him thick congee and well-cooked soup to provide him with strength. He will naturally thrive and be spared diseases. However, do not feed him raw, cold, oily, heavy, or sweet things."[56] Here, Ch'ien I's main concern was in supplying additional foods and the nutritional needs of a nursing infant to give him extra energy to "thrive and be spared diseases." Thus, he believed that six months was a good time to begin. The foods should be soft, plain, and easily digestible, a view shared by many pediatric experts thereafter.[57] Overfeeding or giving food too hard on the digestion should be avoided. Wang K'ên-t'ang (1549–1613) in the early seventeenth century advised people to "feed twice [a day], in the morning and in the evening," but "not to eat chicken before [the child is] three years old," so as not "to cause worms in the belly."[58] Ch'êng Hsing-hsüan (1736–1820) in the early eighteenth century instructed people to boil ground-up "early rice" that had been roasted before hand, adding a little sugar to make a digestible baby food for infants not receiving enough breast milk. He also warned against the danger of feeding meat.[59]

As a whole, gradualism and modesty seem to be the main principles behind ideas of infant feeding in traditional China. Medical literature advocates careful initiation, slow progression, and refined ingredients in its instructions. To stimulate the appetite, or to provide additional food, moderation was the abiding rule, at times even to the point of overcautiousness. Many restrictions were placed upon the kind of food for infants. These guidelines, if followed, promised soft and delicate food but would have deprived a small child of many proteins, vitamins, and minerals other than those contained in soup cereals and a few kinds of well-cooked vegetables. In the same conservative spirit, the Chinese idea of infant feeding appears to have been concerned with digestion (and absorption) of foods, more than with nutrition.

Problems Concerning Nursing and Infant Feeding

Despite expert instructions, there were difficulties. Traditional texts on pediatrics covered numerous troubles encountered by women as well as methods of coping with them. The most common of these problems fell into four areas: substituting food (in the event of insufficient milk supply), a child's refusing to nurse, throwing up milk, and weaning.

SUBSTITUTING FOOD

Medical writings suggested two kinds of substitute foods for infants if a mother's milk proved insufficient and the family was incapable of hiring a wet nurse. One was the milk of animals and the other was thin cereal. Feeding the milk of domestic animals had been practiced in China for a long time. There were no taboos against it, as in the Greco-Roman tradition. After pig raising became common in the villages, sows' milk was often fed in addition to the old practice of using cows' milk. Animal milk acted as a supplement before the mother's lactation began or later on if it appeared insufficient. Many medical experts recommended the practice. Sung pediatricians even wrote a meticulous instruction on the cleanest and most convenient method of procuring sows' milk. They suggested that one should first put a piglet to suckle at the sow. This got the milk flowing vigorously, and then one lifted up the sow's rear legs to let go of the piglet and quickly obtained the clean, fresh milk to feed the infant.[60] When animal milk was unavailable, a frequent substitute was any finely ground cereal cooked in water to produce a thin gruel. This was similar to various supplementary solid foods given to older infants. In fact, medical authors recommended solid foods as substitutes for breast milk.[61]

REFUSING TO NURSE

An infant refusing to nurse, or "not taking the milk," was a problem recognized as early as the Sung. Ch'ien I felt that if an infant showed strong signs of wanting to nurse yet was unable to take the breast, something was abnormal, possibly the initial signs of certain infantile diseases, which should not be taken lightly.[62] Medical texts thereafter tried either to treat the phenomenon or to seek other explanations.[63] Reasons attributed to the infant's "not taking milk" included having caught a cold, overeating, acute ailments, difficulties with excretion, or the effects following a difficult birth, each of which required specific attention.[64] In general, most authors concurred with the opinion expressed in the *Key Methods for Various Diseases in Pediatrics* (*Yu-k'o tsa-ping hsin-fa yao-chüeh*), that "it is only natural that a child nurse as soon as he is born. If he is not suckling, there must be a reason."[65] If an infant continued to refuse, the problem had to be confronted.[66]

VOMITING MILK

Vomiting the mother's milk was another widely discussed problem among late imperial pediatricians. Earlier, during the Sung dynasty, physicians had noticed that there were two kinds of vomiting: the first occurring shortly after birth, the second occurring among sick or feverish infants.[67] After Yüan and Ming times, such discussions grew more meticulous.[68] The famous Ming pediatrician Wan Ch'üan provided particularly perceptive ideas. He identified, according to cause, three different kinds of vomiting. The first was *ou-ju*, or vomiting milk, caused by overfeeding.

Vomiting of milk occurs because the stomach of a newborn infant, being small and fragile, cannot contain too much milk. The nursing mother should thus feed according to degree of hunger, not allowing the infant to be overfed. Whereas the child has a stomach that is small and fragile, yet the mother's milk can be abundant and vigorous. When the child indulges in the milk, his stomach becomes unable to accommodate it, which causes serious vomiting. This [kind of] vomiting occurs with a noise, and [the infant] throws up a large amount of milk, as when pouring water into a bottle, which overflows when too full.[69]

The second kind of vomiting was the accidental "overflow of milk" (i-ju) caused by improper handling or holding of the child:

Milk overflow occurs because a newborn has a weak body and bones. When he reclines to the left or to the right, he lurches toward the front or the rear and depends on people to hold and carry him. If nursed until too full and yet placed in a wrong position, he is bound to throw up two or three mouthfuls [of milk]. As in filling water into a bottle, it will be thrown up when tilted.[70]

The third type was "dribbling of milk" in small amounts for no particular reason: "Dribbling of milk occurs when a child is seen with milk constantly coming out [of his mouth]; it appears often at the corner of his mouth and on his lips. This is like a bottle with a hole, so that water seeps out of it."[71] The author then observed that neither vomiting nor overflow of milk was a serious problem, both easily avoided by better controlling the amount of milk taken and more careful handling of the infant. The child who constantly dribbled milk, however, could be suffering from weak digestion, which should be improved with stimulating medicine.[72]

Wan's analysis identified various problems concerning the throwing up of milk, each one accorded possible causes and different symptoms. It was an attempt to distinguish the ordinary and normal kinds of vomiting from those signaling health problems. Medical works subsequently devoted more discussion to this distinction. The normal kinds of throwing up occurred often and demanded no treatment, whereas those caused by illnesses needed immediate medical attention. Only careful and experienced physical observation and pulse taking could tell one from the other.[73]

Weaning

Weaning takes place at different ages in different societies. Traditionally, Chinese women nursed their children for a relatively long period of time and tended to wean them fairly late. Rarely would anyone wean a child at age one. Most did so when he reached two years, or when he started walking, after which the child began to live solely on solid foods.[74] At times, when a mother did not have enough milk or became pregnant again, a child might be weaned between the ages of one and two.

Weaning often becomes an arduous task, then as well as now. On the one hand, it poses a challenge to the eating habits and health conditions of the nursing child. On the other hand, mothers might be confronted with crying and uncooperativeness that threatens to undermine the purpose of weaning. Thus considerable discussions approved "the recipes for weaning" (*tuan-ju fang*) to help frustrated mothers. Children not yet weaned at two or three back then were quite common and not considered a problem by physicians or others. Only when a child continued to nurse for several more years did the situation warrant correction.[75]

The prescriptions for facilitating the weaning process were mostly based on what seems to have been variations of similar ideas. An example of the latter called for ground realgar and cinnabar made into a powder with the addition of raw sesame oil and other ingredients. The paste was then painted on the child's eyebrows when he was asleep. When the child woke up, according to the recipe, he would no longer want to be nursed. This appeared in quite a number of medical texts from T'ang to Yüan times.[76] Some Ming pediatric texts also suggested that auspicious dates be chosen for successful weaning.[77] These recommendations showed that weaning could impose stress on nursing mothers, who were seeking external assistance, if only for psychological comfort. The recipes indicate that traditional physicians took weaning seriously.[78] Ming medical authors also advised looking after signs of discomfort in the child's digestive tract that could pose additional difficulties in weaning.[79] Others prescribed recipes to decrease lactation and to coordinate better with the weaning process.[80]

Examples from the Medical Records

Actual breast-feeding in practice can be understood in finer details from medical texts and biographical data. Many instances contained in the pediatric records had to do with health complaints related to nursing. *Elaboration on Pediatrics* (*Yu-k'o fa-hui*), by the Ming pediatrician Wan Ch'üan, for example, documented five cases of vomiting infants. Two involved sick children, one was an eight-month-old son of a local (district of Lo-t'ien in Hupei province) educational commissioner, T'ao. The child was said to be "throwing up any fluid that comes into his mouth."[81] The other was a three-month-old second son of Wang Tz'u-fêng, who "took no medicine or milk."[82] In both cases the condition was allegedly improved after treatment with concoctions of pig's gallbladder and the urine of young boys. A third case involved a three-month-old infant girl sick from eating and throwing up milk. Wan Ch'üan diagnosed that her problem came from overeating and food accumulated in the stomach. The family at first denied Wan's judgment but was forced to concede to it when the little girl began throwing up food and rice. The parents later confessed that she must have been fed over half a bowl of rice by an indulgent relative five days earlier. Days later, the rice still gave her "a full and stuffed stomach, making her refuse to eat and drink, also causing her to throw up." Wan solved the problem by prescribing a purgative.[83]

The fourth and fifth cases were newly born infants throwing up milk. One was "a child who has vomited since birth." Wan, reluctant to prescribe anything for the newborn, advised the parents to observe the infant's situation more closely. If the vomiting appeared to be caused by "nursing until being too full," the mother should try to breastfeed her more slowly and moderately. If her vomiting seemed to be caused by having caught a cold while bathing, mild treatments with such recipes as a cup of milk boiled with scallion and ginger, or licorice juice, should restore her health.[84] The fifth case was an infant who "threw up milk constantly after the first month," causing the parents to worry. Wan told the family: "The vomiting was not a regular phenomenon. But now the child throws up milk more frequently, so it must not be caused by illness." The parents were instructed to look for the source of the problem in the mother's nursing habits. If "the mother appeared strong and endowed with abundant milk, but from fear of the child's deprivation indulged in nursing until he became quite full, the milk that he drank would overflow and come out." This kind of vomiting can be easily corrected by better control of the intake or by more appropriate holding positions, such as "holding him more tightly and more carefully." If the child's problem appeared to be caused by a weakness in digestion, "unable to receive milk and digest it," causing "frequent vomiting" and only "throwing up in small amounts," it should be treated with digestive enhancements.[85]

In *More Cases from Famous Doctors (Hsü ming-i lei-an)*, by Wei Chih-hsiu of the Ch'ing period, eight cases were included under the topic "nursing problems of small children." Two involved sick children, one was a two-month-old infant in Hupei suddenly refusing to nurse because of a fever, the other began with the contraction of an illness that caused loss of voice. Both were treated with medication.[86]

Two other instances mentioned children as developing problems after being nursed with "inebriated milk." One was a small child seen by the famous physician Chang Tzû-ho (1156–1228). The child appeared to be "asleep and would not wake up." Other physicians had wanted to treat it as a "sleep fit" (*shui-ching*) and to apply moxabustion. The father of the infant questioned such judgment, asking that if "the child has not had any illness, why this fit all of a sudden?" He then brought the case to Chang. After taking a pulse from both hands of the child, Chang decided that it was not a fit. He questioned the wet nurse privately, "Have you gotten drunk in the

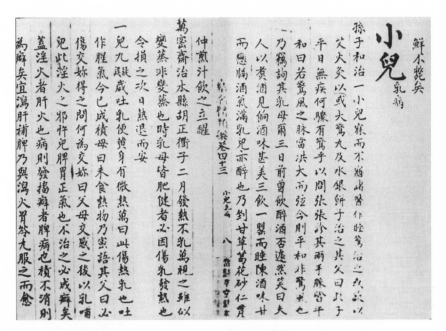

FIG. 16. "The Problem with Suckling" (*Hsiao-êrh ju-ping*), in *More Cases from Famous Doctors* (*Hsü ming-i lei-an*), by Wei Chih-hsiu (Ch'ing dynasty). Human milk was the main source of nutrients for the newborn. This text describes the trouble people had with wet-nursing and weaning. The National Central Library, Taiwan, Republic of China.

past three days?" At which point the wet nurse admitted: "My mistress warmed some wine and invited me to dine. The wine tasted quite good. We drank a number of times, finishing a jar, and fell asleep." Chang's suspicion, that the child had become drunk through his drunken wet nurse, was confirmed.

The other case was a small child of a censor, Ch'ên Chin-lin, who one day suddenly "shut his eyes, ceased to make any noise, and experienced weakness of the hands and feet." A physician invited for consultation suggested that "the child was not suffering from any ailment. It is only because he has been nursed with too much 'inebriated milk' that he became heavily drunk. Prepare some thick Liu-an [green] tea and feed him with a few spoonfuls. He will sober up."[87]

Wei's medical records also include problems of "licentious milk" (milk produced during sexual intercourse). The first of the two cases were said to have produced symptoms of vomiting, yellowish stool, and slight fever. In private, Wan the pediatrician told the father "the child was breast-fed after the parents had had intercourse." In the other case, a child had "slow-

moving eyes and stool with a foul smell." Pediatrician Hsüeh Li-chai diagnosed this as "having given licentious milk [produced] during intercourse."[88] Modern medical scholars also believe that infantile physical discomfort, such as mild vomiting, irritability, and diarrhea, could result from
mothers nursing right after intercourse, but the effect is not as serious or as
pervasive as traditional medical writings claimed.[89]

Wei's final two cases were about children whose mother or wet nurse
gave insufficient breast milk. In one, Wang San-fêng's son of about one year
was frequently sick. Physician Wan examined the boy and felt that he was
"ill from lack of milk." The father at first did not agree with the diagnosis,
insisting that "the child was fed breast milk abundantly." After Wan left, the
mother examined the wet nurse and found out that she indeed had no milk.
When pressed about her method of caring for the child, the wet nurse
replied, "During the day I chew rice to feed him, or treat him to some rice
cakes and fruit; at night I save some water to give him." Little wonder that
the child living on nothing but masticated rice and water would be constantly sick. When his parents went back to the physician for advice, the
doctor responded with deeper thoughts:

Although you are considering changing wet nurses, your child has been close to this
present woman, so you should not change her [abruptly]. But if you do not have a
woman with milk to nurse him, his sickness will not improve. A better way will be
to keep the old wet nurse to raise the child, yet choose a young and strong woman
with milk to sleep with the child at night and to breast-feed him. As time passes, he
will grow familiar [with the new woman] and develop an intimacy toward her.[90]

The idea was to be considerate of both the nutritional and emotional needs
of the child during a period of transition. The case reveals potential pitfalls
in using a wet nurse, as well as the relatively long period of a child's dependence on breast-feeding. The fact that the woman resorted to masticated
rice in place of milk also confirms the information on the kind of usual supplementary and substitute foods found in medical texts.

The second example shows how another small child suffered from inadequate milk supply. When Yao Ming-shui's son reached one, his mother
ceased lactating and began to "feed him with cake, cookies, dates, and per-
simmons." As time passed, the child "appeared to have canker sores in his
mouth and tongue and pus and blood on his lower body. After treatment of
half a year, he was still thin as a stick and hardly ever took in much food or
drink." Only after prolonged treatment did the child's health slowly turn
around.[91] Insufficient milk supply in nursing women, a condition that occurs worldwide in 10 percent of all mothers today, was also a threat to children's health and survival in premodern times. The traditional Chinese use
of thin cereal, sweets, and fruits as substitutes could not have allayed all the
nutritional problems caused by inadequate breast milk.

Ordinary Observations

Medical records represent an expert voice, one vocalized and transmitted in a special fashion. Breast-feeding and infant feeding are such mundane activities, however, that it is interesting to compare the professional
reports with social vignettes from the general population. Biographical and
family records of late imperial China frequently describe insufficient milk
supply or anxiety over feeding and food supplies. Mothers were often mentioned as having difficulties in lactation. Many claimed that ill health or
other psychosocial stress influenced a woman's milk supply negatively. Such
anecdotal passages beg to be restored to their historical context. For instance, was breast-feeding indeed the predominant practice for all classes of
families at the time? If so, did general instructions for nursing in the form
of advice literature or popular wisdom provide the needed practical instruction? Did the prevalent understanding of human milk at the layman's
level correlate to the kind of biophysical problems described in the vocational literature on breast-feeding? What were the most common substitutes
(either in terms of other foods or of a surrogate nurse)? Medical practices
as evidenced in pediatric texts from the Sung period onward present themselves as an interactive site, as well as counter-balancing force operating
within, and against, the historical environment that both gave birth to them
and was constantly altered by their activities.

Nineteenth-century records present a picture of common complaints.
Ch'ên Yen's (1856–1937) mother's milk was said to have dried up because
of an illness during his infancy.[92] When breast milk dried up or became
insufficient, the child's health suffered if the family could not afford a wet
nurse. P'i Hsi-jui (1850–1903) was said to suffer from "immaturity and
frailty" because his mother did not have breast milk to nurse him.[93] For
many families, wet-nursing was not a viable choice. When the leading anti-
T'aiping provincial governor Tso Tsung-t'ang was born, his mother was
said to be devoid of breast milk. To pacify the baby, she fed him rice masticated in her own mouth instead.[94] Ts'ên Yü-ying (1829–1889) was at first
breast-fed by his mother. At age one his mother passed away and he refused
to be nursed by other women, so his grandmother fed him congee.[95] Such
instances show that when a wet nurse was not a choice, thin cereal was the
substitute used most often. Such practices may or may not have been influenced by the instructions in medical texts, but the pictures from the medical
and family records match with each other well.

There were families who could afford a wet nurse when the mother did
not have enough milk or could or would not breast-feed the child for the
sake of her own health or other reasons. For example, Tsêng Chi-fên (1852–
1942) mentioned that her family used to have a wet nurse.[96] Ch'ên Ying-
shih (1878–1916) had to be breast-fed by a wet-nurse because his mother

was constantly ill after delivery.[97] But finding a suitable woman could be difficult. When Shao Hsing-chung (1648–1711) needed a wet nurse, his grandmother went through great efforts before settling on an agreeable choice. Finally, as the biographers put it, "He got a wet nurse after ten women were tried."[98] Hsü Nai's (1810–1867) family also had trouble "looking for a wet nurse [for him]. Many were not to their liking. After a long while they decided on a woman, Sun."[99] Wang K'ang-nien's (1860–1911) mother was so frustrated by the experience of searching for the right wet nurse that she decided to breast-feed his two younger brothers herself.[100] These anecdotes suggest that even the financially able found the search for a wet nurse problematic. Existing medical advice on selecting a good wet nurse might have helped, but it also added to parents' apprehension.

Conclusion

Discussions of breast-feeding in traditional Chinese medical texts are remarkably practical. Although "scientific" analysis of the biochemical mechanisms of lactation or the physiological processes of nursing had not surfaced for most of the late imperial period, the authors' deliberations concerning the right procedure, posture, and the rules of regularity and avoidance appear sensible and minutely technical. The ideas are presented in a matter-of-fact fashion and are in general devoid of appeals to pure myth or folk remedies. Both medical and family records indicate, moreover, that breast-feeding was the predominant way of infant feeding at this time, although substitute foods in the forms of animal milk or thin cereal were used in the event of poor lactation. Wet nurses were employed by the families who could afford them, although not without problems.

The common practice of breast-feeding in China as shown by this medical advice literature was to have wide health and demographic implications. First of all, breast milk provided nutrition and protection against diseases. Second, the prolonged period of breast-feeding (Chinese women usually did not wean their children until they reached two years of age, or when walking began) put added control on marital fertility rates because of the effect of postpartum amenorrhea. Historical family records for late imperial China indicate that general birth intervals were between two and three years, and historical demographic studies have deduced a moderate marital fertility (with between five and six births per woman), which can be viewed as additional evidence of prolonged breast-feeding. Especially since there were no strict taboos against postpartum sexual intercourse, prolonged breast-feeding became a significant and effective contraceptive mechanism commonly understood and resorted to by the general population. Occasional engagement of wet nurses by upper-class families may have shortened birth intervals, thus increasing fertility for wives. The practice of bringing wet nurses into the household and providing them with food and supervision probably resulted in better health conditions than were found in Europe, where babies were sent out to nurse.

Finally, regarding gender and sexuality, medical texts are a special genre of technical literature where women are primarily depicted as functional figures. Nursing women were discussed for their physiological function as suppliers of breast milk. Their needs and feelings in this particular context were measured and understood in relation to the children, not to the men. Nursing mothers were given responsibilities and strict requirements because they were considered to be the physically stronger party in their role as protector of the frail infants, not as the socially weaker or inferior sex vis-à-vis their male counterparts. Breast-feeding as part of the reproductive process was thus seen as something related to, but mostly independent of, considerations of sexuality. The female image that emerges out of this context appears more neutralized and is thus somewhat devoid of the sentimentality often associated with the female sex in other genres of literature.

Part 2

SOCIAL LIFE

Some of the oldest ceremonial bronzes in ancient China from the Shang (1600–1066 B.C.) and Chou (1066–221 B.C.) periods featured engraved, ornamental script indicating that the vessels, and the heritage they represented, were to be for the use of the children and grandchildren of the corresponding estates for ten thousand generations to come (*tzû-sun wan-tai yung pao-yung*). By the high Ch'ing in the eighteenth century, fabricated antique bronzes or real household furniture (a bamboo armrest, for example) in the archaic or antique style could still bear the same inscription. A longing for the perennial founded on familial reproduction runs from one period to the other, though by then the pious desire, from its presumptuous beginning, could claim merely a little more than one hundred generations. For a culture rooted in ancestor worship and a society geared toward cultural endurance, child rearing constituted the key medium for the realization of both. Throughout the three millennia in between, changes in social customs and the coming and going of personal habits were all rooted in and anchored by a conviction and investment in this biosocial reproduction. Particular results, of course, were expected of the children and grandchildren, as well as of their parents and grandparents. The factors of time, whether in personal, family, or larger historical terms, worked their effects through individual lives to produce a result in the aggregate that some argue can be recognized as changing patterns in politics or institutions, in economics or in ideas. Yet they could also be understood as unnoticed traces in the domain of the homestead, a realm that has gone without analysis, without any comment. Child-rearing practices (from the perspective of the parents) and growing up experiences (from the perspective of the children) afford a glimpse of history perceived and acted out from this angle. Lives under the ancestor's shadow, if you would, could be lived for the service, or at the mercy, of their offspring.

4 Modes of Upbringing

Everyday life is the hardest matter to uncover in history. Historical studies on early childhood in China provide an example. Recent scholarship on family in traditional China provides rich information regarding the organization and operation of clans, the political and economic strategies of individual households, career patterns of the gentry, and so forth.[1] Thus far, however, a general understanding of the personal conditions and daily experiences of a particular age group remains unexplored. A host of questions can be posed about the lives of the young in traditional China and at the way boyhood was formulated and experienced among the educated families in Ming-Ch'ing society.

Chinese ideas about childhood seen through the perspective of boyhood is complicated. Basic cultural history materials such as didactics or daily instructions present conflicting impressions. Mencius's understanding of the roots of innate goodness in humanity, for instance, was said to be "like a child, who is bound to love his parents."[2] Such a pronouncement with typical optimism of the Confucian kind accepts a "benign character" of youngsters automatically, though without necessarily being ready to adopt a "liberal" mode in bringing up little ones. On the other hand, there was the popular wisdom expressed in the pedagogical materials such as *The Three-Character Classic* (*San-tzû ching*): "To give birth to a child but not to teach him is the fault of the father, to teach him but not to be strict enough is the fault of a lazy teacher."[3] It suggests a much more stern and "pessimistic" view of children's natural capacity to do well on their own. Should we then conclude from this that most people in traditional China were in fact more likely to assume a disciplinarian attitude toward their young? A classical anecdote claimed that Mencius's own mother moved three times before she could settle her boy in a proper neighborhood.[4] Was Mencius's mother of a pessimistic kind, thus rejecting the optimistic convictions her son was to espouse? What other sources may we approach for certain recoverable patterns in child rearing and the growing up experience of young children in traditional China?

FIG. 17. "Five Children Dancing," by Su Han-Ch'ên (Sung dynasty). In a traditional ritual dance that became an entertainment at festivals, here Sung children dress up, wear masks, and perform roles (of Judge, Gods of Thunders, Medicine, and the Gate). Courtesy of the National Palace Museum, Taiwan, Republic of China.

A useful beginning for teasing out the nuances of the social aspects of childhood experience in traditional China rests in the traces left in the hundreds of *nien-p'u* (chronological biographies) for the late imperial period.[5] Personal letters, poems, diaries, essays, and tomb inscriptions for family members and friends formed the core of the primary materials in the compilation of these *nien-p'u*; they are also partially preserved as cited materials, providing rich firsthand sources of the early years of men and women in the late imperial period. The fact that these *nien-p'u* are chronologically arranged makes them a convenient tool for studying age groups as sociological strata and the growing up process. Such preliminary information then can be verified and complemented by other social history materials— such as diaries, collections of random notes, novels, dramas and stories,

FIG. 18. Children kicking a ball from "One Hundred Children," by Su Han-Ch'ên (Sung dynasty). Playing ball was prohibited by Neo-Confucian philosophers. However, this painting is clear evidence of the fierce social debate taking place in the world of arts and letters. Courtesy of the National Palace Museum, Taiwan, Republic of China.

contemporary accounts of local customs and rituals, folkloric activities, artistic depictions, and occasional legal cases and clinical reports—to approximate a multifaceted representation of the lives of children, hitherto considered inaccessible.

The history of children and childhood in late imperial China must be contrasted to the classical model as first formulated in ancient China, such as Confucianism as a textual and philosophical tradition, on the one hand, and the "recent" renaissance in the medieval period, on the other, including Neo-Confucianism as a transformation and configuration of a particular kind for post-Sung society. Gentry boyhood (or younger years of elite boys) is an appropriate sociocultural baseline for any further understanding of childhood conditions or children's lives in this period.

The Classical Model

China's stated principle of child rearing within family life dates back to antiquity. The classical reference in the paragraph in the "Nei-tsê" section of *The Book of Rites* (*Li-chi*) gives clear instructions on the proper way to raise a child in aristocratic households. The lines read:

As soon as a child is taking solid food, he/she should be instructed in telling his/her right hand [from the left]. Whenever he/she can talk, he/she should be taught the *wei* sound from a man and the *yü* sound from a woman, and that men wear leather, whereas women wear silk. At the age of six, instructions ought to be given on numbers and directions. At seven, boys and girls may no longer eat at the same table. At eight, on entering or leaving a house or when receiving meals, children must be made to follow after their elders. Also, at this time, they need to begin acting with courtesy. At nine, they proceed to receive instructions from a master, at which point they will live away from home and learn to write.[6]

Other than the orderly articulation of these instructions, the *Li-chi* model is impressive on several accounts. First, it described a child-rearing culture with practical steps growing out of particular views on human developmental stages. Second, it placed strong emphasis on the social skills and behavioral propriety expected of children; the differentiation of gender, the observance of courtesy, and reverence for the elderly formed the center of inculcation very early in life. Third, the knowledge that any preschool child (before the age of nine) should acquire consisted primarily of practical subjects such as numbers, directions, and the calendar. Nothing is mentioned about literary skills at this stage. Nor were disciplinary measures suggested for the execution of this ideal.

This basic stage of learning, as sketched in the *Li-chi* passage, was the foundation of proper child rearing among aristocratic families for the first millennium of imperial Chinese history and the source of inspiration and the baseline for discussion of the era that followed. Family instructions by leading Neo-Confucian thinkers in Sung times, such as Ssû-ma Kuang, for instance, represented but adjusted formulae on this classical model.[7] What appears to be new in the emerging post-Sung Neo-Confucian discourse on children and childhood, other than it had grown more elaborate in design and more considerate toward the physical needs of the young, was an unprecedented emphasis upon the importance of an early start in childhood development and upon the value of strong, or even punitive, methods.[8] Training in moral and behavioral requirements still took clear precedence over book learning and intellectual skills. In addition, in these early childhood years, attention was paid to the need for educating (elite) girls on almost equal terms with the (elite) boys before each headed toward different programs after the age of ten.[9]

Women Feed, Men Teach

A distinctive feature in this period is what may be called the "women feed, men teach" mode. Certainly, by the post-Sung period, the women were responsible for physically bringing up the young, for the daily feeding, dressing, and tender care, whereas the men were taking up training, teaching the boys living skills while deciding what the girls should, or should not, learn or do.[10] Since polygamy was not unusual among the upper class, the different wives and concubines from the father's various marital unions often came to one another's assistance in such daily chores. Wang Hui-tsu (1730–1807), for instance, was born into a gentry family of modest means. His natural mother had the status of the second concubine of his father and was mainly responsible for the household chores. His father's first wife, whom he referred to as "formal mother" (*ti-mu*), came to share a good deal of the child-rearing work when Hui-tsu was an infant. It was this formal mother who used to take the baby to bed. When he moaned for milk at night, according to his autobiography, she would bring the boy back to his birth mother to nurse. Hui-tsu's *ti-mu* apparently grew to be quite concerned for the baby.[11] Such close collaboration among the womenfolk did not always come naturally, of course, although practical considerations often enhanced the need of mutual aid.[12] In the poorer houses, female relatives, neighbors, and friends often assisted the child's mother.

Female relatives from the fathers' side, such as the paternal aunts (that is, the father's sister or the wife of the father's brother) involved themselves often in the daily care of a child. Niu Yün-chên (1706–1758) had such an aunt who married his father's younger brother when Yün-chên was two. Always fond of his bright nephew, this uncle could not help talking about him to his bride. Soon, the aunt took a true liking to the toddler. She began sitting him on her lap and combing his hair every day. Delighted to bring fruit and snacks for him, as Yün-chên later remembered, this aunt looked after his daily food and drink, paying particular attention to his health. Her treatment of his painful toothache left a permanent imprint on the boy's memory.[13]

In other cases, cooperation among female relatives was not voluntary, though necessary. Lü Liu-liang (1629–1683), the early Ch'ing political dissident, had to be reared at birth by his third elder sister-in-law (wife of his third elder brother) when his ailing mother was struck by the death of his father.[14] In traditional Chinese families with a large number of children, at times from successive marriages, elder sisters or sisters-in-law were often charged with the duty of raising the very young. Wang Hui-tsu's formal mother on her deathbed entrusted him to his two elder sisters.[15] It was instances like this that gave rise to the old proverbial saying that "one's elder brother is often like a father, the elder sister-in-law a mother" (chang-hsiung ju-fu, chang-shao ju-mu), which in part gave rise to the fierce debate on the propriety of a man's mourning for his elder sister-in-law that old classics used to forbid.[16]

Men could be affectionate in playing with young children, in the lighter moments of life, but rarely would they be involved in daily physical care. Nor were they inclined to deal with the emotionally rough times or unpleasant demands in a child's daily existence. Ming-Ch'ing family records mention fathers caressing and playing with their infants and young children, yet fathers are more typically observed engaging themselves in the more enjoyable and "rational" aspects of a child's everyday world.

Conceived and executed under the Confucian notion of division of labor by gender, the situation cannot be easily framed or understood in the modern delineation between biophysical care versus sociocultural reproduction. Late imperial Chinese mothers and female kin undertook the task of the nursing, washing, and caring of the infants and children in the house because these belonged to the activities of the "inner" (nei) sphere. These were domestic chores, usually, though not necessarily, executed indoors. The fathers and male relatives of these same infants and children were concerned and preoccupied with assuming the duty of inculcating, directing, and supervising the growing up process of the young, for these were seen as the "outer" (wai), external or exterior endeavors, thus understood as social, rather than physical, spaces. This division of roles should never be overstated, since on a daily basis the differentiation in collaboration between the two spheres and between the two parties had always been interactive and fluid. In other words, a gentry father might have looked after the physical needs of his boys and girls in illness, fetched water and medicine, or bathed the body or felt temperature. Nor would anybody have been surprised to

FIG. 19. "A Boy at His Lesson." Literacy was seen as a vital skill and began as early as possible. If the father was not at home, the boy was taught by his mother, elder sister, or grandparents. Reprinted from Wang Lien-hai, ed., *Chung-kuo Ku-tai Ying-hsi Tu-tien* (Chiang-hsi: Chiang-hsi Mei-shu, 1999), p. 35. Based on woodblock print from Shantung. Ch'ing dynasty.

see a happy man walking around with an infant in his arms or hand in hand with a toddler and answering all the practical needs of the child, be it his son or niece. Mothers, grandmothers, aunts, and elder sisters, on the other hand, could mete out instructions for a boy's first few years of primer learning, just as many fathers, grandfathers, uncles, and elder brothers were giving regular lessons to the younger girls in the house. So when a boy was seen helping out with the household chores, as was common in this period, he was taught, helped, and surrounded by his female elders, just as when a girl sat for her first lessons there was a good chance that she would be holding her brush and looking at the book in the company and under the guidance of her male kin.

Learning Takes Command

Stimulated by various vocational opportunities afforded in a rapidly monetarized economy and with increased likelihood of social mobility in either direction, families from this period sought an early start in the preparatory education of their young. The social and cultural background is complicated. To put it simply, an increasingly "free" mobility in Chinese society and the commercialization of the Chinese economy had haphazardly propelled people to be more enterprising. Waves of "entrepreneurially spirited" child-rearing practices first appeared in the landed upper class in the towns, where opportunities hit the population the earliest and most bluntly and were soon seen in other social groups in the outskirts and villages. The "early start" attitude evident in many child-training activities, especially from the sixteenth century onward, bore clear witness to this process at work. Elite families pushed the initiation of literary education on their children at an increasingly younger age.[17] Merchant and artisan families wanted their young to learn the trade, obtain a craft, and start apprenticeships sooner. The better-off peasants instructed and labored together with their boys to work for surplus and cash crops for the market. All wanted their children to have some education, literary or technical. Carpenter boys needed to memorize *The One-Thousand Character Text* (*Ch'ien-tzû wên*) in order to learn the craft and take measurements accordingly. Middle-range farm lads needed simple arithmetic to make sense of prices and keep the accounts. Ordinary households were excited by the prospect of their sons marrying an educated woman who could run domestic affairs intelligently and bring up bright children. Changing contents in the primers for boys and girls, evolving mores in children's stories, and the marketing of educational toys and learning games attested to such a fermentation of economic and cultural forces.[18]

Although women continued to perform most of the nurturing and daily care, alluring opportunities "out there" prompted conscientious mothers (often together with grandmothers, aunts, and elder sisters) to involve themselves more and more closely in the early "preparatory education" that was taking place under most roofs. For the literati families, this meant women folks frequently reciting to their children verses from T'ang poetry, rhymed prose, or simple primers that they themselves knew by heart.[19] This phenomenon presupposes a fair level of female education by this time—at least at a basic level. It also suggests an uneven regional character in popular literacy whereby the poorest in the most "developed" lower Yangtze area were afforded a marked sociocultural advantage over their average countrymen in the rest of the areas that were left behind.

The predominance of female care in early childhood in time yielded to a second stage in which women still took responsibility for physical matters, while the male adults in the house gradually took over formal instruction in the appropriation of elitist or practical knowledge. Families of scholar-official aspirations naturally placed special emphasis on the intellectual development of their boys. The coveted gift of "precocity" (tsao-hui) or the identification as "prodigy" (shên-t'ung) meant real, or imagined, literary skills at an exceptionally early age.[20] To aim for this, a good deal of preparatory learning was felt necessary before the child began pursuing his formal study with a private tutor, at the village or clan school, outside the house. For such "preschool" brilliance, however, no one seemed more trustworthy or convenient as the inculcator than the educated men in the house. As a result, a strong tradition in favor of parental instruction or personal instruction (ch'in-k'o or tzû-k'o), developed among Ming-Ch'ing elite households. These family elders—oftentimes the child's parents or a close relative— would make an attempt to engage their young in learning activities using materials enticing to the beginners. In numerous instances, a father took the trouble, and for some the pleasure, to personally help their boys take their first steps toward learning. This might have involved conjuring up simple couplets during morning walks, learning a few characters from people's door decorations, reciting poems that reminded one of the weather of the day, memorizing lines from a classic that echoed a scene at hand, or learning the names of natural objects in the daily wanderings. Of the biographies revealing such circumstances, the majority indicate the child's father as the first instructor. Some, in fact, did so with affection. The late Ming writer Wung Shu-yüan (1633–1701) was one such lucky child. At the age of three, Shu-yüan later recalled, he often sat on his father's lap. The senior Wung was fond of playing, kissing, and licking the boy's face. Shortly afterward, the father began teaching the boy his first characters while holding him in his arms.[21] The early Ch'ing writer Li Kung (1659–1733) was born into a wealthy household in Hopei province. His father used to recite *The Book of Filial Piety* (*Hsiao ching*) while walking and carrying the four-year-old boy.[22]

Hsia Ching-ch'ü (1705–1787) belonged to a gentry family from Kiangsu province. His father died when Ching-ch'ü was six. Ching-ch'ü remembered his father as a caring man, fond of doing things with the children, especially serving them at mealtime. This senior Mr. Hsia often put down his wine cup when his kids wanted to play. The three-year-old Ching-ch'ü remembered sitting on his father's lap and playing with his beard. He also recalled attractive foods placed on the table, "the hundreds of green peas looked so delicious, I wanted badly to have some." The father would then conjure up a game on the spot. He fetched the wordbooks and started to test Ching-ch'ü, giving the boy one pea at a time as he recognized any single character. "In what seemed no time at all, the entire plate was cleaned of green peas." His father then was said to be throwing the boy into the air with joy, carrying him to the back room proudly to brag to his mother: "Now this child, I say, will not fail the hopes of our family."[23] The same play routine figured in Pao Shih-ch'ên's (1775–1855) memory of learning in his Anhwei residence. Four-year-old Shih-ch'ên, too, remembered receiving his first few sentences on the lap of his father.[24]

These individual accounts refer to a mode of passing knowledge and skills from the older men to the younger generation. Whereas fathers, or their male substitutes, bore the responsibility for personally transmitting, or supervising, the needs of boys to make a living, mothers would do the same with the girls. The general pattern of cultural transmission and social reproduction had been an established one, though changing domestic relations featured parents in an increasingly personal, engaging, and physically intimate fashion. This occurred during the early phase of childhood, usually before the children reached seven or nine, depending on the trade to be learned. For elite families, this meant starting their children toward a literary education. Peasant boys began with the gradual acquisition of farming techniques; sons of merchants learned business skills; and sons of artisans practiced the first inkling of their craft. Girls from educated backgrounds acquired a similar literary education to their brothers (see Chapter 7), whereas the more ordinary among them at a slightly older age began to learn cooking, sewing, and household management from their mothers, older women, or other female instructors. In other words, there appeared a rough conception of childhood in two phases. With the early period of pre-schooling (performed instruction), say before seven or nine, casual preparatory inculcation would be carried out under one's own roof by close relatives in an informal fashion. Depending on the child's station in life, a more structured, serious "education" (of letters, arts, or crafts) would follow, if necessary from a hired instructor at school or through an apprenticeship.

The Duties of a Father

Gentry fathers initiated their boys into learning. A corollary trend had fathers taking their young boys to live with them at their posts away from home. This could mean a father-and-son pair dwelling in one of the official residences in the capital, in a modest house attached to district administration compounds, or in an inexpensive boarding room with the host family of a village class or clan school. The famed Ch'ing philologist Wang Yin-chih (1766–1834) was three when he lost his mother, but the main reason his father, Wang Nien-sun (1744–1832), brought Yin-chih with him the next year when he headed his office in the Compilation Bureau was to supervise his son's primary education and to read the boy the *Êrh-ya* and *Shu ching* classics on a daily basis.[25] The same motivation moved T'ang Chieh-t'ai to fetch his seven-year-old son T'ang Chên (1630–1704) from their home in Szechwan all the way to Wu-chiang in Kiangsu upon taking up his new appointment there as a district magistrate.[26]

As the number of failed and unemployed examination candidates increased in the eighteenth century, many more boys age four to eight accompanied their fathers as the latter hired themselves out as village tutors. At seven, Liang Chang-chü (1775–1849) accompanied his father in another frustrated attempt to pass the examination. His father then became a private tutor around their hometown in the Ch'ang-lo district of Fukien. From then on, for a number of years, the young Chang-chü moved along with his father to lodge at various clan schools—one year in the P'eng residence in Ching-yüan Alley, and the next in the Lin residence in K'ai-yüan-t'ou village. Between 1781 and 1783, when Chang-chü was six to eight years old, the father and son moved through three different clan schools in the area. As a result, Chang-chü, like many other boys in a similar situation, had the opportunity to begin his own education studying along with other pupils in the clan school under close supervision of his own father.[27] The famous special commissioner during the Opium War, Lin Tsê-hsü (1785–1850), also spent a good part of his childhood years with his father away from home. The father, a lifetime failure in the examinations because of poor eyesight, had a job as a village teacher. Beginning when Tsê-hsü reached three, his father started taking him along to teaching posts. So, from a tender age, Tsê-hsü's father could sit the boy on his lap and show him his first characters.[28]

This arrangement between father and son presented a unique opportunity for closeness and for provision and supervision on mental, psychological, and material grounds. Wang Yin-chih's father, as mentioned, took the three-year-old boy with him to his post in Peking. In the mornings on his way to attend the imperial audience, the senior Mr. Wang rode along with his child. Stopping at a breakfast shop to eat, he would give a piece of bread or cake to the boy to munch on in the carriage while waiting. This, we are told, continued for several years. On a business trip Yin-chih fell asleep while the adults were busy with paper work. A colleague of his father's took pleasure in waking the child up to help them remember a character that had somehow eluded them. Everybody was impressed by the boy's quick response.[29] Similar situations of young boys with their fathers and in the company of adults were not unusual among educated families. They reveal a familial aspect of the Chinese male little studied. Merchant, artisan, and physician fathers in this period, too, customarily passed their trade or craft to their boys (a few might consider training their girls as well). The affectionate ties that developed between a young lad and his father often sprang from this daily apprenticeship and the "colleagueship" that followed suit, an association greatly weakened when institutional education took over the role of practical training within the family in the modern era.

Parenting Together

Contrary to the stereotypical impression of gender division in traditional Chinese domestic life, close communication and collaboration often existed between the two parents concerning child rearing. Ch'üan Tsu-wang (1705–1755) was the second child born to a middle-aged couple of modest means in eastern Chekiang. His grandfather had been a local secretarial assistant and his father a village teacher. Tsu-wang's father got married fairly late, at twenty-eight. The first child born to the newlyweds the next year, however, lived for a mere five years. Overwhelmed with grief, the couple was determined to have another child, although it took them another ten years. They nicknamed the baby *Pu*, which means "supplemental." That year, the father was forty-three and the mother thirty-four. Both were anxious to see Tsu-wang (literally, the hope of the ancestors) grow and prosper. When little Tsu-wang reached three, his father started teaching him simple verses. Tsu-wang's performance was not disappointing, though in his parent's eyes he did not compare well with his deceased elder brother, who was said to have shown a brilliantly early grasp of the classics. The father consoled his wife: "This child, though not as intelligent as his elder brother, we should agree, is acceptable." What concerned the parents, in addition to Tsu-wang's seemingly undistinguished ability, was his weak physique. The couple often talked about the child and the future of their household. His father at times would read from T'ang essays, sometimes from Liu Tsung-yüan's (773–819) lament that "having reached the age of forty, I am nonetheless forced to stand by myself in front of the offering altar [to the ancestors] every spring and autumn, fearing that this weakling beside me might not make it to maturity." The parents were said to have broken down in tears.[30] Changing domestic and family life suggests that, from the mid-sixteenth century onward, conflicting trends and new experiences were developing in different regions and among different social groups. Further "civilizing processes," if they may be seen as that, took the form of both the further "ritualization" of domestic activities in southeastern clan organizations and in an intensified "liberalization" and "loosening up" of social mores, especially in the Kiangnan towns. Parent-child ties and husband-wife relationships among China's educated and sophisticated urbanites, by Ming-Ch'ing times, certainly need not stick to the letter of either classic ritual texts or their Neo-Confucian codification. Rapidly changing economic conditions, increasingly varied social practices, and heated debate on cultural norms had preempted any simple, unquestioned exercise of a "business as usual" sort of operation in people's daily affairs. Fathers (often temporarily unemployed) were seen taking a more active part directly, and at times warmly, in domestic affairs and in child rearing. As husbands, too, these men could be acting out an increasingly direct, hands-on style in their domestic engagements, a reorientation well matched to the newly formulated women's culture represented by mothers and wives in this period.

As a proud young father in the sixteenth century, the failed candidate but soon to be famous author Kuei Yu-kuang (1506–1571) recorded how he used to carry his first daughter to approach her mother's breasts for the daily nursing. The baby's infantile fingers used to play with his notes on *The Book of Changes* (*I ching*). Kuei was certainly leading the life of a social pioneer, in fatherhood and manhood. One century later another frustrated literatus, T'ang Chên, reported how several of his classics texts were all stained with cooking sauce and other household oil for the lack of a third room to use as a study. He was still wont to convey the considerably subdued and greatly "modest" fashion of an average gentleman in the physical and material conditions he had devised for his domestic existence. By the end of the sixteenth and the beginning of the seventeenth century, however, the old, haughty air of a "Confucian patriarch" was on the wane. An ethical and aesthetical appreciation for a softer, warmer, socially more domestic and more sociable father, husband, and man had gained a fresh respectability in the sophisticated circles of Chinese society.

The childhood experience of Ts'ui Shu (1740–1816) provides another example of this newly excised domesticity in its more mature form. When Ts'ui Shu was born, in 1740, in the Wei district of Chih-li, his mother was thirty-five. Shu's father, a frustrated "student" of the civil examination system at thirty-two, saw in his son the single hope for life's reward. Carrying the newborn Shu around in his arms, he spoke wistfully to his wife: "I only hope this baby turns out to be a Neo-Confucian scholar one day!"[31] The anxious father certainly did everything in his capacity to bring that dream closer to home. As the boy reached two and began to talk, his father took every opportunity to teach him characters. They practiced reading the red-colored couplets that hung on the front doors, learning the characters on inscribed tablets, and identifying the names of medicine on the labels in local herb shops. Shu's father never grew tired of explaining the meaning of the simpler words they encountered, differentiating carefully for the toddler boy their correct intonations.

As the child grew older, the parents became obsessive in their supervision. When Shu began moving about on his own, the father tried to follow him around wherever the boy went. The idea, according to Shu's own words later, was to "prevent me from mixing and playing with other children."[32] His mother would do the same when the father was away. They could hardly wait until Shu turned three, when they finally had the opportunity to start the boy on some real study. When taught *The Three-Character Classic* (*San-tzû ching*) at three, it was said to have posed no problem whatsoever because he had already learned a good number of the characters. The father spent additional hours daily, however, explaining terms in the calendar, titles of government institutions, the successive order of the dynasties, names of mountains and rivers, and so forth. "Any bits of information useful in my study," Shu wrote, "father was never tired of repeating for me time and again."[33] The senior Mr. Ts'ui took care also to explain to the boy the difference between Buddhist and Confucian traditions, as well as the separate persuasions Chu Hsi and Lu Hsiang-shan expounded within the Neo-Confucian heritage. So accustomed did Ts'ui Shu become to these intellectual activities that whenever his father had other engagements to attend to and was unable to spare time for instruction, he was said to have been able to look at books by himself before the age of six. A scholarly critic was in the making, as Shu discovered early on that other folks from his locality were reciting *The Analects* (*Lun Yü*) with improper pronunciation and diction, a small tribute to the parents' investment. Their experience may be too remarkable to be considered representative of their times, yet the competitive and intellectualizing trend in the development of early education of elite children from this period was a rapidly growing phenomenon. Repeated reports on the grooming of one child prodigy after another become myth-creating, inviting skepticism that extraordinary intellectual performances of young children thrived in an unusually fertile and pressured environment.

For a four-year-old, by any standard, Ts'ui Shu was leading an exceptionally solemn life. In giving instructions on *The Analects*, for example, his father took pains to note for him the phonetic intonations in red ink beside each character so that the child would not be reading the words in their local dialect. Texts were all to be recited one hundred times a day. A string of one hundred copper coins was always sitting on the left hand corner of the desk, one coin was to be moved to the right every time the boy repeated his lines: "It matters less whether I had already memorized it the first few times. I still had to complete my assignment the full hundred times."[34] When that was done, he was allowed a short rest before continuing with the next paragraph. By five years, we are told, Shu was having lessons on Mencius, *The Great Learning* (*Ta hsüeh*), *The Book of the Golden Mean* (*Chung yung*), and other classics. These family teaching sessions had since worked themselves into a daily routine, with one stack of "new works to do" and another pile of "learned works for review." Throughout this preparatory education at home, Ts'ui Shu's mother participated equally. Shu's first lessons on *The Great Learning* and *The Book of the Golden Mean* at age five were, in fact, taken from oral dictation from his mother at dawn.[35]

Among the late imperial elites this trend toward personal instruction and close parental supervision of a child's primary education had a background in both longer and shorter historical trends. For this Ming-Ch'ing era, an old stress placed on the intellectual development of the child had been exacerbated and developed to become a peculiar social fad in admiration of precocity or early maturity in the child. Educated elite families were motivated by the all-important state-sponsored civil service examination, which was growing increasingly rigid and competitive. Personal instruction by the father, or close kin, was perceived as a convenient home guarantee to improve results. The Mencian warning against the negative and counterproductive result of a father's demands (*tzû-fu tsê-shan tsei-ên chih ta-chê*) seems to have been forgotten. The classical Confucian advice to "exchange children in conducting instruction" (*i-tzû êrh chiao*), or that one might avoid the possible difficulties in teaching one's own children, also went unheeded. A general obsession to elicit early intellectual talent surpassed the Sung Neo-Confucian emphasis on moral inculcation and behavioral training of individuals.[36] Gentry families in late imperial China would not acknowledge their decreasing interest in moral cultivation or behavioral correctness in child-rearing, but, in daily activities, literary learning and intellectual pursuits were taking over almost all of a child's time and energy.

When the child's father was unavailable, other family elders would take up the responsibility. In most cases the first relative to assume this obligation was the child's paternal grandfather. Kung Ting-tzû (1615–1673) started learning the classics with his grandfather.[37] The eminent Ch'ing philologist Wang Ming-shêng (1722–1797), at the age of three, began his study of "hundreds of characters per day" from his seventy-nine-year-old grandfather, who was himself a district education commissioner in Tan-t'u.[38] The eighteenth-century historian Shao Chin-han received personal instruction from his grandfather when he was four. The old man took a special liking to him: "He appears bright, even though with a handicapped left eye."[39] Other male relatives under the same roof or in the vicinity, such as paternal uncles, mature elder brothers, or even senior paternal cousins, could function in this "fatherly" capacity to conduct preparatory lessons and be expected to produce similarly effective results. At age five, Tuan Yü-ts'ai (1735–1815) began his primary study with his grandfather, just as he would be tutoring his grandson Kung Tzû-chên (1792–1841) decades later. After the young boy Yü-ts'ai completed the lessons on *The Analects* two years later, however, his fourth paternal great-uncle took over as his private tutor.[40] Liang Chang-chü, at three, had his elder paternal cousin as his mentor, with his mother supervising his study. His father had not yet returned from the examinations.[41]

In Ming-Ch'ing educated circles, in fact, primary education based in the family was so powerful a preoccupation that direct input from the child's mother would not be spared. One of the most influential of seventeenth-century scholars, Ku Yen-wu, was taught *The Elementary Learning* (*Hsiao-hsüeh*) by his biological concubine-mother (*shu-mu*) at three and *The Great Learning* by his formal mother at five.[42] Huang Ching-jên's (1749–1783) father passed away when the boy was only three. His grandfather raised him while his mother supervised his studies, even though at that time he did not show much interest in learning.[43] The late Ming grand secretary Ni Yüan-lu's (1593–1644) mother started him on *The Book of Odes* (*Shih ching*), which he claimed stayed with him for life.[44] Such leading writers as Chang Hsüeh-ch'êng (1738–1801), Yao Ying (1785–1852), Hsü Chi-yü (1795–1873), and numerous others all had their mothers as their first mentor.[45] In most instances where the fathers or male kin served as instructors, mothers remained the supervising and supporting force behind the daily learning activities. Hung Liang-chi's (1746–1809) father even assigned his elder sister the responsibility of teaching the boy his characters when Liang-chi was three. When his father died two years later, Liang-chi continued his study with other tutors but had to report to his mother every evening about what he was learning in his lessons. All these examples show that among educated families, mothers were given a shared duty to oversee the child's early education, while adults of both genders and from both paternal and maternal lines were mobilized to mete out elementary lessons to their children. The participation of mothers and elder sisters suggests that female education had not only made significant headway in late imperial Chinese society, but also carried clear value as capital in social investment.

The compulsive obsession for intellectual prodigies led to the prevalence of oral dictation (*k'ou-shou*) from mothers or female kin. The increasingly tender age of the initiate, the home environment, and the relatively uncomplicated character of the materials (usually one's first rhymed verses were of the simpler T'ang poetry and didactic historical stories) all made mothers a perfect choice for preschool inculcation. Neither should there be much surprise when in records and gossip people marvel at the "special talents" (*ch'i-ying*) of the young as manifested in quick mastery of words and easy adoption to scholastic habits (natural curiosity toward the world of letters, interest in papers and books, heightened concentration). Sun Ch'i-fêng (1584–1675) "spoke late," but according to his biographer, he "knew to point out characters on the gate as soon as he learned to speak."[46] Wang Ming-shêng, obedient to his grandfather, mastered a few hundred words per day at age four or five.[47] The budding geographer Hsü Hung-tsu (1586–1641) was said to have memorized everything as soon as he started to learn anything and proved capable of writing the moment he could hold on to a brush.[48] Kung Ting-tzû never forgot anything that passed his sight, and at age six refused to go to bed before midnight.[49] Lü Liu-liang was born without a father but showed an exceptional brilliance that allowed him to memorize any text after the age of three.[50] Such talents were accorded as strange (*ch'i*), extraordinary (*i*), and even magical (*shên*) or heavenly (*t'ien*). Family elders prayed for young pupils and rushed to do good deeds in petition for them. People boasted and exaggerated about the slightest evidence of brilliance but were envious and distressed if such gifts passed their children and instead developed in the genius of a neighbor. Such evidence can be found in fiction and plays. It was a never fading "social disease" in all walks of life in Ming-Ch'ing China, sprawling over the bustling towns and the connecting villages.

Bookish Boys Against the Rest of the World

The overwhelming concern for a child's intellectual development, fed by a prejudice against physical activity and childish play, represented a fraction of childhoods. Despite the efforts made to promote intellect in elite families, many youngsters could not quite live up to expectations. The Ming Neo-Confucian scholar Sun Ch'i-fêng was regrettably noted as a "late talker."[51] The early Ch'ing classicist Yen Juo-chü (1636–1704), born into a scholar-gentry family of high standards, turned out to be a physical and mental weakling. When sent to school at five, he was said to have appeared awkward and dull. He stuttered and was unable to get much of anything into his head even after hundreds of repetitions. His mother, more worried about Juo-chü's health than his poor performance at school, insisted on allowing the child a few more years to catch up.[52] Rural children from lesser backgrounds, on the other hand, were constantly recorded as having trouble with literary education. Niu Yün-chên was such a boy with learning difficulties. "As a child," his biography tells us, "he seemed inactive, uninterested, and spoke sluggishly. People all thought he was a dumb kid." Only his grandfather, refusing to give up on the child, continued to drill him in words and sentences. He kept the young boy by his side as he drank his liquor at night, flipping casually over pages. If by chance Yün-chên caught the sense of a word, the grandfather would be overjoyed, yelling, dancing, laughing loudly and rewarding the boy with his favorite treat of honey.[53]

Not infrequently then, the child had to be enticed to study. Huang Ching-jên, partly saddened by the death of his father when he was three and partly due to poor health, never became fond of learning.[54] In addition, there were those children who did not accept the expectations of their elders easily. Some were left to continue their childlike sentiments and actions. Chu Tz'û-ch'i (1807–1881), at four or so, was once asked by his mother what he really wanted in life. "Do you, my child, like money?" asked the mother. "Not really," replied the boy. "High office?" "No." "What do you really want?" "I hope everybody loves me dearly, that's what I want."[55] A disappointment to the aspiring parents, perhaps, though an entirely "natural" utterance from a toddler's perspective. In the recording and reporting of such instances, moreover, we witness a more "indulgent" or "loving" child-rearing culture emerging on the social scene.

Within and against this historical context, the Neo-Confucian idea of discouraging physical activities and outdoor play achieved only partial success. For every account of a child's "sitting alone and not going out to play with the crowd," there were many more incidents noted of children rolling about in games for fun. The seventeenth-century essayist Wei Hsi (1624–1680) exhibited an unusual indifference to good times. When his classmates were engaged in noisy bustle, Hsi was said to be sitting quietly all by himself, working on his lessons.[56] For families from conservative classical backgrounds, such as the Wei family from northern Kiangsi, such disinterest in socializing with peers was not viewed as a lack of social skills but praised as an incipient sign of intellectual talent and outstanding character. For others, studious activity did not come naturally, nor was it seen without due ambivalence. As a youth, Shao Hsing-chung appeared at first to be a lively fellow. Once at a family memorial, he was seen fighting with his cousins over dates and chestnuts while others were performing the solemn mourning rituals. The seven-year-old Hsing-chung had to be stopped and reminded of his deceased mother until he too was in tears. He used to be fond of playing kick ball too, only to be severely scolded by his grandmother, who helped in raising Hsing-chung after he had lost his mother at six months of age. She spoke sarcastically to the child: "So your grandfather is not as capable at playing ball. And your talents now certainly exceed your grandfather's." In repentance the young Hsing-chung was said to have no choice but to kowtow until blood was visible on his forehead.[57]

Yet there were also children depicted as endowed with an early sense of purpose and solemnity. Ch'üan Hsieh-shan (1705–1755) was already reading history books like *The Comprehensive Mirror for Aid in Government* (*Tzû-chih t'ung-chien*) and *General Investigation on Important Writings* (*Wên-hsien t'ung-k'ao*) at seven and was quite absorbed in his studies. "When the local string band passed by their residence in the fall, with all the loud music and bright colors, he would not move himself to take a peek."[58] Ma Hsin-i (1821–1870), too, was recorded as being quite diligent at a young age. He was described as a quiet boy, never playing much, speaking to his siblings and peers only slowly and in a calm voice. Whenever a high official went by the village school, "everyone in his class rushed out to take a look, only he sat motionless by himself."[59]

Stories like these, as stereotyped representations, can hardly be taken at face value. Kenneth J. Dewoskin points out also how "famous Chinese childhoods" had existed since ancient times with documents written for moral or political reasons. The earliest section in biographies were there either to show that "the adult in childhood" was "inborn" from the very beginning, or else, the reverse, as a lesson of how careful tutoring and self-improvement could change the odds and make exemplary figures out of unlikely material.[60] Biographical writing and the production of autobiographies by late imperial times had grown more complex.[61] Much unintended information came out of the printed world during this period, while image construction and character building remained key elements in mentioning or preserving the traces of early childhood. Accounts of children and childhood, then, can hardly be assumed to be disinterested projections through some culturally neutral or transparent lens in this historical context, as in most others.

"Model boys" were made to be the exceptions, not the norm. It was their unusual character, in other words, that makes their cases stand out. Most were noted as ordinarily "coarse" children who preferred playing and acting out their boisterous nature. Unlike in other social history materials, children were more often than not indicated in stories and popular arts as joyfully socializing with each other, their family members, and other village elders. Ming-Ch'ing literary sources reveal scenes of festival life and market towns, of toy vendors and children mixing in the crowd watching theater troupe performances. Paintings from this period depict small children picking dates in the fall, catching willow flurries in spring yards, and so forth. Biographical anecdotes concur with these depictions. The sixteenth-century agriculturist Hsü Kuang-ch'i (1562–1633) at age seven or eight purportedly ran around in the snow to trap pheasants and to catch pigeons. The scholar Li Kuang-ti (1642–1718) as a boy loved to go out with his grandfather for chess games or to join his father in meetings of painters.[62] K'ung Tung-t'ang

FIG. 20. "Children at Play in the Hall," by Chin T'ing-piao (Ch'ing dynasty).
In traditional ethics Chinese children were disciplined strictly. However, art
images represented children misbehaving while adults tacitly observed from a
distance. Courtesy of the National Palace Museum, Taiwan, Republic of China.

(1648–1718) remembered a pretty gourd plant growing on the bean shed
out in the garden that produced elegant looking fruits with slender waists.
As a boy of five, he often stood on the shoulders of older children to snap
down a gourd or two to make house decorations.[63] Such fondness for outdoor fun and physical activities, however, grew or diminished in the record
as mainstream social values changed from era to era as they varied according to regional and class differences. Eighteenth- and early-nineteenth-
century biographies portray children of the elite to be limited more and
more to indoor, bookish occupations, leaving less time for physical and
leisure activities. The statecraft thinker Wei Yüan (1793–1861) was a model
studious lad who "loved to sit alone, hardly ever showing a smile, or joining
in the fun." Reading was said to be his favorite pastime, so much so that
upon the rare occasions when Yüan did venture out of the room, his own
housedogs started barking and attacking him.[64] Vignettes like this, real or
half-fancied, crept into biographical and family accounts not as silly oddi-
ties but as shining images. During the decades after Wei's youthful years,
from the mid-nineteenth century onward, a warmer, more relaxed domestic
life and personal intimacy familiar to the late sixteenth and early seventeenth centuries resurfaced. The glimpses of activities of children and child-

FIG. 21. "Young Children in School" (Ch'ing dynasty). Children are shown here as being left to their own devices as the teacher is sleeping or not looking. Reprint from Wang Lien-hai, ed., *Chung-kuo Ku-tai Ying-hsi Tu-tien* (Chiang-hsi: Chiang-hsi Mei-shu, 1999), p. 33. Based on Yao Wen-hang's painting, from the Ch'ien-lung era.

hood found in biographical and chronological data such as the *nien-p'u* represented therefore but part of an evolving textual documentation that reflected this interplay between changing cultural discourses. It also represented and formulated individual and collective experience as well as evolving social realities. These resulted from, but were also part of, contemporary cultural vogues. Little information recoverable from these materials on shifting patterns in family relations and private life should lend itself then to an unambiguous reading or straightforward interpretation.

FIG. 22. "A Lesson in School." Contrasting with the schoolchildren depicted
in Figs. 20 and 21, this picture shows the "model boys," the obedient children
sitting around a table and studying. Reprinted from Wang Lien-hai, ed., *Chung-
kuo Ku-tai Ying-hsi Tu-tien* (Chiang-hsi: Chiang-hsi Mei-shu, 1999), p. 34. Based
on a Ch'ing drawing.

In serious-minded households, concern for intellectual progress appeared
so intense and so specifically focused, for instance, that adults forbade children any leisure reading. To look at "soft" or entertaining books such as
stories, novels, and traditional romances was strictly prohibited in more
than one set of Ming-Ch'ing family instructions; even an occasional glance
at poetry and history was considered unnecessary waste. In his early teens,

FIG. 23. "Plowing and Weaving," by Ch'iu Ying (Ming dynasty). Different from
the children of the rich, most children from Chinese rural families had to perform
farming or do housework even when young. Here, the old and the young, men
and women, work together. Courtesy of the National Palace Museum, Taiwan,
Republic of China.

Wu Ch'êng-ên (1504–1582) had a strong interest in miscellaneous literature
and unofficial history (*yeh-yen pai-shih*). He used to buy them secretly and
share them with his fellow students. Fearful of being scolded or having the
books confiscated by his father or teacher, he had to sneak away and enjoy
them in private.[65] Yin Chao-yung (1806–1822) once, at the age of five,
sneaked a look at the *Romance of the Three Kingdoms* (*San-ko yen-i*), only
to be physically punished for the offense.[66]

Yet this strong concern for a child's intellectual development among
Ming-Ch'ing elite families seems striking when posed against the lives of

children from other walks of life. First of all, girls led a life not exactly the same as that of their brothers.[67] Before age ten or so, they played with their company, sat in the same classes, and went through a learning process similar to the boys. Although approaching older childhood, their regular intellectual training could have come to a halt. The more fortunate among them continued on what was considered "soft learning," or cultural pursuits of a feminine nature—literature and poetic composition, for instance. Only a few of them were allowed to take formal lessons in the classics or history. Most teenage daughters began to be instructed in the feminine skills of sewing, cooking, and household management. The less fortunately situated of the girls learned early on to make sacrifices for the needs of the boys. Sisters were known to do needle work and help with the mother's tasks to earn a small income to put their brothers through school.

The boys from peasant families routinely collected tinder wood, tended water buffalo, cut grass for the cattle, and hoed and mowed the fields. They were obviously physically more active; in fact, the most frequent type of accidents for boys from common households was drowning in rivers and ponds. Children from slightly better-off farming families were beginning to be given a chance at schooling, off and on, in village or clan schools. But in general they went to school at a much later age, not until ten, twelve, or even sixteen years of age. Also, no preparatory instruction whatsoever would be provided. Their parents tended to discipline them according to more strictly traditional ethics; Confucian values such as loyalty, filial piety, charity, chastity, and so on could be taken both seriously and passionately. Social norms and cultural values from both the elitist and the popular strata could obviously function to produce an at once repressive and liberating child-rearing practice, albeit in different areas and for different reasons. Beyond that, ordinary peasant and artisan families simply desired their children to be safe, alive, and productive.

Conclusion

A methodological note to bear in mind following the previous investigation and deliberation is the very "elastic" and flexible, or elusive, nature of the source materials, thus the positively "creative" or "negotiable" character of such a historical exercise. For social historical purposes, the biographies, family instructions, poems, notes, and personal letters could be seen as bearing witness, revealing and reflecting upon the practices and experiences of the day. They are the traces, albeit subjective and positioned refractions, of a time and place that utilized available opportunities (be they the entrenched civil service examinations for the landed gentry or the flowering market economy for the agricultural, mercantile, and artisan sectors).

So an ever compelling tendency to get a child (especially a boy) on the "early-start" program was the game in town, or even in some villages. Mothers and grandmothers might feel sorry for the frail or the sick, so they carried them to school or treated them to warm garments and nourishing soups at night. As for fathers and uncles and grandfathers, the imaginative and energetic among them took the invitation to preschool education upon themselves; they invented playful games, enticed the children with their favorite snacks, and tried to inspire in morning walks and daily storytelling, just as they streamlined the curious minds by constant scolding and unforgiving beating. All of them worked toward the same goal; the few dissenters would have to be found in a different literature. But the same records of a society in a vigorous struggle toward success also revealed intentional or unintentional transgressions. This was a society in conflict with itself, but one that offered the possibilities for success defined in more than one fashion. And, more importantly, it was a society well aware of the attraction of other ways, of alternative views, alternative practices. So the biographers preserved stories of the troubled youngsters, such as K'ung Shang-jên (1648–1718) who eventually persevered and mastered the seductive volumes and lyrics that were robbed and beaten out of his childhood.[68] These complex cultural implications were bolstered by late imperial Taoist naturalism and a revival in the Buddhist sense of liberation, certainly compounded by the radical utterance of Wang Yang-ming's trust in innate goodness.

Upbringing, child rearing, or growing-up and other childhood experiences may or may not be about one and the same thing. "Being brought up," as seen and told from the position of those who were supposedly forming the social environment, is quite different from the experience of those on the receiving end. Modern explanatory models often consider the lives of young children beginning with the social, material, and physical conditions under which they were "raised." Such an approach, of course, is not without its constraints, as the situation also highlights the interconnection of different forces at work, each formulated under different persuasions and defined by different socioeconomic structures. As shown here in part, young children surely had different childhoods due to factors of gender, class, region, religion, or ethnic group. They appear to have been leading different existences, not simply by the forces of the time but also by the forces that penned the records. Subjectivity and agency are extremely important and yet acutely thorny problems when applied to the case of children and childhoods in history. For this reason a comparison over time and space may provide an indispensable inspiration in spurring further investigations.

5 Domestic Bond

As a self-statement commemorating his fiftieth birthday, Generalissimo Chiang Kai-shek (1887–1975) released an essay entitled "Serving my Country and Remembering my Mother" (Pao-kuo yü ssû-ch'in), in which the staunch nationalist pronounced that toiling for his country and paying tribute to his mother (an illiterate Chekiang village widow who remarried) were the goals that gave meaning to his life. The two were in fact, as he put it, intertwined and connected. The latter, while personal, stood as the inspiration at the root of the former, the larger public cause. Another well-known piece in twentieth-century Chinese literature was an essay later entitled "My Mother" (Wo-tê mu-ch'in), taken from the *Self-Account [autobiography] on my Fortieth Birthday* (*Ssû-shih tzû-shu*) by the influential intellectual leader of the Republican era, Hu Shih. In this work, Hu Shih gave a typical account of his life as a young boy growing up with his widowed mother. She (another uneducated but morally upright woman) used to wake him up every morning at dawn for school, reiterate his wrongdoings, recount his father's legacy (with the ancestors' expectations) and whip him when his naughtiness got out of hand. Ch'ên Tu-hsiu (1879–1942) and Ch'ü Ch'iu-pai (1899–1935), forefathers of the Chinese Communist revolution, were fatherless sons with young widowed mothers in the same stormy period in modern Chinese history. Both gave their versions of domestic misery to show what had sewn private seeds of social discontent and political revolt. Four centuries before them, Ku Yen-wu (1613–1682), leading thinker and, some would say, precursor to China's protonationalist sentiment, was also a young child of a widowed mother. It was she (not his biological mother but his father's second wife in an unconsummated union, a woman in love with the classics and infatuated with glimpses of national politics) who starved herself to death demanding his loyalty to the collapsing Ming dynasty to which the youthful boy Ku swore his personal allegiance.

Such anecdotes from Chinese history beg for elucidation beyond the perspective of social statistics on widowhood and orphanage from the late imperial period onward. Biosocial reproduction should not be limited to mother-child or mother-son bonds alone. Yet as a core family the domestic sphere of women and children was where most childhoods began, as the mother-son bond illuminates in a more dramatic manner the interconnection between the characteristic of motherhood and the formation of personhood (even the link between personhood and nationhood), reminding us of the artificiality of the separation of microlevel individual or "private" sentiments formation and macrolevel changing modes of public consciousness.

The relationship between mothers and sons has attracted much scholarly interest from historians as well as from social scientists and psychologists, especially since Sigmund Freud (1856–1939) put forth his theory of the Oedipus complex. It remains worthwhile, nevertheless, to examine the particular case of mother-son relationships in the Ming-Ch'ing household, to depict the environment that nourished most childhoods, the interaction mothers often had with their children, the specific expectations Chinese mothers came to have of their boys, as well as to reflect upon the wider emotional and historical implications this bond had in that society.

Sociologists and anthropologists studying Chinese families in modern times posit that a woman in China needs to have sons to secure her position in the family and in society.[1] Under such conditions women's futures often depend on the quality of their relationship with their sons. For upon these relations lie the mother's single hope for care in old age.[2] From these field investigations, it seems plausible that the mother-son relationship is of particular significance in Chinese social relations and one that does not obviously stop at the birth of a son. To ensure that this relationship works properly, and to gain the exact effect the mother wishes, requires additional human effort—a certain kind of identity building and emotional construction. Past records reveal this portion of the emotional contours of the mother-son bond in its formative stage. How did this mother-son relationship came about in the first place? And how did the people concerned want it to function? If possible, such a formulating process ought to be examined not only from the point of view of the party who appeared to have an upper hand in constructing it (that is, the mothers), but also from the perspective of the ones who were experiencing and participating in the same process presumably at the receiving end of things (the sons). Therefore it is important to consider not just at what point and in what ways the mothers instilled their needs and their will into the minds of their young, but how the boys managed and lived out in their childhood and later came into their adulthood. The following examination, in other words, hopes to delineate the formation of the domestic bond between mothers and sons as a specific case to illustrate the kind of inner constructions at work below the surface of the usual social aspect of parenting. The point is not simply to demonstrate the general human environment a young child often grew up in during the late imperial period, but also to show how in actuality moral values and personal interest could be translated into the daily grind of parent-child interaction, thus making possible the realization of particular social aims through the process of carefully constructed, respectively articulated, and mutually defined human emotions.

The main historical source employed here is information culled from more than eight hundred *nien-p'u* (chronological biographies) from the Ming-Ch'ing period, supplemented by personal writings (letters, memorial essays, and autobiographical accounts). Since the compiler of a better *nien-p'u* often makes free use of any bits and pieces of materials he can lay his hands on to reconstruct the yearly events as they took place in the life of his character (*p'u-chu*), a wide array of poems, family letters, and personal diaries could, therefore, find their way into the *nien-p'u* in direct quotation form or as indirect references. In addition, by the Ch'ing period, self-compiled *nien-p'u* (*tzû-ting nien-p'u*) had become a format of increasing popularity. This was a genre of a particular kind of autobiographical account, with all the advantages and flaws inherent in such literature.

In these accounts, mothers in late imperial China were represented, much like those in traditional societies elsewhere, as symbols of virtue and suffering. And no one could have known this better than their own children. The sons witnessed their mothers' daily toil as the daughters did, and yet they were in a special position to show their sympathy and gratitude and to redress grievances with their own successes. The Confucian moral code of filial piety enabled and in fact required the sons to remember their mother's dedication and misfortune in life through emotional terms and practical means. With both parties appreciating the reciprocal nature of the relationship, the generally intimate and mutually reliant mother-son bond took on powerful dimensions in the emotional and gender context of Ming-Ch'ing China. The situation was further complicated by the fact that the person a child considered as his mother did not refer exclusively to the woman who had biologically given birth to him. In the case of a child born to a secondary wife or a concubine, his formal or official mother, called *ti-mu*, was actually his father's first wife (who might not have a son of her own). The *ti-mu* often participated in the daily rearing and disciplining of the child and socially performed a role that was like a mother and thus could come to expect the same reciprocal relationship from the child as his "natural mother." In the words and deeds of many Ming-Ch'ing characters, the mother who came to mean so much and made a great impact on a person's life could actually be his *ti-mu*, the "social mother," rather than his biological mother. The woman who made a vehement loyalist of Ku Yen-wu, the woman whom Wang Hui-tsu (1730–1807) wanted to name his collected writings after, or the one pressing Liang Chi (1859–1918) to reward her with his success, indeed, were, or included, their "social mothers." The relationship between a

FIG. 24. "Illustrated Classics of Filial Piety" (Hsiao Ching), by Ma Ho (Sung dynasty). In Chinese settings, children were often asked to kneel down before parents, showing respect and willingness to listen to the lesson seriously. This activity also represented the continuance of generations both culturally and physically. Courtesy of the National Palace Museum, Taiwan, Republic of China.

ti-mu and her "social offspring," or between a stepmother and her step-child, revealed by historical literature, reinforces many social scientists' convictions that motherhood is largely a socially and culturally constructed phenomenon that can be separated from the biological linkage.

Chinese men felt compelled to write profusely about their mothers, living or deceased. It is through their collective memory and from their particular perspectives that historians gain a special access to the lives of mothers and their relationships with their children. A close reading of this memorial literature allows one to untangle the human and emotional world that once belonged to married women (as mothers) and growing or grown men (as sons). One should be careful, however, not to take the contents of this memorial literature too literally. In a society where personal ambitions and private desires were never considered legitimate motives, people tended to claim a higher motivation for their careerism. This notwithstanding, it remains to be explained why, among all the motivations men could possibly claim and among all the persons they could identify as their inspiration, the overwhelming majority chose to honor their mothers as the single human force driving their experiences.

Model Mothers

The life of a mother in the Ming-Ch'ing household, not unlike that which awaited a married woman elsewhere in history, was seen as a product of the unfavorable and demanding role allotted to her in society. The ordinarily laborious housekeeping and tedious child-rearing responsibilities, as observed by a seventeenth-century critic, demanded much yet rewarded little even in the best of situations.[3] Mothers from gentry-families could not be spared the onerous and oftentimes distressful duties expected of them. Fathers seldom shared the domestic chores of raising the young.

The daily work of the ordinary household no doubt dominated the lives of countless Ming-Ch'ing mothers. They were described as constantly burdened by daily toil, especially while nursing the young and caring for the sick. The famous Ch'ing classicist Tuan Yü-ts'ai (1735–1815) realized the fate that befell his mother when he was merely a child of seven:

At the time both my grandfather and my grandmother were already in their seventies. To serve them and to manage the entire house, my mother was constantly burdened by the supply of rice and salt, by endless cooking, grinding [of cereal], washing, sewing, and even the cleaning of the portable toilets. Since there was no servant in our house, mother had to do it with her own hands. There were, in addition, small children to nurse and feed. Everyday counted, she was never left a moment to catch her breath. . . . Only with such hard labor and meticulous attention was mother able to please my grandparents.[4]

Although objectively, the situations depicted were hardly deplorable by any means, subjectively many sons seemed to feel remorse over their mothers' daily labor. They spoke appreciatively and regretfully of a situation in which maternal compassion was fueled by personal sacrifice to achieve a comfortable home life. The eighteenth-century philologist Wang Ming-shêng (1722–1797) spoke of a cold winter when he was eleven; because of the family's indigence, the boy was deprived of a quilted garment. One evening, Ming-shêng's mother (née Chu) made up her mind to remedy the situation. That very night, she sewed him a jacket, as a result "her hands were freezing and cracking and left stains of blood visible [on the cloth]. Yet the next morning, mother got up early as usual to pump and carry a bucket [of water from the well] with the same pair of hands. There was not a word of complaint."[5]

Matters as basic as nursing could turn out to be arduous. When the high Ch'ing essayist Wang Hui-tsu was born into a gentry family of modest means in eastern Chekiang, for instance, his father was a distance away in the capital. Once she delivered the infant Hui-tsu, his natural mother continued to carry out all the daily chores around the house. Seeing her being overburdened by housework during the day, Hui-tsu's formal mother (ti-mu) shared in the care of the infant at night. She always put him to bed in the evening, ready to bring him to nurse at his own (natural) mother's breast whenever needed. This was done a few times every night, followed by a diaper change.[6] Recollections like these bring to mind the ordinarily draining task of child rearing along with the heavy housework that was the mother's lot even in the most well supported and uneventful of situations.

Under less fortunate circumstances, the motherly duty of a woman was to be discharged with more effort and pain. For one thing, not every child was endowed with a strong physique. The fifteenth-century Neo-Confucian scholar Ch'ên Hsien-chang (1428–1500) was born a weakling suffering from constant illnesses. His mother was, of course, the one to bear it all and, among other things, breastfed the boy until he was nine.[7] Then there were many other mothers who, owing to years of arduous housework, were themselves deprived of good health, which became an additional liability. Hsü Tzû's (1810–1867), Ch'ên Yen's (1856–1937), and Ch'ên Ch'i-mei's (1878–1916) mothers were all recorded to be deficient in breast milk because of poor health or other physical weaknesses.[8] Bearing and raising the children (both girls and boys) alone, in fact, made up a large part of a mother's domestic burden; Tsêng Chi-fên's (1852–1942) mother was said to be physically exhausted from bearing too many children. She did not have enough milk to nurse her infant daughter.[9]

Childbearing became such a hard fact of life for women that some of them sought medical intervention to avoid or end pregnancy. The sixteenth-century scholar Kuei Yu-kuang (1506–1571) noted that his mother lost her voice, and later her health declined once she took "the drink with two snails" for contraceptive purposes.[10] P'i Hsi-jui (1850–1908) recorded that his mother too suffered from poor health due to an unsuccessful attempt to end her pregnancy.[11] Once a child was born, however, the mother's commitment to rearing the infant could turn into another ordeal. As mentioned before, the late-Ch'ing provincial leader Tso Tsung-t'ang's mother did not have breast milk to nurse him when he was born. Nor did the family have the means to hire a wet nurse. Tsung-t'ang's mother chewed rice until it became thin cereal to feed the infant boy.[12]

Small children, on falling victim to health problems, brought added worry and work to their mothers. Some Ming-Ch'ing biographies mention physical weaknesses of the young that required the parents, especially the mothers, to tender additional care to the sick child. The renowned seventeenth-century writer Wu Wei-yeh (1609–1671) confessed that: "While young I often lay in illness, leaving my parents with the work of extra care. As a result [of this sheltered existence], I knew nothing about the outside world until I was fifteen or sixteen years of age."[13] Shên Chao-lin (1801–1862) also remembered that he had "some problems with phlegm [t'an-chi]" and thus a tendency to faint and fall around the age of six. Small children from his native Hang-chou area usually sat on high chairs while reading but Chao-lin would suddenly erupt into a seizure and pass out, falling along with the high chair, with his head crushing on the ground. This highly dangerous problem had his mother worried and troubled for years. She exhausted herself in the daily care of such a vulnerable child, trying everything she knew, including prayers, to prevent the accursed disease from recurring. This, needless to say, was extremely demanding on her both emotionally and physically. In addition, Chao-lin seemed to have some sort of an ear infection constantly. There was always fluid coming out of his ears, causing a hearing impediment. His mother lived with the difficulty of caring for this sick child until conditions finally improved after he passed ten.[14]

A sick child was often recorded as subjecting his apprehensive mother to nervous prayers and laborious care. The late Ch'ing painter Ch'i Huang (1863–1957) revealed the price his mother paid for his sickness-stricken childhood. Between two to three years of age, as Huang later recalled, he kept on falling ill. Oftentimes driven out of her mind by worry, Huang's mother sought every possible healing measure. After consulting every physician, exhausting all the drugstore supplies, and sinking the family into debt, his mother made sure to try every folk method or magic treatment. When ordinary doctors and medicine brought no effective result, she traveled to temples near and far, returning with her forehead all swollen and red from devout kowtowing against the hard floor in front of various altars. The witches in the villages, too, were invited into the house with their dazzling tricks. Huang's mother, in constant fear of losing the boy, spared neither money nor pain in weathering these years of anxiety and drudgery.[15]

In her painful and costly experience, naturally, Huang's mother was by no means alone. All mothers with a sick child in their arms were revered for sharing the toil and the same sense of helplessness. Chü Chêng (1876–1951) confessed that not long after birth he was always suffering from various ill-nesses. At first he had difficulty with breathing and had chest pains. Then he suffered from a certain abdominal pain. The infant Chêng became rest-less, bawling day and night from the physical distress. His mother had no choice but to carry him on her back, pacing and circling the bedroom through sleepless nights. The ordeal lasted more than a year until he was finally relieved of the affliction by a miraculous prescription.[16]

Among the diseases that preyed on Chinese children in the late imperial period, smallpox still stood out as the preeminent threat despite attempts at inoculation. There were quite a few detailed accounts of mothers drudging through the demanding days with small children bedridden with the pox. Wung Shu-yüan (1633–1701) contracted smallpox in the third month when he was eight: "In tendering intensive care to me, for many days and nights, my late mother did not have a chance even to change her own garments," Shu-yüan later recalled. There was a time when the boy's eyes all of a sud-den turned up to the whites, and he himself appeared out of breath. Des-perate and terrified, his mother called all the women to circle the boy and cry out his name until he finally came back to his senses after what seemed a very long while. Less than three weeks later, Shu-yüan's younger sister, who was born after their father passed away, also had the pox and unfor-tunately died shortly thereafter. "It was because mother was all too atten-tive in looking after me," Shu-yüan regretted, "and could not spare enough time to care for my sister."[17]

Many biographers of this period tell similar stories. Sun Hsing-yen (1753–1818) got smallpox when he was nine. For twenty days his mother was said to be taking turns with the grandmother, caring for him day and night with-out a rest.[18] Wang Hsien-ch'ien (1842–1918) had the pox when he was merely eight months old. "With the depleting pain and toil of my mother, I was at last spared death and my life was saved."[19] Even those children who were inoculated could develop serious symptoms because of the unreliable nature of the procedure. Miu Ch'üan-sun (1844–1919) fell seriously ill after he received the traditional smallpox inoculation when he was four. His mother was said to have wept incessantly, anxious about the boy's condi-tion. Together with a maid, she did the utmost in caring for her boy, who at last recovered from this adversity.[20]

Widow Mothers

The ordinarily demanding life of a mother became many times more difficult when she lost her husband. Since in this society the remarriage of men occurred more frequently and was considerably easier than that of women, the loss of the father brought far graver consequences for the welfare of the child than the loss of the mother. Yet, precisely because men often contracted multiple nuptial relations (either at the same time or subsequently), there appeared a higher chance for a relatively young woman to lose her husband of an older age than for a man to lose all his wives. Therefore, a child was much more likely to grow up without a father than without a mother (including stepmothers and other maternal substitutes).[21] Thus, there emerged numerous accounts of widowed mothers trying to bring up the young single-handedly while keeping the family together with meager resources. Such lamentable circumstances often left a despondent feeling within both the mother and her children and further generated a sense of solidarity among them.

The late Ming thinker Liu Tsung-chou's (1578–1645) father passed away before his son's birth. Tsung-chou, born a posthumous infant (*i-fu-tzû*), was to have a hard and solitary childhood. His mother, apparently unable to support the family unaided, was forced to return with the children to her own family to get through the years.[22] Chao Yü-ching's (1652–1707) father died after a dining and drinking banquet in a famous local restaurant, T'êng-wang-ko, with the district magistrate of Nan-ch'ang in Kiangsi province. The senior Chao left behind him two partners (his second wife, then twenty-five years of age, and Yü-ching's mother, presumably a concubine at twenty-three). Between them, there were six young children, none of whom had reached ten. A typical family with widowed mothers and helpless young children, "it was clear that they would not be able to make it on their own." The paternal grandfather, located in the distant Shantung province to the north, decided to take them in to assist the mothers in bringing up the children.[23]

The difficulties suffered by a widowed mother often left an indelible imprint on a child's memory. The father of the high Ch'ing provincial official Liu Pao-nan (1791–1855) died when his son was merely five, "a weakling," in Pao-nan's own words, "who could not even put on his own clothes. Everything I came to have in my later days was due to my mother's thoughtful care and close protection." Pao-nan's mother, as he remembered, was strict in disciplining the children, although not without a sense of compassion. The intimate years of struggling through life together created a strong bond between the mother and her children. Pao-nan remembered the days well when his mother had to labor hard to provide him with both tender care and stern instruction. In later years, he composed poems describing the sober days and his mother's tender care: "As I took my first steps, it was mother who led me with her own hands; while I lay ill, it was mother who treated me with medicine from her own mouth. Thus when I grew strong, she appeared exhausted and weak, for the strength she gave out was all absorbed by her own child."[24]

Furthermore, there were verses about the way his mother tried using her limited ability to conduct instruction sessions for her boy:

As I turned five, she started to teach me *The Book of Odes*, and when I was seven, she gave me lessons on *The Book of the Rites*. Every time the whips fell upon my body [for not meeting her standards], it was her heart that received lashes more than my skin. For, alone in a dark room, she wiped away the tears streaming down her face.[25]

In personal accounts like these, a widowed mother's relationship with her children was shown to have developed out of specific conditions. A few major themes seemed crucial to this particular context. First, without the materially pivotal role of the father, the mother's task of raising the young and keeping the house together became greatly more arduous. The Republican politician Hsü Shih-ch'ang (1855–1939) spoke of his fatherless childhood in the mid-nineteenth century as follows: "Father died when I was merely seven and my younger brother five. The condition of the family immediately declined, although mother [née Lin] persevered in maintaining the household and bringing us up to be independent."[26] Many strong-willed single mothers, furthermore, insisted on carrying out their duties on their own, winning limited, though perhaps precious, autonomy at a dear cost. The early-twentieth-century educator Ts'ai Yüan-p'ei's (1868–1940) father died when Yüan-p'ei was eleven. Relatives and friends of the family suggested raising funds to assist in bringing up the children, only to be firmly declined by Yüan-p'ei's mother. She pawned clothes and other articles in the house, running a tight budget to feed her three boys. Her motto was "rely on oneself [and] never count on the aid of others."[27]

A second feature of widowed motherhood was that the experience of sharing a hard life and struggling through some particularly harsh and often humiliating times together nurtured a strong and unbreakable bond between the mother and her children. The renowned mid-Ch'ing demography-scholar Hung Liang-chi (1746–1809) lost his father at seven. Deprived of an adequate livelihood, the boy, his mother, elder sisters, and younger brothers moved in temporarily with his maternal grandparents. The grandparents' house, nonetheless, was itself not much better off. Liang-chi's widowed mother, therefore, led the girls in doing needlework to help provide for the family and to save up for the boy's schooling. Well into his adulthood, Liang-chi could still recall vividly those long evenings when his mother, surrounded by the girls with their sewing and the boy with his

FIG. 25. "Mencius's Mother Moving the House," by Chin T'ing-piao (Ch'ing dynasty). The story of Mencius's mother moving the house three times became a classic model of a parent's guiding role in molding the social environment of a child. This picture shows that this model still affected Chinese in the Ch'ing dynasty. Courtesy of the National Palace Museum, Taiwan, Republic of China.

homework, worked until the wee hours every night.[28] The late-Ch'ing classics scholar Liu I-chêng (1880–1961) remembered, too, the special sense of hard-pressed yet intimate feeling the children grew to cherish by surviving difficult times along with their mother. I-chêng once spoke of the poor meals they had daily after his father died. "Those days when we were little, we could hardly afford to be concerned about nutrition. A piece of preserved tofu in red sauce was all that we could afford on the table. That was what mother, elder sister, younger brother, and I had to go with our rice every day."[29] Solidarity nurtured by common suffering and shared strife hardly diminished through time.

A third feature created by necessity in the experience of a widowed mother was that she often found herself taking up additional responsibilities left behind by the children's deceased father. (While in the reverse case, a widower hardly ever had to perform the duty of a mother due to the prevalence of the remarriage of men.) Huang Fu (1880–1936) recalled the change that took place after his father passed away, leaving behind six young children. "From then on," he confessed, "mother had to take up both the responsibility of feeding and of teaching us all by herself." Fu himself was then seven. He remembered clearly the seriousness with which his mother discharged the added duty of supervising his studies. "Whenever I was found inattentive to my studies, I was badly scolded and punished without any mercy." Occasionally, when the tutor reported a good performance by the boy, his mother only exhorted him to continue to be diligent and never to be easily taken in by self-satisfaction.[30] In these and similar stories, widowed mothers sustained a house through its crises and raised their sons, who were of decisive value to the survival of the family as well as to the mothers' personal welfare.[31]

The Dual Role of a Mother

The added responsibility taken on by a widowed mother is a phenomenon of particular interest because it highlights the dual role mothers often played in traditional Chinese households. Even when the father was alive, he could be away or simply unavailable to execute his family duty. Mothers, it appeared, were always ready and capable of carrying out the additional burden in the children's, especially the boys', upbringing: nursing, feeding, as well as disciplining and instructing. The mother's task was of course made heavier because of the absence of the father. The family fortune of Wei Yüan (1794–1857), the nineteenth-century statecraft thinker, declined severely after his grandfather passed away when Yüan was ten. However, Yüan's father was serving hundreds of miles away in Kiangsu, unable to look after the practical needs of the house. Everything was left as

usual to his mother, caring for the aging grandmother who demanded assistance all the time as well as making ends meet under financial constraints.
"Thanks to Yüan's mother [née Ch'ên], who strove in all directions, things
were dealt with to bring about a bare balance. The boy, furthermore, was
never forced to interrupt his studies."[32]

This dual character was most clearly evident in the mother's involvement
in the instruction of her sons. In elite families, the mother participated in the
disciplining, character-forming, and skill training; in the lower classes she
helped to decide on the choice of trade for apprenticeship. Indeed, mothers
from Ming-Ch'ing elite households were known to give instructions to their
boys in the formative stage of their education.[33] Especially suitable learning
activities were acted out by these mothers with their sons in early childhood,
with lessons carefully chosen and instructing methods astutely employed.

In the opening lines of The Three-Character Classic, it was said that "if
a child is raised well but not taught properly, it is the responsibility of his
father." But in reality, the mothers in Ming-Ch'ing households exhibited a
strong, and in many instances a stronger, interest in the sons' education and
career development than did the fathers. Both parents were concerned
about proper training and achievement for the son and their shared obligation to the future of the family. Yet a mother differed from a father in some
particular desire to assist and push a boy for success. For in the social hierarchy of Ming-Ch'ing society, a woman could hardly acquire any public
acclaim for herself. Her personal ambitions and public recognition was
achieved through men, and her son was the most promising candidate for
realizing her wishes. Her father and her brothers could rarely do much for
her welfare once she was married. Her husband might attain accomplishments that would add to her satisfaction, and indeed she often made a conscientious effort to contribute to his success. However, he was often a grown
man when they met, leaving less for her to improve upon. A man's affection
and gratitude, moreover, was not to go first or foremost to his spouse. The
husband-wife relationship was one laden with duty, allowing little room
for free affection or open acknowledgement. The husband had his own
mother—the wife's formidable mother-in-law—to obey and honor above
all others. Only on the boys whom she nursed and cared for since day one
did she have an unshakable first claim. A nineteenth-century biographical
account recorded a dramatic showdown and a mother's rage over her son's
favoring his wife. The occasion was when Yang Tao-lin's (1837–1911) father returned home from his Hai-chou office when the boy was five. Upon
entering the house, Mr. Yang made the mistake of passing by his mother and
delivering the two leather chests he purchased directly to the chamber of his
wife. His mother, the old Mrs. Yang, was seriously offended by her son's act
of imprudence. She immediately summoned her adult son to her presence

and scolded him for his "shameless indulgence" of his wife. In her fury, the old Mrs. Yang scratched her son's face with her fingernails. All the while, her scholar-official son was made to kneel down on the floor, continuing to apologize, not daring to utter a word in his defense. Nevertheless, the cut on his face was so deep, we are told, that this Mr. Yang had to be excused from receiving any guests for a whole month under the pretext of an illness.[34]

A mother felt she was entitled to her son's first allegiance not simply because traditional ritual and moral propriety prescribed it, but also because she felt she had invested heavily and counted on this reward all her life. Many a mother, in fact, did not shy away from letting her boys know, as she was giving her time and energies away, exactly what was expected of them and how as a mother she was holding her sons liable for a long-term yield. The nineteenth-century provincial official Liu Pao-nan gave a straightforward account of his hard-driven childhood in the absence of a father. (His father had died in the imperial capital when he was five.) His mother continued his instruction even though the family's financial conditions had taken a turn for the worse. As the boy was reciting and memorizing the classics dutifully at night and as the lantern was running out of fuel, Mrs. Liu often left her son with these words to consider:

I work hard every day and still may not have enough to eat, yet I never complain of hunger. At the year's end, I have often not had any warm garments to put on, but I never spoke of the chill. If only you, my boy, would work as hard on your studies, I could swallow every bit of bitterness without a single world of discontent.[35]

In pressing the boys to work hard, the mothers made it clear that on their performances lay not only the future of the family, but also the single hope of vindication for their dedicated and suffering mother. In an autobiographical account, the mid-Ch'ing scholar Wang Hui-tsu recalled the sad conversation his two mothers (his father's second wife and his own mother, who was a concubine) often had with him after his father died when Hui-tsu was ten. As the two women labored hard in weaving and other manual work to provide for the family, they also took every opportunity to remind their son what was expected of him. These exhortation sessions often took place late at night while Hui-tsu's two mothers were still toiling over their work. In great fatigue and in tears, they would remind the teenage boy: "If you do not study hard, there will be no way for you to make it in this world [wu-i wei-jên], and your late father will have no worthy descendants [wu-hou]. In that case, the two of us would much rather die than continue living [shêng pu-ju ssǔ]!"[36] The impact this would have had on a twelve-year-old boy is not difficult to imagine.

Such emotional outbursts probably took place far more frequently than

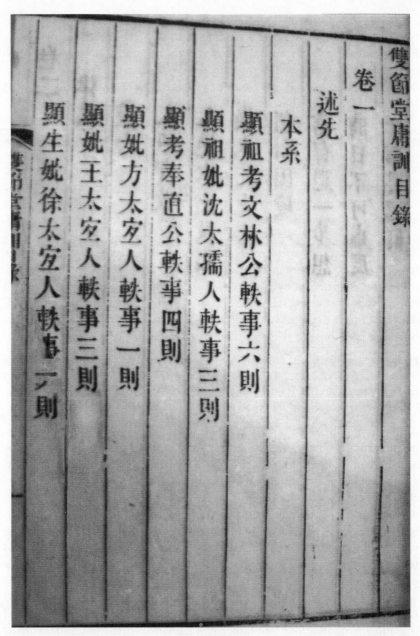

雙節堂庸訓目錄

卷一

述先

本系

顯祖考文林公軼事六則

顯祖妣沈太孺人軼事三則

顯考奉直公軼事四則

顯妣方太宜人軼事一則

顯妣王太宜人軼事三則

顯生妣徐太宜人軼事八則

雙節堂庸訓

FIG. 26. *The Humble Instructions from the Hall of Two Chaste Women* (*Shuang-chieh-t'ang yung-hsün*), by Wang Hui-tsu (Ch'ing dynasty), shows a son's tribute to the various motherly figures in his life. Here both his official mother and his biological mother are formally acknowledged. Courtesy of the National Central Library, Taiwan, Republic of China.

FIG. 27. Autobiographical account from *A Dreamlike Record by the Sick Bed* (*Ping-t'a mêng-hên lu*), by Wang Hui-tsu (Ch'ing dynasty). It shows Wang Hui-tsu's presentation of his mothers' roles in his self-narrative as quite different from the treatment given in his collected writings, as show in Fig. 26. Courtesy of the National Central Library, Taiwan, Republic of China.

the written record attests. Many mothers did not hesitate in venting their frustrations and personal grief upon their young sons, making it their sons' sole obligation to bring worth and joy to the mothers' lives. The modern Confucian scholar Liang Shu-ming's father Liang Chi had a childhood filled with his grandmother's suffocating devotion and unrelenting demands. Chi's mother (née Liu) had not only handwritten the first characters that her boy was to learn, she also hand-copied and personally bound the texts. Every evening, in addition, she double-checked every piece of schoolwork he completed during the day. Often these home tutoring hours were then followed by lengthy exhortations of the how-to-become-great-in-life sort. At that moment, Chi's mother was inclined to ask the boy what he wanted to become when he grew up. "I was then quite devoid of any ambition," Chi later confessed, "so what I came up with was often some menial little thing that fell far short of her expectations." In great distress and disappointment, his mother (his father's first wife) often closed the books in front of him and wept. Covering her face with her sleeve as she sobbed, she would go to Chi's natural mother, squealing: "This boy seems so dumb and stupid, I am afraid Heaven has finally let us down in life. What is there left for the two of us to hope for from now on?"[37]

The Suffering Mother and Her Obligated Son

Viewing her son as the person to bring her vindication in both psychological and material terms was not a habit limited to widows, although a widowed mother might have felt and expressed this more keenly. The majority of ordinary mothers shared the same desire. The famous special commissioner, Lin Tsê-hsü, grew up in a modest home. His father, having failed to pass the lowest level of the official examinations, remained a village tutor for life. As a result, his mother did additional needlework to bring in strings of copper cash to supplement their income. The young Tsê-hsü used to follow his father to the village school to study. Upon returning home in the evening, however, the boy was always confronted by the cold little room surrounded by four undecorated walls and a small table, with more studying to do for him and endless embroidery for the mother, all around this same short table. As Tsê-hsü was at last to go to sleep late at night, his mother still would not retire. According to him, she often could not lie down until "the cocks began to crow at dawn." There were, in addition, other hardships that his mother endured, "which were beyond ordinary standards of bearing." The boy was constantly disturbed by what he witnessed. He often begged to take over the hard labor for his overburdened mother, or he would save some food for her yet was only reprimanded by his toiling mother. "A boy should aim at something lasting and be farsighted," she would admonish her son: "How could you concern yourself with these petty matters and consider this to be an expression of filial piety? Only if you study hard and honor your parents by your success might my pains not have been suffered in vain."[38]

Voices like these speak eloquently from the heart of a Ming-Ch'ing mother. For her, the future of her sons had an irreplaceable intrinsic value that was entirely hers to claim. Some mothers would claim it through their bitter complaints, others might choose to remind their sons in milder tones, but their emotional and practical goals were essentially the same. The nineteenth-century official Chao Kuang's (1797–1865) father worked away from home in a secretarial position while Kuang was little. Kuang remembered that during those years the family was often hard-pressed financially. He lacked the money for studying with a tutor, and his mother and elder sisters were always doing needlework to help provide for the family. "For all the summer and winter days, mother, sister, and I worked side by side until midnight and we would all rise up again early the next morning.

'Though this house is poor,' my deceased mother used to say, 'so long as we have a son who is willing to study hard, I shall have nothing to be distressed about!'"[39]

The Voices of the Mother

The hard work of daily house chores, the tedium of child rearing, and the sad situations in which they often found themselves were all realities in the lives of Ming-Ch'ing mothers. But what is also intriguing was the fact that many of them also made deliberate efforts to impress their dedication and suffering in the minds of their sons. Many sons lived out their lives with a strange sense of regret for never being able to quite repay their mothers what they felt they themselves or the family owed. In numerous instances, it was in fact the mother who tried to make good use of the intimate and emotional bonds between her and the boy to generate or to stimulate that sense of guilt. In so doing, she was to transform her own sadness or frustration into her son's lifelong sorrowful and seemingly unredeemable debt.

The nineteenth-century secretary-advisor Lo Tsê-nan (1807–1856) recalled the day when his mother personally brought some rice to the village school for his lunch. In seeing Tsê-nan, then still a teenage boy, the mother reminded him that: "I hope in the days to come you will never forget this hardship I have gone through." Tsê-nan admitted later that, indeed, these words often rang in his ears as he grew up, leaving an unsettling feeling in his heart. His mother, he remarked on a different occasion, was the daughter of an "untitled scholar" (ch'u-shih) by the name of Chê-p'u from the same district. Born with a considerate and kind character, as the son Tsê-nan observed, she led a diligent and frugal life once married into the modest Lo family. She worked industriously to serve to the needs of her father-in-law and to instruct her boys and girls in a disciplined way. Tsê-nan recalled clearly the admonishments she always had for him on his occasional home visits from the village school. These often came in the form of the mottoes of some famous scholars or the acts of certain historical figures. "Those were what your grandfather once taught me when I was a girl," his mother told him. "You should take them to your heart and do not forget about them." Tsê-nan's mother died at forty-one, when he was nineteen. He later confessed that it remained a deep regret for him that his mother left them when the house was still quite indigent, and that he was never given the opportunity to repay her properly as a filial son. The remorse was so great, Tsê-nan said, that whenever he came to think of it, the pain became quite unbearable.[40]

Such unbearable remorse, in many instances, was exactly what the mother feared she could not instill in her son. It was often the most effective tool to goad a son toward success and it certainly served to deepen the lifelong indebtedness that a mother would not prevent her son from feeling for her.[41] The famous nineteenth-century provincial leader Tso Tsung-t'ang's case, mentioned briefly already, is particularly revealing. It shows how a son's personal narrative may yield a literary acknowledgement of the effect of his mother's daily reminders on his conscience. "Mother often talked about her difficulties in raising me," Tsung-t'ang conceded, "about the laborious chores she had to go through to masticate the rice in her mouth all the time to produce the thin cereal [mi-chih] that I lived on as an infant [because of a deficiency in breast milk]. To this very day, her voice continues to ring in my ears every time the thought occurs to me, with her grumbling voice always disconcertingly resonant."[42] The May Fourth icon-oclast Ch'ên Tu-hsiu (1879–1942) said that in his childhood, "mother's tears always worked much more forcefully than the spanks from grandfa-ther. It was the tears of my [widowed] mother that were the most effective motivation, pressing me constantly to work harder in my studies."[43]

The Mother Within the Son

The compelling reality that emerges out of accounts such as these is not simply that of a pitiful child being vigorously chastened by his strong-willed mother. What took place in addition was often a family of young children receiving and confronting the harsh demands of life from, but also along with, their suffering mother. The tears of Ch'ên Tu-hsiu's mother were shed, in fact, not because he had been behaving badly, but because of the hard life she and her children were thrown into together—a young widow with her growing child (ku-êrh kua-mu), a most devastating situation in tra-ditional Chinese society. Under such circumstances, as the instances we have examined and many other similar accounts reveal, the shared misery and humiliation bound the young children more closely to their mother. The es-sayist Wang Hui-tsu described the financial condition his family suffered im-mediately after his father died when Hui-tsu was ten. Many clansmen sus-pected that his mother had private savings hidden away somewhere. Incited by local gamblers, they pressed Hui-tsu's uncle to continue requesting money from his widowed sister-in-law. When she declined, they used to beat up the young boy in retaliation. At times they even grabbed Hui-tsu away from his mother, as the two widowed women (Hui-tsu's father's second wife and his own natural mother, who was his father's concubine) were bor-rowing money desperately to pay off the blackmail. With experiences like these, it is not hard to appreciate why, when Hui-tsu finally made a position for himself in society, he would want to entitle a collection of his works The Humble Instructions from the Hall of Two Chaste Women (Shuang-chieh-t'ang yung-hsün).

Many autobiographical accounts from the late imperial and modern period tell such tales of children striving through life with their suffering but persevering mothers. Wung Shu-yüan tells us:

My late father had never been good at concerning himself with the material welfare of the family. He was generous and liked to involve himself in philanthropic activities. In contributing food to the hungry, clothes for the cold, as well as helping with burials for the destitute, he never realized that our family did not have enough for provisions. The few hectares of land along with a row of houses that we owned, as a result, were mostly sold to support his donations. Thus, when he passed away, when I was six, the family had relatively little to live on. My mother, left a helpless widow with three small children, did her best to hold the family together and to make ends meet. Countless days passed when we rose up in the morning not knowing how we were going to get through that very night. Four years had gone by like this when we were hit again by a famine. A peck of rice cost over one thousand copper cash. Mother and the four of us were hardly able to feed ourselves with bran and chaff, after which we began to peel the bark from the elm trees to fill our stomachs. Yet there was no one from among our kinsmen who would take pity upon us.[44]

Children of a widow were by no means the only ones to have to bear the cruel facts of life with their mothers. Boys and girls of every ordinary household first encountered the realities of life and society with their mothers. These realities were often quite dismal and troubling. Tung Hsün (1807–1892) described the circumstances of his childhood thus:

The old house we dwelled in was all broken down and inhabitable, yet my grandmother, mother, my small brother and I did not have anywhere else to turn to. We had moved from the Eastern Temple Alley by the canal, to the Southern Barn Alley, and on to the east side of North Street. During those years, mother sold off her hairpins and earrings to add to what she made in needlework to send me to school. It was by following her orders that I came to study with my teacher Yü Hsiao-ming.[45]

The shared experience of going through hard times together gave rise to a special intimacy toward the mother in the hearts of her children. Many sons came to exhibit an emotional attachment to their mothers even in their adulthood. A Confucian ethic advised all "not to travel afar while the parents are still living" (fu-mu tsai, pu yüan-yu). Yet in the literature, we learn of men staying behind mostly due to a concern for their mothers. This was evident not just in the gentry class. Materials from merchant and artisan backgrounds suggested the same pattern of a strong emotional bond between mothers and sons. Lo Shih-yang revealed the attitude his merchant grandfather had toward his great grandmother. In the year 1866, Shih-yang later recorded, his grandfather ran a Prosperity Rice Shop (Jung-hsing mi-hao) on the High Street of Hsing-ning-ssû. Mr. Lo did not want to move away to any distant places. He decided, therefore, to establish his shop in the locality. "Thus, when my father was born into the house that same

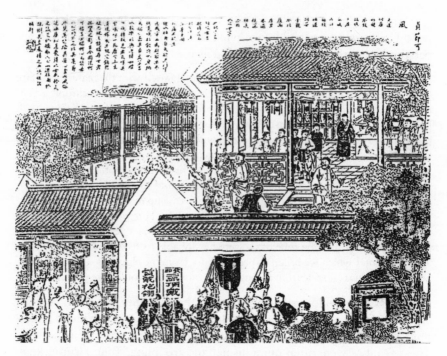

FIG. 28. "Honoring a Chaste Woman." This scene shows both the social capital of chastity and the promotion of Ch'ing government for women's honor. Marriage and child rearing being the main career opportunities for women, their achievement often lay with motherhood, which in turn became a driving force behind people's memory of childhood. Here is a late-Ch'ing depiction of the officiating procession, as reproduced in Chang I-ho, *Chên-chieh shih* (Shanghai: Shanghai Wên-I Press, 1999), p. 5.

year, my great-grandmother was overjoyed to receive him—her new born grandson."[46]

From the large amount of biographical and autobiographical data from the nineteenth and twentieth centuries, it is clear that the strong emotional ties between a mother and her son continued to hold up in a changing society. Shared hardship created a special intimacy as well as an intensified solidarity between mothers and sons. Both parties understood that the mother was to manifest her will through the deeds and accomplishments of her son. Many a mother labored hard to prepare her son for his career in which she was assured recognition. She also never stopped telling her boy what she had gone through in life because of him, reminding him explicitly of what she expected in return. From this were derived the numerous confessions of eminent men and humbler folk in Chinese history who openly admitted that they were living out their lives primarily according to their mothers' wishes. Ku Yen-wu vowed to be a Ming loyalist his whole life because his step-mother (née Wang, who remained chaste) pledged her own life to the collapsing Ming dynasty. She starved herself to death, leaving behind her wish that her son was never to serve the new court. This is a woman who used to delight herself, late at night after she had done her weaving, with readings of history: *The Records of the Grand Historian* (*Shih chi*), *The Comprehensive Mirror* (*T'ung chien*), and various dynastic histories. Her given name was "Chaste-Piety" (Chên-hsiao), and she was determined to continue reflecting her character through the acts and thoughts of her boy—who turned out to be none other than the leading seventeenth-century statecraft thinker Ku Yen-wu.[47]

Altogether too many men proclaimed that their mothers were the driving force behind their lifelong endeavors. They achieved success mainly to realize the ambitions and vindicate the frustrations and sufferings of their mothers. The late Ch'ing local official Liang Chi wanted people to recognize that "his character and his integrity were all due to the instruction of his mother"—a woman "who for two decades fulfilled fatherly duties in addition to her motherly obligations." Chi himself was born a premature infant in the seventh month. What his mother had to go through in order to rear him physically and emotionally gives his narrative added poignancy.[48]

Even in the rapidly changing society of the early twentieth century, a remarkable number of historical figures testified that, like Ku Yen-wu and Liang Chi, they too owed everything they came to achieve to the sacrifice, inspiration, and hard work of their mothers. The politician Huang Fu, for example, publicly acknowledged the toiling, and at times bitter, woman who single-handedly raised four boys and two girls. (At age seven when his father died, Fu had three elder brothers, one elder sister, and one younger sister.)[49] And there were many like Kuo Mo-juo (1892–1978) who wished to convince us that "in my entire life, it has been of course my mother who has had the greatest impact upon me, especially in my early childhood. My mother loves me dearly, and I love her as well." It was a powerful relationship that exceeded and transcended far beyond the innocent little T'ang poem that Mo-juo's mother dictated to him that he had since taken to heart.[50]

Thus, in matters grave and small, a mother could live on within the life of her son. It was a natural outcome of shared fate and mutual affection as well as a result of active cultivation. Ku Yen-wu admitted that he persevered in his loyalty for the falling dynasty because his mother sacrificed her life for the Ming cause and demanded similar faithfulness from her son. Three centuries later Chiang Kai-shek proclaimed that the force that drove him to a nationalistic commitment for his country was also a personal longing to pay tribute to his illiterate, but devoted, widowed mother.[51] Others spoke of the influence of their mothers in lighter, yet just as significant, terms. Chang Kung-ch'üan (1889–1979) ascribed both his forceful character and his persistent endeavors to his uneducated mother who, in times of want, had never spoken of poverty but only encouraged him and his brothers to work hard in their studies and in their deeds to make something of themselves.[52] Mo Tê-hui (1883–1968) admitted that throughout his public life, he planted willows everywhere he went because his mother used to breast-feed him under the red willow trees at his grandfather's house. Among friends he called himself Liu-ch'ên, "the Willow-Adorer." He also managed to decline alcohol and cigarettes all his life because his Muslim mother advised her children against the vices even though she did not insist on their religious adherence.[53] The renowned linguist and accomplished lyricist Chao Yüan-jên (1892–1982) attributed his fascination with music and verses to his gifted mother who filled his boyhood evenings with his first taste of rhymes.[54]

From Ku Yen-wu to Chiang Kai-shek to Chao Yüan-jên, the values, integrity, and interests of a mother played out and lived on within her son. It is a mother within a son, but also a woman in a man—the most powerful transcendence of gender boundaries in traditional China. It is a historical saga of biological and social reproduction in personal terms.

In Memory of Mother

In Chinese history, a woman was often forced to express herself through the men in her life. And the man (or men) she could rely on most to make her voice heard and her acts count was her son (or sons). She left traces in society through her performance as a faithful wife, but even more as a dedicated mother. In her motherly performances she was remembered by her children, receiving public recognition and respect if her son achieved success in society. The glimpses of the lives of mothers are derived mostly from their sons' memories. The biographical materials of women, as a matter of fact, are not just the lives and thoughts of women as told by men, but the recorded feelings of sons about the deeds of mothers. There is understandably a particular strand of emotional and sociopsychological prejudice built into these narratives.

Sons who wrote about their mothers and acknowledged their personal debts were presenting constructed memories. Few would have the ability to remember the days of nursing (as Tso Tsung-t'ang and Mo Tê-hui did), of diaper changing (as Wang Hui-tsu did), of being cared for as a sick infant (as Wung Shu-yüan did), of being led to take the first steps (as Liu Pao-nan did), and so forth. In the old China, when the Confucian culture of filial piety ruled, relatives, servants, and neighbors could all inform a son of his hardworking mother to instill gratitude. But more than anything else, it was the mother's own efforts in the endless telling and retelling of past experiences that became basic building blocks in the son's memory. In the memory-creating process, no doubt, experiences were sieved and retrieved and some real life stories were selected while others were deleted. Indeed, historical evidence of the lives of women in traditional China comes primarily from this commemoration literature about mothers produced by their socially obligated sons. Thus the kind of womanhood we have come to recognize was mostly about the lives of married women, of the hardworking and suffering provider from her twenties to her forties. Missing in this same historical literature are glimpses of a cheerful and innocent girlhood, or of an accomplished, secure, and powerful older motherhood, grandmotherhood, or mother-in-law-hood.

The world of mothers as presented was one filled with toil and misery, yet deprived of any satisfaction or joy. The reality for a married woman in traditional Chinese society, more often than not, consisted of many burdensome obligations dictated by a frustrating familial role that promised little contentment or gaiety in return. Yet it is still surprising that few historical accounts from men's points of view allow for cheerful women or happy mothers. This was attributable not only to the objective facts of the lives of Chinese women but also to the subjective wishes of both the women and their boys. Many mothers wanted people and their children to remember them for their virtue and suffering. Indeed the misery in many instances defines the very nature and content of their virtue. Thus in the biographical literature of women, their sons documented their days in toil, in pain, and quite literally, in illness and in death.[55]

The sick and dying mother forms the other favored motif in the memorial literature. The mid-Ch'ing classicist Yü Yüeh (1821–1906) noted that his mother fell gravely ill the third day after giving birth to him. "The ailment nearly took her life and kept her in bed for over twenty days. Yet as the date for the first full month [of her infant boy] was approaching, she insisted on sitting up in bed to sew the [ceremonial] cap for him."[56] A few months before Ch'ên Yen was born on the eighth day of the fourth lunar month in 1856, his family had moved to a new residence at the foot of Mt. Dragon (Lung-shan) inside the North Well Quarter (Pei-ching-lou) on the northeast side of town. When they first moved into the house, the deserted backyard was full of bushes, grass, and dirt under hazelnut trees. Against much good advice for her own health and that of the fetus, Yen's mother, in advanced pregnancy, trimmed the bushes and cut the trees for firewood with her own hands. Not long afterward, Yen was born, a healthy newborn with a smooth delivery. Four months later however the mother began to show signs of illness that developed into dizziness that caused her to pass out frequently. At first when she fainted, Yen's father, who knew something about medicine, was able to bring her back around by forcing a reviving concoction down her throat. Nonetheless, soon after these fainting episodes, her milk gradually dried up. The biographical account then gave the story of how, since the family was too poor to afford a wet nurse, his various aunts had to take turns feeding the four-month-old Yen with thick cereal before weaning the boy prematurely.[57]

In addition to portraying sick mothers, many accounts depicted mothers dying. There were those such as that of the late Ming radical thinker Li Chih (1527–1602), whose mother died soon after his birth.[58] The mother of the early Ch'ing scholar-official Shao Hsing-chung contracted a disease and passed away while Hsing-chung was a mere six months.[59] It was emotionally devastating when a mother left her children at a vulnerable, young age. An official of the K'ang-hsi reign (1662–1722), Huang Shu-lin (1672–1756), lost his mother while he was seven or eight, shortly after which his father also died. He was adopted by the brother of his stepmother and changed his surname from the original Ch'êng to Huang. Decades later, he could still recall a familiar scene with his late mother. One day standing, outside the door, Shu-lin saw a few students arriving to visit his father, who was then the district educational administrator of the Ch'ü-yang district. That day his father happened to be away somewhere. Shu-lin plucked up courage to approach the visitors and discovered that they had traveled quite some distance. Thus, like a man, he entered the house and asked his mother to prepare food for the guests. That year he was six, one or two years before his mother left him.[60] Lo Ssû-chü (1764–1840), who later made a career in military service, grew up as a village boy. He spent his childhood years tending water buffalo, collecting wood, and farming the fields. His mother, an uneducated country woman, died when he was ten, leaving hardly anything inspiring for her boy. Yet he did remember the year before when he was rescued at the third attempt from drowning in the stream. His mother, together with his father, gave him a lecture: "Three times you were engulfed, yet by god's mercy were rescued. Now you should really look after yourself as a worthy person, to take on the affairs of others as that of your own. To learn from the righteous deeds, acting upon loyalty and filial piety as the ancients did. And remember not to be greedy or to cheat." Ssû-chü confessed that it was from that moment on that he began to comprehend something of life, making up his mind to do well in this world.

Many remembered the virtues of their mothers, the sacrificing character they had and the sad situations surrounding their death. The mother of mid-Ch'ing official Liang Chang-chü (1775–1849) died when Chang-chü was ten. She was the person who initiated Chang-chü in learning when he was four. He also wrote of her as a filial daughter who, while unmarried, had once cut flesh from her own arm to try to bring about a miraculous cure for her father.[61] Hsü Han (1797–1866) grew up at the turn of the eighteenth century in a rural part of the Jih-chao district in Shantung province. While young he used to tend water buffaloes as many boys did in the village. When his mother died, he had just turned nine. In a piece of "family memorial" (chia-chi-wên) composed later, he remembered the disconsolate days leading to his mother's death. His father had been an unsuccessful student-candidate who earned a meager income by tutoring. That year of 1805, when his mother fell ill, the family was also forced to divide the property with his uncle. The house-dividing incident apparently added much distress to his sick mother, though all that he was willing to convey was that "as a result, mother died soon thereafter." That day when his mother left them, his father happened to be in the prefectural capital making yet another attempt at the civil service examination. "When he finally [received the news and] returned home," Han noted, "the cover of mother's coffin had been sealed for several days."[62]

Others mentioned the obviously shocking impact their mothers' death left on them in their youth. Chu Yün (1729–1781), who later rose to be imperial editor in the late eighteenth century, lost his mother in 1743 while he was a young teenager. She died in the seventh month that year, after which Yün and his younger brother "decided to sleep together, so that both could read classics, copying and reciting well into the night, never lying down until the rooster crowed at dawn."[63] Fang Shih-kan's (1772–1851) mother (née Têng) passed away on the nineteenth day of the eighth month of 1783, when he was twelve. Born physically weak with many ailments, Shih-kan appeared to take the bereavement hard. Even though his grandmother (née Hu) immediately took over his care, he became so sick that he was unable to attend his mother's funeral, after which the boy began to throw up blood. He never quite recovered from the impairment until his thirties, when he would still occasionally cough up blood and appear somewhat neurotic.[64]

Many boys had difficulties getting over the pain and grief of losing their mothers. Some wondered about the lives of married women in that society, such as that of their unfortunate mothers. The bittersweet, and at times ambivalent, mother-son relationship thus influenced stages of social criticism as well as intellectual and political upheaval in both traditional and modern China. In the lives and shadows of their mothers, men came to realize, in part, the injustice done to a woman even the social ills of China. Generations of sons, who had trouble getting over their longing for their suffering or deceased mothers, may be stirred to use their words and their deeds to present a personal agenda for all to consider the repressively dark forces of the patriarchal, authoritarian, and hierarchical ancient regime.

The sixteenth-century scholar Kuei Yu-kuang wrote, in various ways, about his affection for his toiling mother who died when he was eight, and the hard and abused life she had as a married woman. Then he went on to compose essays protesting against "virgin chastity" (*chên-nü shou-chieh*), the kind of social tyranny he viewed in the lives of contemporary women.[65] Four centuries later, the forerunner of the modern Chinese social and political revolution, Ch'ü Ch'iu-pai (1899–1935), admitted that it was his mother's suicide that brought home to him the abhorrent reality of women's lives. Through the tragic fate of his mother, who was forced to take her own life on a bitter winter's day by poisoning herself with matches and strong tiger-bone liquor, he began to see the tyrannical society that was driving many people to destitution and desperation. The life, and later the death, of his own mother gave him enlightenment and truth, which thereafter directed his mind and his actions in the Chinese revolution.[66]

Intellectual, social, and political historians should begin to appreciate the human dramas that have been taking place behind the scenes of centuries of social protest and political rebellion in Chinese history. Indeed, a historical figure such as Ch'ên Tu-hsiu opened his gripping autobiography by stating the first thing people need to know about his life: "I am a fatherless child." He then described the miseries of his widowed mother and her pitiful children.[67] Life and society seem especially unjust from the experience and perspective of the suffering women and their children. A son, while young, bore the facts of life and society along with his mother. As he grew up he might, understandably, feel compelled to speak up and to act upon these evils on behalf of his mother, who was denied a proper voice and a place to act for her own cause.

Conclusion

In the context of gender relations in traditional China, a man's mother, ironically, was too often the only woman he knew well and could openly and unabashedly love. For a woman, likewise, her male offspring were the only men she could both adore without any reservations and secure loyalty, affection, and gratitude. The emotional bond between a mother and her children was established in the intimate years of childhood. Out of this relationship a child not only recognized the details of his mother's fate, he was also made to identify himself with her grievances. The unique Confucian ethics of filial piety, moreover, allow, or really require, a son's absolute and permanent homage to his mother. The mother had good reason to put additional spiritual and material investment in her boys and to expect, or to demand, faithful return when they grew up. The peculiarly abundant memorial literature for women and mothers serves as an eloquent testimony to this psychological burden and social heritage.

Although the historical sources reviewed here are mostly from the elite (referring primarily to educated families, though not necessarily the socio-economic upper class), the general mode revealed, as confirmed by various anthropological and sociological reports, is not limited either to the late imperial period or to that social class. Women in rural Taiwan and Hong Kong continue to invest and formulate their relations with sons in basically the same fashion as their elite counterparts from the past, and will continue to do so, at least until socioeconomic changes bring about new choices of old-age security and material rewards independent of those provided by their children. For women from a lower socioeconomic class, the emphasis can lean toward material returns more so than toward the social recognition and personal gratification desired by elite mothers in the late imperial period. As China entered the tumultuous modern era, furthermore, the "feminist" feelings embraced by male personalities became a clearer force in China's social and political forum. It is well to recognize that this could be a phenomenon grounded also in the older psychological dynamics of the culture of children and childhood in late imperial Chinese society.

6 The Emotional World

In 1730, when Wang Hui-tsu was born in the east room of the family residence in Ta-i village of the Hsiao-shan district, Chekiang, his father, was more than a thousand miles away in the capital (waiting to be assigned a post). His grandfather, then fifty-nine years old, overjoyed at the new arrival, decided to call him "Garbage" (Lê-sê)—the most abundant and useful material in rural life. This was not to signify that the boy would "fertilize" the family line, but to hope that the undesirable, valueless designation might help the newborn to escape the jealousy of the gods and thus safeguard his life. Since Hui-tsu's own mother had to carry out all the household chores, it was his formal mother who took him to bed in his infancy. Whenever the boy woke up crying for milk, this *ti-mu* would bring him to nurse at his own mother's breast and then change diapers for him. The formal mother, however, died when he was three. On her deathbed she asked Hui-tsu's two elder sisters to help care for him. The grandfather soon arranged for a *chi-mu*, the toddler boy's second formal mother. The next year, this stepmother accompanied his own biological mother and Hui-tsu to his father's post, so that the four-year-old boy could be initiated by a private tutor. The father was a local history compiler in Honan. The family stayed at his father's official residence for four years before his father retired. Returning home, his father discovered that the family property had been depleted by his uncle's indulgence in gambling. Later that year Hui-tsu's grandfather died. After the burial, on his way to seek employment opportunities to the south in Kwangtung, Hui-tsu's father too passed away. Hui-tsu was less than ten.[1]

Shorn of specific dates and places, this account has all the major features of a child's early years in late imperial China. First of all, in contrast to their modern counterparts, the young then tended to grow up in a complex human environment. Various adult relatives other than the parents, such as the formal mother, the grandfather, and the elder sisters in Hui-tsu's case, participated and shared in the daily child care, interacting closely and regularly with the child. On the other hand, given the demographic reality of the day (an average life expectancy at birth of between thirty and forty years), children often experienced the death of family elders at a very young age.[2] These two facts, when compounded, made a child's emotional world at once rich and insecure.

A Variety of Adults

European social historians have observed the constant presence of persons not belonging to the immediate family, such as visiting relatives or servants, as a distinctive feature of the premodern household in Western Europe.[3] But in general, the households in early modern Europe, in which the natal parents were the main adults responsible for bringing up the young, were simpler in composition, if not in size, compared with their counterparts in late imperial China. For one thing, Western and Central European couples were used to setting up their own residence, while their Chinese counterparts almost exclusively remained with the man's parents, forming what is called a "joint" family. A child growing up in late imperial China was, therefore, often surrounded by many different people. The structure of the extended household meant that a child was born amid a group of patriarchal relatives dwelling under the same roof. The operation of the extended family resulted in the involvement of other clanspeople in the child's life. The care given by grandparents and aunts, the discipline supplied by uncles, and the company of cousins became a significant part of a child's experience.[4] In addition, the average ages at marriage of both men and women were lower in late imperial China than in Europe. Most young couples began having children before they themselves were financially independent or physically separated from their elders. Practical needs made the new child dependent upon the economically more viable larger family, while his youthful parents were adult dependents themselves.[5] The structure of village and community life allowed friends and neighbors easy access and an active role in family affairs, not the least of which were the ways the children were raised.[6] Together, the above factors produced a human environment that was much more varied for the young and more crowded and noisier than the situation would have been elsewhere, or later.

Lo Tsê-nan, a leader in the anti-T'aiping campaign, was often cared for by his paternal grandfather when he was young. His maternal grandfather, living close by, also came to visit with the family regularly. Upon noticing the boy's strong intellectual curiosity, the latter commented to the parents: "This child appears to have a special talent. Though pressed by extreme poverty, you ought to find a way to afford him some education. In the future, it will be this child who brings fame and honor to the house."[7]

As a child grew up, the person most intimately involved in caring for him and in forming his childhood was often someone other than his parents, such as an uncle, an aunt, or a maid. The eighteenth-century historian Chang Hsüeh-ch'êng (1738–1801) used to follow his maternal uncle around when he was less than two. This uncle's favorite daily activity was to take the little nephew Hsüeh-ch'êng to a neighborhood shop for liquor. As part of this routine was indulgence in alcoholic beverages, the toddler was frequently given a sip. Early childhood roots, Chang Hsüeh-ch'êng later claimed, were to blame for his personal weakness for drinking in later life.[8]

Since the parents were not socially or economically independent at the time of reproduction, the status of their children became one of "double dependence." Involvement of other family members seemed natural and unavoidable. Many children were recorded as being born in the residence of a grandfather or a paternal uncle, indicating that their parents were still provided for by their fathers' own parents or their fathers' elder brother. This was just as much the case with the country's landed elite families as with people from the poorer lower classes. When Huang Ching-jên (1741–1783) was born, his father was still a "district student" with no career or income of his own. Ching-jên thus lived in the residence of his grandfather, who was then an instructor of the district magistrate of Kao-ch'un county.[9] Chang Liang-chi's (1807–1871) father was already forty-three at his birth, a middle-aged man with no fixed employment. Liang-chi's mother, therefore, gave birth to him at the house of his elder uncle, who worked in a local administration.[10] Children in such circumstances grew up recognizing the fact that domestic authority often rested with someone other than their own parents.

Grandparents, Aunts, and Maids

Two kinds of relatives actively shaped late imperial Chinese childhood experience: the child's grandparents and female relatives. Many biographical sources mention grandfathers with a strong affection for the grandchild; they carried, held, and caressed the child. Traditional notions of the division of labor dictated that men took charge of activities outside the home, whereas women attended mostly to domestic affairs. To a certain extent, the grandparents' involvement with the child followed the same pattern. The grandmother usually assisted or replaced the child's mother in caring for the child's physical needs and supervising daily activities. The grandfather, on the other hand, paid close attention to intellectual or farming activities. He also played with the grandchild much of the time, taking him around for social occasions. In this regard, the grandfather appeared to be a special figure among the male relatives, the rest of whom maintained a rather aloof and solemn relationship with the young. In certain instances, the grandfather took the child to bed with him. Hu Lin-i (1812–1861), one of the major officials in the T'aiping era, was born to a thirty-five-year-old father, a mere "student" striving to climb the social ladder and establish himself. Most of the time Lin-i's father was studying in academies away from home. The child, therefore, grew to be deeply attached to his grandfather. When the old man traveled around the village, Lin-i insisted on following him, his little hand holding on to his grandfather's gown. The grandfather was apparently very fond of his grandson. In 1816, when Lin-i was five, his grandfather wrote a letter to his father, conveying affectionately: "Lin-i has been quite good, except he likes to talk a great deal, and also to follow me around constantly. When I go on social visits upon the invitation of our neighbor, he has to come along. He insists on sleeping with me at night as well." The homely letter was closed with the postscript that he was in fact holding the little grandson Lin-i as he wrote.[11]

Maternal grandparents, though usually not living together with the child, could also provide assistance, if residing within a short distance. Traditionally, marriages often took place between families within the same locality or from nearby villages. The maternal relatives in many instances lived within walking distance or not much farther. More important than the geographical distance was that, psychologically, children were used to being with their kin, since married daughters' relationships with their natal families appear to have been strengthening in this period.[12] Both the old and the young felt comfortable about regular contact, which was certainly more frequent than would be the case in modern times. Youngsters were therefore apt to seek shelter with relatives during times of practical or emotional stress. Lo Ssŭ-chü (1764–1840) was a peasant boy. While growing up, he was often punished for getting into fights with other village children. Around age seven he once ran away from home to hide in his third maternal aunt's house some distance away, where he stayed for more than a year before returning home. The aunt did not treat him as a guest; soon after arrival, he was put to work, "sent to the hills to tend the water buffalo." For the child, living together with parents or relatives did not seem a big difference.[13] Accounts told of arrangements for grandchildren to stay with maternal grandparents to acquire initial education. The young Chiang Yu-tien (1766–1830) was always taken to the village school by his maternal grandmother, who liked to prepare special treats with medicinal concoctions to strengthen his health.[14]

Admittedly, most of these cases come from educated elite families, though the general pattern was by no means limited to that social stratum. Like similar situations in many other premodern societies, extended family, early marriage, and a relatively "open" community life were as much part of the peasant's and artisan's way of life as that of the official-gentry. Sociologists and anthropologists confirm this same child-rearing practice in their studies of most rural societies. Evidence from postwar rural Taiwan suggests to Margery Wolf that a close female affinity together with friends and neighbors played a part in a mother's efforts in reproducing her uterine family.[15] Martin Yang notes in his study of village life in Shantung in the first half of the twentieth century of how a child's grandmother, elder sibling, sister-in-law, or older cousins figured in the daily care of children, especially in the event of larger numbers of children.[16] It is obvious that the special family structure, marriage pattern, and rural social organization created an at once broader, more intimate, and yet fluid and flexible human network—a particular kind of relationship pattern for a child's growing up in traditional Chinese society. Children from all walks of life were born into and became accustomed to the close association of relatives, domestic help, and neighbors.

The "Motherly" Assembly

All in all, however, child care remained primarily women's work. It was the various women who took part helping one another with the task, especially with daily, physical care. Among them were the aunts by marriage, often dwelling in the same living quarters. Niu Yün-chên (1706–1758) was less than two when his paternal uncle (the father's younger brother) married. The uncle was proud of this promising nephew and enthusiastically introduced Yün-chên to his bride. This paternal aunt soon grew tenderly close to Yün-chên. As he remembered later:

When I was three or four, my aunt was the one who would take me on her lap and comb my hair for me everyday, constantly peeling a pear or giving me dates, paying close attention to my food and drink. Whenever minor illnesses occurred, it was this aunt of mine who would most carefully tend my needs, fearful that otherwise something unfortunate might occur. One time, when I got a toothache, the pain was so bad it prevented me from eating for a day or two. Aunt tried hard to take care of the cavities somehow, which made me feel a lot better indeed.[17]

For upper-class families, other than paternal aunts, another kind of "motherly" figure often present came from the various "wives" the child's father had wed at different points of time and under different circumstances. The example of the young Wang Hui-tsu, cited earlier, was such a case. Whereas he himself was the son of a "concubine mother" (shu-mu), his two "elder" or "formal mothers" (sequentially married to his father) took responsibility for his physical needs and planned for his education. These different women married to the same man, under better circumstances, were supposed to live together like sisters. Practical needs drew not a few of them close to one another in carrying out household chores and child rearing. From the child's perspectives, his life often had as much to do with these various motherly figures (chu-mu) as his own biological mother (shêng-mu).

This is not to say, however, that affection or goodwill among them always prevailed. In some situations, feelings among different wives of the same man were anything but cordial, creating a distressful emotional environment as well as destructive living conditions for the young. The story of late Ming intellectual-activist Chang P'u (1602–1641) serves as such an example. P'u himself was born of a mother who used to be a maid in the house, and the humility of his birth won him nothing but degradation from the relatives. As a boy he was often treated rudely, even by the more powerful servants in the house. As a result, Chang P'u grew up with bitterness and resentment, vowing revenge.[18] Children born of a first wife, on the other hand, were not guaranteed attention and affection either. The political reformist T'an Ssû-t'ung (1865–1898) was born to his father's first and official wife, who witnessed an amorous relationship developing between her husband and his young concubine. As a boy, Ssû-t'ung bore coldness and neglect from the household under the concubine's sway. His mother would leave home for extended periods of time, during which the young Ssû-t'ung was left to endure prejudice himself. At around seven, he was said to have developed a habit of sitting quietly all day, never opening his mouth to respond to people's greetings.[19] In bleak pictures like this, one realizes that for the children of this period, life was conditioned by many different people besides and beyond the realm of their own parents. These people could help to provide for their needs, but they could also add sadness and resentment. In either case, there existed a complex human environment, one that tended to acquaint the young to adult society earlier and in a more complicated manner than if it were otherwise.

A child's elder sister, or sisters-in-law, when old enough, could also be given the task of bringing up younger siblings. The little boy Hui-tsu, discussed earlier, was entrusted to his two older sisters on his formal mother's deathbed.[20] The famous dissident intellectual Lü Liu-liang (1629–1683) was raised by his third elder sister-in-law from infancy when he was born, without a father and with a sick mother.[21]

In middle- and upper-class families, wet nurses, maidservants, and other women in the household also played a vital part in shaping a child's experience. Unrelated by blood to the family and having the low status of servants, yet caring for daily physical and emotional needs, they built strong bonds with their charges. Appreciating the importance, contemporary medical and pedagogical literature recommended that special attention be paid to choosing wet nurses and nannies.[22] Shao Hsing-chung's (1648–1711) grandmother tested and tried out no fewer than ten women before deciding upon a suitable one. A few months later, his natural mother, about to pass away, expressed her last wish to her son by giving him over to the special care of his wet nurse. It showed a common recognition of the vital importance of a wet nurse and the trust she might earn from the child's mother.[23] These female servants in some instances not only nursed the child, but were themselves housemaids with an intimate tie to the family. When Miu Ch'üan-sun (1844–1918) fell seriously ill as a result of a smallpox inoculation, a maid servant of his mother's helped to care for the child day and night. Out of this grew a deep gratitude and an emotional bond comparable to a parent-child relationship. Miu later looked after the needs of this maid Wang to the very end of her days.[24] Many maidservants ate, slept, and organized their work schedules around the child. The child's own mother was still the one to keep an eye on what was going on and to supervise the nursemaid's conduct. Wung Shu-yüan (1633–1701), when about three, was once carried to the doorway by his wet nurse for a walk when they suddenly caught sight of a "beggar woman pleading for food with an infant in her arms." The young Shu-yüan, clearly affected by the scene, broke out crying. Not only that, he started weeping badly, waking every morning murmuring something about the beggar woman. His own mother, when told of the incident, instructed the wet nurse never to carry the boy to the doorway again.[25]

Some wet nurses developed a cordial relationship with the child's mother. As mentioned earlier, one wet nurse got merrily drunk one night along with her hostess and was said to have therefore produced "drunken milk," believed to be harmful to the health of her nursling.[26]

The Whereabouts of the Father

In the memorial literature related to family elders in late imperial China, there was often the conspicuous absence of the father, and this not just regarding the upper class. The classical model, it is true, calls for the Confucian gentleman to stay away from the quarters of women and children, to maintain a formal distance so as to enhance ritualistic dignity and personal authority as the family head. Biographical data from Ming-Ch'ing sources suggest that this strictness and rigidity no longer prevailed in all homes. For those many fathers who were missing from people's narratives on their childhood years, it was absence due to occupational needs, traveling for official posts, trade, or military duties. More significantly, those who had the opportunity to be with their young did not refrain from picking them up, hugging, and teasing them. Indeed, an increasingly affectionate father seemed to be looming large from social documents at this period. When Li Kung (1659–1733) was four, his father used to carry the boy around in his arms, sometimes reciting *The Book of Filial Piety (Hsiao ching)*.[27] Wung Shu-yüan was another lucky toddler who enjoyed the affection and company of his father. When three or so, as Shu-yüan later recalled, his father often played with him by kissing and licking his face. Shortly afterward, his father began teaching him his first characters while holding him in his arms.[28] Hsia Ching-ch'ü's father was also fond of doing things with the children. He liked to feed the children, encouraging them to eat more during the meal. When Ching-ch'ü was a toddler, as noted before, he used to line up green peas to motivate the boy in learning.[29]

"Softer" sociocultural trends in the domestic realm signified newly appreciated values in the cultivated man from the sixteenth century onward. For educated elite families, the inculcation of the Neo-Confucian philosophy enhancing a more rigid social order and personal conduct, which reached its climax by the first half of the sixteenth century, seemed to be on the decline. On the contrary, many economic and social forces functioned behind the scene in structuring a reorientation in domestic arrangements, a redrawing of gender relations, and a reconsideration of individual morality, normative ethics, and political institutions. Within such a context, a more "softened," "flexible," or relaxed family life began to creep in to the new sentiment, especially in urban settings in search of a "naturally" inclined, "genuine" personhood and cordial masculine style. For the middle or lower social class in the mid-Ming, however, continued efforts to propagate and proliferate rigid strains of Neo-Confucian ideals through the same printing culture helped clan organization and popular arts to reap their first harvest from mass circulation. Enhanced social mores and an unprecedented value attaching to propriety in behavior were certainly evident in the representations of the elite and lower-middle classes in small towns and rural villages from this period. The craving for liberating the "uncivilizing" process of the upper echelons of society in cities and big towns juxtaposed majestically with the inclusion of the "edifying" process in the lower stratum of society in the rural community.

So, from the late sixteenth century onward, fathers from educated backgrounds were depicted as both resisting and longing to form emotional detachment or physical separation from their children. Their interaction with their young exhibited these ambivalent traits in this ambiguous struggle. First of all, a father was more easily inclined to approach a child during his early childhood. When a child became physically independent, and before he entered into learning (whether at school, as an apprentice, or in the fields), his father found him adorable, and the two often developed a close association. Yet since the role of a father was defined in the "traditional" context of family life as the party most appropriate for handling the formal and presentable—therefore rational and pleasant—aspect of a child's daily existence, apart from emergencies, he could rarely get involved in the daily feeding and bathing of his progeny, in illness or emotional distress. Happily or not, for parties on both sides the more laborious aspects of child rearing, in the manner of the old division of labor, continued to be left to the mother or other women in most circumstances. As an extension of this arrangement, a father had the responsibility to supervise and oversee the learning activities of the boys, be it to initiate a child in his intellectual development, teach him his first few characters or lessons, engage him in a certain craft, or simply take him to work in the fields. A father or a fatherly figure was the one to train a boy in becoming a man. He might engage himself or approach this in any traditionalist or innovative fashion he chose.

What was stressed was a strong sense of duty; one's duty not to oneself, but to one's ancestors and family line, for both parents and children, for both the instructive father and the student son. In most instances, at the center of these values was a functional understanding of life: fathers worked as officials, clerks, teachers, artisans, merchants, or peasants to provide for the family. They kept their sons by their side to learn a trade—also to learn the roles expected of them in the social chain—so that in the long run they would take on the vocation left behind by their fathers. In this profile, children, or childhoods, were not a focus of value in and of themselves. Adults lived to work, and children lived to become adults. No child learned to be, or was allowed the luxury of enjoying being simply, a child; every child was there to acquire the manner and skills of the grown-up in order to be prepared to take the place of their elders in due course. Yet, many male adults brought their young boys along when they took up bureaucratic appointments. T'ang Chieh-t'ai made his seven-year-old son Chên travel with him all the way from their home in Szechwan to Kiangsu when Chieh-t'ai was assigned to be district magistrate. Even more commonly, young boys accompanied their fathers to their posts when the latter were hired out as village tutors or in clan schools. Liang Chang-chü (1755–1849), when seven, used to lodge with his father at one clan school or another for quite some years.[30] Lin Tsê-hsü (1785–1850), too, followed his father around at age four.[31] The reason for doing so, ostensibly, was so that the young boy could learn along with all the other pupils under his father's instruction. The seven-year-old Chang-chü began his education on his father's lap. But this trend represented as an older mode, when parents of the same gender bore the responsibility to pass to their children "the trade" in life, also ensured an extended bonding time between the young and the old through the personal transmission of the skills to help the boys make it in this world. The elite fathers liked to teach their boys words and literacy, and some quite affectionately, just as the artisans would their crafts, the peasants their farming, and the mothers the cooking and sewing skills to their growing daughters.

Regardless of or in addition to the presence of the father, the main thing was that many different adults continued to move through a child's youthful years. Depending upon circumstances, a child could be cared for either by a grandparent, an aunt, a sister-in-law, or maid-servant. Children from poor peasant families would not have had as many wet nurses, housemaids, and formal or concubine mothers, but their relatives tended to live close and be involved in the daily life of the young. Old neighbors, too, frequently joined hands with family elders to provide for the needs of the children, along with their liberal interference, amid which a more personable father was striving to take a hold in the country's social life from various different corners. In this kind of "communal" atmosphere, the one or two figures who came to occupy the most precious space in a child's mind or heart could well be persons other than his or her own parents. Traditional childhood, in this sense, was spent in a human environment with more varied elements than the modern nuclear family implies. It is associated more with, and more closely resembles, the adult society, deemed ultimately to be the only "real world."

The Power of Death

Another aspect of traditional childhood experience that set it apart from its modern counterpart was the factor of mortality. English demographers have confirmed the common impression that average life expectancy for the early modern era was markedly shorter—for the most part, between the thirties and forties—for the population of Western Europe.[32] The demographics for late imperial China were categorically similar, placing life expectancy approximately in the upper thirties and lower forties for males and females. This fundamental structure meant that it was fairly common for a child to lose his or her parents or other intimate family elders at a very young age, and vice versa. A rough estimate shows that, among the more than eight hundred cases collected, more than one-third of children lost at least one parent by the age of eight. If one adds to this the deaths of grandparents and siblings, a large majority of children experienced death in their families at a young age.

What could this have meant for a child? Of all matters, the loss of a parent had, of course, the gravest impact. The death of a father, however, implied quite a different set of changes in a child's life than the death of a mother. When a nursing child lost his or her mother, chances were that he or she would perish with her, except when the most favorable conditions prevailed. For most young children beyond infancy, moreover, a psychological blow resulted from the loss of physical and emotional intimacy. But in terms of practicality, the children's life could carry on since most fathers soon remarried. Shao Hsing-chung lost his natural mother (who died of postnatal complications) when he was six months old. His grandmother immediately took on the responsibility of child rearing, and a wet nurse was hired. Within a year or so, his father married again. Thus, Hsing-chung grew up with the care and supervision of his stepmother, until nine years later when she passed away as well. As his father had to seek employment away from home at this point, the ten-year-old Hsing-chung was sent to his maternal grandparents to be raised and educated.[33] The experience of Hsü Han (1797–1866) was another such typical story. Hsü Han's mother died when he was eight, and shortly thereafter his father took a new wife. The young Han was said to have received his stepmother respectfully and helped in looking after the four subsequent brothers.[34]

The loss of a father presented grave economic problems, as only a minority of women at this time had the financial independence to support a family. In cases when the mother had been better accepted by the conjugal family, the paternal grandfather or other male relatives could "take in" these children, providing food and shelter. Such was the case of Huang Ching-jên (1747–1783), whose father died when the boy was three. His grandfather came to his father's former post to fetch the mother and children. He took them back to their family home in Kiangsu and helped to raise his grandchildren.[35] Wang Fu (1667–1732) is another example of someone who was also only three when he lost his father. By age six, after some initial confusion, he ended up living with his paternal uncle.[36] Although according to Confucian ethics, paternal kin were expected to bear some responsibility for the children of a deceased man, family relations were often strained and went sour by the departure of the head of a particular branch because they were deprived of the extra financial contributions and often had trouble keeping their status. The children were quick to sense such changing attitudes. Often realizing that without their father, they were at the mercy of the relatives, they became "outsiders" among their supposed family. When Chao Yü-ching (1652–1707) lost his father, his mother had to take him, together with five siblings, all under the age of nine, from Hopei back to Shantung to live with his grandparents. Yü-ching, the eldest male among them, knew the need to be particularly humble and submissive in order to invite sympathy and tolerance. Their grandmother unfortunately was a rigid and cruel woman, he remembered. "When anything slightly displeasing occurred, she would be seriously upset and not talk to anyone." The five-year-old Yü-ching would kneel down in front of her weeping for mercy. His pleading was said to have often moved his authoritative grandmother to forgive whatever minor domestic irritation had occurred.[37]

If the paternal family was incapable of aid, by later imperial times more and more fatherless children and their widowed mothers were seen turning to their maternal relatives for help. Hung Liang-chi (1746–1809), a scholar interested in demography, lost his father. His mother soon took the five-year-old boy to live at her own parents' house.[38] In other instances, moreover, the maternal uncle might take the children in, especially if both parents passed away. Ku Kuang-ch'i (1766–1835) became an orphan at the age of five. After the boy properly observed his father's funeral, his maternal uncle took him away to raise him in the capital, where the uncle had a post.[39] Given the old Chinese patriarchal tradition, a married daughter returning with young children to her own family, though now happening more often, could not be spared social pressure and gossip. Such was the case of Shao Hsing-chung. Shao, as mentioned earlier, lost his own mother in infancy and was brought up by both his grandmother and stepmother. Unfortunately his stepmother also passed away when he was ten. Having to seek employment elsewhere, Hsing-chung's father decided to send Hsing-chung and his younger half-brother to their respective maternal grandparents' houses. His half brother, as it turned out, encountered a chilling reception. At the time, not even two years of age, he was given separate lodging and was often ridiculed by the unsympathetic maternal relatives. Once when both brothers met again at their own house, each just returning from their foster homes, the younger brother held on to Hsing-chung and wept. "Uncle has always resented me," he cried. "He once hit me with a metal stick, shouting that I am after all a child bearing a different surname." A young child with such suffering often had nowhere and nobody to turn to. The only thing Hsing-chung and his younger brother could do was to console one another.[40]

In the event that none of the above choices were available (that is, neither the paternal grandparents, uncles, nor the maternal grandparents and uncles were there to help), the family had to consider putting the orphaned children up for adoption. Under such circumstances, people usually went first to relatives on either side. In the case of a child being adopted by a maternal relative, he oftentimes changed his surname to become a member of a different clan. Huang Shu-lin (1672–1756), for instance, originally had Ch'êng as his surname. When both his parents died within a short period of time, the seven-year-old boy was adopted by his maternal uncle, who raised and educated Shu-lin. In addition, the uncle changed the boy's surname from Ch'êng to Huang in accordance with his new family identity.[41] Chao Kuang (1797–1865), too, recalled his mother having to switch her family name from Chu to Han when she lost her mother at a young age and was adopted by her maternal uncle.[42]

As a last resort, some family elders would even try to contract a marital arrangement for the orphaned child, passing on to the prospective parents-in-law a share of responsibility for the welfare of their future son-in-law or daughter-in-law. Li P'ei-ching (1826–1886) was one such orphan. P'ei-ching was only seven months old when his father died. His grandfather, after raising the child until about age five, decided to arrange a marriage for the boy. The idea, unfortunately, did not materialize as planned, as the head of the family chosen by his grandfather met an untimely death himself the next year.[43]

But in-laws could certainly be a source of assistance and protection. When the late Ming political leader Yang Chi-shêng (1516–1555) lost his struggle with court politics and faced execution, he penned a final letter to the two sons he was leaving behind. Among other things, the adult boys were instructed to remember to go to their fathers-in-law for help and advice in times of need.[44] Yang's words to his boys Ying-wei and Ying-chi were later printed, circulated, and included in numerous collections of famed family instructions and self-cultivation literature, as one father's last thoughts became public advice. Marriages, people realized, were hardly ever contracted without strategic consideration. Yang's case simply reminded all of how ironically close the fate and needs of the better positioned in society can be with those of the least favored.

Still, if no external assistance was forthcoming, the widow had to raise her children on her own. Weaving, sewing, doing handicrafts, and hiring herself out as a maid or wet nurse were ways a woman could bring in valuable income. The educated could also hire themselves out as tutors, find bidders for their calligraphy and paintings, or take in cash as scribes. Under such circumstances, older girls often joined their mothers in doing needlework or crafts, as the boys hired themselves out tending water buffaloes to get their meals or collecting firewood and wild vegetables for a few coppers. Tung Hsün and his three-year-old brother did just that in an orphanage as no relatives offered aid. For a while his grandmother and mother were scared of the future, he recalled, and did nothing but cry before his mother gathered her senses and started selling her dowry followed by working on needlework and handicrafts.[45]

Sadness and Fear

Whether or not it meant an immediate financial crisis, the lost of a parent or surrogate, especially at a minor age, often shocked a child. This was so even though a child might not comprehend the matter fully at that moment. The famous Ming essayist Kuei Yu-kuang (1506–1571) lost his mother at seven. As he recalled, at the time he and his four surviving siblings (out of six born) barely understood what was taking place. They were weeping simply because others in the house were doing so. Yet as he grew older, a strong longing for his mother's presence gripped his heart. In his teens, he confessed, he got into the habit of holding onto a family elder's gown and asking about anything and everything that occurred in the house when the young mistress was still living. Information gathered in this fashion, he explained, helped to heal personal wounds. "Losing my mother at a very early age, I often feel uncomfortable when left alone," he wrote after he grew up. "I find myself always thinking about the lives of those who are gone and wondering what I never knew about them. I also worry constantly about people who are still alive, that there may not be enough time to know them fully—all because of that tragic event, which still hurts me so very deeply."[46]

To protect children from the initial shock, many surviving elders tried to conceal the fact from their young initially. As Wung Shu-yüan recalled the event one day in the springtime of his fifth year:

As I came in from the outside, I saw father lying on the ground with his face up. I pointed at him and asked the maid what he was doing there. The maid tried talking to me, saying that father was asleep. "Why is mother crying, then?" I asked. "Because your father has been sleeping and won't wake up, that is why." I then lay down beside the body, touching my father's face with my hand. Nothing moved. Breaking into tears, I cried, "Dad will never wake up now."[47]

This little boy Shu-yüan continued to weep over the next year and thereafter, whenever his mother remembered his father in mourning rituals. The long, hard grieving period produced a lasting imprint on the child's memory.

Feeling deserted, some children turned religious. They chanted Buddhist sutras every morning and night from the day they became orphans. The young boy Chiang Tun-fu (1808–1867), when his mother was "sent home" (divorced) by his grandmother and his father passed away shortly thereafter, found it hard to get over his sorrow. He left home to "wander about" in his adolescence before deciding to enter a Buddhist monastery.[48]

Most such children went through life with sadness buried deep in their hearts; some mused that devastating loss had given them a special appreciation for the sentimental in literature as well as in real life, though they could also become easily overwhelmed by melodramatic scenes. Others expressed their frustration in more direct and forceful ways. Young brothers and sisters admitted vowing to work their hardest, either in their studies or out in the fields. Toiling seemed the way to prove to the world their wounded determination not simply to survive but to excel.

The fact that death could occur at any time did not appear to have accustomed the young any better to loss. Learning of a parent's sickness continued to prompt children to dramatic acts. In depression, they approached folk religions for comfort and salvation. Yin Chao-yung (1816–1882) was seven when he discovered that some "quack" doctor had made his father's sickness worse. He got up the courage and later confessed to having made a trip by himself to the local Ch'êng-huang (city god) temple to seek divine intervention. The divination, as he received it, however, brought the sad prediction that "the life is at an end, what else can one do?" The boy broke out crying in despair.[49] Others were compelled to take even more drastic measures. Chu Tz'û-ch'i (1807–1881) was ten when his father "came down with a stomach illness that appeared difficult to cure." Filled with horror, he hand-copied a special prayer to the Household God (tsao) and kowtowed to plead for his father's health until blood streamed down his forehead.[50] Li Kuang-ti (1642–1717) was another such child. When his father fell ill with a hernia, he said, he secretly pushed open the window in the middle of the night and knelt down to pray for his father's recovery.[51] Wung Shu-yüan, as we learned, lost his father when he was five. Five years later, his mother was confined to bed by a "chill in the back." This condition of his widowed mother who meant everything to Shu-yüan after his father's death brought added apprehension. He waited by her sickbed day and night, deciding eventually to take matters into his own hands. "I threw myself prostrate over mother, using my mouth to blow warm air onto her back." The strenuous effort worked somehow. After several days of this his mother appeared to have improved. The experience, however, became a haunting nightmare, leaving a permanent mark in Shu-yüan's memory. As an adult, he often had dreams of himself lying down and panting desperately over his mother's back, only to wake up crying in dread.[52]

These feelings, to be sure, were not confined to child-parent relations in the narrow sense. The sentiment and devastation could have occurred with any parentlike figure since a child often developed intimate ties with the grandparents, aunts, and uncles, even siblings and wet nurses. Accounts abound about children praying to "lend" a few years of their lives to a sick sibling or a dying elder. Demographic realities in late imperial Chinese society were such that similar events constituted a fairly common experience. Fang Shih-kan's (1787–1849) mother died in childbirth when he was five. One month before that, his one-year-old brother perished. Within the next few years, three other young siblings had died.[53]

The Joys and Pains of Growing Up

Traditional Chinese biographical literature might be lacking in vivid human emotions, but traces of childhood happiness and sorrow can still be detected by pooling multiple sources. In everyday life, it appears, what delighted a child the most was nature, food, and play; sweets and snacks appear to have pleased children then as now. There is never a lack of accounts of children fighting over dates, as Shao Hsing-chung did, or brothers and sisters struggling over cracking a walnut shell, as Ssû-ma Kuang did.[54] Food was obviously a powerful attraction, so much so that elders could hardly prohibit themselves from employing such lures as honey or green peas to move a child to do what was desired.[55]

Games, too, brought cheer to young lives, as children in late imperial China were beginning to possess toys of the commercial sort. The few toys they had in the form of kites, dolls, or simple daily objects were made of common materials like bamboo sticks, wooden strips, paper, or mud. Meanwhile, children invented social amusement from their surroundings just the same. Getting together with siblings, cousins, and neighbors, they ran to nearby hillsides and swam in streams and ponds, although these activities were discouraged under threat of severe punishment. Young girls and boys also continued to play with small animals, keep pets, play with balls, and at times even gamble, which moralists like Chu Hsi openly scorned. Children got scolded for gambling. Others simply chased one another in the yard, as with Ssû-ma Kuang, whose playmate climbed up a water urn, fell in, and almost drowned.[56]

Child activities varied most clearly according to region, class, and the agrarian calendar. They liked kicking balls when the weather permitted, trying their hand at simple gambling games in the winter recess, even though the more stern of the parents frowned upon both activities.[57] The young Chou Tun-i enjoyed "harvesting games," such as fishing; Hsü Kuang-ch'i trapped snow hares and pheasants.[58] Similar scenes were represented in a variety of art and paintings.[59] Productivity, or pretension to "real work" attracted especially those in comfort and ease and thus became the subject of representation in enviable anticipation. Other youngsters liked to draw animals and furniture on the wall with chalk, as Wu Ch'êng-ên (1504) did as a toddler.[60] Or they could delight themselves with children's rhymes and songs.[61] School children were known to steal time to play hide-and-seek while the teacher was away, as Kung An-chieh's (1382–1467) friends did. Such children were also seen humorously depicted in paintings from the Sung period onward.[62] In seeking or having fun, children managed to find room for spontaneity and resourcefulness, either by themselves or with siblings, cousin, neighbors, and schoolmates.

They also took part in pleasurable activities along with their elders. This was most evident at festivals, when they attended theater shows and visited family friends and relatives. Lo Ssû-chü watched plays with his grandfather. Shao Hsing-chung accompanied his great-grandmother on family visits to relatives in the city. At festival time and occasions for popular entertainment, children mingled with adults to enjoy food and games like everyone else. In daily life and amusement, there did not seem to be a constant need or artificial force to separate or create a world of the young from that of their elders, the adults. Children in late imperial China played and worked with pals from their own age group. In enacting naughty jokes or mischievous sabotage, they possessed a certain solidarity among people of their age and rank. Yet on other occasions, they appeared equally comfortable being

FIG. 29. "Gathering Dates," artist unknown (Sung dynasty). In this stylized painting, young boys and girls are shown collecting dates from a bountiful tree. A sight of delight, it also celebrates reproduction as the fruit symbolizes fertility. Courtesy of the National Palace Museum, Taiwan, Republic of China.

FIG. 30. "Children Playing in a Garden in Autumn," by the leading Sung court painter of children, Su Han-ch'ên (Sung dynasty). Here we see a boy and a girl using the stone from the date tree (as depicted as being gathered by children) to make a toy, a common game for children in north China. Courtesy of the National Palace Museum, Taiwan, Republic of China.

with their elders, and were often mentioned as participating in "adult matters" (*ch'êng-jên chih-shih*). The idea that, somehow, the existence of a youthful identity ought to include an "either-or" character in the conducting of people's social life may be mostly a modern invention.

Seen in other terms, a child in the late imperial Chinese setting could be made to learn the cruelty of "adult existence" with minimum pretension or protection from a childhood in innocence. A parentless child often suffered insults and discrimination from relatives and neighbors similar to those suffered habitually by children of concubines or maidservants. As a child born

FIG. 31. "Children Roasting Buns Together," artist unknown (Yüan dynasty).
Associated with symbolic foods (the bun as a warming wrap) and activities
(preparing things together), children are shown to represent the auspicious signs
in life. Courtesy of the National Palace Museum, Taiwan, Republic of China.

of a maidservant, the late-Ming intellectual Chang P'u grew up with humiliation and abuse.[63] Children were, therefore, in need of group support, social recognition, and friendly acceptance. Yet they appeared also ready to
wage individual struggles to escape despair and/or to obtain favorable conditions in case little outside assistance was forthcoming. The modest humility and harmonious subservience expected of children in the Confucian

FIG. 32. "Children Playing with Toy Boats," artist unknown (Sung dynasty). The word for "river (water)" puns on that for "harmony," showing the harmonious relations of generations to come. Children symbolized harmony and solidarity between the generations, a collective wish in the abstract. Courtesy of the National Palace Museum, Taiwan, Republic of China.

mode could never produce total surrender to adversity from the high and powerful in the social hierarchy. Nor could it completely rationalize, comfort, or prevent personal alienation or revenge from the most junior of the members on a one-child to one-adult in one-house basis.

Ordinarily, most children longed for the warmth and comfort of a homely existence. Even when such was not uncommon, children continued to be recorded as reacting to their parents' temporary absence strongly. The late Ch'ing reformer T'an Ssŭ-t'ung had a difficult time seeing his mother off from their residence in the capital. Ssŭ-t'ung confessed later that upon returning to the house, he would not answer people's inquiries, soon fell sick, and became increasingly thin.[64] Granted that T'an's was a case aggravated by domestic conflict, nevertheless, it was not unusual for young children to be understood as vehemently attached to their parents, especially their mothers, and therefore despairing of physical separation.

Other than the sudden occurrence of unfortunate events such as illness, death, or the departure of loved ones, the harsh realities of life appeared in Ming-Ch'ing childhood in mainly two fashions: material stringency and family friction. In terms of the first, other than the poorest in society whose young were in constant want, children of all walks of life were noted as sensitive to the pressure of material need, above or under the subsistence level. This became devastating at times of crises such as flood or famine especially for the underprivileged groups such as fatherless children with their widowed mothers. Conflict within the family or unfavorable treatment by kin constituted another big shadow in literature on childhood. For a child living under Confucian morality that prescribed strict hierarchy and prohibited active revolt on the part of the young, life could be particularly frustrating when witnessing and suffering from such conflicts. As a boy, for instance, Huang Shu-lin was sadly aware of the bad relationship between his mother and grandmother.[65] Though friction between mother-in-law and daughter-in-law were infamously common, Huang could find no condolence in the social ill. Discord between the father and the mother also caused grave anxiety. This was especially so when the situation worsened to the brink of causing—or actually caused—the breakup of a marriage.[66] In a society like that of the late imperial Chinese gentry, where divorce was far from any accepted norm (as termination of a marriage, other than by death, could only take the form of a husband rejecting and "sending away" a wife), children were caught up in additional bitterness, with their deserted and bickering mother and their stern and equally helpless father. As was often the case, the father soon would take in other companions, which the polygamous Chinese society condoned. The young, be they the disfavored children of the first and formal wife (as in the case of T'an Ssû-t'ung), or those of the demeaned secondary wife or concubine (as in the case of Chang P'u), were invariably documented as the suffering, either from the abuse of the powerful or from humiliation as the product of ambivalent associations.

In addition, children were recorded as living under the whip of corporal punishment. Disciplinary measures, though expected to be employed under control in elite families, and arguably less prevalent than in puritanical early modern Europe, were by no means a rarity in late imperial China.[67] Although in this instance daily corporal discipline fell mostly to the mother. Chinese biographical and autobiographical literature includes more than a few memories of disciplinary measures, often recalled with a biting sense of irony. We observed earlier of Liu Pao-nan's recollection of the lashes he received when failing to meet his mother's wishes.[68] Beatings may have occurred more frequently from mothers in distress, such as the widowed mothers of Liu Pao-nan, Hu Shih, and Chiang Kai-shek.[69] Fathers, too, employed the rod to press a child to learn his books, apprenticeship, or farming skills. Some did not hesitate even to spank a child in sickness or frailty. Hsü Nai (1810–1867) was said to have been a child of weak physique who often lay sick with asthma. This, however, did not prevent Nai from being naughty by wrestling around with his brothers. Once caught at play while neglecting his lessons, his father gave him "punishment by the whip."[70] Grandfathers too employed whips and sticks on grandsons because of their common involvement in child rearing. Wang Hui-tsu, while ten, sneaked out on a boat to watch the bridal chair on his elder sister's wedding day. When Hui-tsu fell out of the boat by accident and almost drowned, his grandfather was outraged and gave the boy "a severe beating." On another occasion his grandfather got angry and hit Hui-tsu heavily when he was found making inappropriate jokes.[71] Ch'ên Tu-hsiu remembered his grandfather's stick as well, though he said that it was not as effective as his mother's tears.[72] Most records however took note of physical punishment toward the male children. Beatings of young girls seemed conspicuously absent in texts and in principle.

Other than family elders, teachers and masters were also seen exercising physical punishment as authorities by extension with the same power or responsibility toward their pupils or apprentices. Individual methods and degrees of harshness varied. Some nonetheless turned out to be deadly brutal. The mid-Ch'ing scholar Chang Hsüeh-ch'êng had the misfortune to study, along with his cousins, under a violent tutor in the village school. Their teacher, though "a clumsy person who did not know much about anything," had a tendency to "frequently beat the students." One student by the name of Tu was the most frequent victim. "Once [the beating was so cruel that] his temple was seriously hurt, from which he almost died." "Later on, the wound was finally healed," it was reported, "but as a result a lump was left on top of his head that no longer appeared as smooth as before."[73]

As suggested, corporal punishment in traditional China appeared to carry with it a significant gender prejudice. In which instance, young boys, as presumably the favored sex, were made to bear most of the blows, while social decency and behavioral modesty toward the female body may have worked to deter beating of young girls. (It seems then, regarding "negative" behavior traits like neglect and abuse, class and gender could be exhibiting a "reverse" correlation, whereas in "positive" behavior traits like pleasure-seeking and physical indulgence, such would actually manifest a mixed or positive correlation, showing a sociopsychological compensation or a "tipping-over" effect of the normative.) Just as an infant girl from poor working-class families of, say, Su-pei (northern Kiangsu) might have had her toes

FIG. 33. "After the Poetic Line 'Leisurely Watching the Children Collect Willow Flowers,'" by Chou Ch'ên (Ming dynasty). Chou Ch'ên captured the details of children's play and the adults' envy. The painting shows a T'ang poem painted by a Ming artist in the Sung style. Courtesy of the National Palace Museum, Taiwan, Republic of China.

bitten off by ferocious mice when her toiling mother was forced to tie her to the furniture. Gentry boys slightly to the south in the Kiangnan (Lower Yangtze) region were made to endure more lashes, though far less play, than the girls in the same house or neighborhood.

Conclusion

Children's existence, whether in everyday life or in their literary and artistic representations, appears at once richly complex and notably unstable in late imperial China. On the one hand, children were surrounded with many different sorts of people, resulting in a varied, active interaction with any number of relatives, neighbors, and friends. On the other hand, the constant presence of death rendered their days insecure and vulnerable. Practically and psychologically they could hardly afford to lose their elders, yet demographic reality made this a relatively inescapable occurrence. Society resolved this uncertainty and crisis by deeming the world of children and childhood as transitory. In which view, a child was welcomed as an extension to one's family line. In order to better carry out a child's duties in the future, childhood was to be treated as nothing more than a transitional phase, though treasured and recoverable beyond the biophysical age. Food and games, as well as pains and punishment, made up the usual happiness and sadness of youthful years. Though in and of themselves these years were not necessarily deemed as representing any independent value. Childhood simply marked the successful passage of each minor to the adult, and real, stage of human life. The sooner it did so, the better. Except with such an outlook, the varied and unpredictable nature of a child's social environment was actually seen to resemble closely that of the unrelenting world of adulthood. Thereby, the presumably ultimate benefit of rapid maturing of the child and the quick phasing out of the tender aspects of childhood is balanced out by a built-in admiration for the precious innocence it symbolized and the eternal possibility of rejuvenation promised in philosophical aesthetics and popular Taoism.

Part **3**

MULTIPLICITY

Childhood and children are about variation, change, and fluidity. The experiential, existential, and expressive aspect of a child's everyday life and the notion of his or her childlike years are mostly a social construct, thus, like most other human affairs they are prone to the influence of such factors as class, region, gender, ethnicity, religion, and historical changes. Also, a "child" or "childhood" is, biologically and sociologically, an impermanent position, unlike most statuses or identities derived from the list of categories cited above. Most males remain men, most females, women; the majority of lords and masters stay privileged, as most servants keep to their humble station. Yet few children are young for life unless they perish early. The following chapters discuss the built-in forces of change for this first phase of human existence, and thus demonstrate the interplay between the malleable with the less malleable elements of history. Methodologically and conceptually, they also point out and address the need and possibility of considering the nontextual, nonverbal expressions of human existence, the very meaning of participation in absence, when examined and appreciated with due care and comprehension.

7 *Girlhood*

Street folks under the sway of Yang Kuei-fei's (719–756 C.E.) charm in high T'ang Chang-an were not the only people in imperial China murmuring wistfully, as in the lament Po Chu-i (772–846 C.E.) dashed off, that nowadays having boys is not nearly as sensible as giving birth to a girl. One millennium later, the country offered a perplexing array of sounds and scenes regarding the fate of young girls as opposed to young boys. Among middle-class families in the seventeenth century, parents advocated indulgence, spoiling their young daughters to counteract the downward journey that lay ahead for grown women, while at the same time scolding and beating their boys for the important duties expected of men. In fact, basic civil decency at the time discouraged corporal punishment on young females, and even the poorest of rural peasants would clothe their daughters before they would their naked sons. During the eighteenth century, teenage girls or young women were known to have been bought for thousands of copper cash, while young boys were left to no one's taking.

The Analects (*Lun yü*) state, "To recognize that which is known as knowing, while confessing to that which is not-yet-known as not-knowing, this is understanding [*chih-chih wei chih-chih, pu-chih wei pu-chih, shih chih yeh*]."[1] Admitting to limitations in knowledge is always a challenge. For it is often not only a confession of inadequacy, but also an admission of deep remorse over a certain long-standing incapacity, persistent carelessness, or even prejudice that hints at the possibility of collective ill will. The lack of understanding or attention to girlhood to this day is one such subject. At a time when children and childhood are more often studied by specialists in medicine, psychology, and education, the female section of a populationis still gravely unattended and relatively elusive.[2] Nor, unfortunately, has the recent wave of women's studies rallied enough enthusiasm to illuminate the very first phase of a girl's existence. In the case of China, the few studies of children and childhood have, until recently, almost all been works of social scientists with a clear contemporary orientation. While initial attempts to look at the subject with a historical perspective have been fruitful and stimulating, Jon Saari's study on the experience of growing up in rapidly changing modern China (late nineteenth and early twentieth centuries) or Anne B. Kinney's edited volume on the various views of childhood throughout Chinese history, as examined before, have not paid particular attention to the gender issue.[3] Contemporary research on the lives of Chinese women, represented by such illustrious scholars as Patricia Ebrey, Susan Mann, Dorothy Ko, Charlotte Furth, Francesca Bray, Ellen Widmer, and others, though making clear the importance of viewing their subject with a keen sense of the stages of life, has thus far only marginally touched upon female existence in its earlier phases.[4] Girlhood as a distinct phenomenon—be it separate, different from, together with, or the same as its male counterpart—remains therefore a neglected topic.

Definition of Girlhood

The traditional Chinese understanding of girlhood, reduced to canonical references, derives primarily from two sources. In terms of behavior and rites, *The Book of Rites* (*Li-chi*) reads, "At seven [years of age], boys and girls shall not sit on the same mat, nor shall they dine together."[5] Before that stage, instructions for child rearing and early socialization made no such delineation. Age seven appears to be the first socially conceived gender difference. The next age marker of significance is fourteen for young women and twenty for men, when they received the *chi* (pinning up of the hair) and *kuan* (capping) rites, respectively.[6] These signified the time for both sexes to contemplate marital prospects, though other passages of the same text pronounce thirty as the appropriate age for men to marry.[7] Therefore, according to ritual texts, the demarcation of genders began at age seven, before which there was a period of "general childhood" when girls and boys seemed to be socialized doing similar activities, devoid of gender-specific considerations. A second point worth noting is that there seems to have been a notion that life courses moved in units of seven for females, whereas males experienced units of ten. For men, ages ten, twenty, thirty, and so forth marked *yu* (child), *yu-hsüeh* (elementary learning), *juo* (youth or capping), and *chuang* (adulthood or marriage). Whereas age seven was the time when little girls began to be set apart from their male siblings and friends and age fourteen when, as young women, they prepared for conjugal engagements and family making.

In contrast, *The Yellow Emperor's Inner Cannon* (*Huang-ti nei-ching*) sets forth a different understanding of life phases. Among other matters, it presents a chronology for the onset and end of girlhood, boyhood, childhood, and youth different from the chronology found within the ritual texts. Here, the seven-year phases were again conceived physically for the females. A seven-year-old girl thus had "flourishing vitality from the kidney" (*shên-*

ch'i shêng) with "teeth changing and hair growing," while at fourteen the presence of "reproductive capacities" (*t'ien-k'uei*) moved through key veins and conduits that promoted timely menstruation and the capacity to bear children, until age forty-nine. A biophysical understanding of girlhood therefore perceived two subperiods: an "early girlhood" between birth and seven years of age and a "later girlhood" between seven and fourteen. By comparison, male life courses were divided by eight, from birth to sixty-four.[8] Each phase of the man's life was extended one year longer than that of the woman, not only yielding at least a fifteen-year difference in their total life span, but also a one-year (from age seven to eight) and two-year (fourteen to sixteen) childhood extension over those of their female counterparts. Therefore, from a strict biomedical reading, the periods before seven, eight, or sixteen appear to be the potentially "sex-free" years in the human life course, to a higher or lower degree.

If one was to patch together the various denotations of girlhood, boyhood, and childhood from different sources, a few comparative problems would quickly emerge. One has to do with the existence of a possible "general childhood" or "nonsexual stage" in the early phase of males and females. Almost all ritual texts, beginning with *The Book of Rites* and instructional literature such as Ssû-ma Kuang's renowned *Miscellaneous Rites for the Family* (*Chü-chia tsa-i*), attest to the segregation of sexes beginning with separate seating and dining at the age of seven. As the ideal for the elite, it leaves ordinary folks to their own devices at home, in playgrounds, or during hours of feeding, dressing, and medical treatment. Still, theoretically it allowed for a sexually unimportant period of seven years at the beginning of human life. Closely examined, infancy indeed comes closest to this sexually undifferentiated phase. Observations on infant physiology in the "changing and steaming" (*pien-chêng*) theory, for instance, made no distinctions whatsoever based on sex.[9] Nor did pediatric advice for breastfeeding or infant feeding distinguish instructions according to the sex of the baby.[10]

Special features marked the key difference between early childhood (one to seven years of age for girls; one to eight for boys) and later childhood (seven to fourteen; eight to sixteen) in the females or the males. For girls the numeral seven was a benchmark, evident in both ritual and medical texts. Whereas for boys, the medical discourse relied on the number eight while the ritual texts adopted a decimal progression. Here again, certain gray areas emerge, such as the time lapse from seven to eight when social etiquette asked that girls be separated from boys and when girls were already embarking on the socially complicated process of later girlhood, yet boys were not yet ready to enter the separate arena of later boyhood. Similar problems existed for the period between seven and ten, or eight and ten, when girls were dictated both by the ritual authors and medical authorities to be entering maturity, yet boys still had two or three more years to go before formal schooling or the onset of maturity. This differential age period widens as the female and male life courses go on, as the difference between seven and ten becomes ten and fourteen, or fourteen and sixteen or twenty, and so on, when girls and boys were not in synch.

The Upbringing of Young Girls

Both the structural formulae for young girlhood in traditional China and biographical and family data from the same period indicate a substantial influence from didactic literature. In fact, the literature not only influenced the lives of elite daughters but also penetrated the lives of girls of merchant, peasant, and artisan families by way of the theater, religion, proverbs, and social ambience.

With regard to primary sources of socialization for girls, one didactic work from the sixteenth century stands out. *Words for Little Girls* (*Nü hsiao-êrh yü*) by Lü Tê-shêng, written and circulated since the first decades of the sixteenth century, distinguished itself from other works of the genre in several ways.[11] First of all, among dozens of instruction materials for children (*mêng-yang* or *mêng-hsüeh*), this is the prominent one composed explicitly for girls. The rest were produced for the needs of "the children," hypothetically including both girls and boys, though in fact having mostly the latter as their main audience.[12] Second, against the long tradition of instruction literature for women (*nü-chiao*), which began with such renowned works as Pan Chao's *Instructions for Women* (*Nü-chieh*) and Liu Hsiang's *Biographies of Exemplary Women* (*Lieh-nü-chuan*), this is the first, and unfortunately the only one, aimed ostensibly at the younger group of that gender.

Thus, the brief and compact contents of *Words for Little Girls*, in four-word verses or short proverbial phrases, deserves further examination on several counts. For instance, how young was its intended audience? Or, put another way, which of its contents spoke about the needs or the molding of girls before age seven? Age is a pertinent issue here both for the conceptual framework behind this material and for the potential influence such a text may have brought to bear on the lives of young girls. Furthermore, which of the instructions may have had a direct effect on a younger girl's everyday life? Or, which of the moral sayings in the long run may have become, by reference or implication, modifying forces in a girl's character? All of these questions, if possible, need to be posed against the comparable situation of the boys.

Judging from the language, analogies, and structure of the treatise, the intended audience of the *Words for Little Girls* included very young girls. Yet in terms of its contents and behavioral models, a lot of what it addressed to girls could be read similarly to the requirements for boys and children in general as presented in the *Words for Little Children* (*Hsiao-êrh yü*). For girls in the former were expected to be diligent, to rise early and to rest late, to be earnest in work and modest in consumption; they should be clean and thrifty, quiet and humble, respectful and obedient. Yet none of this would have been bad advice for a young lad. As a matter of fact, in the majority of circumstances, the latter text by the same author exhibited behavioral rules almost indistinguishable from the former.[13] The instructions for boys, as representatives of all children, were worded somewhat differently from those for girls, but the essence of the messages was quite similar. These, in other words, were the demands asked of a youngster situated at the lower end of the social ladder for whom, because of age, gender made less difference. It is true that in time, age and status shall gain their importance to form order and propriety, as indicated by the Chinese term *chun-pei chang-yu* (high versus low and old versus young). But the difference between females and males comes into increasing consideration only when puberty moves sexuality and reproduction to the central stage and as the next stage in life brings both parties closer to betrothal. Marriage shall place the wife as the inferior (*pei*) to her husband. In other words, the differentiating factor between a girl and a boy emerges and develops as both grow older and come closer to physical and social maturity. Toward the other end of the life span, gender and sexuality close to a neutral phase as old age arrives, in a late imperial Chinese biosocial trend.

Moral dictums in the *Words for Little Girls* spoke in somewhat different tones. Here the fostering of such virtues as softness and tenderness (as opposed to vulgarity and frivolousness), prudence and kindness (as opposed to meanness and cruelty), contentment (as opposed to calculation), and agility (as opposed to sluggishness) did appear to carry a "feminine" flavor.[14] The protagonist was steered toward a visibly domestic existence, the transition characteristic from the life of a daughter to the positions of a wife and mother, a contrast to the more steady existence of a boy and man. Comparable advice on the attitude and values expected of a young boy promoted virtues cast in different terms. A boy, from the viewpoint of the *Words for Little Children*, ought to be calm in his motions and quiet and stable in his words, and brave in admitting error; he should not be hasty or reckless. He should be ready to compromise, yet motivated enough to look for good friends, seek a useful occupation, and hone valuable skills. Emphasis was placed upon the positive and constructive, not so much on accommodation or passive endurance, though it could be argued that admonishments to boys implied similar values as expected of girls. The idea

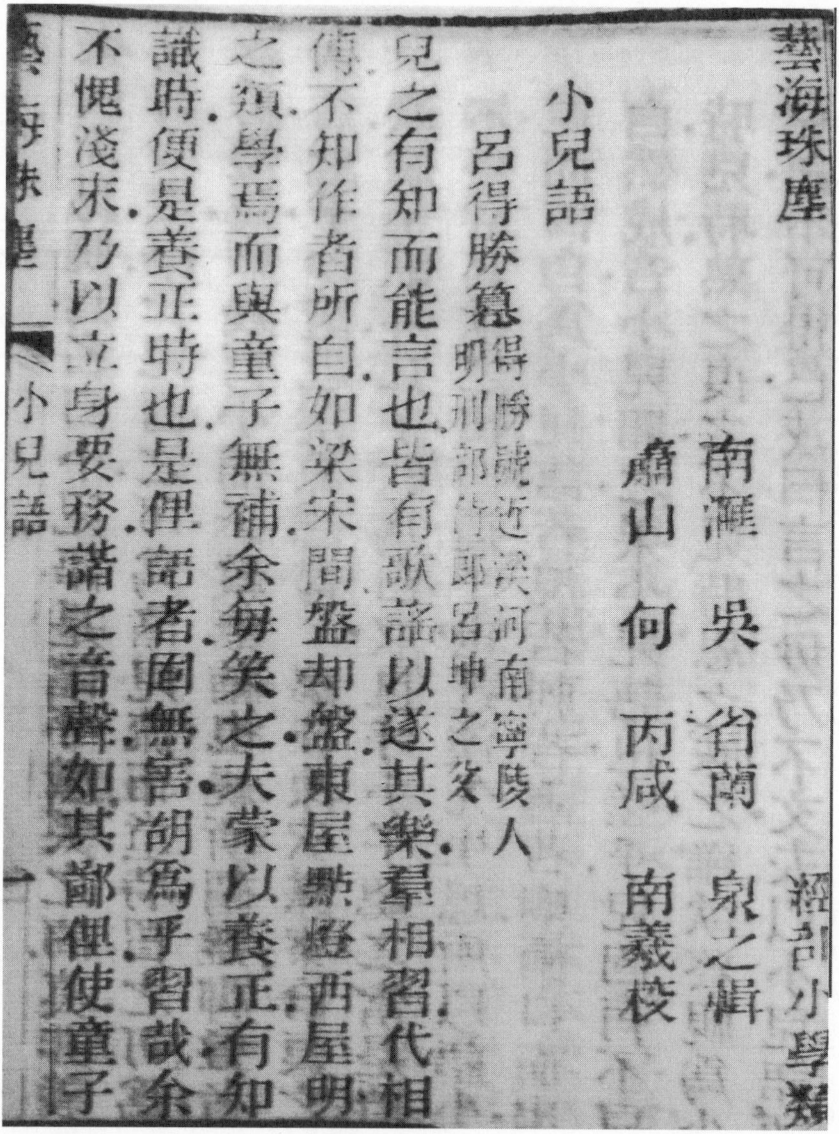
藝海珠塵　　經部小學類
南匯　吳　省蘭　泉之　輯
蕭山　何　丙咸　南羲　校
小兒語
呂得勝纂　得勝號近溪河南寧陵人明刑部侍郎呂坤之父
兒之有知而能言也皆有歌謠以遂其樂羣相習代相
傳不知作者所自如梁宋間盤却盤東屋點燈西屋明
之類學焉而與童子無補余每笑之夫蒙以養正有知
識時便是養正時也是俚語者固無害胡為乎習哉余
不愧淺末乃以立身要務諧之音聲如其鄙俚使童子
藝海珠塵　小兒語　一

FIG. 34. "A Page from *Words for Little Children* (*Hsiao-êrh yü*)," by Lü Tê-shêng (Ming dynasty). Courtesy of the National Central Library, Taiwan, Republic of China.

of viewing a male life cycle in stages, however, appears far less evident. The text expects a boy to maintain the virtues of a good son for his entire life. Although the text discusses how to become a good wife and dedicated mother, lessons for a commendable husband and fine father are glaringly absent.

There were, nonetheless, overlapping areas in this instruction literature. Both young girls and young boys, for example, were asked to be quiet, respectful, obedient, diligent, and vigilant. They were indiscriminately instructed to be careful and thrifty, kind and calm. Differences are kept to a minimum except when training girls to prepare for betrothal. In everyday deeds girls were reminded especially to value *ch'iao* (skillfulness), a virtue needed for a maturing woman to perform *fu-kung* (woman's work). The same was never promoted in the training of boys, presumably because most early education primers were geared toward elite consumption with a customary disdain for manual labor. Both girls and boys were to be neat and clean. Furthermore, girls and boys were all warned against laziness, carelessness, and frivolousness. Girls were especially warned against the ills of "slowness in hand" (*shou-man*), "coarseness in heart" (*ts'u-hsin*), and loudness in laughing, while boys were cautioned to guard against indolence, mindlessness, and vulgarity. The impact of such dictums in the daily rearing of girls and boys is anybody's guess. The principles prescribed and perceived in these instruction materials suggest that, for this society, the lines separating grown-ups from children were immeasurably clearer than those distinguishing gender in early childhood. Furthermore, class or socioeconomic status was unquestionably the second leading factor in formulating these rules and codes, much more so than the separation of the sexes.

Therefore, if any period during a person's life can be deemed as "asexual" in traditional China, when gender differentiation seemed least important, this early childhood period would come closest, with venerated old age coming as a significant second. Both classical texts on rites and late imperial family instructions profess as much. Didactic literature for children during the Ming and Ch'ing periods sustains this proposition as well. Compared to texts written for boys and men, instructions for girls and women contain more illustrative allusions pointing to the progressive nature of femininity and gender. To prepare young girls for future tasks in reproduction and childbearing, texts such as the *Words for Little Girls*, together with the various versions of domestic teachings (*nei-hsün*) and the compilations of biographies of exemplary women, were pouring out in ever increasing numbers. They advised on such issues as womanly virtue, womanly deportment, womanly speech, and womanly work, as defined vis-à-vis rules and performances expected of boys and men. On the other hand, materials such as the *Words for Little Children*, together with children's primers like the *Be-*

ginners Book for Children (T'ung-mêng hsün) and numerous formulae for manners and social etiquette such as *Collected Admonitions for Children* (*Yu-i tsa-chên*), offered almost no particulars that can be identified as especially designed for boys.[15] Not only was incipient "masculinity" hardly laid out in letters, there were not many discussions describing the art and secrets of being a man, a husband, or a father. Nurturing literature for masculinity concerning courage, bodily strength, assertion, decisiveness, or aggression were scarcely advocated in late imperial Chinese instruction texts for boys, or for children in general. When girls were taught the specifics of the approach and means to being a woman (*fu*), a wife (*ch'i*), a concubine (*ch'ieh*), and a mother (*mu*), boys were given rules mostly for being a son and very rarely about being the head of the house. As a result, the humility, wariness, and dedication anticipated of sons proved ironically close to those demanded of a subservient female, young or old. Indeed, all instruction literature composed for "children" could be presumably suitable and was indeed used in the education of girls. If one dared to train young boys using materials like the *Words for Little Girls*, scarcely anything would have turned out to be inappropriate.

Besides "natural" gender inclination, most families and adults would permit girls to play together with boys at this early age. Left to themselves, girls could be more inclined toward dolls, puppets, or animals made of cloth, straw, and clay; boys, for the most part, occupied themselves with shuttlecocks (*chien-tzû*), climbing trees, and swimming. A preference for activities of a quieter and more indoor nature seems clear among the elite children, as opposed to the outdoor, physical type favored by their rural, lower-class counterparts. From the perspective of socialization, the former did enjoy such things as singing, rhyme chanting, hand clapping, string netting, and playing house. Different activities may have been encouraged by parents and seniors with different values from different backgrounds. Under the sway of Neo-Confucianism, warnings against vigorous physical and outdoor activities became pronounced: they were unwelcome "coarseness and wildness" as was mingling with wild gangs.[16] Herein perhaps lay one of the areas where codes of tactfulness, prudence, soft speech, and respectful inactivity in the instructions for girls (for example, *Words for Little Girls*) and women (many kinds of materials for female inculcation) could have trickled down to the younger age group. Ostensibly these rules could have applied just as well to boys. In fact the instructive literature for Chinese men or boys (such as *Words for Little Children*) hardly offers any explicit encouragement for a powerful, domineering, or dependable leadership character.

Contemporary narratives note with admiration model boys said to embrace the essence of "an adorable girl." Kuei Yu-kuang, as a young lad, was

FIG. 35. "Lantern Festival," artist unknown. Phases of life varied according to gender. As shown here, the youngest boys and girls are playing together in a garden, while the teenage girl refrains from physical activities and stands under the eaves. Courtesy of the National Palace Museum, Taiwan, Republic of China.

affectionately referred to by an old housemaid as leading a life "mostly in the likeness of a girl."[17] Tsêng Kuo-fan (1811–1892), at three or four, was said to have been a quiet, sweet boy who habitually followed the women-folk around, "gazing softly all day at the weaving machine worked by his mother, with an innocent smile like that of a lovely girl."[18] Even Wei Yüan (1794–1857), who led a childhood life so reticent and reclusive that his oc-casional coming and going made the family dogs bark, was admired for his passiveness and femininity.[19] None of these servile, passive, and reclusive boys were chastised for becoming "unmanly." The moral character and the real identity of an ideal child defined along gender lines appeared very much blurred. Asexual games, such as hide-and-seek, did exist, as did mixed plays, storytelling, and theater attendance. These were accepted for girls and boys at an early age and lasted until household training surfaced in a young woman's daily schedule in rural and less "cultured" communities.

Nor were female children instructed on women's work (*nü-kung* or *nü-hung*) in those earliest years, for girls from wealthier families did not begin

FIG. 36. "A Girl at Her Lesson." Girls from rich families were taught not only to learn of woman's work (*nü-kung*) but also to acquire a certain level of literary education. This picture shows an older woman teaching a younger girl on the skills of woman's work. Reprinted from Wang Lien-hai, ed., *Chung-kuo Ku-tai Ying-hsi Tu-tien* (Chiang-hsi: Chiang-hsi Mei-shu, 1999), 36. Based on woodblock print from Shantung, Ch'ing dynasty.

this training until they turned ten or later. For families with lesser means, as young girls were called to work the land along with their widowed mother, boys could not be spared child-care responsibility or other domestic chores.[20] The labor that young boys were likely to undertake exclusively was animal herding; girls worked shoulder to shoulder with their brothers for tasks such as tinder collecting, grass cutting, cooking, and washing. In such households, little labor distinction was made along gender lines.

The Daily Provision

As one moves from the normative to the realistic plain, sources conducive to an understanding of young girls and early girlhood become frustratingly scant. References to girlhood are at times included in the prefaces and postscripts to literary works by female authors, as well as in letters written, published by, or exchanged among educated women.[21] When patched together and contrasted against accounts of their early childhood as perceived, overheard, remembered, and written by male relatives or acquaintances, they can yield meaningful reflection to a girl's existence. By Ming-Ch'ing times, such accounts were no longer social rarities. Kuei Yu-kuang left biographies of his mothers, three wives (in succession), numerous female relatives and acquaintances, and two deceased infant girls.[22] Hsü P'u (1428–1499) wrote about his mother and wives as well as his daughters.[23] Wei Hsi wrote elaborately about an adopted daughter.[24] Many of these compositions were done with affection and drama. When seen in conjunction with or in comparison to the women's own voices they help illuminate a historical reconstruction of early girlhood.[25]

Archives in Chinese pediatric medicine offer a view from another angle, as medical deliberation on disease and treatment, individualized prescriptions, and minute case records on both female and male patients provide information on the daily diet, clothing, sleeping, and other conditions of daily existence. Remarks on the health of children from different regions, social classes, towns, and villages culled from the collection of notes and local gazetteers yield the details of young lives led in gender-specific or generic terms.

Information regarding the daily provisions and actual sex-differentiated treatments of young children, be they of a material or psychological nature, are key issues open to interpretation and debate, as sketches of a girl's daily existence that do survive are often too sporadic and anecdotal to allow for any systematic answer.[26] The many instructions and clan rules, for instance, yield no explicit evidence about sex-differential treatment of young children in matters of eating, drinking, clothing, or resting. Discriminating principles were more likely formulated for manners, games, and behavior aimed at boys and girls of an older age. All in all, the sociocultural understanding of gender, not biophysically defined sex, appears to bear the essence of such differentiation.

Generally speaking, different and unfavorable treatment of young girls in terms of material needs was rare in adequate and normal times.[27] Even less difference was shown in the provision of food than in the matter of dressing, propriety not economics being a core concern in the latter case. Elite and culturally conservative families may have had their girls and womenfolk eating at separate tables or at different sessions, but the food served was not categorically distinguishable from that for boys and men. Peasant families had girls dine together and fight over dishes with their brothers because girls labored as hard in the fields and at times rendered contributions more valuable to the collective well-being.[28] Real differences in diet between girls and boys, or other family members, occurred at times of scarcity and crisis.

Clothing for toddler girls, as shown in paintings and illustrations, was made in different styles from those for boys. But this does not necessarily mean that discrimination existed in terms of the quality or the amount of the materials used. For most, the gender distinctions in garments, when affordable, focused on the styles and designs, not so much on the sufficiency of coverage and warmth. In fact, after functional and practical concerns were met, more serious attention was paid to the clothing of young girls than boys, for considerations of decency and social etiquette, whereby the separation of classes was certainly more grave than the differences between gender. In warmer seasons and in rural settings boys up to age ten or so were known to go completely naked; nothing near this would have been contemplated for girls of a comparable age from similar backgrounds.

Sex-differentiated treatment or gender-specific experiences of young children became more evident in times of crisis such as sickness and famine.[29] Sick girls, as both family records and medical documents suggest, received nursing and medical care not completely at variance to those for boys in places where these treatments were available. Here the main question was accessibility of health care in terms of family means and regional medical development, not necessarily gender specificity of patients. In villages and towns that had herbalists, drugstores, general practitioners, or a pediatrician, families above the poverty level were noted as seeking comparable treatments for their sick girls and boys. For the truly indigent, accustomed to survival according to the whims of nature, gender made little difference, nor did generation or age. That class and regionality, rather than gender, dictated childhood experience emerges from thousands of family records with good data on small children and from hundreds of local pediatric texts in this period. Such information might contradict people's stereotypical impression. Pediatric texts repeatedly revealed families of average means who sought a physician or drugstore that gave sick children of both sexes medical attention.[30] In these texts all medical impairments were discussed in nonsexual terms; almost no categories of diseases in the voluminous case record included male patients only. For all health problems, the occurrence, treatment, consultations, and records of young girls were always present along with those of the boys. Crudely speaking, the cases of boys may appear somewhat higher in prevalence, but the gap is not a grave one.[31]

Potentially gender-specific information found in the pediatric texts concerned the occasions where different diagnostic analyses and pharmaceutical prescriptions were given to girls and boys with identical health complaints. Such incidents were rare and by no means constituted the bulk of Chinese pediatric discourse, yet nor were they simply of a random or senseless nature. The issue here had more to do with a physiological theory based upon the concept of yin and yang in ebbs and flows throughout the human life course. Its implications for pediatrics practiced in later times allow the possibility of identical health problems manifesting different symptoms for girls and boys, in anticipation of what laid ahead for women and men in adult medicine. A practitioner might have decided that instances of fever, vomiting, or diarrhea could elicit slightly different signs in a girl patient than in a boy. Such assumption then led to different diagnostic judgments regarding their pathologies and remedies. As a result, different treatments at times came to be prescribed for children of different sexes with seemingly similar health problems.[32] A most pertinent point was a medical tradition that dwelled heavily upon the notion that the yin and yang are different and their implication and influences upon the human body ascended in age (*yin-yang yu-pieh*) or men and women are different (*nan-nü yu-pieh*), not upon the principle of favoring a man or boy over a woman or girl (*chung-nan ch'ing-nü*). This may be examined in a few additional ways. First, in the medical discourses where different symptomatic information and pathological and physiological hypotheses were discussed along sex lines, the emphasis was always on the biological and somatic difference, not on any superiority or inferiority of the gender in a social sense. The language did not necessarily carry any derogatory tone toward young patients of the female gender. Here the difference in values and attitudes demonstrated between pediatrics (*yu-k'o*) and gynecology (*fu-k'o*) deserves special attention. Gynecology's discriminatory approach to the female body and women's health was associated with functional differences between men and women and closely tied to maturity and reproduction. Second, in the places where slightly, but not substantially, varying medication was prescribed for girls and boys, pharmaceutical ingredients for girls was not inferior in quality or price to that for boys. Therefore, variation in treatment for boys and girls was not dependent on perceived financial burdens of girls or gendered notions of social hierarchy.

Biographical and autobiographical sources do reveal that attention and care could favor boys when more than one child in a household fell ill and competition for intensive nursing and human resources, not for general medical care, was involved. Wung Shu-yüan contracted smallpox when he was seven. Soon after, his young sister of less than two also caught it. The lives of both children were in grave peril. At one point, Wung passed out and his eyes turned up. His widowed mother screamed, summoning other womenfolk in the house for help, and the boy was revived after what seemed a long while. In the meantime, the sister died of a certain "fright" from the pox. No direct evidence suggests that her death was a result of neglect, but decades later Wung's autobiographical chronicle admitted the sister perished "because my late mother, pressed by my own condition, was left with less to care for her."[33]

Stories like this need not lead one to believe that the lives of little girls were of no concern to the parents. However, demographic statistics from this period do show an unbalanced sex ratio of boys versus girls, with infant and child mortality disfavoring the female.[34] A significant part of the general growth in necrological literature after the medieval period was the inclusion within that genre of an increasing number of mourning essays, memorial poems, and burial laments composed for young girls.[35] Kuei Yu-kuang, for example, wrote an elaborate grieving essay on the untimely death of his sixteen-year-old son. Yet he also mourned vividly and painfully for two of his very young daughters who died in 1535 and 1539. Both were given a full burial, in a section of the family cemetery set apart particularly for the prematurely deceased (*shang*).

For the first of them, Ju-lan, Kuei noted:

Those despondent plots strung together to the north of our ancestral graves in Shü-p'u were the spot for burials of the prematurely deceased. The pit in the south corner with new dirt was that of my daughter Ju-lan. It was on a midautumn day of the fourteenth year of the Chia-ching reign (1535) that she died and was buried. She was by then over one year of age and capable of calling for me. Alas! Her mother is such a humble woman, and it was such a difficult birth. I never tendered her any special affection for knowing that she was from a good mother. Only on the verge of her death did I give her a hug. If Heaven knew fully well that this is what it would come to, why in the world would it want to bring forth her life![36]

Kuei's protest against Heaven shows the personal frustration and inconsolable loss his daughter's death brought him. His regret over the missing "special affection" was a wail from a father's heart. He might have felt better had he invested more love and care like the kind he had shown for his first daughter born six years earlier. The birth of this first girl bought tears of joy to Kuei and his new bride, with Kuei himself still missing intensely his late mother who had personally sealed their marriage. In a preface he later wrote for an edition of *The Book of Documents* (*Shu ching*), he recalled warmly the scenes in which he came to memorize the text so well.

In 1531 I again returned from Nanking [after failing the civil service examination]. Keeping the door shut and my house clean, I rarely entertained any guests. Nor had we any spare room. So during the day I would always carry our little daughter around the bedroom and play with her. When she fell asleep or wanted to nurse at her mother's breast, I then used to open my *Book of Documents*. As I read, moreover, she liked to play with the pages, using her tiny finger to point at the lines and making sounds as if she understood something of it as well. This was how I came to study this classic constantly without wasting any time.[37]

A father's joy with his infant daughter flows out of plain yet unabashed language. Kuei took note of his daily carrying and caressing of his daughter while trying to work and study at the same time. The story attests also to an example of undeniable parental devotion toward a girl. The sentiment was echoed again in Kuei's burial note for his other infant daughter, the little Êrh-êrh (Little Two-two). This Êrh-êrh, born in the first month of 1538, when Kuei was thirty-three, passed away the next spring. Her death brought deep grief as well as sweet memories of intimacy and fondness. Kuei's burial inscription relived his feelings from the hour of her birth to that of her death:

My daughter Êrh-êrh was born in the *wu-wu* month of the *wu-hsü* year (1538), the hour and the date of her birth happened also on the *wu-wu* of *wu-hsü*, which I thought was a wondrous coincidence. That year I had been staying in the Kung-fu Mountain. Êrh-êrh, not seeing me, [was said to be] calling frequently for me. One day, I returned from the mountain and saw my eldest daughter was already carrying this little sister of hers; I was quite delighted by the scene. At the time when I was about to step out of the door again, Êrh-êrh wanted to jump into my arms.

A few days then passed since I had last been back on the mountain. One day, in the late afternoon, while reading *The Book of Documents*, all of a sudden I lifted my head and saw our house servant in front of me. Surprised, I asked him: "Is there something (wrong)?" Unwilling to tell me right away, he started talking about other matters. Standing there for a while, he then uttered: "Êrh-êrh died on the hour of the fourth drum [one to three A.M.]." So she died after having lived for a mere three hundred days, on the *ting-yu* day in the third month of 1539.

After that I returned to see to her coffin and burial. On such a month and such a day she was laid to rest in the graveyard of the old Ch'êng-wu. Alas! I had spent most of my time away since 1535, thus neither knowing my daughter's birth, nor witnessing her death. How very sad![38]

Parental affection for girls, like most ordinary human emotions, is difficult to ascertain. So here a reader discovers the unintended revelation of a father's thoughts and feelings for his infant daughter. Kuei wondered about the fortuitous meaning of Êrh-êrh's birth, was pleased by the news about her while away from home, and remembered fondly her joy. Disheartened by her sudden death, he returned to shroud and bury her, sending her off with a lament, which left traces in his memory. Kuei's burials and inscriptions for his daughters could be seen as both revolutionary and "modern"; such practice would have been deemed strictly improper in pre-Ming orthodox terms yet was gathering momentum by late imperial times. Literary evidence from the mid-sixteenth century onward abounds with parental passion for the young and the tender care for daughters. One reads about fathers especially, playing dotingly with their girls, attending physically to their illnesses, and mourning deeply for their demise.[39] The eminent Ch'ing philologist Wang Ming-shêng (1722–1797) lost all five of his young children (including an eldest daughter at ten, a pair of twin girls at six, and two sons at eight and three) to a smallpox epidemic. In a long poem with one hundred stanzas composed in their memory, he wailed over the early withering of his girls as much as the unfair destruction of his boys. From this grieving father there appeared little sign of a preferential attitude. Wang's remorseful confession showed that he adored both his daughters and sons and that he had sought to save them all by every means, medical and otherwise.[40] The next entry in Wang's biography spoke of the following autumn when he felt blessed again, by the birth of another child who brought joy back to his life—it was a baby girl.[41]

In a survey of daily treatment of girls and boys for this period, degradation and scarcity may be the forces that press prejudice to the surface, as general references to sex-specific behavior are not easy to pin down. In the early stage of a nonthreatening food shortage, for instance, there were mentions of families providing better or more food to the boys, allegedly in consideration of their different consumption levels. When worse famines hit, however, even this gender discrepancy quickly diminished. As desertion and selling of children occurred, boys were given away or put up for sale along with their sisters. In the late 1780s, for instance, when famine struck some of the Shantung regions along the Yellow River to the point where corpses lay exposed on roads, people fled from their homes and dug up graves to devour carcasses after the depletion of wild edibles. Girls of eight or nine were left for anybody to take, as husbands begged for bids on their youthful wives. When life degenerated to such an extent, the usual gender differentiation did not hold out above everything else. A scholar passing by witnessed an old man taking one girl and one boy to be sold. For the teenage girl, the grandfather received two thousand copper cash, one half of what a ferryman had just paid for a man's wife in her twenties, he noted. All this time, the little five-year-old boy went without any bids. Stressed over the sight, the scholar-observer jotted down two poems in anguish. In the one entitled "The Selling of an Orphan" (Yü-ku p'ien) he grieved that "the younger the girls, the further their price diminishes"; nothing compared with the fact however that "mere boys invited no one's pity." This, the observer explained, hit him hard. "Only now do I recognize the [folk] notion that having a boy can actually be far worse than bearing a girl." The postscript to the story described how a green-turbaned soldier on the next boat finally took the little boy out of pity, agreeing to keep him as an adopted son while placating the grandfather with three hundred copper cash.[42]

Unfortunately, the indiscriminate abandonment and selling of children are not strange themes in the history of the poorer regions of China. In the above case, the older girl was valued at almost seven times the price of the young boy. Were girls valued more as brides, concubines, maids, or even entertainers and prostitutes? Could it be that in times of need, a family already with male offspring to carry on their ancestral line tended to eschew additional children, males included? How would this "marketability" of young females be translated into or reconciled with the general terms of late imperial Chinese social reality?

One usually assumes that a patriarchal society favors sons and therefore distributes goods and emotional investments to males. However, empirical data can surprise investigators with information that leads to the opposite conclusion, especially for the youngest age group. To begin with, late imperial Chinese parents tended to be warmer and more lenient in their treatment and training of young girls. As a notable testament to this, the Neo-Confucian thinker Ch'êng I (1033–1107) presented this eulogy for his mother: "[As a girl] her father loved her more than his sons."[43] The implications behind such a pronouncement may be manifold. Subjectively, girls could have appeared to adults as having more of a natural charm, as if born with softer and more tender characters as people's personal confessions often intimated. To adults in the house, a girl was always reported as outshining the boys in physical appeal, reticent manners, and finer sentiments. Physically and emotionally she also stayed closer to the parents, receiving messages, answering requests, and attending to their daily needs. The contrast this entailed, or was meant to imply, vis-à-vis her male counterparts hardly needs elaboration. The famous Yen Family Instruction (Yen-shih chia-hsün) warned family elders against the habitual tendency of adoring younger children against their older siblings. Uneven parental preference had obviously been a fact and a problem. The Instruction did not mention favoritism of girls over boys, but most private records from late imperial times mentioned the favorite child in the house being a girl, hardly ever a boy. Some even argued approvingly of the practice.

In the usual domestic arrangements, a girl was likely to take up more

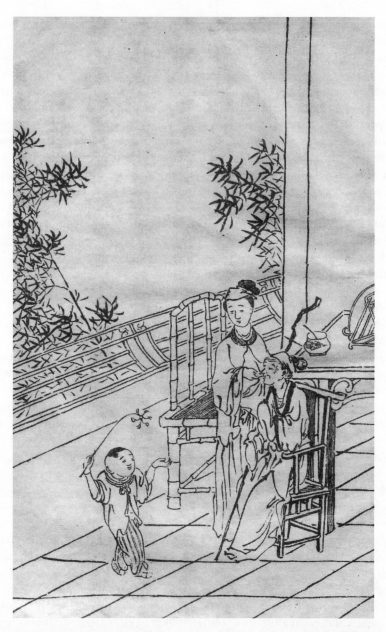

FIG. 37. "Breast-feeding One's Mother-in-law." Narratives or pictures showing a daughter-in-law breast-feeding her mother-in-law illustrate how in the late imperial Chinese culture of filial piety, young women in place of their husbands served their in-laws in the role of adult children. Reprinted from Hu Hai-ch'ên ed., *Twenty-four Stories of Filial Piety* (*Êrh-shih-ssû hsiao Tu-shuo*) (Shanghai: Ta-tung, 1925), p. 12.

household chores. For this the parents felt obliged. Eulogistic literature and family writings often acknowledged this. In the popular mind and by social custom, the bridal dowry was often understood and measured against this contribution, symbolically and arithmetically.[44] A daughter's undertakings in domestic work could have begun fairly early on in her life, three or four years of age would not be too young as the starting point, five or six was probably the rural average. Against which, the skewed representation of devout adult sons, as opposed to that of young daughters, in such moral tracts as *The Twenty-Four Stories of Filial Piety* (*Êrh-shih-ssû hsiao*) painted but a stereotypical picture of China's culture of filial piety, gradually institutionalized and sensitized to cover or take in the spheres of women and children.[45]

Third, ironically, quite a sizable number of late imperial Chinese parents began to love and indulge their daughters in early childhood precisely as a private compensation or a personal antidote against the public and social ills leveled at women. The seventeenth-century provincial critic T'ang Chên (1630–1704) captured the flavor of this mentality:

I once stayed with my friends the Wang family, during which time Mr. Wang reprimanded his young boy quite a number of times. "Do you care for [*ai*] your boys, or your girls [better]?" I asked. "My girls," he replied. "Equal as children are," I remarked, "I have always had more tenderness [*hsü*] toward girls than boys." He wanted to know why. I told him: "Though favoritism toward the inner quarter [that is, women] has never been an accepted virtue, violence toward wives is certainly a great vice. Nowadays wife battering [*pao-nei*] is so widespread that I feel especially soft-hearted toward girls."[46]

T'ang was a father without a surviving son; a single daughter of his grew to adulthood. His words might therefore be dismissed since he had little choice in the matters. The larger environment of T'ang's conversation and his other intellectual positions however suggest his argument in support of daughter preference was hardly a case of heart over head. Nor was the contemporary notion of daughter indulgence mere lip service. The idea of treating one's small girls more favorably than the sons occurred in a social milieu where prejudice against women tightened its grip in their adult life. Attempts to activate human counterjustice to "balance out" whatever injustice (*pu-p'ing*) lay inherent in the assumed "natural way of things" thus became the vogue in certain elite circles, exactly in the terms T'ang Chên and his kind used to put to their audience.[47] In other words, some of the more conscientious parents in late imperial China, witnessing the rigid gender prejudice, deplorable social bias, and abhorrent restraints and hardship that daughters had to endure beyond their girlhood, decided to "even things out" on their own. Not unreasonable in notion or in deeds as social bargaining, though hardly adequate to right the wrongs, this could be seen as an attempt born out of a private wish to counterfeit social conventions in the double negative.

This "compensation" of young girls to balance out a difficult womanhood also created a complicated situation for young boys. When parents and elders gave their girls extra latitude in place of normative "pressure," they felt they also had to "give" additional attention to their boys, the favored party in China's gender system. T'ang Chên's story serves as a double-edged example. Mr. Wang, the friend T'ang mentioned, expressed his proper son-preference by submitting his young boy to hard demands and repeated admonishments. Concerns came not with warmth or compassion but with harshness and punishment. Modern psychology has acknowledged that inattentiveness or negligence could bring out not just enmity but perhaps also passivity. This notion had in part worked itself out in China's premodern social dynamics. Late imperial popular wisdom held that severe discipline in child training was a proxy for parental attention and social importance. The most-favored child literally bore the heaviest blow.[48] Parents believed that the deepest of pain and horror not only demonstrated supreme concern but also ensured permanent memories, gave irreplaceable lessons, left unique psychological imprints, and in the end perhaps yielded virtue, talent, and even gratitude. Such stark reminders as "filial sons emerge only out of a heavy rod" (*pang-t'ou ch'u hsiao-tzû*), or "severe teachers produce meritorious disciples" (*yen-shih ch'u kao-t'u*), applied unfortunately (or fortunately for our female protagonists) to boys only. Girls were also free of the application of social principles such as "raising yet not teaching (a child) is the fault of the father; teaching while not severely punishing is the indolence of the master," as such was understood as aiming mostly at boys. Discrimination this certainly was, but rendered in a twisted form, it could provide a strange escape, an unasked reprieve from the childhood predicament of the least favored—a ludicrous testimony to the country's long-held heritage of "valuing the boys while despising the girls."

A combination of some or all of these factors could be responsible for constructing an oddly accommodating, even indulgent, parental attitude and social treatment toward young girls. The practical implications included customs that would have the boys conceding to the girls in the house when it came to receiving food or favors, or in requiring the former to back down in domestic disputes. Even though general principles of seniority ruled that an elder child should yield to a younger sibling regardless of sex, instances can be found of rural households where boys were made to give way to their sisters at all times, elder sisters included, citing the latter's daily contribution or their eventual pitiable fate to leave for "the house of others" (in marriage) as a cause for parental sympathy and brotherly compassion.

By a similar implication, significant differences existed in the physical treatments of children as well. Far less corporal punishment was applied to young girls as opposed to their male counterparts. Many families made it a rule never to strike a daughter. A little understood ramification of Neo-Confucian social ethics and body culture allowed openly gazing at, or striking, a boy much more readily than it would tolerate peeking at, or touching, a girl. For ordinary households, if girl beating was not absolutely unheard of, instances of it were incomparably rarer than those for boys. Whatever impact physical punishment might have produced in a child in this context, boys were its main victims.[49]

To further confront the superficial impression that gender prejudice could have worked only to the advantage of boys, it is useful to look at the privilege a young girl might have had in affective ties and emotional warmth from family elders. Despite an ideology of preference for boys and the fact that many sons did develop fairly strong bonds, especially with their mothers, parents from this period, fathers in particular, appear to have treated their daughters with increasing affection in the early years and often wanted to continue these affectionate ties for the rest of their lives. Most families, if made to disclose, indicated their favorite child to be a daughter, rarely a son. The number of Ming-Ch'ing parents who went about adopting girls specifically to fill an emotional void ceased to be a rarity. In her autobiography, Tsêng Chi-fên, the daughter of late Ch'ing viceroy Tsêng Kuo-fan, mentioned on at least two occasions deliberate adoption of young girls within the clan for no reason other than to "please" (ch'êng-huan) a couple with no shortage of boys but feeling, deep down, "empty at heart." One was the adoption of her fourth elder sister (Chi-fên was the sixth) by an uncle. The other occurred when this adopted sister, married and without any children of her own, decided to adopt two daughters, not a single son.[50] Incidents like this were not idiosyncratic and are not difficult to decipher. When Ch'ên Shih-i's (1856–1930) younger brother lost his only boy, Ch'ên agreed to give the brother his own little boy, but asked to have the brother's daughter in return.[51] The famous seventeenth-century Kiangsi scholar Wei Hsi, failing to produce any child of his own, decided to adopt a baby daughter whom he held dearly in his affections. "For me, you were always just like a boy [yu-tzû]," he exclaimed when she passed away after marriage.[52]

There are also forceful reports of the development of a "daughter loving" culture in this society of son-preference, which carries material, physical, as well as emotional and psychological ramifications.. The eminent eighteenth-century official and social reformer Ch'ên Hung-mou (1696–1771), in his preface to the Collected Instructions for Girls (Chiao-nü i-kuei), saw this practice as both a favorable precondition and the imperative reason for wanting to bring young women into his educational scheme. What struck him, he said, was the social fad of indulging and spoiling one's daughters without providing them with any training or proper cultivation.

Though parents loved their girls deeply, all they [the parents] were accustomed to do for them consisted of nothing but provisions of practical needs, daily comforts, fine clothing, and plentiful food. As they [the girls] grew older, instructions in needle-work and embroidery were furnished, and a fine dowry prepared. As to whether their characters and hobbies were of the erroneous or correct kind, whether their speech and movements were appropriate to old propriety, little of the sort was ever contemplated.[53]

Ch'ên said that personally he did not approve of the spoiling of girls, but viewed it as fertile ground for their improvement, hoping that parental in-dulgence might fortuitously support female education. Verified by family records and private notes, what Ch'ên voiced was less rhetorical than people might assume. Parents, especially in the "progressive enclaves" of south China and various urban centers, compensated for the low status of their daughters with sympathy and compassion; many showered their girls with favors, not the least of which included education that would guarantee their welfare in the long run. By the post-Ming era, moreover, this was becom-ing more than the dream of the elite or the wealthy.

It wasn't surprising then that "obstinate" young ladies were noted at this time as a growing phenomenon. For one thing, the potential gap or conflict between prospective expectations of a dutiful wife, subservient daughter-in-law, and hard-working mother, on the one hand, and the intentionally groomed and lavishly nurtured young girls, on the other, could hardly be closed up easily. The sad marriage of Yüan Mei's (1716–1797) presumably talented sister and the alienating experience of the late Ch'ing rebel Ch'iu Chin (1875–1907) were but the better known examples of frustrated daughters turned unsuccessful housekeepers in the rank and file; their sto-ries attest to the sociopsychological forces at work behind, or within, China's patriarchal framework when gender intersected with generation, age, and conjugal ties.[54] In other words, the overindulgence granted these girls might have inadvertently worked against the odds of their survival and social adjustment in the longer run. For many, like Ch'iu Chin, there could be more than an accidental link between "winning deep affection from her parents" in early girlhood, and the sudden depression she claimed to have suffered in marriage and womanhood.[55] By comparison, for the few good boys who had enjoyed tender care along with the girls, nothing near this kind of an abrupt downhill slide in human emotion awaited them in adulthood. Socially and psychologically boys were never as sheltered or nurtured, nor was their life course or the social process of maturing as dra-matic or clear-cut as that of women.

Transformation and Personal Escape

Opportunities to transport or escape the mundane existence of girls beyond the boundary of age and gender carried special significance. The most valuable aspect of such, no doubt, consisted in practical training and book learning, in what was understood as women's education. Recent scholarship has shown how two distinct tracks of training existed for girls or women: *chiao* (instruction or inculcation) and *hsüeh* (learning or study).[56] The former was geared toward moral inculcation and social ethics, while the latter aimed at intellectual pursuits, the learning of classics, history, literature, arts, and philosophy.

In terms of literary education, female literacy was on a gradual but clear rise in the second millennium of imperial Chinese history, with the greatest acceleration occurring in the last four centuries. Since a disproportionate majority of the estimated 10 to 20 percent of literate females (yielding a total of millions) was concentrated in China's southeastern region, places like the Lower Yangtze area were saturated with women who possessed a classical education.[57] The era not only saw the publication, circulation, and marketing of poetry, drama, novels, calligraphy, and paintings by women, but also gatherings of female associations brought together by epistolary exchanges.[58] Most of these women educated or supervised the education of their children, both boys and girls, managed family estates, and gave advice in politics and on battlegrounds, albeit to or through their husbands, fathers, sons, or brothers. Thus these women of learning had to have received a classical education, like their brothers, beginning at a very young age, between four and five years if not earlier. This occurred because it was the "trendy" practice of the day and because of the way female lives were managed in gentry families. The sociocultural elite (not necessarily the most privileged families economically) who provided such an upbringing for their daughters were quite conscious and conscientious about the cultural cultivation and practical achievements of their children, regardless of gender. Parents from this background, especially the fathers as the main decision makers, tended to be of the mind that for girls a classical education was valuable, even indispensable. Pressed, they were ready to contest slogans like "a woman's lack of talent is a virtue" (*nü-tzû wu-ts'ai pien-shih tê*) to say that, quite to the contrary, talent constituted the very essence of feminine virtue, more so than her beauty. For them, a good education was of essential concern and the best guarantor for their sociocultural standing, especially as such was lived out and carried on by their daughters, who would become wives and mothers. Therefore, a girl had to begin book learning at the same time as her brothers, which, for the anxious adults, should be as early as possible—no later than when the toddlers were able to walk, sit still, and concentrate. Similar to the fate of their brothers, "gentle girls" were being initiated at an ever younger age.

Crudely speaking, almost all young girls received their preliminary or preparatory education from their relations, not much different from the experience of the boys.[59] Here affinity within kinship lines would prioritize the choice of a girl's teacher. Parents came before anyone else, in most cases, followed by other relatives under the same roof or close by (uncle, aunt, elder brother, elder sister, and others), according to their affinity, ability, and availability. Contrary to the conventional assumption that social propriety dictated the segregation of sexes or the teaching of girls by mothers or other female kin, historical evidence from the late imperial period presents a different picture. Granted that educated mothers, elder sisters, aunts, sisters-in-law, grandmothers, and so forth did form a reservoir of literary instructors for young daughters, as they did for young sons, their learned male kin represented the most important source of instruction when it came to classical education. The eminent Ch'ing historian Shao Chin-han (1743–1796) told of his mother as coming from a scholarly family, specializing in historiography. According to her son, she gained her life-long erudition by "receiving instructions as dictated to her as a little girl in sentences and chapters by her own mother."[60] Shao Nien-lu (1648–1711) also remembered that his grandmother, while teaching him, was also initiating her great-granddaughter (his niece) at a similar age.[61] So mothers, grandmothers, and close female kin could teach and did instruct.

However, because of the association of intellectual pursuits with "public" and formal arenas, and hence with the male domain, fathers, elder brothers, uncles, and other male kin in fact performed the more significant roles in education. The late Ming philosopher Liu Tsung-chou (1578–1645) insisted on giving lessons to his two young daughters (the older of whom was nine) while bedridden by illness. His chosen ritual and philosophical texts were rigorous, yet he persisted in teaching for quite some time.[62] Convenience and expedience were as much a factor as predisposition in intellectual strategy: be it a female-to-female, a male-to-female, even a female-to-male transmission. The late Ch'ing reformer Liang Ch'i-ch'ao (1873–1929) taught his daughters himself, yet his younger sister, decades earlier, began studying under his wife, her sister-in-law.[63]

The conditions under which young girls began their study varied considerably as well. The majority experience (albeit the majority among the privileged minority) was the placement of young daughters together with their brothers in the same room under the same hired tutor (shu-shih) after the girls had been initiated in character learning, poetry memorizing, and the first technique of coupling (tso-tui). Li P'ei-ching (1826–1882), a prodigy from an old clan in the Changsha district of Hunan province, spoke of his elder sister, who, as a little girl, used to receive lessons in *The Analects* from the same family tutor as his elder brother.[64] In the1880s, Fêng Kuo-chang's (1859–1918) daughter obtained her primary education from a teacher who was engaged to instruct both girls and boys in their house.[65] Such arrangements, naturally, were not free of problems or constraints. In the 1860s, Tsêng Chi-fên used to go with her elder brother to study with their family tutor. Encountering difficulties at first, Chi-fên said an easier curriculum was designed for her, replacing *The Analects* they were using with simpler primers. After a while the tutor decided, customarily, to bring his own boy along to learn in the same class. At which juncture, "considering the difference between the inner and outer spheres [that is, the separation of the sexes]," Chi-fên confessed that she was forced to "interrupt my formal learning [*tu-shu*]." For an eminent and strict household as that of the Tseng's, classical training of girls could have started at a lower level or moved at a slower pace than that of the boys in exercise and in expectation. Although in her autobiographical account, Chi-fên conceded apologetically that in her situation the lag was more a result of her own "indolence in study, with lesser accomplishments." She was speaking against an elitist view on intellectual comparability regardless of sex as a high and obtainable ideal in children's education.[66] The segregation of the sexes nevertheless remained a factor; as the mixed group of students increased in age, it was handled in a more conservative style. Such confirms the earlier observation that the relatively "liberal" or open learning environment afforded young girls at home or in the "domestic" scene (family, clan, village) in the Ming-Ch'ing era marked a new development in history, whereby women's intellectual growth had been granted a greater opportunity, depending on people's socioeconomic, geographic, and thus cultural positions. Yet all this education still had to be implemented before the force of sexuality and marriage set in.

Another, less widely practiced, although no less important, provision of literary education for one's daughters was to hire special tutors, even setting up a separate "family school for girls [*nü shu*]" at home. These had in their ranks both female and male teachers, as literary references from the seventeenth century on mentioned associations of "female instructors" (*nü hsien-shêng*), "women teachers" (*nü shu-shih*) giving out lessons to their "female pupils" (*nü shu-shêng*).[67] Biographical data recorded instances of parents from the socioculturally developed Kiangnan region in the late imperial era, mothers like Ku Juo-p'u or parents like that of Ch'iu Chin's, who relied upon special teachers to provide a structured education for their daughters.[68] By mid-Ch'ing times, some women had made a significant income from offering elementary education and the teaching of "girls' crafts." When the time came for her boy to receive formal schooling, for example,

Liang Chi's formal mother hired herself out as a "woman teacher." She used the handsome fees, she admitted, to fund her son's own schooling.[69] Male tutors could be asked to tutor daughters as well, especially on classical subjects, such as *The Book of Filial Piety* and *The Analects*, the two most widely used primer texts for both girls and boys. Conventions did dictate it preferable for female teachers to be engaged for girl students and males for boy students. Yet, by the last two centuries of imperial Chinese history, quite a number of tutors of both sexes were teaching young students in mixed groups. Nor was it unheard of for a male teacher to be tutoring girl students only, or for an all-male family, clan, village, or charity school to have a woman as its instructor.

A further step in the family commitment to educate girls was to set up a private study group, securing the service of a tutor to teach on a long-term basis. The school that Yen Hsiu (1860–1929) established at the turn of the century is one example of such operations for gentry daughters. In 1903 the Yen family had in operation within their family compound a school especially for girls. Daughters, nieces, even youthful daughters-in-law, nieces-in-law, and "other girls of close relatives, good friends and the four [related] surnames" made up the student body. Other than the regular subjects common to the curriculum, similar schools of earlier times might not have had mathematics, English, or Japanese as this one had by the early twentieth century. In addition, classics, Chinese literature, and music in the form of rhymes and verses constituted the core of the syllabus in such schools.[70] Parents and family elders played a decisive role in determining the curriculum and designing the daily activities in these schools, as they often did with most "private" educational institutions in premodern societies. Moreover, like the boys present, the age composition of the girl students and the state of their academic levels varied greatly, ranging from newly initiated pupils in their teens or even early twenties to fairly advanced young girls. In time, after age ten or so, training in women's work and domestic skills could be added to the academic program, with special instructors for these technical subjects employed on the side.

A third type of formal study for young girls was "secret learning" or stealing lessons through unofficial channels. P'i Hsi-jui (1850–1908) spoke of his mother, who "had never learned to read or write from a teacher, yet by privately listening to what was being taught as my uncles [her brothers] were studying, was able to learn *The Four Books* [*Ssû shu*] as well as the *Mao Annotation of the Book of Odes* [*Mao-shih*], and get a good grasp of the main ideas." Like numerous other gentry women before or after her, P'i's mother's "secret learning" not only made up the core of her own intellectual world but also formed a cultural reservoir from which she drew to initiate her single son Hsi-jui decades later. At four Hsi-jui learned the

FIG. 38. A photograph of a girls' school in the Ch'ing dynasty. Reprinted from
Shan-tung Hwa-pao, ed., *Old Photos* (*Lao chao-p'ien*) (Chi-nan: *Shan-tung Hwa-
pao*, 1997), p. 25.

same texts that his mother had memorized secretly to embark on his journey toward scholarly eminence. Late imperial Chinese sociocultural reproduction was carried out in the crisscrossing of an intricately formed generational and gender matrix, whereby intelligent girls, sensible of the privilege
afforded their brothers, seized whatever opportunity to benefit themselves
from the world of letters and then passed that on to their boys and girls in
the next generation.[71] Tsêng Chi-fên described a baby daughter of two in
her family who, barely able to walk, helped to fetch and hold the "character tray" (*tzû-p'an*) for her own elder brothers while the latter were learning their first words. This curious toddler girl unfortunately died shortly
thereafter, taking with her the handful of words which could have started
her on a life with some measure of learning.[72] Thus, young girls expediently
hitched on to the literary track in lessons not necessarily intended for their
consumption. For those resorting to this latter channel, deep immersion in
classics or literature, though attractive, could rarely materialize. For most
purposes, these "on-the-side lessons" could never measure up to formal instruction. They did not last long, nor could they be substantial or extensive

enough in a structured sense. The circumstances under which these occurred were already predicated on the trespasser being pushed toward a different orientation in life. A girl's chance of barely and discreetly benefiting from her brother's schooling marked her out as coming from a family that did not take their daughter's education seriously enough. Since family attitude was critical in arranging privileged intellectual pursuits for a woman, a negative one considerably compromised her chances of success. This is not to say, however, that her learning became negligible or less valuable. A survey of biographical and family records yields the opposite picture, suggesting this unofficial channel functioned at least as significantly as the formal ones in presenting educational opportunities for girls toward the end of the late imperial period.

The known cases unfortunately provide no conclusive indication as to the relative prevalence of the three types of formal study, although ample biographies note girls or women as "immersed in books and history since childhood, with an ability in literature and art." Liu Pao-nan's mother "was acquainted with books and understood literature" (chih-shu chieh-wên).[73] The classicist Wang K'ai-yün's (1832–1916) wife was revered as a woman who "appreciated poetry and books and was accustomed to the great meanings [of things]."[74] The eminent nineteenth-century scholar Yü Yüeh's (1821–1906) second daughter was described as "a bright and intelligent girl while a child [yu ts'ung-huei], capable of producing poetry [shih] at ten, and lyrics [tz'u] at twenty."[75] Remarks like these present but a crude picture of the much mentioned growth of female literacy and women's culture in this period. Except for regional and class characteristics, it is devoid of systematic microlevel details.

Records do indicate that better-off and conscientious families in Ming-Ch'ing Kiangnan were among the most determined to make educated women out of their daughters. For this group, early girlhood was the time to start, because in the later years of girlhood (age ten or later), formal instruction was restricted to such "womanly" skills as needlework, weaving, shoemaking, culinary arts, accounting, and domestic management.[76] A good grounding in basic reading, writing, and the classics therefore had to be laid before academic matters got "pushed aside" as these little women gained in age. The intellectual achievements of the better-situated girls and women were comparable to those of boys and men, except for the shorter duration of their academic careers and the limitations imposed by society. A girl's teenage lessons in "female inculcation" (nü-chiao) were the unavoidable "interruptions," as the older boy's learning in examination essays led him to a particular field of performance. For those girls blessed with the knowledge of the classics, history, and the like, the toddler years were filled with soft songs and enticing music, morning walks with their hands in the palms of an affectionate parent or grandparent, and endless recitals of verses and texts. Theirs was an existence much akin to that of the "gentle boys" in their house, a far cry from the overwhelming majority of Chinese children, of either sex, from the lower echelons at the time.

Still the social, cultural, and even political and economic implications of educated girls are more significant than immediately apparent. By late imperial times, various employment opportunities for men had increased far beyond anything previously known, while marriage remained more or less the main career for most women. The increased need and opportunity for education and literacy affected the two sexes differently. With men, vocational choices dictated that a variety of nonclassical literary and technical training existed outside the elitist track of classical learning and civil service examinations. For a young boy whose family wanted him to enter into commerce, medicine, carpentry, or other crafts, a few years of elementary education were needed to afford the basic literacy to move on to special manuals or to practical accounting. The primary education he received may have been based on the usual primers commonly referred to as the *San-pai-ch'ien* (namely, *Three-Character Classic, One-hundred Surnames, One-Thousand Character Classic*), beyond which point this vocational education (still mostly literary) varied from occupation to occupation. Thus, the "degree" of intellectual or literary sophistication in boys and men covered a much broader spectrum than that in girls and women, resulting in a marked discrepancy between their world of letters and the void experienced by the female population. This was the sharp cliff that separated the accomplished writers of elegant poems from the ordinarily capable housewives, who had few meaningful or structured vocational choices.[77] Female entertainers and religious women of various sorts existed in between the two extremes, as did the small number of female shopkeepers, healers, and crafts women.[78] However, the amount and nature of their training fell far short of the kind of training that produced practitioners, artisans, or merchants in men. In these latter categories vocational training for women was not unheard of, but it never matched that afforded the boys. While the literacy and education of males by this time resembled a gradually scaled-down continuum, that for females still represented a much sharper drop between the world of the educated and the overwhelming masses of the completely uninitiated and totally illiterate. For any girl destined for a cultural upbringing, a classical education came very early in life and with much intensity. In time, this investment would usher her into an arranged marriage. As for other daughters upon whom fortune did not fall in this fashion, not much could be hoped for in their later girlhood or young womanhood, a stark contrast to boys headed toward various vocational choices in the trades. The segregation between educated girls and their uneducated "sisters" was therefore of a graver nature than either that between them and the elite males, or that between the best educated boys and their relatively less educated "brothers."

Like the case of young boys, it is difficult to have a reliable or comprehensive grasp of young girls' day-to-day learning materials at this level.[79] The "curriculum variations" for girls seem to have been far less than those for boys, as explained before, because of a more strict "single-career" pattern for women (for example, marriage and motherhood) and because education for most females was even more of an act of "learning for learning's sake" than for their male counterparts. Thus, the formal education of girls tended to carry a far more "idealistic" cast than that for boys.

Categorically speaking, young girls received two kinds of curricula: that in the classics and that in literature and the arts. Engagements in the two were not mutually exclusive and could overlap, though ordinarily the study of the classics came before that of literature in schedules and in importance. In studying the classics, the intellectual path of young girls was little different from that prepared for gentry boys. In other words, after character learning and mastery of a few basic primers (such as *San-tzû ching*, *Ch'ientzû wên*, *Pai-chia hsing*, *Hsiao-hsüeh*, and so forth), students were invariably given items out of *The Five Classics* (*Wu ching*) or *The Four Books* (*Ssû shu*) as introductory materials to lay the ground for further academic advancement. Here, the sequential order reflected the judgment of fathers and tutors, though the total pool of selection was not too big. As in the case of boys, the two texts most frequently used were *The Book of Filial Piety* (*Hsiao ching*) and Confucius's *Analects*. Both works, and especially *The Book of Filial Piety*, were likely selected for purposes of female moral inculcation and thus served both the purpose of women's intellectual training (*nü-hsüeh*) and that of moral indoctrination (*nü-chiao*). They were also the most favored texts in the standard classical curriculum for young boys, albeit with a heavy moral connotation. The fact that girls were taught with identical reading materials provides additional evidence that guidance for children toward classical letters entailed little gender differentiation at this incipient stage. When Li P'ei-ching's sister joined her brother in schooling, *The Analects* was her text, no different from any boy student in her class.[80] P'i Hsi-jui spoke of his mother's attempt to benefit from her brother's learning activities; what she succeeded in "stealing" from the boys' classes came from the usual curriculum of *The Four Books* and *The Book of Odes* (*Shih ching*).[81] Families that provided a formal education for their daughters not only gave them the same classical literary training as the boys, but also schooled them in exactly the same classics, in the same order, and by the same schedule. For such an elitist education *The Book of Filial Piety* and *The Analects* were always preferred over such gender-specific renditions as *The Book of Filial Piety for Women* (*Nü Hsiao-ching*) and *The Analects for Women* (*Nü lun-yü*). The latter, together with such women's texts as *Instructions for Women*, *Biographies of Exemplary Women*, and *Standards within Women's Quarters* (*Kuei-fan*), constituted "female moral inculcation," not the core or foundation for "women's education." Even for conservative families, a structured development of female inculcation would not have been set up without a fair grounding in literary education. The selection of learning materials with a specific and explicit female orientation signals a relatively conservative and narrow-minded sociocultural position as opposed to the pure, classically minded, elitist background of the highbrow.

The schooling and indulgence of girls in literature and arts was one area that significantly set their intellectual orientation apart from boys. By late imperial standards, literature and the arts were considered superfluous to career development for boys. Boys instead focused on preparing for the civil service examination or other trades, rendering knowledge or pleasure in poetry, novels, calligraphy, and painting as somewhat dilettantish and licentious.[82] The absence of any serious professional or vocational considerations for girls and the presumed soft, or "feminine," character of literary and artistic sentiments however cast these disciplines under a quite different light for the instruction of females. Skills in composing and appreciating lyrics and in conducting and pleasing oneself in leisurely brushworks appeared especially apt for early girlhood education as these could become valuable assets in maturity. As small boys were ushered off to be drilled in prose composition, rhetoric, and on to the eight-legged examination essay, their sisters older or younger continued to be immersed in T'ang poetry, lyrical writing, calligraphy, and painting. Kuei Yu-kuang's second wife (née Wang) and Ni Yüan-lu's (1593–1644) mother were women skilled in *The Mao Annotation of the Book of Odes* (*Mao-shih*).[83] Kung Tzû-chên's (1792–1841) mother allowed her child the loving experience of hearing reams of poetry through a maternal voice while reclining him between her legs.[84] Such instances in and of themselves may not be substantial, but the image was one that drove an ever larger number of families to offer their daughters a literary and artistic education that resulted in cultivated daughters, erudite wives, and learned mothers.

The acquisition of artistic skills came one scale below that of literary ability and was held in slightly less, though still respectable, esteem. A sizable number of gentry girls from this period did receive formal instruction in brushwork, painting, and calligraphy, and some came to be known for their accomplishments.[85] Biographical information attests that Li P'ei-ching's stepmother had talent in poetry and painting.[86] Ts'ai Yüan-p'ei's (1868–1940) wife, educated in the late nineteenth century in Kiangsi province, too, was said to have a good hand in calligraphy and painting.[87] Chang Ta-ch'ien's (1899–1987) mother and sister were not only capable painters, Chang himself, a modern master of the old school, received his first lessons in brushwork from them.[88] For families versed in the tradition, arts were passed on in the same manner as letters.

Female artists did not all live out their lives simply as gifted wives and cultured mothers. By the eighteenth century at least, cases are known of women calligraphers and painters getting fair prices for their work. Shên Ts'ai (1752–?) had a local market for her work in calligraphy and painting, enough to be a vital support for her family after her father's death. In addition, she traveled to distant towns, from Kiangsu to Nanking, to Shang-tung, and even to the capital in Peking to seek better prices. That there should exist forgeries of her work (done by men) proves further that female talents in art did not go unappreciated, nor were these artists secluded in the inner quarters only.[89] The pertinent point here is that a woman's skill in brushwork had to have begun very early on in her girlhood. Like her train-ings in classics and literature, artistic ability was both a luxury and a prac-tical asset in a girl's life. Special teachers of arts and crafts were hired for girls whose families valued such abilities. Female artists possessing local fame but still shy of national celebrity found careers as woman instructors (*nü chiao-shih*) in painting and calligraphy for the next generation of gen-try girls. Lessons of this nature took place while the girl-disciples were young, well before teenage preoccupation with domestic crafts intervened and certainly before marriage "clouded their sky." The cultivation of other feminine abilities, such as skill in dancing and music making, like the ac-quisition of the art of flirtation and courtship in Renaissance high society, were only part of the instruction of girls aiming at the entertaining career in imperial China, albeit at a distance from the strict gentry upbringing.[90] Training in music could be added to classical learning, literary creativity, and art, yet for the orthodox of the day, bodily charms subverted the very core of feminine qualities, much as frivolous leisure literature was frowned upon in the breeding of upright boys.

The larger implications, whether personal or social, that literary educa-tion might have brought for girls, and later women, are complicated to sum-marize. At an individual level, the hours spent in the studio studying *The Four Books* and *Five Classics* and poetry under the guidance of a teacher set the educated female's life miles apart from daughters of ordinary sta-tions occupied with duties of cooking, cleaning, and other household chores. The very existence of a child of letters was such a rarity that for the female gender it only enhanced an enforced loftiness and solitude. From the early age of four or five, she became enclosed in a world of intellect, values, sentiments, and sensuality that was literally a world away from most of her gender or age group. In her mind and in her experience, she had more to share with educated boys than with uneducated girls in her society, regardless of how the future course of life might impress upon her the elusiveness of both. Many a gentlewoman did speak of the uniqueness that a literary education gave them, and the separate path that this imposed on them. There were ambivalent remarks warning people of the tragedies awaiting talented women in a life that constantly threatened to engulf them. Conservatives like Chang Hsüeh-ch'êng criticized vehemently the dangers posed to female virtue by intellectual interests and literary pursuits (albeit of the wrong kind).[91] Ultimately, though, few forces actually worked to stop the rapid growth of women's education in this period.

Not all educated investments of time and money for a female were made with an eye on spiritual and cultural rewards. In the search for, or marketing of, prospective brides, a literate candidate no doubt placed herself well above the rank and file who could merely take pride in their moral virtue, manual work, or physical appearance. Men, or their families, from modest gentry or merchant backgrounds were known to seek educated women as spouses. Li P'ei-ching, as mentioned above, praised his second wife for her talent in painting and poetry.[92] Wang K'ai-yün, too, admired his betrothed as one who "knew poetry and books and understood larger principles."[93] Even a social radical like Ts'ai Yüan-p'ei was openly pleased that his wife was gifted in the old way, in calligraphy and painting.[94] Prospective groom's families could be concerned enough to urge the bride's family to try improving on what she lacked and to brush up her talents. A chosen daughter, after the engagement, might be demanded by the groom's family to embark on a few subjects of study, upon which request her father was forced to give her an intensive course on *A Chronological View of Official History* (*Kang-chien chêng-shih yüeh*). One such girl found unsatisfactorily educated, was none other than the granddaughter of the late Ch'ing viceroy, Tsêng Kuo-fan, her father being imperial China's ambassador to England, Tsêng Chi-tsê (1839–1890).[95] Less extraordinary households found practical returns from the education of their daughters as well. Educated women could make money earning incomes as scribes, copying documents or putting together contracts and deeds of transactions for illiterate villagers, as did Wung T'ung-ho's (1830–1904) mother as a young widow trying to bring in extra cash.[96]

A proper literary education furnished the majority of girls with the skills and intelligence needed to be capable spouses and resourceful mothers. The kind of excellent house managers that Kuei Yu-kuang exhorted his mother and his wives to be were women who could keep a family content and the estate prosperous without worrying or concerning the men.[97] Or perhaps the ideal should be the sort of mother (and grandmother) who need not rely

on anyone but herself to teach her children the first thousand characters, as
Lu Pao-chung's (1850–1908) mother did with him when he was five, as Hsü
Chi-yü's (1795–1873) mother did with her boy when he was six, as Yang
Tao-lin's (1856–1932) mother did with him when he was four, as did Ts'ên
Yü-ying's stepmother, Yin Chao-yüng's (1806–1883) grandmother, and
many nameless others. Some of these learned women found themselves giv-
ing lessons to their children on *The Elementary Learning (Hsiao-hsüeh)* and
The Great Learning (Ta hsüeh) less than ten years after they imbibed the
texts themselves. Ku Yen-wu's stepmother taught him when he was six. In
those days any woman like her, who after the day's chores were done, was
used to "reading books at night, with a special love for *Records of the
Grand Historian [Shih chi]*, *The Comprehensive Mirror [T'ung chien]*, and
Chronicle of the Present Dynasty [Pên-ch'ao chi-shih]," would have had her
interests formulated and nurtured while very young. The same may be said
of the numerous other mothers who taught their children classics, history,
and poetry.[98] Many more reviewed, supervised, and kept a close watch on
their boy's study under the lantern at night, like the mothers of Ch'üan Tsu-
wang, Ts'ui Shu, Huang Ching-jên, Yao Ying (1785–1852), and their sort.
Education was a valuable asset for women, bestowed on them in girlhood,
confirmed and made to bear fruit in their productive and reproductive
maturity.

Girls who did not have the opportunity to acquire a literary education
found other less elegant "hidden curricula" that were not devoid of their
own "world of signs and symbols."[99] They shared with their elitist sisters
the deep moral and cultural foundation beneath "female inculcation" (*nü-
chiao*) and "women's learning" (*nü-hsüeh*)," which instilled in a girl's mind
the basics to follow the "greater meanings" (*ta-i*) and to know "the reasonable in emotions and rationality." Indicating the separation of the highly
educated from others was the boundary as well as the blur between China's
classical Confucian heritage and late imperial popular culture.[100]

The practice of foot binding for upper-class girls inevitably raises questions. As Dorothy Ko points out, the wrapping up and reshaping of the female foot was regarded as an act of civility long before it was deemed a sign
of barbaric cruelty. In symbolic and cultural terms, foot binding was conceived and executed in conjunction with the fine breeding of elite women,
who strived for femininity of a particular kind.[101] As this practice spread
down the social hierarchy to influence the lives of middle-class merchants,
artisans, and commoner families in the last century or so before the modern era, it entered the lives of an increasing number of girls. The anti-
foot-binding literature of the nineteenth century or the admiring lyrics and
narratives from the previous hundred years form a disjointed chorus that
suggest the practice as targeting ordinarily acceptable small feet, with the

binding beginning when a girl reached eight or nine years of age. Regulations from the anti-foot-binding associations from the late Ch'ing period stipulated that for girls aged eight or younger, bound feet ought to be freed, whereas for those nine years or older, there was no need to attempt to loose what must have been already accomplished. The whole question is a complex story that falls outside of the proper domain of this study, both in terms of age and focus of concern. For the fraction of the most ambitious parents and guardians trying to bring forth a pair of small feet with exceptional "beauty," the unreasonably small size and severe degree of arch of the foot (*kung-hsien*) demanded action be taken as early as four or five years of age. These most severe cases of bending and deforming a girl's feet, according to personal memoirs and instructive manuals, required the daily aggressive reshaping of the young girl's feet for "a number of months." For these chosen girls, most probably from the extremist families falling for the fad, the hundred or so excruciating days of proper "feet treatment" had to be endured together with the charm of serene studies in the early morning hours. Not a few of these elitist young girls were remembered being carried about with frail smiles and temporary laughter mixed with tears. In the more unfortunate cases, infections and other health hazards resulted from the activity. Medical assistance and actual casualties were not unknown for these "select few" in prescription books or family records.

Conclusion

The study of early girlhood in late imperial China is an exploration of female life experience in its earlier phase, on the one hand, and a look at the depth of gender differentiation in that experience, on the other. The convergence or divergence of the two test the limits of the notion that "men and women are different" (*nan-nü yu-pieh*) in historical China without exaggerating the case. The engagement and negotiation between them also contextualize China's culture of "male preference" (*chung-nan ch'ing-nü*) in the "personal time" of lives of boys and girls, the "family time" of families and communities, and the "historical time" of history. An examination of the evidence of a gender-specific upbringing for girls helps one to determine how the separation between the female and the male penetrated down to the youngest age group. In the case of late imperial China, sources on early girlhood appear to point at a gender-specific culture that increased with age for preadulthood (and diminished similarly as people entered old age). Notions and practices of a sex-discriminatory nature, in other words, may be quite sensitive to age. Children under seven or ten were viewed and treated, in theory and to a high degree in practice, as a group with relatively less gender differentiation.

This then meant that female children might not have had experiences significantly at variance from that of their male counterparts. For the better-off, and the most "cultured," dress codes or behavior standards may have applied differently to girls than to boys, but the virtues cultivated, the activities designed, and the general physical care provided were fairly similar. The possible androgynous nature of early childhood in traditional China is indicated by the many references to children (*tzû*) in the classical texts, which were meant to include girls (thus gender-generic), as opposed to those that referred to boys only. The cultural or class background to age specificity and gender differentiation are matters carrying myriad implications of interest well beyond history and historians. Times of crisis and scarcity are what sharpened the division, no doubt, as did the socioeconomic conditions of the family.

Girls faced a future of increased gender differentiation, and thus book learning, intellectual pursuits, and cultural interests acquired in early girlhood provided their only means of temporary escape or respite. Such opportunities were not furnished solely for their spiritual value since much practical good could flow out of these investments. Elitist and cultured families sought a general classical education for their girls. The more conservative and relatively "low-brow" among the gentry would confuse inculcation with literary training and make do with the pedagogue of the materials for female inculcation. Ironically, in the end, education brought girls closer in spirit and temperament to their elitist male counterparts while setting them decisively apart from the rest of their unfavored "sisters."

As to whether a girl was allowed a period in life called "childhood" (that is, the existence of a girlhood vis-à-vis boyhood) depends to a large extent on how children or childhood is understood experientially and conceptually. According to modern psychology, philosophy, and sociology, childhood is viewed not simply as a phase in the life course of the youngest age group but also as a period of spiritual freedom, indulged naiveté, and innocence. Girls in traditional China could have had a life much closer to this modern notion of a child and childhood than that of their male counterparts. She may have been less valued and less important in the long term, but her very insignificant status also granted her this special "breathing space" while young. Her prospective hardship in life encouraged parents to take pity or rule in favor of her temporarily or whenever the situation permitted.

Taken as a whole, however, early girlhood in the late imperial period is inevitably complicated. Put more straightforwardly, if one was to ask whether the lives of young girls had become better or worse in the last few centuries before the modern era, the question could hardly be answered without qualification or delineation. On the positive side of the scale, chances of education had indisputably improved for all classes of young girls, though most markedly so for the elite in the developed regions and urban centers, due to a general increase in child literacy, a thriving publishing business, and a lively print culture. Continued developments in pediatric medicine in almost all regions of China proper also meant better opportunities for health care for the youngest population, girls included. On the negative side, continued intensification and institutionalization of the Neo-Confucian orthodoxy brought increasingly rigid and unfavorable treatment for the female gender throughout this period. Due to the relatively "asexual" character of early childhood, the destructive impact on young girls at this phase in their lives was not as pronounced as that which they were to confront as they aged. Aggressive advancement toward the ultimate inculcation of a woman's place in society certainly did not prevent conservative families from lowering the age of sex-differentiated treatment to infringe upon an even younger population. The occurrence of foot binding before age seven is one case in point. On the other hand, precisely as this sex-discriminatory treatment of women was taking place, a selective sociocultural revolt against the tyrannical mainstream presented society with a fashionable and intensified indulgence of their younger girls at home. It was a reaction to compensate for the prospective suffering of women once they moved beyond the temporary refuge of these first years, as well as a conscious protest, on the part of the sensitive, against the unfortunate and tragic destiny of their daughters.

The few studies on childhood in Western history, important and illuminating as they are, lump the long stretch of preadult human life in one category. All young people are placed under the general category of children or childhood, with little distinction for age or gender within that sixteen- to twenty-year period of infancy, childhood, and youth. Most studies have focused on later childhood, schooling, apprenticeship, and advanced socialization, neglecting early childhood as distinct from the teenage experience. In addition, Western studies hardly ever provide materials for considering the regional and historical character of gender as a means for verifying or contradicting what has been uncovered here about early girlhood in late imperial China. Whether deductively or derivatively, many questions may be posed around the theorization of age. Yet, until further detailed studies are complete, these questions and others remain only profound curiosities.

8   Concepts and Realities

If Philippe Ariès had known Chinese and the world of China, he probably would have hesitated before making his assertion that until relatively recent times people had little notion of children or childhood.[1] A casual perusal of China's historical materials leaves one with the unmistakable impression that this was a society wherein close care and nurturing were consciously devoted to the very young. Without considering for the moment sources in medicine and related fields, which are arguably of a technical category, such materials as philosophical deliberations, literary notes, family records, and biographical accounts abound with concerns for and opinions about children. We need not consider whether Ariès or any hermeneutics of mentality would attribute the specific nature of childhood to this wide range of Chinese literature. What we may begin to do is to reveal what Chinese childhoods could have been like, from a normative as well as an experiential perspective, to allow for conceptual and methodological questions posed at more than one level and from more than one perspective. Juxtaposing the construction of childhood from the normative as opposed to the experiential perspective begs the issue of agency and subjectivity in history. In so doing, the familiar, modern notion of an adult-centered-versus-child-oriented discourse must be reexamined under critical consideration, which may open up an understanding of children, childhood, or the course of human life itself, in historical and cultural terms. Furthermore, historical representations of children's lives and childhood culture have to be appraised together with, or against, the process of record generating that had woven together personal experience and subjective private sentiments with retrospective memory, collective mentality, and cultural sanctions. Elements related to microlevel individual existence and those of macrolevel cultural values, institutional setups, and social operations need to be seen thus reinforcing or conflicting with one another in creating and recreating history. Records in history therefore demand a mental exercise of peeling away while piecing together at the same time the "historical" and historiographical effect of each of these social, cultural, and psychological forces. An additional challenge comes when the subjects one deals with are below the age of "legible expression" in writing and speech—a problem constantly faced by modern child psychologists, early education specialists, and pediatricians. With innovative methods or inventive approaches, recorded gestures and facial expressions of young children, the sounds and kicks of small infants that may have intentionally or accidentally entered the texts, should, for example, be carefully evaluated to allow for an approximation of a child's life relived, a return to the sounds and scenes of the young. The academic skills and mental processes involved in such an anterior performance can never be free of questions or doubt, nor should they be exempt from suspicions of ultimate validity. The perspective one gains as a result, however, will always outweigh the limitations and flaws. For one thing, this whole matter of reassessment brings into sharper focus the overassertiveness of the latest science on children and their self-fulfilling prophecy concerning modernity. Infants and children at different times and from different places tell neglected but vital stories that can be equally compelling to the modern social sciences and natural sciences.

The Normative View

Normative statements about children and childhood appeared early, perhaps *too* early, in Chinese history. *The Book of Rites* for instance laid down detailed instructions for the very first phase of human life. As soon as a child takes food or begins to talk, the adults are to initiate him or her in basic matters, such as direction, yin-yang (concepts of contrast and complement), numbers, and social etiquette.[2] As time progressed, such instructions increased in meticulousness. A comparison of *Li-chi*'s model with a later passage from Ssû-ma Kuang's *Miscellaneous Rites for the Family (Chü-chia tsa-i)* gives one an idea of the cumulative process and evolving character of what may be termed China's culture of child cultivation.[3] Before, and certainly after Ssû-ma Kuang, there was never a lack of deliberation about children, the correct attitude toward them, and the methods for teaching them. These writings of "instructive literature" are examples of the assumptive frame concerning children and childhood.

Cautions need to be made, however, so that one does not draw a direct equation between this long heritage of "treatments for juniors" and the modern notion of child rearing or children's culture. To begin with, the "children" (*tzû*) spoken of in the instructive literature, like all junior members of a family, or pupils to a master, were not necessarily understood in any mechanical or biophysical sense as relating to age. That is, the nature, characteristics, strengths, and weaknesses of this "child"—referred to as the *tzû*, or the *yu*, or the *pei*—were not derived from an empirically observed stage in the phase of life as a linear progression nor were they based on any practical consideration of blood kinship. They could hardly carry the standardized implication of age or the life course in a modern sense. Instead, they came from inferences anchored in cultural and ritualistic schemes that emphasized ethical order and social performance over biological reproduction. As principles in social reproduction dictate, the junior (*yu*), the young (*hsiao*), and the child (*tzû*) were prescribed materials for elementary education (*mêng-hsüeh*) by family instructions and targeted by the advice literature for child rearing and youth training. These were the same subjects defined within the patriarchal hierarchy that spoke of having superiors presiding over inferiors and the old over the young. The issue was never simply the modern task of raising and "socializing" children in order for them to become "themselves," to achieve a personal goal in the individualistic sense, but rather, to mold and lead them into a culturally meaningful shape with whatever materials were present at birth. It was about the cultivation, treatment, handling, and nurturing of the upcoming social group (one may also call it the next generation), yet less in a biophysically defined reproductive sense than a socioethnic, ritually transmitting sense before they can assume and take on the status, role, and function of the presiding senior group. In fact, the complete or matured person (*ch'êng-jên*) that appeared as the significant and managing Other to the child or the youth in Chinese had always laid more stress on the "completing," "becoming," or "fulfilling" of the potential incipient in the human development process. It should perhaps never have been rendered or understood as the equivalent of an "adult," especially in the modern Western cultural-linguistic connotation. It is the classical Chinese meaning of the junior in front of the senior that Kuan Tzû addresses at the beginning of the celebrated piece, *The Duties of a Disciple* (Ti-tzû chih). It discusses the obligations of the young (*shao chê chih shih*), which consist mundanely of going to bed late, getting up early, dressing oneself before the master arises, washing and brushing, and running miscellaneous errands whenever needed.[4] Kuan Tzû's "disciples" included young people of various ages who had entered into apprenticeship, though its focus was probably older children or youths. While late imperial family instructions and teaching materials continued to copy and cite *The Duties of a Disciple* as their model and inspiration, the pupils and disciples (*ti-tzû*) were of a much younger age, of a more massive number, from diversified backgrounds, and bound toward a myriad of trades and purposes. This was a far cry from the old days of the ancient aristocratic past. By late imperial times, the emphasis on the same sense of obligations, duty, and propriety had encountered the compelling new challenge of the Wang Yang-ming school's advocacy of men's, or children's, natural inclinations, innate goodness, and individual liberty. In this older school of thought, disciples (read children) in society submitted to masters (read adults). As *The Duties of a Disciple* advised:

What the master teaches, the disciple follows. He [the disciple, almost always a male] should be moderate, gentle, and humble, accepting what is given to him. He should emulate the goodness he sees, and admire the righteousness that he hears. He is to be kind, filial, and with brotherly compassion, never to be overbearing with his gifts. He wants to be void of haughty evil, and to act according to the correct and the straight. He should dwell upon and move about in an amicable manner, to approach and receive influence from the virtuous. He should always dress neatly and pleasantly. His mind should be in the proper place. He should rise early and go to bed late, be attentive that his clothes and belts are properly worn. He should try to improve himself in the morning while continuing to devote himself to learning in the evening and be watchful and prudent at all times.[5]

The piece is obviously part of the normative, classical culture. It tells of the young in terms of "should be" and "ought to," with the anticipation that they submit to parents and teachers. The view differed from the way children "already are" or "can naturally be," as later followers of the Wang Yang-ming school or a modernist would ponder it.

The Adults Envisioned

The instructive literature from the classical orthodox or the late imperial progressives were nevertheless in agreement on one issue: in order for the young to become what they ought to be, the elders responsible for their upbringing and education were to be of the first importance. The pronounced opinion appeared in the form of famed quotations from Ssû-ma Kuang, speaking in the tone of a conscious and conscientious social engineer:

The elders of a family [*chia chang*] must follow the rules strictly to manage and lead the many young and other members in the house. He should assign them duties, give them tasks, and demand from them accomplishments. For all the humble and the young, regardless of matters big or small, they should never act upon their own will; they must submit in all matters to the decision of the family elders.[6]

Ssû-ma was speaking of a time, indeed, when everybody's father ruled. The family elders spoken of here represented the generic "ideal adults" (as complete or completed persons, *ch'êng-jên*), a condition expected of all parents and teachers as a qualification for their social status and practical roles. From this and similar texts, it is clear that such adults were thought to have not only the intelligence and ability to lead and mold the young under all circumstances, but also the maturity to sustain themselves through difficult times. For on adults alone lay the possibility of producing children in keeping with the foreseeable or unforeseeable future of society. The grown-ups imagined in this scheme, therefore, had to be no less a fanciful construction than the children. As a matter of fact, since the character of adults was frankly conceived as less than perfectly ideal, they were also perceived with an endowed ability to compromise or nullify their social mission.

When such irony suggested itself, therefore, the instructive literature in fact exhorted young students to act heroically in the face of fallible parents. In Ssû-ma Kuang's words, following the classical Confucian model, a child who realized that his/her parent had committed an error (*yu-kuo*) had but one choice: to try to remonstrate with him (or her) humbly, with a pleasing expression and a soft voice. In the event that the parent did not respond favorably, the child was still to maintain a respectful and filial attitude. If, later, the parent appeared somehow more amenable toward mending his/her ways, the child could then remonstrate again; if on the other hand, the parent became irritated and grew upset, there was "no need to offend clansmen and neighbors by continuing." Furthermore, should the parents "beat the child to the point of bleeding," still the child should never hold a grudge.[7] Although of a prescriptive nature, the possibility remained that parents, or adults in general, could be the wrongdoers in society, discernible as such even to their own children, and yet recalcitrant enough to reject the children's cautioning, at times to the point of violence.

More seriously, not only could parents or adults commit personal mistakes, they could also give incorrect orders and commands regarding the action of their children. Ssû-ma Kuang, for one, advised children to heed their parents' orders, complete the task efficiently, and report back immediately. In the event that the parents "approached the child with unadvisable instructions [*ming yu pu k'o hsing*]," the latter should try presenting his own view, with as pleasant an appearance and as soft a voice as possible, on how best to distinguish right from wrong and to separate beneficial from harmful thoughts, all the while wishing for, and laboring toward, the parents' understanding. Yet, and here is where an ethical confusion arose, if the parents simply failed to approve of the child's expositions and expostulation, the child should accommodate his parent's orders (*ch'ü ch'ung*), given that it was not a matter of grave harm (*shih wu ta-hai*). The social ill or ethical flaws such actions may produce in real life is a dilemma Ssû-ma Kuang did not pursue. He did, however, note that a child who chose to act upon his own judgment with the conviction that his parents were erroneous would be considered a disobedient child, even if he were to stand on perfectly justifiable ground, making it plain that the old ideal of a harmonious, hierarchical order was essential. So long as social order continued to be envisioned in such a manner, disagreeable qualities of the leader could never be translated into a questioning of his qualification to lead, nor would bad decisions create a right to challenge or a reversal of roles. Ssû-ma Kuang ended the discussion with a bewildering contemplation that "what the child insists upon might not be ultimately correct," leaving behind a disconcerting ethical impasse.

In concept, and by implication, such considerations open up more than one interesting issue. The most significant is the close interconnection, as well as the potential disparity, between the social meaning of the child (as a status and a role vis-à-vis the parents or elders), its narrower biophysical meaning in everyday life (as the earliest phase in one's life course), and its abstract, philosophical connotation (as an existential state and natural quality denoting innocence, purity, and innate goodness).

The Good Children

In traditional Chinese instructive literature, children bore remarkable responsibilities. They were requested not only to comply with parental demands and social requirements but also to be wise enough to distinguish right from wrong (often at a higher order than their elders). Records do not indicate how they became intelligent enough to be aware of parental errors, but children needed to be gentle enough to remonstrate humbly, even at the risk of inviting a good whipping from their dumb, irritated, or ashamed parents. The humanity perceived, and the ethics required here, seen comparatively, are extraordinary. Yet from each of the very young, presumably the most inexperienced members of society, such expectations were held. How does one argue for the innately superior (the child) to be molded by the potentially fallible (the parent)? Further still, through what process and at what point did the child begin to lose such intelligence, goodness, and amicability or become muddle-headed one after another, in time to become the socially corrupted and morally inferior adult?

Latter-day Neo-Confucian thinkers, in fact, had pondered hard on such questions in relation both to early education pragmatically and the nature of children philosophically. Wang Yang-ming, for one, argued for a liberal and liberating attitude toward elementary education, asking people to adopt methods of encouragement and to use materials of enticement (such as rhymes, songs, and ritual activities) to instruct children. He believed working with children provided an opportunity for nurturing and cultivating the innately good, not an occasion for molding and constriction, which he believed led to resentment of teachers and bitterness toward learning.[8] The sixteenth-century radical Li Chih, too, wanted people to recognize a child's heart (t'ung-hsin) as the only true heart (chên-hsin) a person could possibly have. Once this heart became polluted and contaminated by "false" book learning, pretentious social customs, ordinary worldly evil, or civilized self-cheating, a numbing blindness set in. To Li's mind a child was endowed with a good heart, upon which external teaching and acculturation could only produce a superfluous and harmful effect. A person ceased to be a true man (*chên-jên*) the moment he lost the child's heart, the second he left his childhood behind.[9] The false person (*chia-jên*) that took the child's place was the result of this artificial cultivation and deceptive education, the product of which society commonly referred to as an adult.[10]

Such deliberation and debates on children's nature and early education in wishful and rhetorical statements posed subjectively against other observations by various subschools of the acclaimed Wang Yang-ming philosophy of the heart (*hsin hsüeh*) from the mid-Ming onward constituted also a significant sociocultural movement by no means unprecedented in Chinese history or unique in comparative terms. Neither the joyful, curious mind in Wang Yang-ming's scheme, nor the innocent heart in Li Chih's argument, seem any closer to the representation or the ideal of a "real child" than the assumption imagined in Ssû-ma Kuang's or Chu Hsi's disciplinary terms. Historically and cross-culturally, pessimists had always perceived that children should receive proper education from adults, even as they conceded that there were moments when children knew better and acted more agreeably than their elders. Optimists across culture and history, on the other hand, advocated that children were born with a superior purity and precious innocence. Although they also admitted that in the end little could prevent humans from being corrupted by the environment as life moved on. So are children basically inadequate yet in possession of a miraculous potential? Or are they fundamentally good but ultimately doomed?

In Search of Historical Children and Childhoods from the Late Imperial Period

Inquiries into information regarding or related to the lives of real children in traditional China bring back tantalizing variations but also ample incongruity. Ordinary family instructions, for example, asked one to mold and lead children and not to be weighed down by their irritating behavior. In other words, children and childhood in China's long discourse of family presented humanity with coarse and crude forms to be improved and cultivated. Biomedical evidence seen in pediatric texts, on the other hand, tended to emphasize the importance of understanding infants and accepting children as they were, treating them accordingly in a relatively "child-oriented" framework. Paintings depicted children idyllically, at play with toys, pets, and tricks, approaching vendors, enjoying themselves at festivals, or having a mischievous time at the village school while the master napped. In such depictions, the moralists' prohibitions against pets, rowdy play, and physical activities were nowhere to be seen. Hardly is a child shown quietly at a desk or following an elder in neat robes with a bowed head or folded hands, as our Neo-Confucian theorist would have him. Were these simply sights and sounds from different corners, at different moments, presented from a different perspective and for a different purpose? Or could they actually be created and intended as some form of cultural dissent, an aesthetic dig at the serious-minded social mainstream? The autobiographical literature, diaries, poems, and letters, furthermore, remembered childhood days as often filled with delights involving food and play, on the one hand, mixed with the fear of illness, death, loneliness, and frustration, with the pain of punishment and discipline, on the other.[11] These were obviously different cultural discourses, talking over one another in a multifaceted history. The representation, pieced together, shows a picture made up of jigsaw puzzles, not necessarily forming any coherent design.

In treating children's experiences as a legitimate and significant concern in history, we may, in the case of China, want to refrain from mixing accounts of the process relating to growing up with the social and material conditions in which it took place. Therefore we should not substitute the state of children and childhood experience with the attitudes toward, or treatment of, children. This latter investigation and interpretation considers children as the recipient and passive objects of changing rearing practices, varying educational methods, different social mentalities that are really parts of "the history of adults." Instead, we should reflect upon the very character of a "children's view in history," that is, the possibility of including children's understanding of themselves, their feelings and attitudes toward others, their perspectives on matters near or far, and their voices of joy and pain.

Here issues regarding concepts and methodology are inevitably intertwined with questions of substance and source materials. There are clearly different kinds of material available for the study of children. In the case of China, the familiar information includes family instructions, genealogy, teaching materials, and pediatric records. Representations in paintings and crafts also demand consideration, but viewers should bear in mind philosophical and religious movements before arriving at any understanding of the composite and complex world of children. Biographical and autobiographical sources can form an important starting point, yet they should not be employed without properly contextualizing the social and cultural circumstances of their production and reproduction.[12]

A World of Interactions

The changing discourses of children and childhood have long been associated with people's notions of human life (as either having an innately benign nature or being a hopelessly sinful beginning) and assumptions about nature. This should not be a surprise as philosophers Eastern or Western, modern and ancient, have inclined to see children as the beginning of life, as an individual in a purely innocent state. Others, however, identify a child's daily, mundane activities as anything but pliable materials at the disposal of others. In this latter view, neither humanity nor nature is purely naive, passive, or unintentional at the very beginning. Throughout Chinese history, adults of either camp argued and acted upon these views in education, medicine, social ethics, and popular religion. Late imperial Chinese pediatricians, after the eleventh century, believed that frightful, distressful, or unhappy experiences could result in a child's serious illness, in part because they thought he or she usually remained in a state of natural serenity.[13] The thirteenth-century physician Chang Ts'ung-chêng instructed parents to present small infants with toys floating in a water bucket as useful stimuli to an active mind and body since he was convinced that they were receptive and impressionable.[14] Clinical observation and therapeutic experience suggest to other medical experts however that even small infants could be endowed with some kind of a willpower, a character, or at least certain signs of preference and dislikes. Working with, rather than going against, these inklings and attitudes seemed sensible and of benefit to their well-being.

Family records and biographical sources yield concomitant pictures for both views. Records showed that an infant or a child was by no means devoid of personal will, or lacking in self-expression. Ample biographical accounts tell of the difficulties caretakers encountered in nursing. When Shao Hsing-chung's mother failed to nurse the baby herself, her mother-in-law was compelled to look for a wet nurse. "Ten women had to be tried before he finally sucked at a breast."[15] Hsü Nai (1810–1867) provides another example of a baby having trouble with nursing. His family "looked at many women still unable to find anyone suitable." It is interesting that, at the level of both practice and cultural representation, the problem people encountered—retaining suitable nurses—should have been related to the child's preference and response to the nursing.[16] Ts'ên Yü-ying's (1829–1889) mother passed away before Yü-ying reached the age of one. His grandmother ended up feeding him congee because they failed to get any other woman to succeed in nursing him.[17] Family opinions and other factors may have played negatively into these troublesome situations, but the child's own reception or rejection were often observed as the key element that people could not rule out in these decisions. Biographies and family notes mentioned cases of a small child's refusing to nurse, or refusing to eat, seemingly for no obvious reasons. The discursive implication these "difficult kids" represented points toward a society wherein the infant's will was taken as a given.

Late imperial Chinese medical texts and family records speak of small

children who did not want to be weaned. As a result, pediatric and gyne-
cological manuals gave out "recipes for weaning." Medical cases noted examples of children at four and five years of age "who should have been
weaned but rebuffed any such attempts." Biographies describe actual circumstances where children of five, six, or even eight, were still nursing. Children who resisted nursing, feeding, or weaning were described, and to a certain extent recognized, as having "independent" minds of their own.[18] Infants and children were not seen as being devoid of some sort of a will,
whether it was a taste rooted in their original imprint, a preference as part
of their innate character, or an inkling of their individual endowment. Then
as now, people thought that in choosing to eat or sleep, a child was acting
out an intention as a subjective response to his objective physical and social
environment. It is true that the adults around the child might form a vital
part of the human environment, but they were not the sole factor or overwhelming element. The so-called difficult infants, or troublesome children
in Ming-Ch'ing society were considered by many to have a "mind" of their
own. Daily events were the sites of demonstrable communication and performance, when willful interaction could be but ordinary parts of these ne-
gotiations. Seen from this perspective, it mattered less how negligent adults
were, or how "adult-oriented" a society or a culture appeared to have been.
When infants and children were not taken to be passive recipients of rules
and treatment, of socialization and acculturation, the records of their acts
show the impoverishment of modern psychological assumptions and social
theories.

Ssû-ma Kuang, who later dictated model family instructions as an expert
moralist in the Sung, was said as a child to have delighted in food and play
and was known for arguing with his sister about how best to crack walnut
shells. He was depicted as a boy who loved running around. Once, with a
quick wit, Kuang rescued his pal who fell into a tall water crock.[19] The Neo-
Confucian philosopher Chou Tun-i (1017–1073), too, was said to have
liked to fish.[20] The famous Ming scholar-official Hsü Kuang-ch'i (1562–
1633) was also noted for his enjoyment in catching hares as a child.[21] The
great Ch'ing dramatist K'ung Shang-jên (1648–1718), for his part, was said
to like to climb the racks in the garden to snatch gourds to decorate his
room.[22] The late Ch'ing scholar Ch'ên Tung-shu (1810–1883), when about
four, used to play with his sister a lot, keeping birds, feeding fish, and following drama troupes around.[23]

So if even model characters and great names in the same late imperial
Chinese history were not presented as having merely childhoods under restrictive discipline or of the quiet type advocated in Neo-Confucian book
learning, what kind of a social scene or cultural message were they delivering? Chu Hsi's (1130–1200) *Essential Knowledge for School Children*

FIG. 39. "Children Playing in Autumn," artist unknown (Yüan dynasty). In the adult's portrayal of childhood, children frequently project a childlike innocence independent of their gender, region, or class. Thus, children at play became a common motif in traditional paintings of children. Although Confucian philosophers such as Chu Hsi advocated that children be self-disciplined, frugal, and avoid nonsensical activities (indulging in snacks, playing games, or keeping pets), such themes did not disappear from Chinese art. Courtesy of the National Palace Museum, Taiwan, Republic of China.

(*T'ung-mêng hsü-chih*) cautioned children "that they should not go near the hustle and bustle. Never gamble, keep birds or pets, play with balls, fly kites, or be involved in any such useless activities [*wu-i chih-shih*]."[24] Ts'ui Hsüeh-ku's *Instruction for the Young* (*Yu hsün*) also prohibited "catching bugs, treading upon ants, snatching flowers, or playing games [*tso wan*, literally,

FIG. 40. "Market in the Spring" (Ch'un-shih t'u), by Ting Kuan-p'êng (Ch'ing dynasty). The general festivals of the Chinese or markets were places where people of all generations enjoyed themselves together. This picture shows the old and the young going out, chatting with each other, and watching the entertainment, including a puppet show. Courtesy of the National Palace Museum, Taiwan, Republic of China.

having fun]."[25] But on the other hand, celebrated Sung paintings portrayed children at play (ying-hsi t'u), children surrounding venders (huo-lang t'u), and children in festivals and markets (ch'un-shih t'u). Does the historical record suggest troops of children taking to the outdoors in their gentle or boisterous play? Does such a picture argue for the existence and prevalence of a "children's culture" since medieval times? Should modern intellectual assumptions be adopted at all in evaluating young lives in late imperial China?

To help us wrestle with such questions, evidence from Ming-Ch'ing sources presents information of a bewilderingly broad range and wide variety. Elders indulged, praised, and admired children's inclinations, hinting at a more "lax" attitude some had toward child training that was quite different from that depicted in instructive literature with uninhibited approbation. The famous Ming official Hsü P'u's (1428–1498) uncle, for instance, often spoke admirably of a child he knew who loved to sing beautifully.[26] The sixteenth-century novelist Wu Ch'êng-ên (1504–1582), who produced Journey to the West (Hsi-yu chi), was noted also as a child who loved to draw animals on the whitewashed walls in the house.[27] So a few "perfect boys" might stand out in this society to confirm orthodox theories about a stylized and formulaic childhood under the Neo-Confucian ideal, even though a general survey quickly reveals a mixed sociocultural discourse that accepted childhoods of a far more complex, fluid, and lively kind.

Such pondering begs conceptual and methodological reflection of early childhood education. For every well-bred, precocious, and diligent lad who appeared in the first pages of famous men's biographies, there were many more children in number and in representation who failed miserably and hopelessly, or simply were ordinarily unintelligent (*pu hui*). Thriving beneath the rigid formality of conformity in social acts or in literary recordings was the mass of boys and girls in Ming-Ch'ing China whose inappropriate interests, unconventional hobbies, and usual "problems" taxed the patience of elders who would sooner overlook the mediocre reality. The late Ming loyalist Chang Huang-yen (1620–1664) was said to have a passion for songs and verses. His father, "worrying that [Chang's interests] might get in the way of [his study in] classics and history, often warned against it." Though merely eight, Chang had managed to "immerse himself secretly in them."[28] The early Ch'ing scholar Shao Hsing-chung's grandfather, in bringing him up, made sure too that "non-Confucian books [*fei ju chih shu*] would not be seen."[29] So, on the other hand, the more strict aspect of late imperial elite culture was known for its disapproval of licentious literature, songs, stories, novels, plays, and even poetry and history that could be placed off-limits to the young. Fang Pao (1665–1749), at six, used to have to wait until his father was out in order to read his favorite history books.[30] Yin Chao-yüng tried the same but was discovered by his father and given a severe beating.[31] Wang K'ai-yün (1832–1916) regretted later that his early passion for *The Songs of Ch'u* (*Ch'u tz'u*) was nipped in the bud. This prevented him, he claimed, from pursuing other kinds of reading.[32] Yet, as with social misfits, reports about the personal characters of "stubborn" or "mischievous" children of any kind were not made without a trace of admiration and approval. Therefore not only were the qualities of living and struggling children beneath the normative surface preserved in a contradictory manner, the social environment that bred and tried to deal with them was also seen in its ambivalent complexity. By the same token, children were thought not only to be born with varied intelligence and particular aptitudes, but also had distinguishable personal traits before the onset of indoctrination. Here no one began, to be sure, as a clean slate upon which adults and society might write at will.

This complicated assumption of the natural endowment of humanity, moreover, did not necessarily (or was not understood to) carry a built-in class prejudice. Peasant boys and artisan lads were not expected to be deeply involved in social etiquette or book learning, but their social isolation amid nature allowed them to develop manners and avoid moral corruption. Parents and elders of lower-class families were noted therefore to have asked their children to be obedient, reliable, hard working, and not to make trouble or to invite disaster. Swimming or playing in ponds and rivers, for instance, was frowned upon. The anti-T'aip'ing general Lo Ssû-chü (1764–1840) came from an ordinary peasant family. While young, he almost drowned himself three times playing in the water. After each rescue a severe beating followed.[33] Physical adventure and love for food and play were assumed to be at the core of a child's being, regardless of their social standing. Reform-minded moralists perceived restriction in this regard as a unifying factor that put children on an equal footing against the shifting adults at the other end of the social spectrum. Hsü Nai was reported as being physically weak and often ill but liked to have fun. Wrestling with his brothers however resulted in a flogging for everybody.[34] Wang Hui-tsu's enjoyment of jokes and humor earned him the same treatment from his grandfather.[35]

Enjoyment and fun continued to be presented as the concealed world of the young lurking behind orthodox child-rearing models of late imperial China. Chu Hsi used to admonish youth that "when it comes to food and drink, [they ought to] receive what is available, and not to desire or beg [for what is not there]. There should be congee and rice to fill one's stomach, but [they should] never fight for more or be allowed to choose the favorite over the disliked dish."[36] Lü Tê-shêng's *Words for Little Children* instructed the little ones to try to control their physical needs or material preferences, not to demand good food or pretty clothing: "Those with full stomachs and warm clothes who run around with silly words and useless games have nothing but confused and delirious days, [leading lives] worse than cows or horses."[37] *Rules for the Pupil (Ti-tzû kuei)* required that students not be choosy when it came to eating or drinking, and to take only the appropriate amount.[38] *Instruction for the Young (Yu hsün)* said that young people should satisfy their hunger mostly with congee.[39] But biographical literature continued to flood people with tales of active children having a ball fighting over snacks. For those taking note of these scenes, the highbrow expectations in everybody's mind seemed to function as the best cultural background to present individual, interesting characters. As mentioned above, Ssû-ma Kuang had serious discussion with his sister about cracking walnuts.[40] Seven-year-old Shao Hsing-chung too was scolded for grabbing the dates at a family mourning ritual.[41] Yet, mixed with these moral tales were the humorous and ironic stories of parents, grandparents, tutors, and examiners who used material rewards and snacks as the recognized "lure." As, in the example of Niu Yün-chên's (1706–1798) grandfather, honey was given to the little Niu whenever good memorizing work was accomplished (despite Niu's constant trouble with a toothache).[42] These elders appeared to accept a child's natural inclination for food and sweets as legitimate tastes and a convenient motivating force. For them and the social act that they represent, voices from instructional literature did not merely confirm the gap that usually existed between lofty ideas and daily reality; they taught

all the human ways to work daily matter out, thus affirming a deeper una-
nimity beneath.

So for the educated of this period, what was the average childhood like?
It was said that Lu Shan-chi (1575–1636) was "born with a serious and
solemn outlook, never taking part in play."[43] Huang Tao-chou (1585–
1646) "appeared graceful at a young age, took no pleasure in any of the ordinary things, being inordinately quiet," and preferring "always to be by
himself."[44]

People familiar with the political, social, economic, military, intellectual,
or religious history of late imperial China will recognize immediately many
of the protagonists in the above-cited stories. All left impressive marks in
their later years on history, one way or another. The fact that we have to resort to (accidental) biographical information on the early years of "great"
or "important" figures (heroes or villains) tells us much about the adult-
oriented and "functional" nature of history and historical pursuits as well
as the very "utilitarian" and "calculating" approach societies have taken to
children and childhood. Few families of these infants or children were truly
obscure, although varied career choice patterns and increased social mobility (both upward and downward) meant that these children, and the adults
they later became, represent sociologically a multistrata and cross-regional
group for this period. In any event, both the food-indulging, fun-loving, and
active (the "natural" by the liberation-centered modern standard) kids and
the seriously virtuous, model children represented through a premodern
outlook an evolving image of childhood that was at once lively and confined
both in practice and in representation. The social fabric that produced
and/or accommodated such multiplicity and fluidity came from an intellectual heritage and everyday custom that calls for "contextualization" concerning childhood and children's culture that would take into consideration
both the complex and changing social life of obscure existences (children
and childhood as an "objective" phenomenon) and the multifaceted and
conflicting discursive culture (the depiction and discussion on such matters
as a constantly evolving subjective force). At the same time, this very attempt may throw a reflective light back at the oftentimes discerning character of historiographical undertakings (in concept and in methodology) as
an inept attempt to meet up with this peculiar challenge of making sense of
and bringing together both the objective and the subjective, the at once rational and emotive aspects of humanity.

Stories often showed that model children were able to control themselves
in spite of the lure of noise and fun from the outside. Yin Hui-i (1691–1745)
at five was commanded to contain himself and "not to play with the rest of
the children."[45] Ma Hsin-i (1821–1870), while young, "was of a quiet character, and did not like to play." At the village school, when some famous
personage was passing through and his schoolmates were distracted, he was

said to be the only one to remain in his seat.[46] Wang Hsin (1825–1857) as a child also "declined to venture out."[47] Yet, without the actions of their undistinguished, but no less representative, counterparts in groups and crowds, the special character of these inactive model children would not stand out. Without the background of children at play, how else could the self-contained child appear praiseworthy? In other words, this narrative, not necessarily a result of complete fabrication, tells us both how society and biographers believed perfect children and commendable childhoods could be made to distinguish themselves from the common crowd, and what could be made of their lives. The mentality behind the words was namely part of the force that was driving and performing the reality in a not always seamless collaboration.

If one follows the Wang Yang-ming philosophy or the Taoist advocacy in believing that adultlike seriousness was a result of training, not of innate goodness, why or how might society continue to reward and credit the achievements of most children for their natural attributes? The Ch'ing philologist Ts'ui Shu's parents followed their son around beginning with his first steps, determined that "he would not play with other children."[48] In this depiction, Tsui did not seem to be staying behind because of his own will; the act was a hard-won achievement of his parents, against the "liberal" trends and other justifying social inclinations at the time. The famous statecraft thinker Wei Yüan was said to have been "a child of few words or smiles." By five or six, he was "sitting alone a lot." Outside, the family dogs barked furiously at him, as though he were a stranger.[49] How should historical figures and scenes like these be related to the various evaluating and propagating forces lurking in their background, in the context of contemporary cultural, philosophical, religious, even physiological and medical debates, for them to have achieved status as anecdotes of the extraordinary? Tsêng Kuo-fan came from an established gentry family. He was praised as an unusually composed boy who would occupy himself by watching the movements of the weaving machine, standing by the working woman with a shy smile "like that of a girl."[50] Self-motivated and well-mannered children, from virtuous families, surely there were, yet they were also made to bear more of the burden (real or imagined) of cultivation and social liability in place of the large, blurred majority. Biographies want us to remember the child sitting solemnly in the classroom rather than the many more who were outside raising hell in the same picture, but not without due appreciation of the ambiguity and mixed sentiments in both situation and representation.

The Circles of Life

At an early age Chinese children were taught to learn and to recognize the reciprocity of their roles in the family and in society. Adults were

represented as being committed to raising children properly so as to continue the clan and promote prosperity, and concomitantly children appear
to have assumed their duties as necessary correlates in this social enterprise.
It was hoped that they would understand their place and gradually fulfill
the long line of "shared responsibility and the countless daily acts." For example, the Ming general Ch'i Chi-kuang's (1528–1589) father warned him
against ruining luxury when he was said to have showed a liking for silk
shoes.[51] Ho Hui-kao (1865–1930) is reported as having studied hard for the
civil service examination, "knowing that nothing else could bring satisfaction to his father."[52] Wang Hui-tsu's two mothers—his formal stepmother
and his biological mother—would implore the young boy to work hard in
his study, lecturing the fatherless boy that "there is really no other way for
you to make it in this world, in which case your father shall have no worthy descendant, and the two of us would rather die than continue living."[53]
Such speech and petition would be of no avail unless children were perceived as subjective agents who could be made to understand larger duties
and to act upon them, in spite of their spontaneous fun-loving instinct and
inclination to innocence, which might have favored other choices.

From letters and essays of the nineteenth century, in fact, one encounters
references to a child's ability to identify with group goals and to share collaborative burdens. Tuan Hsi-p'êng (1897–1948) went out to get loans for
his impoverished family.[54] Peasant children, such as Ts'ai T'ing-k'ai (1892–
1968) and Ho Lien (1895–1975), were accustomed to helping their fathers
and grandfathers in the fields.[55] Hsüeh Kuang-ch'ien (1910–1978) while
young was said to have realized the implications of a business setback in his
father's wine industry.[56] Not all children were assumed to be able to respond
with the same degree of duty, lest the moral in the tale should lose its effect.
But children's spontaneous engagement and participation in the larger
world of the adults also showed them to have a will of their own, occupy-
ing and securing a place in family and sociocultural networks vital in composing the great circles of life, materially and spiritually, by nature and by
choice. In other words, in this scheme of things, innocence may be the natural attribute that defines the very essence of a child and his or her childhood, but a youngster demonstrating an ability to transcend his natural
limitations was recognized as precious and exceptional.

Another area that reveals the meaningfulness of children's broader participation concerns their support and care of elders. Conventional biographies no doubt impress readers with stories of adult devotion to their young
in trying circumstances. But the same story is often discernable from the opposite side. For example, as the demographics of premodern China dictate
high mortality for both young and old, the young frequently lost their parents and others close to them, just as adults kept on losing their infants and

children.[57] More than a few, like the Ming essayist Kuei Yu-kuang (1506–1571), composed prose and verse that expressed the shock and grief they received as a child with the death of parents. In his mourning essay composed for his mother, Kuei not only remembered vividly his mother's daily bond with her seven children but also confessed that the thought of having abruptly lost the intimate relationship filled him with ever recurring remorse. As a child he had been shattered by his mother's death, he confessed, and as a man he longed for any bits of information on her life, which, he claimed, brought tears to his eyes.[58] Wung Shu-yüan, as quoted before, told a similar story of bereavement.[59] Hsia Ching-ch'ü lost his father when he was seven. Years later, he said he could still recall the impact of the funeral, with his mother recovering from recent childbirth, wearing a raw linen mourning gown and his infant sister crawling around the straw mat unattended.[60] Liu Pao-nan, whose father died when Pao-nan was five, later wrote about how the family's livelihood suffered as a result, and how his mother worked hard to overcome her grief.[61] Struggling through harsh luck or memorable times together, as discussed in Chapter 5, forged a special sense of solidarity and a "bond." In any event, in their own memory, and in the collective memory of late imperial China, children could be represented as experiencing ups and downs more deeply and sensitively than the adults around them.

For the numerous children devastated by the loss of a loved one, or showing anxieties about the sickness in the family, the observation of their reactions eradicate any remaining doubt that they or their culture might be identified as but innocent receivers of events. The late Ming philosopher Li Yung (1627–1705) was a teenager when his father was killed in battle leaving behind his mother, who wanted to take her own life. The young Li was said to have grabbed at his mother's girdle, pleading for her to stay. Weeping, he returned her to her senses saying that he would in turn have no choice but to sacrifice his life over hers, thereby ending the family line.[62] As discussed earlier, the Ch'ing grand secretary Li Kuang-ti prayed for his father's hernia.[63] Ying Chao-yüng sought divine intervention from the deity on behalf of his father's illness.[64] Chu Tz'u-ch'i resorted to long sessions of kowtowing and praying for his father's health.[65] The relationship that existed between elders and children was understood, depicted, and no doubt often acted out as a construction of connected reciprocity, which cannot but yield a twisted picture, if rendered in one-dimensional polarity, of either adult-oriented hierarchy or child-centered modernity.

This support and sentiment children showed for and shared with their parents can also be extended to other familial or social relations. Huang Shu-lin (1672–1756) was observed as being saddened by his grandmother's dislike of his mother.[66] Chiang Tun-fu (1808–1867) took it to heart, too, that his mother was "not received well by her mother-in-law."[67] It was recorded that other children took life's miseries no more easily or passively. The late Ming political leader Chang P'u was born of a mother who used to be a maid, which brought poor treatment from the nastier of his clansmen. One day, witnessing his father's suffering from his uncle's servants, Chang swore that "if this enmity is not one day revenged I shall not be called the son of a man." When his father died, the teenaged Chang managed to move his despised mother out of the residence of the spiteful paternal clan— an ironic reversal of the famed story of Mencius's mother thrice moving from bad neighborhoods for her son's sake.[68] The late Ch'ing reformer T'an Ssû-t'ung, the son of his father's first wife, could not but be depressed over his father's falling in with a young concubine. When Ssû-t'ung was seven, his mother decided to leave their house in the capital for their old residence hundreds of miles to the south in Hunan, ostensibly to arrange for the marriage of his elder brother. The young Ssû-t'ung, as mentioned before, knew full well what was taking place and insisted upon seeing his mother off. As her carriage went out of sight, T'an "had tears filling up in his eyes, though he kept them from falling down his cheeks." The emotional frustration and the bitterness within the boy prevented him from opening his mouth for more than half a year.[69] Discord among mothers and daughters-in-law, fighting among a man's wives and concubines, and jealousy among relatives were all familiar themes in Chinese society. Children were shown, or themselves reported, having survived these experiences, bearing the pains and sustaining group solidarity in due course. Childlike naiveté, the *t'ien-chên* that aroused admiration, envy, and debate among generations of Taoist naturalists, radical Neo-Confucianists, and other-worldly Buddhists, not withstanding, late imperial Chinese social portraiture presents a bewildering array of deeply complex and at times profoundly disturbing cultural images of the world of adults and children in their "undelivered" state, untouched by the call of emancipation or a psychoanalytical understanding.

It is also known that parents and elders could consult their children about personal matters. Wang Hui-tsu's father, traveling with the nine-year-old boy on a boat, talked intimately about the tough luck he was having making a living, about the frustration of seeking small jobs, and about the sad trip they were both making yet again to seek help. The conversation, reportedly, moved both father and son to tears.[70] Chao Yü-ching, when forced to return to their grandparent's after losing his father at six, always knew how to "throw himself on the ground, sobbing alone ahead of the rest," until their grandmother's mood changed.[71] Parents revealed their inner thoughts, the bleak and depressing ones along with the less mentioned better times, to their young as they and their children together belonged to a circle made of mutually liable and reliable companionship in an age that understood individuality, intimacy, and personal rewards within their homestead, as defined in its own terms.

In the Eyes of the Young

To appreciate the lot of children, it is imperative to try to see from their viewpoint and feelings or to consider the feasibility of such an endeavor. Chinese culture and Chinese biographies at first glance lend little hope for such an investigation. The supposedly patriarchal, hierarchal, and formal structure of that society permitted little in the way of lively reflections and rarely documented daily feelings of any age stratum in detail. Although certain hidden characteristics and the embedded texture of these materials could disclose unexpected signs, beyond uniform eulogies and stifling formality. One may in fact learn to detect children's views, within and among themselves, toward the people and events around them, especially toward parents and family matters. Their views are not necessarily as comforting or respectful as the homilies had it or as the moral literature would like us to believe.

The Ch'ing grand secretary Li Hung-tsao (1820–1897), for instance, wrote of his father's cowardly character. Once, when Hung-tsao was four, the biographer recorded, his father saw his servant struck down by lightening. So shattered, he had to quit his job as a local official. Fleeing to their residence in the capital, he "fell down with a sickness of the mind." In the process, the father left behind dozens of family members in Kuei-lin with no arrangements or plans whatsoever. In the end, Li's mother was forced to pawn her clothes and hire carts and boats to take everybody home.[72] Wang K'ang-nien (1860–1911), too, spoke of his father as someone who was "inexperienced in the bureaucratic lifestyle, never successful due to his rigid and snobbish habits." To make up for this shortcoming, and to get on a better footing, family jewels were sold to purchase a lucrative position for him, which would allow an easy and early retirement. According to the information his son's biographer was able to discover, here was a father who wanted to be "spared the tough competition in the administration." The plan unfortunately was sabotaged when the middleman ran away with their money. The loss sent Wang's father into a deep depression, thereafter he became "a flimsy soul, sinking deeply into sadness." Wang, only five at the time, observed the unfolding of events not without a sense of irony.[73] The ambivalence that this biographical literature purposefully or unintentionally contained, the ambivalence that the children consciously or unconsciously remembered about their supposedly dutiful yet often dysfunctional elders, and above all the very ambiguous social space that Chinese culture allowed for both attributes to be put on display entails more layers of con-

structed sentimentality and interlocking ethics than can be thoroughly considered here. Suffice it to say that there was never a shortage of ill-per-
forming, failing adults in either objective documents like Chinese biographies and family records or subjective revelations such as personal letters,
poems, or self-narratives. The salient fact is that children seemed quite
aware of, and were granted the liberty to act upon, the unpleasant reality,
even at a young age. Youngsters were reported as having dealt with these
matters alone, developing perceptions in the process of their own recognition of the unbrilliant, incapable, and less-than-brave elders, who were witnessed running away from obligation and deserting families and social
responsibilities.

Many children, we are told, therefore learned at an early point in life
to rely on themselves and to meet hardship on their own terms. Chu Yün
(1729–1789) and his younger brother swore to study hard after their
mother passed away. They slept and rose together, reading classical prose
deep into the night, hand copying and memorizing until the cock crowed.[74]
Chao Yü-ching made the resolution to "surpass all his schoolmates" after
his father died when he was six.[75] Some of this "willpower of orphans" (ku-
êrh chih chih) represents, of course, standard products of normative Confucian ethics enhanced by social reinforcement. Beneath the surface of self-
motivation and high morality, children were seen as active agents with their
own willpower, as bearers of subjective sentiments of determined acts and
"independent" responses. They revealed at times an understanding and
sense of obligation related to their particular age and social circumstances.
The young Wang Hui-tsu heard about his family's dark moments listening
to his father's talk of failure and humiliation. When his father died, the more
predatory among his clansmen came pressing for money from this weaker
branch of the group that included his widowed natural mother and his formal stepmother. Whenever the two widows failed to satisfy the exacting demands, strongmen would come and grab Hui-tsu literally from the arms of
his mother and hold the boy hostage.[76] When Hsüeh Kuang-ch'ien's father's
brewery suffered a setback, the boy said, "[I] felt a heavy burden immediately thrown upon me which propelled me to work harder from then on,
daring not to take any break."[77] Children reported, or were spoken of, as
not only capable of comprehending and absorbing family calamities but
also being resilient enough to contribute their own strength and labor. The
very young in late imperial China could be made—or looked up to as—
pillars that weathered storms and supported the emotional and practical
needs of their elders.

The adults in children's lives, furthermore, could appear more than simply feeble, pitiable, or vulnerable; at times they could be cruel and outright
rotten. The renowned Ch'ing scholar Chang Hsüeh-ch'êng remembered the

people who filled the days of his childhood when he was two or three. A maternal uncle used to come to take him wandering. Usually the uncle ended up coaxing liquor from neighborhood shops. The uncle habitually poured some down his nephew's throat. This, Chang later conceded, was the root of his life-long suffering from alcoholism. A few years later, starting his student life, Chang was dealt another blow. The village schoolteacher was a creature of uncommon incompetence and vice. None of the children escaped his curses or floggings. After one horrendous beating, Chang later revealed, a fellow student name Sun passed out and almost died.[78] Thus, late imperial Chinese children not only came from a society that heaped abuse and beatings on them, they also lived in a culture that somehow created the atmosphere that trusted their judgment and survival as a young individual. Similar difficulties and brutality in changing social sentiment and historical contexts were to generate a separate discourse that would soon make room for, or manufacture, a more explicit movement that proposed to represent the voice and position of the underlings.

Even in the earlier conditions of Ming-Ch'ing times, this burbling consciousness was nourished by conventional warmth mixed with timeless naiveté. When Chu Tz'u-ch'i (1807–1881) was four, his biography has it that his mother asked what he desired for his life. Unencumbered by expectations, the boy responded that "so long as everyone loves me, I shall be happy."[79] The story of Liang Chi half a century later provides an interesting contrast. Liang's formal mother used to "lecture to him and encourage him to make something of himself and become a great person" as he got back from school and was memorizing his homework. "Then quite devoid of any ambitions," Liang later admitted, "I had only petty and unworthy replies for her," which "sent her dropping [his] books and breaking into tears." This formal mother, endowed with the duty of instruction, would go to the boy's natural mother, her sleeve covering up her face in shame, squealing that life had dealt them such despair that this depraved child of theirs should turn out to be so hopeless.[80] Many knew that an unmistakable gap could open up between the young and the old. Various instruction manuals attempted to bridge this, indicating ways to orient children toward worthy goals. Outpourings from moralists and educators presupposed that children in their temporary state could nevertheless embody, or manifest, personal attributes different from the adults that they would one day become, and that they could possibly arrive at and live through the transitory stages of life somehow holding on to these particular perceptions.

What constituted the special perspective and peculiar sentiment that belonged to or represented this age or status? How was it related to the experiences or station of children? From a variety of evidence, it seems that there was a conviction that children's views derived from something more than

accidental encounters or random individual sentiments. Activities particular to this age and status group, such as picking fruit, fighting over snacks,
flying kites, and swimming in ponds, mixed with the special attributes of a
mental and emotional state, were sources of formation, people thought,
leading toward a philosophical and existential quality defined as "a child."
Toys and children's rhymes and stories point to a world filled with motion
and noise. Personal biographies speak of the young living their lives in
groups and with a sense of togetherness. Wu Wei-yeh (1609–1671) once
wrote about four or five friends with whom he "shared the same alley,
learned from the same teacher, and therefore always hung out together and
ate in each other's company." These childhood companions remained, he
said, his associates for over five decades, having formed life-long bonds.[81]
Hung Liang-chi followed his mother to live with his maternal grandparents
in the Wu-chin district of Kiangsu province after his father died when he
was six. That same year, the boy Huang Ching-jên also returned to live with
his paternal grandfather on the other side of the same river after his father
died. Fate brought together the two boys, three years apart, both having just
recently lost their fathers. "From meeting at ferrying times, [we] became acquaintances." Empathy for each other's sad destiny tightened the mutual
grip on two young hearts. At a young and impressionable age, the helplessness they felt owing to similar circumstances gave special depth and affinity
to their comradeship. The special tie that helped them console each other as
childhood pals formed the basis for a lasting friendship after they grew up.
Even though, soon thereafter, Huang's mother took him back to his paternal home, therefore ending the daily company between the two drifting
boys, a life-long affection had been secured.[82]

The Voice of the Young

The many toys discovered in archeological excavations and those exhibited in museums and private collections represent but a small fraction of
the material traces of a lost world of uproarious activities. The special genre
in Chinese painting called "children at play" (ying-hsi t'u) gives, in its stylized compositions, embellished clues of the type of play children had in their
ordinary activities. Children revealed their enchantment when engaged with
peddlers as depicted in "traveling vendors'" (huo-lang t'u) pictures. Several
traditional plays also told of "child heroes" to amused and excited audiences, young and old. The brave and self-sacrificial Mu-lien in "Mu-lien
Saves His Mother" (Mu-lien chiu-mu), the spirited and rebellions Nuo Cha
in "Prince Nuo Cha Stirring up the Sea" (Nuo Cha nao-hai), and Monkey
King (Sun wu k'ung) in Journey to the West all capture the robustness and
innocence of their protagonists in spirit, together with a youthful energy and
childlike naughtiness. There were countless songs (more than two hundred

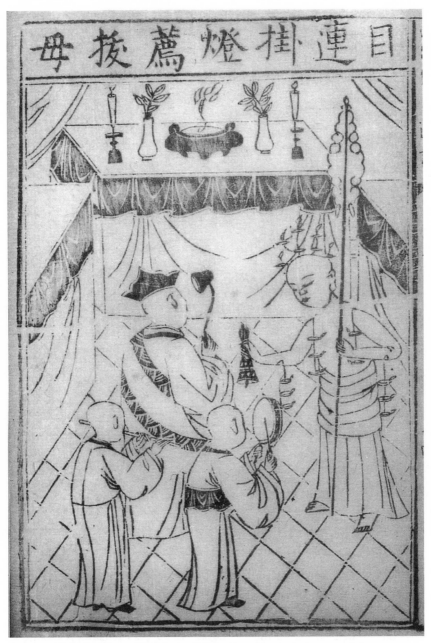

FIG. 41. "Mu-lien Saves His Mother" (Mu-lien chiu-mu) was one of the most popular themes among children's entertainment in late imperial China. Here is a woodblock representation of an episode in this famed Chinese Buddhist story. Reprinted from National Central Library ed., *Hsi-ch'ü Hsiao-shuo Hsüan-ts'ui* (Taipei: National Central Library, 2000), p. 73.

FIG. 42. "Prince Nuo Cha Stirring Up the Sea" (Nuo Cha nao-hai) was another well-known and well-liked story from traditional Chinese literature that had gripped the hearts of young and old alike. Here is an artistic representation of the fiery rebellious boy from the late imperial period. As included in Chou Hsin-hui, ed., *Ku Pên Hsiao-shuo Tu-lu* (Beijing: Hsüeh-yüan, 2000), p. 358.

FIG. 43. Some imaginative materials from Chinese traditional literature, such as "Monkey King" (Sun wu k'ung) in *Journey to the West*, represent the perceived view of the disposition and character of children. It was also a most familiar and admired character of youthful mischief in late imperial China. Reprinted from Chou Hsin-hui ed., *Ku Pên Hsiao-shuo Tu-lu* (Beijing: Hsüeh-yüan, 2000), p. 379.

in the category of "children's ditties" [*t'ung-yao*] are included in the twenty-four Chinese official histories), rhymes, verses, and stories that were labeled as being created by or for children. These material objects, artistic depictions, and literary creations with childhood-related motifs hinted at an environment wherein people understood youthful years as a particular phase, and thus infants and children a different category of social existence. They also recognized that children tended to carry with them character traits and personality qualities associated with their inexperienced status as social novices (innocence, purity, care-free attitudes, gaiety) that were at variance with older members of the population. Moreover, this incipient, inferior, obedient, or submissive role had a complicated, complementary nature in relation to their immature status in the biophysical state, on the one hand, and a happy, naive, and genuine sentimentality, on the other.

Individual biographical data and random self-narratives contain or disclose a child's "voice" (whether as daily utterance, occasional verbal expression, or ideas in action). Pao Shih-ch'en's (1775–1855) biography tells us that studying Mencius while young made a deep impression on him. It also upset him that all the bureaucrats he knew fell quite below the Mencian standard, which made the boy want to turn politics around and put Mencius into practice when he grew up.[83] Wang Hsin (1825–1857) was seven years old when his father, hearing the news that a candidate from their village passed the civil service examination, asked him half seriously about whether he might harbor any envy at heart. To which Wang allegedly responded: "Regarding examinations, these are things beyond one's control. I only wish that someday everybody may benefit from my good work; that is what really interests me!"[84] These were obviously model and stereotypical gestures, yet they suggested the world that produced them, which literally or philosophically conceded to the possibility of a child's intellect and a youthful will. The child Ma Hsin-i (1821–1870) was said to be studying at school one day when eminent officials passed by. When all the other school children ran after the procession for a peek, only Ma sat motionless. When asked why, he replied: "Dropping one's study to fight for a look at others, how can it compare with working harder now so as to let others admire me later?"[85] Portraits of brilliance somewhat overdrawn, these were nevertheless children who were assumed to have had a determination and character of their own, not entirely copies of model adults or indoctrination in the abstract. They were perceived and recorded as historical characters imbued with preference and choice, even though the views expressed might sound disturbingly like duplicates of the received Confucian formula. The priorities and options so revealed, moreover, were meant to leave traces of individual dispositions as well as the evidence of continuous interaction and negotiation between a young person's inner motivations as they unfolded within circumscribed cultural spheres.

In recorded children's views packaged within prescribed ideal types as examples of "good offspring," where does the possibility lie of recovering anything related to historical childhood? Surely, the examples cited noted children aiming at something worthwhile. Other instances tend to aggravate the problem of narrative and representation, particularly when children were documented as speaking, remembering, and paying tribute to their parents. Ku Yen-wu disclosed that he was determined to be a loyalist because of his mother's request.[86] Hsia Ching-ch'ü told people he missed his father, who used to add rice to his bowl, carry him around, and allow him to play with his beard. This senior Mr. Hsia even gave up drinking out of his son's urging.[87] Liu Pao-nan's mother led him to walk with her own hands, fed him medicine with her own tongue, and tearfully beat him when he failed.[88] Tso Tsung-t'ang could not—and in fact was not allowed to— forget his mother's difficulty in nursing him with masticated rice.[89] The Buddhist monk Hsü Yün (1840–1959) murmured that his mother died giving birth to him.[90] Chang Yü (1865–1937) told of his father's stingy habit of saving in order to buy a few books for him.[91] Mo Tê-hui showed his endearment for his mother by nicknaming himself after the red willow tree she used to nurse him under.[92] All these stories, as suggested before, seem to be repeating familiar themes in a culture that prizes filial piety founded on family loyalty. Even if the various scenes and noises can be "sanitized" and "cleaned up," so the narratives appear less consciously pretentious, the sources of trouble come as much from the inquirer as the inquired. If both the lives of children and the discourse of childhood, which formulates and presents them, come from the same sociocultural ecosystem, are we left with any intellectual scheme that allows us to take on both social practice and its representational products? In fact, the interactive and interconnected relationship between narratives, representation and social life, and daily existence begs for a nuanced, multifaceted approach to the formation of children and childhood culture.

Of course, the question of whether children's feelings and expressions were mere redundant repetition or extensions of those of adults remains. As junior and dependent members of society, they were subjected to endless mental manipulation and influence. However, no individual or group exists in a vacuum. The youngest infants and children, like other obvious "dependents" of society, may live to a higher degree as recipients of tangible assistance. But even the most powerful and seemingly "autonomous" members of humanity operate as dependents and receivers of the people, forces, and institutions surrounding them. The weakest of weaklings, the lowest of the underclass, viewed from a less hegemonic angle, produce influences just the same, albeit of a different kind. Internalization and socialization, furthermore, never stops at any age; the ideas and conduct of adults might not be any more "mature," "accountable," or "fixed" in themselves so as to warrant any more serious attention or any less ambivalent suspicion.

This lack of information on children in words or deeds appears therefore to be mostly arbitrary. Chang P'u's bitter revolt against his father's clansmen is one example of an unusual or nonconformist act. The late Ming thinker Huang Tsung-hsi saw his father's faction in vicious fights against a eunuch's party and vowed to take revenge when he grew up.[93] Yang Jên-shan (1837–1911) was another boy who found himself unable to condone the conventions of society. He was born as the only son among five daughters and enjoyed tender care and indulgence. Yet from his early years, Yang said he always argued against the unfair treatment given to his sisters.[94] Early twentieth century revolutionary Hu Han-min (1879–1936) witnessed his father dying from the malpractice of a quack doctor and resented that he could not take the offender to court with his youthful hands.[95] These children were either outraged by the persecution and injustice their parents and siblings suffered or wanted to right the wrongs in society and its practices. Their ideas and reactions were not those strictly prescribed by tradition and thus could not be said to have matched perfectly with expectations. The adults on their side, furthermore, were either victims or weak and vulnerable, thereby quite incapacitated to serve as models or leaders or to set a straight course for their young. In any event, the reactions and responses from these youthful actors were too obvious and distinct, either in words or acts, to gain any single interpretation or historical—even psychological—configuration.

Other youngsters took action to make their disagreement and repulsion known. The early Ch'ing thinker Yen Yüan (1635–1704) had to go find his biological father thousands of miles away.[96] Hsüeh Kuang-ch'ien opted for schooling between six and twelve, despite his weak physical condition, because he felt that "life at home was far too complicated. One can never move without stirring up jealousy or receiving blame. It was so much worse compared to the freedom we gained at school."[97] General Ts'ai T'ing-k'ai (1892–1968) recalled one childhood incident when, playing with a lantern, he set his father's medicine handbooks on fire. Discovering the accident, Ts'ai's peasant and amateur-druggist father submitted him to a relentless beating. As the strokes fell, Ts'ai begged for forgiveness, but with no avail; his hope for rescue from his mother further vanished with her approval of the father administering a "good whipping." Amid the brutality and helplessness, Ts'ai said, "I absolutely hated them." He was forced to admit his wrongdoing afterward but "wailed and refused to eat."[98] Children were not recorded or perceived as simply docile recipients of conventions and adult motivations, without a willful mindset of their own. When a child was said to have fled from home, escaped to the classroom, or endured a senseless flogging, his (occasionally her) actions and his voice spoke for itself, of his thought and his culture in action. The child's independent perspective is as disconcerting as it is exciting. The thoughts, feelings, and voices of children could hardly have been mere reflections, copies, and repetitions of those of others, simply because they were not presented as living identical, or even agreeable, lives with those around them.

The question of children's choices and their understanding or exercise of a certain realization of their stations was known in many ordinary settings. The early Ch'ing philosopher Fu Shan (1607–1684) told the story of how he was intrigued by his father's passion for religion and the mystical when he was little. He decided to follow the chanting, even drugging himself with the "yellow essence for eternity" (*pu ssû huang ching*).[99] Perhaps his later revulsion against sex and a life-long fascination with Taoism and medicine was an overflow from these childhood experiments. Thus children could be consciously looking, processing, and observing the world around them in ways similar to an adult. Adults of course formed a large part of the reference of children, but children also made up a big part of the meaning or the environment of the adults. For example, General Fêng Yü-hsiang (1882–1948) always felt that he was born a loner. He took in things according to his lonely, yet sharply watchful, eyes, a trait he thought was possibly inherited from his father.[100] As a child, the politician Hsü Yung-ch'ang (1887–1959) revealed the instance when he took a look at the scratches of his own handwriting and said to himself that unstable styles seemed to be part of his natural inclination, whereas perseverance might be difficult to expect of his character in the long run.[101] Chang P'u said that he knew his father's clansmen were haughty and prejudiced. T'an Ssû-t'ung realized that his mother had lost the love and the attention of his father to his father's new love. Kao Chien-fu (1879–1951) said he was aware of being born of a concubine mother on a date considered inauspicious. He had always been received as a child of bad luck. He told of family members wanting to abandon him in an orphanage, but the act was intercepted by his father.[102]

Specifically, what sort of a social environment existed in the late imperial Chinese family formation or cultural consciousness that would allow for, or breed, these seemingly detached observations of a youngster toward his environment and shrewd comments on himself? Which sort of elements were in place from their religious beliefs, social ethics, or daily activities that might give rise to a reflective sentiment that would encourage their expression and preservation? The imitation or internalization theory within the framework of socialization does not answer all our questions. Nor do the crude assumptions of the nature-versus-nurture model of psychology speak eloquently for the interaction between the subjective self-agency of a child in late imperial Chinese terms and the influence of an external environment

FIG. 44. "Children Bathing Buddha," by Su Han-ch'ên (Sung dynasty). Late imperial Chinese children usually worshipped with their parents; burning incense and reading scripture were frequent activities. In this picture, four children bathe Buddha and pray. Courtesy of the National Palace Museum, Taiwan, Republic of China.

that defined human nature and collective nurturing from different philo-sophical-religious bases. The existence of these suggests a tradition that ac-corded a certain demeanor and resolution on the part of a child.

In a world of human sentiments and historical practicality, where the meaningfulness of the adult often depends on the existence and fate of their juniors, both objective forces and subjective feelings could function differ-ently. As the general social need of biophysical or sociospiritual reproduc-tion rendered infants and children literally the answers for deep prayers and ultimate deliverance, the meaning and gratification they embodied and rep-resented came to have a mixed status to their elders and benefactors. The Confucian notion of the two-sidedness of filial behavior, the Taoist expla-nation of rejuvenation, and the Buddhist conviction in Karma as endless retribution and rebirth all taught late imperial Chinese parents and children, elders and youngsters alike, that offspring could be as much "givers" of joy and meaning as they were "recipients" of care and assistance. To the women waiting to become mothers, to the men longing for the continuance of the family line, to the masters hoping to transmit teachings and skills in what-ever trade or craft: infants and children promised the only elevation and "salvation." As seniors, adults could be reliant, anxiously wishful that their young would duly arrive, and survive, to rejuvenate energy and revitalize spirit, to carry on and extend life into the next phase. Not only were the mischievous children known as half-wits, but also as the "little ancestors" (hsiao-tsu-tsung).

Conclusion

In Ming-Ch'ing China, children and others were leading lives differ-ent to those previously lived. Society became increasingly varied and en-gendered increased competition. For the gentry elites, the civil service exam-ination paved the way for social mobility but also demanded heavy human investment. For merchants, the broadening of domestic and overseas trade presented new opportunities mixed with economic fluctuation and chaos. For peasants and artisans, the emergence of local and long-distance markets meant that they needed to figure out smart strategies in electing to produce cash products while maintaining a stable supply for self-sufficiency. For all walks of life in towns and villages, people were approaching life in a more hard-driven fashion. Children, with parents of different stations in life, were more likely to be molded toward narrowly defined goals; they worked harder and were more committed to high achievement. Better preparation and skilled labor might not lead to obvious returns in the short run, de-spite glorious accounts of elite children who were (or were made to be) con-scientious students and who appeared "with a solemnity almost like that of

an adult" as unusually young boys laboring in the fields or as girls participating in weaving and other handicrafts all year round. Along with these
"positivist" phenomena, there are accounts of children from all backgrounds running away from homes and workplaces, of gentry children forbidden to paint or engrave, play sports, or even read novels and plays. Some
model children tacitly complied, but more trembled in fear, while still others resisted, escaped, or defied. Their obedience, depression, obtuse difficulties as troubled children, or young troublemakers—like their rebellion—tell
a story of childhoods in tumultuous transformation.

People were familiar with the notion that children had always lived along
with others while maintaining a world apart. Adults and children alluded
to this schism in different ways. When Chang Chih-tung (1837–1909) was
a child, his father used to say, "Those of you in your childhood [child years,
t'ung-nien], how are you able to understand this [the trouble of an
adult]?"[103] Certain adults admitted that in terms of emotions and mentality, there existed an unbridgeable gap between them and their children. Parents complained of the difficulty in raising proper children; teachers were
frustrated by impasses in disciplining students. In their struggle to devise di-
verse approaches, adults tried to lead children away from where they were
(the state of being a child) to where they were to be (the state of being adult
men and women), and all the while they were puzzled by the difficulties of
the endeavor. By the "dawning" years of the modern era, Ch'ên Hêng-chê
(1890–1976), as a little girl, had a maternal uncle who liked to share news
and fresh ideas at his niece's bedside. Listening attentively, Ch'en said, her
imagination carried her off, "passing unknowingly, from the small world
of a child to the outskirts of the world of adults."[104] It was a modest acknowledgement for one single girl but a remarkable comment on the long
march that youthful self-consciousness had traveled from the centuries
before.

The kind of history that has almost no space for children is similar to that
which neglects the lower classes, women, workers, and popular or folk religion. By now it should be clear that a history of children and childhood,
even if just of the Chinese past, hardly entails only questions of source materials or methodology. The old historiographical problem of its feasibility
is tangled with the larger question of its value or the intellectual significance
of this undertaking. As yet another frontier in history, in social, cultural, as
well as political, economic, intellectual, and institutional history, this history of children and childhood offers many new rewards and fresh attrac-
tions. But that which it has to offer to historical studies that may prove valuable, indispensable, irreplaceable, not just complementary or supplementary, still needs elucidation. Certainly, it will illuminate the importance of
"age" and "phases of life" as categories and subjective construction blocks

for individuals and society. Thus, like the other, once unduly neglected, perspectives of class, gender, or ethnicity, childhood, youth, middle, or old age, can and ought to be fields of vigorous investigation. More than other cases, a historical examination of the world of infants and children in the rapidly changing, yet basically orthodox, larger sphere of late imperial China reveals to us the interconnection and mutually defining nature between this biophysically conceived youthful stage, thus sociologically junior status, and the philosophically and religiously apprehended innocence at the onset of human existence. The constant playing out, remaking, and recreating of each one among these three layers, or three aspects of the meaning of a "child" or "childhood" in Ming-Ch'ing times is what may help us to renegotiate with psychologists and social scientists the peculiarity of many of the cultural assumptions behind modern intellectual exercises that Western scholars in family studies have insightfully pointed out, though hardly ever resolved.

Afterword

Life, as described and perceived by those experiencing and witnessing it, is constrained by the choices people make and the circumstances in which they find themselves. It is in this sense that infants and children, whose history is presented and represented here, become intertwined with their physical and social environments. In the case of late imperial China, the practice and characteristics of pediatric medicine were much supported and influenced by the value system that produced it. In fact the very birth and development of the pediatric specialty within Chinese medical and health culture, from the Sung onward, owed a great deal to the scientific and technological extension of the Confucian humanist tradition. Buddhist compassion for life and the Taoist understanding of nature each, in its own way, stressed the interconnectedness of humanity under the auspices of Heaven. Much of the evolving substance of Chinese views and treatments on infants and children continued to be molded by the external environment; the specific biophysical forces at work; demographic trends; and the everyday conditions under which most had to operate. Parts 1 and 2 of this book, though not preconceived as such, can be read as complementary pieces that present some key components of such basic frames. The interplay of these constituted the fundamental structure of the world of the youngest children in late imperial China in all its diversity, as is partly shown in Part 3.

The Perspective of Children and Childhood in History

Much of what we learn (or try to unlearn) from contemporary research on infants and children (for example, early education, child psychology, or pediatrics) is based on the notion of the "modern, scientific child"—a certain universal, standardized quality in the abstract—that is historically specific, yet whose particular complexity in cultural terms remains unknown. We realize this as we read back and forth between modern theories and past records on children. More critically minded scholars in developmental psychology, cognitive studies, autistic children's centers, or children's courts also recognize this when they reflect on the particularity or temporality of their own expertise and the intellectual validity they represent.

Past research by historians on children and childhood has scarcely offered any creative dialogue or independent assessment to close this gap, widened by one-sided admiration and uncritical reference. The complex substance and profound ambivalence represented by Chinese source materials, partly disclosed above, promises an intriguing set of both counterarguments and comparative insights of an unusual kind. Debates on children and childhood based on Chu Hsi's or Wang Yang-ming's views from this perspective may be just as relevant and revealing as any theses or surveys modeled after the moral philosophy of, say, David Hume.

Ample evidence indicates that one-sided and arbitrarily "modern views" have become the "common outlook" based on "objective" studies of children and continue to dominate both the academic and popular worlds. However, a review of the subject in recent or distant history reveals, casts doubts, and raises fundamental questions. The pioneering works produced by Western historians of children and childhood have not quite fulfilled the expectation as intellectual mediation between modern, scientific understanding and other experiences. Most have shown themselves to be committed followers of contemporary children's studies at a time when modern disciplines such as developmental psychology, early education, sociology, and demography appear to have held a certain "common" analysis in matters related to human development on life course or age factors. These have offered numerous "theoretical frameworks," but serious evaluation of more complex human records got lost in the shuffle. Investigations into medieval European or early modern French child-rearing practices mostly documented the anticipated historical developments leading up to "the rise of the egalitarian family" and the "discovery of the (modern) notion of childhood" as they corresponded to expected patterns in historical developments and manifested themselves under the sway of linear progression. The humanities could hardly, then, turn the table around and begin to query the applicability of much of these nineteenth- or twentieth-century assumptions, less still engage in any serious conversation, any deeper negotiation, with contemporary pediatricians, child psychologists, or children's court judges regarding potentially alternative views on childhood or human existence at large.

Some of the material presented in this book, in the case of Chinese history of childhood and the child, should make it clear that the prevailing modern stance on children and the life course inherits many striking characteristics of modernity that beg for reassessment. One assumption is that human existence is understood as a process, as biophysically fixed stages in a mechanically irreversible journey toward some common end point (be it physical fatality or spiritual salvation). Any progression or "advances" in this journey (that is, phases in the life course) are thus conceived as objective, standard movements in common areas of humanity whether individually or collectively. These different sections in a human life (infancy, childhood, adolescence, adulthood, and old age) are then taken, without a blink, to be biophysically, therefore "scientifically," founded (be it socioculturally constructed and personally lived). With these inherently modern notions of human existence, a "child" could not but be identified as the dialectic opposite of the "adult." Infancy and childhood become irrecoverable, sweet memories or nightmares in a person's past. One's hypothetical ability to experience or behold the child state and adult character simultaneously as Taoist philosophy assumed, or classical Chinese aesthetics advocated, can only become a logical nonsense. Social and cultural conditions in the later imperial period in China, as yet unacquainted with the European Enlightenment, manifested some of these older premises. The Chinese population could hardly dream of the sociohistorical transformation it was about to experience in this regard. The old Taoist idea that a human life is existentially a cyclical procession, or some fluid state with no definite end or any fixed later phase, carried the potential to allow people to return to their first, innate, original infantile innocence. It had a curious revival under joint state sponsorship, Neo-Confucian reification, and popular religious movements in post-Ming China. The Confucian conviction of interconnected generational relations and the Mencian belief in the "completeness," "maturity," or "cultivatable goodness" innate to any newborn on the other hand formed a central theme in the Neo-Confucian social and cultural ethos. In Ming philosophical eclecticism, or the Ch'ing development of clan organizations later, one witnesses the manifestation of these abstract notions as concrete social dynamics combined with the growth of material consumption and a market economy (in children's goods and ritual commodities). As a sociocultural force, the idea that a child carried something innately "completable" and on its way to "adultlike" qualities continued to operate in the daily practices of late imperial China. The Chinese term commonly taken to mean adult, "ch'eng-jen," translates literally as "complete person," emphasizing the "mature" and "fulfilled" nature of a human being rather than some assumed mechanical advancement in the physical phases of ageing. Similarly, any adult could retain a childlike state within him or her, including any natural attributes usually present at the beginnings of human life that philosophical idealists or Taoist followers admired and cultivated. A sage, in this light, could be someone who managed never to have lost his childlike purity to worldly decadence in the rough and tumble of harsh reality. Physically, if someone exercised and cultivated this infantile energy and vitality, he or she could approach immortality in the material and spiritual sense. Bearing this in mind, the difference between children and adults could hardly be fixed, as neither state has yet been defined and delineated by the universal "scientific" understanding of humanity.

The Question of Memory and Representation

Views of childhood inevitably lead to questions of memory and representation. Since infants and children under the age of six are unable to speak or express themselves coherently or articulately through the usual means of communication, they are often rendered "voiceless." Their ability to bear direct witness in their daily lives becomes blatantly problematic. Although people habitually recall events from earlier points in their lives, often in ways suggesting a "historical present tense," recollections of those experiences cannot be taken at face value. Tso Tsung-t'ang recalled time and again, as related earlier, of the days his mother used to chew rice to feed him when he was a six-month-old infant. Mo Tê-hui wanted everybody to know that the nickname he later gave himself was chosen to commemorate the red willow tree under which his mother breast-fed him. In searching and re-searching traces of life in this earliest, blurred stage, one constantly confronts the ambiguity of the creation, transmission, recording, preservation, and circulation of memories. The occurrence, preservation, presentation, and representation of these events constitute a perilous process for the historian. With the rapid development in cognitive studies and neural sciences, a historian is compelled to look at both the data and the thinking behind the old humanist's methodological questions while wondering about newly informed ways of deciphering these increasingly "classical" codes and traces. As the past retreats from us in physical time, moreover, this task becomes simultaneously alluring and unattainable.

The rediscovery and mapping out of the history of Chinese infants and children offer a few stimulating thoughts. One, in its historical and socio-cultural configuration, which varies substantially from the familiar modern, Western norm, the nature of human existence is not necessarily a single, progressive procession. One of the implications, then, is that an individual self may be endowed with a certain "multiplicity" from the beginning to the end. The Chinese notion of a person's life carries both a "self" in the limited, individualistic sense (called the "small self": *hsiao-wo*) and some existential state with its broader, extended character (called the "larger self": *ta-wo*). Two, in a similar vein, time in a personal manner or on the abstract physical level does not move in a linear fashion. In other words, before modern standardized "physical time" came to dominate and impinge on the comprehension and management of personal lives, myriad sociocultural

FIG. 45. "Children Carrying Children," attributed to Ch'iu Ying (Ming dynasty). Courtesy of the National Palace Museum, Taiwan, Republic of China.

timetables allowed for multiple tracks of time via human existence simultaneously—even as certain forms of reversible "fluidity." Three, the long Chinese tradition of compassion (*tz'u*) and filiality (*hsiao*), when erected upon these conceptual premises, created a particular kind of continuous interplay of human existence in ways seemingly both bewilderingly "modern" and hopelessly "traditional."[1] In a society that stressed intergenerational connectedness, youths could anticipate the peculiar character of the older generation, while the seniors could rejuvenate and return to "infancy" within their own worldly journey. This reversion was even possible for deceased ancestors at the sacrificial altar. Both parents and children, amid the "cultural allowances" or social resources of life found in premodern Chinese, could live out a historical existence that moved with multiple constructions whereby more than one human time track was imagined and executed.

Listening to Silence and Seeing the Void

When approaching conditions of infancy and early childhood in the past, one must decipher silence, both real and metaphorical, in human existence. This need or possibility suggests itself in the context of Chinese children's history on at least three levels: First, the documentation of nonverbal expression as recorded in conventional historical sources demands a more serious and systematic elucidation. The facial expressions, vocal sounds, bodily gestures, physical motion, daily activities, and even motionless inactivity carry complex social, political, cultural, and psychological messages. Second, nontextual evidence of human existence requires, as a result, vigorous assessment of what anthropologists call objects or materiality: food, clothing, furniture, architecture, toys, plants, and animals. Together with other traces of ordinary interaction, these objects could reveal powerful messages about the outlook, attitudes, strengths, and vulnerability of individuals and their social environments, about which young lives were but among the less familiar examples. The implications these may unearth however are far from insignificant.[2] Third, in a fundamental way, we must recognize that what is missing, both literally and figuratively, gives meaning to what turns out to be present. The ability to imagine, articulate, and reconstruct what has been absent (for example, lives lost in infanticide) leads to a less arbitrary understanding of what is familiarly present or has been crudely and cruelly excluded.

Such conceptual and methodological questions relate to the question of historical subjectivity and agency. If infants and children are to be accorded any subjectivity in history, and if there is to be any serious discussion over their historical presence, one must confront the notion of "participation" in history. Many people have always been missing from historical records and

FIG. 46. "Children at Play," said to be by Su Han-ch'ên (Sung Dynasty). This picture is typical of a genre of art where children were represented as the sole focus of attention. The children in the painting appear realistic rather than formulaic. Courtesy of the National Palace Museum, Taiwan, Republic of China.

historiography; infants and children could be the most blatant, intellectually innocent, and professionally overlooked among the unrepresented (some would say unrepresentable). Their nonappearance and ambiguity hangs heavily on the conscience of the intellect of the collective. The silence or absence can no longer be considered hopeless, thus "natural," with the spread of liberalization and democratization. In this regard, high infant and child mortality in the past can hardly excuse omission. The frail and silent character of this earliest phase in humanity, the preverbal and preliterary condition, admittedly deprived infants and children of an opportunity to produce on their own recording in the conventional fashion. Such deprivation might inhibit direct access to that world of the young, but the historian's indirect representation points out some glaring characteristics of modern academic orientations. Other factors contributing to the silencing and absence of children in history also bear witness to the human-made environment of history (for example, infanticide, neglect and prejudice, and selective historical consciousness). Infants and children do not stand alone in their buried state and "forgettability" in time or in the industry of knowledge production.

If one were to dig up and sort out these "silencing" and "vacating" effects, the voice of silence would become "audible" and evocative. As in music or linguistics, the occurrence, duration, and peculiar characteristics

FIG. 47. "Traveling Vendors" (Peking, 1930s). Traveling vendors were an artistic genre from the late Sung onward. This photograph shows children as the sole customers, as evidenced by the toys and other children's novelties from the 1930s and 1940s. Reprinted form Hedda Morrison, ed., *A Photographer in Old Peking* (Oxford: Oxford University Press, 1985), p. 98.

of the "silent" moments carry powerful significance. Similarly, inactivity has always been a natural and indispensable part of activity for humanity. The historical world of the infant and small child is characterized less by the subject's limitation in expressive vehicles than by the historian's glaring intellectual ineptitude and conceptual oversight. Acknowledging preconceived barriers and vocational baggage as part of a broader social prejudice and human inadequacy might lead to restoration of historical awareness. The history of the strong and powerful is often recorded at the expense and absence of the remaining sociopolitical order. As any architect, sculptor, or art historian can testify, the empty space has as much to do with the deeper meaning of the entire composition. The fundamental flaw in the contemporary humanities is that modern men and women of letters compromise the intellectual value of the less functionally sensible. At times unexplainable and obviously untidy complications in the world of lives represented causes them to act as overzealous followers of the normative and positivist mentality of social and natural science.

In late imperial China, the moment leading up to birth—or as some back then would call the very "consent to descend"—marked already an undeniable participation in the world of humanity, until then made up of parents and ancestors, a communal existence including also the seniors and adults, plants and animals, rocks and stars, and gods and ghosts. The very likelihood of this physical world, made of the possibility to inherit any form of life, also presented a picture for contemporary members of society that was constantly negotiable and alterable, with the addition and subtraction of any elements related to the cosmos. One of the best examples of this view is the transforming power that pregnancy and childbirth had on Chinese women, allowing them the prospect of elevating themselves from the humbling status of a wife to the ultimate achievement of the mother. The same may be said of men who were bachelors or were married without children. Like most other normal couples, they prayed with vehement hope for offspring, presenting eternal gratitude and offerings for those born safely and on good health. The action or inaction of any infant and child were therefore acts of socioecological empowerment in this never-ending human chain, in that larger circle of life. In this sense, the hows and whys of the history of children and childhood become one, speaking volumes about the physical and material conditions as well as the attitudes and values that gave rise to it.

Meetings of Different Minds

A few reflections on the "Ariès thesis" are in order. Much scholarship has challenged Ariès's observation that the notion of children and the awareness of childhood is a relatively "modern" phenomenon. Studies on children and childhood in medieval, even ancient, history have since revealed to us what may be learned of the lives of the very young before the "dawning" of the recent past, which reminds us all of the precarious tendency in viewing any "absence of modern" inclinations as the equivalence of "premodern ignorance" and "absence." Ancient historians show that parents in Greece and Rome were not without feelings toward their young.[3] Passionate bonds, it was demonstrated, existed between individual adults and their offspring.[4] Information with regard to medieval attitudes and practice toward children was in fact so abundant that a leading scholar was prompted to reject Ariès's theory completely. Still this revisionist literature is not as widely read as Ariès's bold pronouncement, especially in fields outside history.[5]

More than anything else, then, the "discovery of childhood" by pioneers like Ariès and the attentiveness to the young by his predecessor and kindred spirit Hu Shih (who preceded him in raising the May Fourth critique on people's attitude toward children as the key measurement for the progression of civilization) represented a conscious effort of a particularly "enlightening" kind to direct "modern" attention to some of society's most vulnerable and neglected. Family historians, demographers, researchers on social welfare, education systems, and children's mental and physical health in this regard could be considered as similar agents of modernity in the academia. Some may even be willing to identify the birth and development of Chinese pediatric medicine, the evolving characters of Chinese family life, and the spread of early education from the Sung through the Ming and the Ch'ing era as certain familiar characteristics of a complicated manifestation of a certain kind of "progress" in history. Although this need not be the logical implication, as it is certainly not the conclusion intended by this study.[6]

While the previous chapters do reveal that ample materials about children existed in premodern China, this study also makes clear, I hope, the numerous areas that await exploration. The value of such endeavors in intellectual archeology, furthermore, does not have to lay with a confirmation of a separate, independent, autonomous, subjective world of children, though the latter may be validated to a surprising degree in the case of late imperial China. Nor should the history of children be simply yet another latecomer in the seemingly endless string of historical puzzles recently uncovered. Even though adding the factor of age or life course to the historical perspective, like the categories of ethnicity, class, and gender before it, is an important enhancement.

As a collection of essays, the eight chapters grouped in three sections, reworked for the purpose of this release, can hardly satisfy the need for a monographic treatment of a history of Chinese children or childhood. Other than perhaps a multivolume representation that addresses the changing physical, social, emotional, and cultural environments of the young, any basic introduction to such a history must unravel the structural elements pertaining to these constructions and consider the usual analytical perspectives themselves as anything but self-validating. While documenting historical developments in the conditions of children's health, family bonds, social relations, as well as the gender, class, and regional variations lurking behind these forces, the current investigation may still be short of a balanced appraisal, not just as the result of conventional methodology but due to the habitual omission of interest from the historical agenda. If there remain any doubts as to whether, or when, children or childhood has been "discovered" in history, then recent developments in modern historiography come indeed shockingly late—a subject of concern and serious interest in itself, as surveyed in the introduction to this book. As a rejoinder to this intellectual exercise, this study welcomes further deliberation and investigation in unattended areas both in historical studies and the studies on children and childhood.

REFERENCE MATTER

Notes

PREFACE

1. Hu Shih, "Tz'u-yu tê wên-t'i," *Hu Shih wên-ts'un*, p. 739.

2. Ping-chen Hsiung, "Konzepte von Kindheit im traditionellen China." In Heike Frick, Mechthild Leutner, and Nicola Spakowski (Hrsg.), *Die Befreiung der Kinder: Konzepte von Kindheit im China der Republikzeit*, pp. 21–34 (Hamburg: Lit Verlag, 1999).

3. Hsiung Ping-chen, *T'ung-nien i-wang: Chung-kuo hai-tzû tê li-shih* (Childhood in the past: A history of Chinese children); idem, *An-yang: Chung-kuo chin-shih êrh-t'ung tê chi-ping yü chien-k'ang* (Ill or well: Diseases and health of young children in late imperial China); idem, *Yu-yu: Ch'uan-t'ung chung-kuo tê ch'iang-pao chih tao* (To nurse the young: Infant care in traditional China).

4. Hsiung Ping-chen, "Êrh-t'ung wên-hsüeh" (Children's literature), in William Nienhauser, ed., *Indiana Companion to Traditional Chinese Literature*, vol. 2, pp. 31–38; idem, "Hsi-shuai shih-tien: Ying-hsiung pu-lun ch'u-shêng ti (The epistomology of a children's game: Cricket fight in China's cultural lexicon)," in idem, ed., *Tu-wu ssû-jên* (Viewing the Humanity through Things), pp. 55–96.

INTRODUCTION

1. The French version of Philippe Ariès's book, *L'enfant et la vie familiale sous l'Ancien Régime*, appeared in 1960 in Paris. Its widely circulated English translation, entitled *Centuries of Childhood: A Social History of Family Life*, appeared in 1971.

2. Out of the group, Linda A. Pollock's *Forgotten Children: Parent-Child Relations from 1500 to 1900* is the earliest full-fledged attempt to confront Ariès's thesis and "reexamine" the existing attitude toward children, adult-children interactions, and early childhood experience in early modern England. Mark Golden's *Children and Childhood in Classical Athens*, Thomas Wiedemann's *Adults and Children in the Roman Empire*, and Shulamith Shahar's *Childhood in the Middle Ages*, though not as critical of Ariès's views as Pollock, all show cultural conditions of childhood in the West in earlier times.

3. See Philip J. Greven Jr., "Life and Death in a Wilderness Settlement" and "Independence and Dependence in Mid-Eighteenth-century Families," in *Four Generations: Population, Land, and Family in Colonial Andover, Massachusetts*, chaps. 2 and 8, pp. 22–41, 222–61. Greven, like quite a few other scholars, went on to conduct further investigations on childhood experience and children's culture in American history, indicating that family historians who acknowledge such perspectives in fact carry a special concern for the "children's question" in history. See Philip J.

Greven Jr., *Spare the Child: The Religious Roots of Punishment and the Psychological Impact of Physical Abuse*.

4. Most of John Demos's coverage on Plymouth colony was written with a keen awareness of children's interest in mind; see Demos's *A Little Commonwealth: Family Life in Plymouth Colony*, esp. chaps. 6, 9, and 10.

5. According to Lawrence Stone, the "restricted patriarchal nuclear family (1550–1700)" in England tends to "reinforce" patriarchy by having a combined "permissive" and "repressive" mode in their parent and child relations. Whereas when "the closed domesticated nuclear family (1640–1800)" emerged later on, a "child oriented, affectionate, and permissive mode" of parent-child relations were developed, see Stone, *The Family, Sex, and Marriage in England, 1500–1800*, pp. 109–35, 254–302.

6. Two out of four chapters in Steven Ozment's book, *When Fathers Ruled: Family Life in Reformation Europe*, are devoted to conditions of children's existence; see chaps. 3, 4, pp. 100–177; Michael Mitterauer and Reinhard Sieder, *The European Family: Patriarchy to Partnership from the Middle Ages to the Present*, chap. 5, pp. 93–119; Section 3 (pp. 111–76) of Beatrice Gottlieb's *The Family in the Western World From the Black Death to the Industrial Age* is a discussion on "procreation and education"; Ralph A. Houlbrooke, *The English Family, 1450–1700*, gives a good documentation of young lives in the English family of the period; see chaps. 6 and 7, pp. 127–201.

7. Recent studies on women's history bearing some general significance for history of children are too numerous to cite. Those focused on motherhood and domestic conditions can be of particular relevance.

8. In this regard, Randolph Trumbach's coverage in *The Rise of the Egalitarian Family: Aristocratic Kinship and Domestic Relations in Eighteenth-Century England*, for instance, appears to be an early example; see chaps. 4, 5, and 6, pp. 165–286. By the 1990s, studies on social life in classical times are also giving due attention to children's conditions. See Keith R. Bradley, *Discovering the Roman Family: Studies in Roman Social History*, chaps. 3 and 5, pp. 37–75; 107–24; Margaret L. King's detailed account, *The Death of the Child Valerio Marcello*, is a good example; David Hunt's book, though named *Parents and Children in History: The Psychology of Family Life in Modern France*, is primarily a case study of the early childhood of the future King Louis XIII as told through his attendant Heroard's journal.

9. Viewing infanticide as a primitive practice associated with the heathen tribes and the backward oriental societies has been an unexamined assumption long in existence in the West. Samuel K. Cohen Jr. began his edifying discussion of infanticide in the lives of Renaissance women with the explanatory observation that in fact recent "essays have suggested that infanticide was not a birth control practice peculiar to Asian populations alone but a normal recourse of families . . . throughout Western civilization," a suggestion that he said still "met with biting criticism"; see Cohen, *Women in the Streets: Essays on Sex and Power in Renaissance Italy*, p. 149.

10. Peter C. Hoffer and N. E. H. Hull, in their study on infanticide in early modern England and New England, included children under eight or nine as "infants" in contemporary social and legal practices. Child murders as well as parental neona-

talticides are both considered in their investigation. The quantitative evidence in their study is also quite revealing. It placed "over 25 percent of all murders heard in the early modern English courts . . . [as] infanticides," and "90 percent of all murderous assaults by women were directed at infants"; see Hoffer and Hull, *Murdering Mothers: Infanticide in England and New England, 1558–1803*, pp. xvii–xix.

11. John Bowell's moving book on the abandonment of children in Western Europe from late antiquity to the Renaissance, entitled *The Kindness of Strangers*, and David L. Ransel's judicious study on child abandonment in early modern Russia, *Mothers of Misery*, serve as good indications of the historic as well as geographic range of these recent works.

12. Joseph Robins's study of "charity children" in eighteenth- and nineteenth-century Ireland, entitled *The Lost Children*; Ruth McClure's study on the London Foundling Hospital in the eighteenth century, *Coram's Children*; and Rachel Fuch's study of foundling and child welfare in nineteenth-century France, *Abandoned Children*, though searching and presenting the question from different angles, as their topics suggest, all tell the tales about both the "giving-up" as well as the "taking in" of youth.

13. In this regard, changing contemporary concerns are obviously both informing and formulating historical studies. Quite a few studies on family life or childhood history have recently included sections devoted to the questions of child labor or children at work. John Demos's and Philip J. Greven Jr.'s respective studies on colonial America and Lawrence Stone's study on early modern England each provide information on children's work. David Herlihy's *Medieval Households* and Peter Laslett's work on England before the industrial age, titled *The World We Have Lost*, also give glimpses of young boys and girls laboring (pp. 16–17). Thomas Wiedemann, in his account of the lives of adults and children in the Roman Empire detailed quite interestingly the work children performed in the fields and in the vineyards, and the training processes for such skills; see Wiedemann, *Adults and Children in the Roman Empire*, pp. 155–64.

14. Ivy Pinchbeck and Margaret Hewitt's study, *Children in English Society*, particularly vol. 2, is a good example that views the problem of child labor together with, and in the context of, the development of social legislation.

15. Studies into the pedagogical materials or children's primers can also reveal the world of "children's literature," or the interplay of the literary and the world of children. See, for instance, the number of quite fascinating essays included in *Infant Tongues: The Voice of the Child in Literature*, edited by Elizabeth Goodenough, Mark A. Heberle, and Naomi Sokoloff.

16. Several book-length analyses on the lives of school children and the changing conditions of schooling highlight the pedagogical experience of youngsters in historical times. Paul F. Grendler's *Schooling in Renaissance Italy: Literacy and Learning, 1300–1600* is a rich treatment of the subject, covering the education of girls, working-class boys, as well as vocational and technical training. Raymond Grew and Patrick J. Harrigan's *School, State and Society: The Growth of Elementary Schooling in Nineteenth-Century France: A Quantitative Analysis* gives a good structural explanation to the changes in primarily education. The gender and class aspects of schooling are again interestingly illuminated.

17. The examples par excellence are the works produced over the decades by the Cambridge Group for the History of Population and Social Structure, whose very name serves as the best indicator of historical demographers' understanding of their population analysis in relation to the broader and larger process of social change. E. A. Wrigley's *Population and History*; Ronald Demos Lee et al., eds., *Population Patterns in the Past*; and E. A. Wrigley and R. S. Schofield's *The Population History of England, 1541–1871: A Reconstruction* are among the best examples.

18. Peter Laslett and R. Wall, eds., *Household and Family in Past Times*, for instance, gives the mean household size, changing family structures, and residential arrangements, which all bore importantly upon the daily existence of the young. Peter Laslett, in his acclaimed book, *The World We have Lost*, also estimated that, given the shorter life spans and different demographic structure in premodern times, children could have made up to two-fifths or more of the total population.

19. Among historical demographers, the works of the family historians and scholars studying the historical ups and downs of local communities are especially keen in making such points. Tamara K. Hareven's introduction to *Family History at the Crossroads*, edited by herself and Andrejs Plakans, provides a good overview on the field's attempt "to connect small-scale life with great structures and transformations," and to consider social change from all three perspectives of "personal time, family time, and historical times."

20. In addition to those attempts at deciphering history in entirely psychological terms, such as the work by Lloyd Mause and his associates at the Institute for Psychohistory ("an evolutionary, psychoanalytic theory of human history"), almost all examinations on social life, family history, and, not the least of all, childhood history, are found to be observation and analyses perceived and conducted under certain Freudian and general psychological terms. See Mause, *The History of Childhood*. Conceptual exercises to look into the "conditions" of childhood in its "formative" stage filled the pages of such works, often without further questioning of their deeper cultural historical implications. For a typical example of the psychoanalytical application in the study of "successive child-rearing modes" as "a new paradigm for the understanding of historical change," see Glenn Davis, *Childhood and History in America*, pp. 13–33.

21. Contemporary knowledge in developmental, cognitive, and social psychologies has played an important force behind historical observation of children and childhood. It is possible that historical discoveries can be used as materials to reflect upon some basic assumptions in developmental psychology and child psychology as well, which to this point is both a product of nineteenth- and twentieth-century history and an influential intellectual and social force in formulation of the historical development of that period. A group of scholars drawn to the field of "indigenous psychology" (*pên-t'u hsin-li hsüeh*) in Taiwan have been exploring such possibilities with their series of conferences and a biannual journal, *Indigenous Psychological Research in Chinese Societies*.

22. See Jon L. Saari, *Legacies of Childhood: Growing up Chinese in a Time of Crisis, 1890–1920*; Anne Behnke Kinney, ed., *Chinese Views of Childhood*.

23. See C. John Sommerville's brief foreword to the volume, pp. xi–xiii.

24. Ann Behnke Kinney's essay, the first in the volume, lays out the specific Han

dynasty notions around the moral development of children based on the ancient Chinese concern for "auspicious beginnings and ritual correctness" of humanity. Elegantly entitled "Dyed Silk," it provides a useful foundation for the Confucian attitude toward children and early education; see Kinney, "Dyed Silk: Han Notions of the Moral Development of Children," in idem, *Chinese Views of Childhood*, pp. 17–56; Wu Hung's discussion, focusing on the issue of "private love" versus "public duty," moves through a host of sociocultural problems implicated in the artistic and hagiographic representations of the image of the child; see Wu Hung, "Private Love and Public Duty: Images of Children in Early Chinese Art," in Kinney, *Chinese Views of Childhood*, pp. 77–110.

25. Beginning with general remarks based on scant information revealed by Chinese biographies, autobiographies, and accounts of wet nurses, Pei-yi Wu's essay moves on to the rewarding and barely noticed materials of parents' writings on children, relating the obvious growth of necrological literature of children to what he perceived as an emerging "cult of the child" in late Ming China; see Pei-yi Wu, "Childhood Remembered: Parents and Children in China, 800 to 1700," in Kinney, *Chinese Views of Childhood*, pp. 129–56.

26. Charlotte Furth's contribution to the volume builds on her earlier studies on traditional Chinese gynecology and birthing culture to consider the interrelatedness of biological reproduction with social reproduction. The beginnings and evolution of human life and the birth and growth of infants and children were understood and managed physically and practically, assisted by China's biomedical discourse. Yet, as Furth shows, this tradition itself had always been embedded in a particular set of cosmological notions and sociocultural concerns; see Furth, "From Birth to Birth: The Growing Body in Chinese Medicine," in Kinney, *Chinese Views of Childhood*, pp. 157–92.

27. Waltner's article connects the gender-specific character of infanticides with the rising dowries in late imperial China. She considers social factors such as the marriage system with the status of children and the treatments they received; see Waltner, "Infanticide and Dowry in Ming and Early Qing China," in Kinney, *Chinese Views of Childhood*, pp. 193–218.

28. Angela Ki Che Leung shows the development of such organization as the Pao-ying hui (Society for the Preservation of Babies) and the changing character of Chinese foundling hospices as activities manifesting a new approach to child destitution as well as a new concept of the child as a complex social being, both at the expense and as a partial result of the declining state leadership; see Leung, "Relief Institution for Children in Nineteenth-Century China," in Kinney, *Chinese Views of Childhood*, pp. 251–78.

29. Lucien Miller's piece discusses "the adolescent world" in *Hung-lou Mêng* (Dream of the red chamber) while Mark Lupher's essay examines the social behavior of "rebel youth" in the 1960s; see Miller, "Children of the Dream: The Adolescent World in Ts'ao Hsüeh-ch'in's *Hong-lou Mêng*," in Kinney, *Chinese Views of Childhood*, pp. 219–50; and Lupher, "Revolutionary Little Red Devils: The Social Psychology of Rebel Youth, 1966–1967," in Kinney, *Chinese Views of Childhood*, pp. 321–44.

30. In the introduction to her book on adoption, Waltner gives a thoughtful and

broad consideration on the issue from both a cross-cultural and theoretical perspective, which establishes her findings in Ming China in the context of procreation and heredity in historical comparison; see Waltner, *Getting An Heir: Adoption and the Construction of Kinship in Late Imperial China*, pp. 1–81; Hui-chen Wang Liu, *The Traditional Chinese Clan Rules*; Charlotte Furth, "The Patriarch's Legacy: Household Instructions and the Transmission of Orthodox Values," in Kwang-ching Liu, ed., *Orthodoxy in Late Imperial China*, pp. 187–211.

31. See Angela Ki Che Leung, *Shih-shan yü chiao-hua, ming-ch'ing tê tz'u-shan tsu-chih*, chap. 3, pp. 71–102.

32. For instance, see Ts'ui-jung Liu, *Ming-ch'ing shih-ch'i chia-tsu jên-k'ou yü shê-hui ching-chi pien-ch'ien*; Lee and Campbell, *Fate and Fortune in Rural China: Social Organization and Population Behavior in Liaoning, 1774–1873*.

33. In her analysis on Lü K'un's writing for women, children, and the poor, Handlin explains Lü's work for children. The *Words for Little Girls* (*Nü hsiao-êrh yü*), *Words for Little Children* (*Hsiao-êrh yü*), and *A Sequel to Words for Little Children* (*Hsü hsiao-êrh yü*) are efforts embedded in his populist preoccupations and are geared especially for the young audience; see Handlin, *Action in Late Ming Thought: The Reorientation of Lu K'un and Other Scholar Officials*, pp. 143–60.

34. Much of what I am summarizing here can be found within the systematic treatment in the three monographic studies I have published in Chinese: Hsiung, *T'ung-nien i-wang: Chung-kuo hai-tzû tê li-shih* (Childhood in the past: A history of Chinese children); idem, *An-yang: Chung-kuo chin-shih êrh-t'ung tê chi-ping yü chien-k'ang* (Ill or well: Diseases and health of young children in late imperial China); idem, *Yu-yu: Ch'uan-t'ung chung-kuo tê ch'iang-pao chih tao* (To nurse the young: Infant care in traditional China). *Yu-yu* and *An-yang* use centuries of pediatric records to show the biophysical, physiological, and material conditions of this childhood experience.

35. Hsiung, *Yu-yu: Ch'uan-t'ung chung-kuo tê ch'iang-pao chih tao* (To nurse the young: Infant care in traditional China), pp. 5–24.

36. Hsiung, "Chung-kuo chin-shih êrh-t'ung lun-shu tê fu-hsien" (The emergence of the discourse on children in late imperial China), pp. 139–70.

37. A good example is Chu Hsi, *T'ung-mêng hsü-chih* (Instruction for children), p. 12.

38. Lü K'un, *Hsiao-êrh yü*, pp. 1–3; Lü Tê-shêng, *Hsü hsiao-êrh yü*, pp. 1–7; Lü K'un, *Nü hsiao-êrh yü*, pp. 430–32.

39. See Pei-yi Wu, "Education of Children During the Sung," in W. Theodore de Bary and John Chaffee, eds., *Neo-Confucian Education: The Formative Stage*, pp. 307–24.

40. See Hsiung, "Chung-kuo chin-shih êrh-t'ung lun-shu tê fu-hsien" (The emergence of the discourse on children in late imperial China), pp. 139–70.

41. See Hsiung, "Êrh-t'ung wên-hsüeh" (Children's literature), pp. 31–38.

42. See Hsiung, "Shei-jên chih-tzû: chung-kuo chia-t'ing yü li-shih mai-lo chung tê êrh-t'ung ting-i wên-t'i" (Whose children are they? Reflections on the status of children in the context of Chinese family and history), pp. 259–94.

43. The category of the National Palace Museum's exhibition *Ying-hsi t'u* (Paintings of children at play), for instance, included the Ming painting *Hua Hsien-*

k'an êrh-t'ung cho liu-hua chü-i. This work was based on the T'ang poetic line: "Leisurely watching the children catching willow flowers," in which its young protagonists were reduced to small figures with mere bodily gestures but no visible facial expressions; see National Palace Museum, ed., *Ying-hsi t'u*, p. 32.

44. In a comparative review essay, I have laid out the ambivalent nature in attending to children's interest in the early modern period; see Hsiung, "Ju-ch'ing ju-li: Ming-ch'ing yu-hsüeh fa-chan yü êrh-t'ung kuan-huai chih liang-mien hsing" (To be rational and to be sensible: The contradiction in the early education development and concerns for children in the Ming-Ch'ing period), pp. 313–25.

45. Compare, for example, Ariès's perspective as laid out in the second section of his *Centuries of Childhood* and my own treatment of the sociopolitical implication of elementary education in Ch'ing dynasty China in *T'ung-nien i-wang: Chung-kuo hai-tzû tê li-shih* (Childhood in the past: A history of Chinese children).

46. Hsiung, "Hao-tê-k'ai-shih: Chung-kuo chin-shih shih-jên tzû-ti tê yu-nien chiao-yü" (Getting off with a good start: Early childhood education of elite families in late imperial China), pp. 201–38.

47. My conclusion in *T'ung-nien i-wang* (pp. 329–38) tries to dwell on this point.

48. In the introduction for the anthology *Childhood and Family in Canadian History* (pp. 7–16), Joy Parry explains how "childhood and family are mostly shaped by historical rather than biological process," which are only minimally founded in nature.

49. For instance, see Chêng Hsüan, *Li-chi chu-shu*, chuan 28, p. 243; Ssû-ma Kuang, like *The Book of Rites* (*Li-chi*), drew a plan of the ideal upbringing for a child from his infancy to his adulthood, only adding still further programs with more specified activities. Ssû-ma, *Chü-chia tsa-i* (Miscellaneous rites for the family); see also Hsiung, *T'ung-nien i-wang*, pp. 80–81.

50. See Ssû-ma, "Chiao-nan-nü" (Instructing boys and girls), *Chü-chia tsa-i* (Miscellaneous rites for the family), chuan 19, p. 333; see also Hsiung, *T'ung-nien i-wang*, p. 81.

51. There is thus far no study on family instructions relating to children. For a general analysis on traditional clan rules and family instructions, see Liu, *The Traditional Chinese Clan Rules*; Furth, "The Patriarch's Legacy: Household Instructions and the Transmission of Orthodox Values," pp. 187–211.

52. For a brief introduction to children's primers and other literary productions intended for young readers in premodern China, see Hsiung, *T'ung-nien i-wang*, pp. 16–24.

53. For a brief explanation on the genre of *nien-p'u* and its use in understanding personal lives, see Hsiung, "Constructed Emotions: The Bond Between Mothers and Sons in Late Imperial China," p. 88.

54. For an introduction to Chinese pediatrics and the source materials it left behind, see Hsiung, "Treatment of Children in Traditional China," pp. 73–79; see also Hsiung, *T'ung-nien i-wang*, pp. 16–24.

55. I discuss the values pediatric texts may have had for approaching historical epidemiology in "Case Histories in Chinese Pediatrics and Their Bio-medical Value," a paper presented at the conference on "The Case History in Chinese Med-

icine: History, Science, and Narrative," Jan. 1998, UCLA. In *An-yang: Chung-kuo chin-shih êrh-t'ung tê chi-ping yü chien-k'ang*, I analyze major patterns of health and disease of young children in late imperial China.

56. See Hsiung, "More or Less: Cultural and Medical Factors Behind Marital Fertility in Late Imperial China," paper presented at the IUSSP workshop on "Abortion, Infanticide and Neglect in Historical Populations," Kyoto, Japan. Oct. 1994.

57. See, for example, Tu, "Ku-hua chung tê êrh-t'ung shih-chieh" (The world of children as seen in old paintings), pp. 4–15.

58. Hsiung, "Treatment of Children in Traditional China," pp. 73–79; Hsiung, *T'ung-nien i-wang*, pp. 16–24.

59. Such assumptions are quite common in family history works in European and American studies. See Stone, *The Family, Sex, and Marriage in England, 1500– 1800*; C. John Sommerville, *The Rise and Fall of Childhood*.

60. See Wang, "Hsün-mêng ta-i" (The principles in child education), pp. 57–58; Li Chih, "T'ung-hsin shuo" (On the heart of the child), pp. 22–24; see also Hsuing, *T'ung-nien i-wang*, pp. 192–216.

61. See Nieh, *Tou-k'o Tz'u-hang*.

62. *Tz'u-hang* was originally a Buddhist term denoting the human life experience as a passage in the ocean of pains and hardship (*k'u-hai*) in need of constant guidance and compassion from the merciful Bodhisattva. By the late imperial period, the concept was borrowed to represent the special innocent and frail existence of infants and young children, as for instance, expressed in the title *A Tender Voyage*.

CHAPTER 1

This chapter has been adapted from chapter 2 of *Yu-yu: Ch'uan-t'ung chung-kuo tê ch'iang-pao chih tao* (To nurse the young: Infant care in traditional China) (Taipei: Lien-ching, 1995).

1. Ariès, *Centuries of Childhood*.

2. For example, Shulamith Shahar's *Childhood in the Middle Ages* is an attempt at correcting Ariès's view that the Europeans did not acknowledge the category of childhood before the early modern era. Its conclusion gives a more extensive review of this scholarship on children and childhood in Western history.

3. Two books and a number of articles have resulted from systematic readings into these pediatric documents. See Hsiung, *Yu-yu: Ch'uan-t'ung chung-kuo tê ch'iang-pao chih tao*; idem, *An-yang: Chung-kuo chin-shih êrh-t'ung tê chi-ping yü chien-k'ang*; idem, "Case Histories in Chinese Pediatrics and their Bio-medical Value."

4. *Lu-hsin ching* was said to be written by Sorcerer Fang, in common opinion a late T'ang–early Sung work. It is accorded as the oldest text known specifically devoted to pediatrics. *Lu* is the skull, and *hsin* is the soft top of the skull. The discipline that the text represented was supposedly interested in helping with the very young, including the infants whose skulls had not yet solidified at the top. Their physiology and pathology are thus recognized as different from those of adults. The title *Lu-hsin ching* (Classic on the soft skull) thus can refer to infant pediatrics. The edition available today, gathered together from scattered citations of later texts, is collected in *Ying-yin wên-yüan-ko ssû-k'u ch'üan-shu*.

5. Ch'ao, *Chu-ping yüan-hou lun*, *chuan* 45–50, pp. 1237–1392; Sun, *Ch'ien-chin fang*.

6. Wang, *Wai-t'ai mi-yao fang*.

7. *Ku-chin t'u-shu chi-ch'êng* KCTSCC, *chuan* 501, p. 1.

8. Liu, *Ch'ien Chung-yang chuan*, p. 1.

9. Ibid., p. 1.

10. Tung, *Hsiao-êrh pan-chên pei-chi fang-lun*.

11. For a discussion of the general development of Chinese pediatrics from ancient times up to the Southern Sung dynasty, see Ch'ên, *Chung-kuo i-hsüeh shih*; Shih, *Chung-kuo i-hsüeh shih*; Ch'ên, *Chung-i êrh-k'o hsüeh*; Wang and Chiang, ed., *Chung-i êrh-k'o hsüeh*.

12. Ch'ien, *Hsiao-êrh yao-chêng chih-chüeh*, pp. 1–2.

13. Ibid.

14. The *Catalog of Clifford G. Grulee Collection on Pediatrics* in the special collection division of the University of Chicago's library contains an extensive holding of Western pediatrics texts. The earliest items were Latin and then German treatises on children's health from the late fifteenth and sixteenth centuries. See pp. 27–32.

15. The founding figure of American pediatrics, Abraham Jacob, learned his craft in Germany, the forerunner in modern European pediatric medicine. See Cone, *History of American Pediatrics*, pp. vii–x, 99–107.

16. See the preface by Hsü Tsan, in Lu, *Ying-t'ung pai-wên*, p. 5.

17. Ibid.

18. See Lu, *Ying-t'ung pai-wên*, *chuan* 1, 4, 5.

19. Such as Wan, *Yu-k'o fa-hui*, *chuan* 1, pp. 4–7.

20. Wang, *Yu-k'o chun-shêng*.

21. See Hsiung, "Ch'ing-tai chung-kuo êrh-k'o i-hsüeh chih ch'ü-yü-hsing ch'u-t'an" (A preliminary study on the regional characteristics of Chinese pediatrics under the Ch'ing), pp. 17–39.

22. Consult also Unschuld, *Medical Ethics in Imperial China*.

23. Wan, *Yu-k'o fa-hui*, p. iii.

24. Ibid.

25. Ibid.

26. Ibid.

27. Ibid.

28. Ibid.

29. Ibid.

30. Ibid.

31. Ibid., p. iii; see further discussion in Hsiung, "Ch'ing-tai chung-kuo êrh-k'o i-hsüeh chih ch'ü-yü-hsing ch'u-t'an," pp. 17–39.

32. Wan, *Yu-k'o fa-hui*, p. v.

33. See Needham, *Clerks and Craftsmen in China and the West*; Unschuld, *Medicine in China*; Chao, *Chung-kuo ku-tai i-hsüeh*; Hsiung, "Ch'ing-tai chung-kuo êrh-k'o i-hsüeh chih ch'ü-yü-hsing ch'u-t'an," pp. 17–39.

34. *Su-chou-fu chih*, *chuan* 109, p. 28; Shih, *Chung-kuo i-hsüeh shih*, pp. 130–32.

35. Wang Ch'i's foreword to *Pao-ying ch'üan-shu*, in Hsüeh, *Pao-ying ch'üan-shu* (Complete writings on infant protection), pp. 8–10.

36. See Leung, "Organized Medicine in Ming-Qing China: State and Private Medical Institutions in the Lower Yangzi Region," pp. 134–66.

37. The accomplishments in both medical skills and medical studies by the father and son Kung T'ing-hsien and Kung Hsin as well as those of the father and son Hsüeh K'ai and Hsüeh Chi were all closely related to the institutional power of the Imperial College of Medicine.

38. Hsüeh, *Pao-ying ch'üan-shu*, pp. 13–26.

39. Wang, *Yu-k'o chun-shêng*.

40. See Kao, *Ku-tai êrh-k'o chi-ping hsin-lun*.

41. "Wu Chieh Chuan," *Ming-shih*, *chuan* 299, p. 7649; Shih, *Chung-kuo i-hsüeh shih*, pp. 130–32.

CHAPTER 2

This chapter has been adapted from chapter 4 of *Yu-yu: Ch'uan-t'ung chung-kuo tê ch'iang-pao chih tao* (To nurse the young: Infant care in traditional China) (Taipei: Lien-ching, 1995).

1. *The Diseases of Children and Their Remedies* (1764) by Nils Rosén von Rosenstein (1706–1773) was most often cited as the first important text that devoted special medical attention to children. Although before that, in the late seventeenth century, there began to be discussions on the diseases of infants and children, such as Walter Harris's (1647–1732) *De Morbis Acutis Infantum* (1689) and William Cadogan's (1711–1797) *A Essay Upon Nursing* (1748). See Cone, *History of the Care and Feeding of the Premature Infant*, p. 4.

2. See Cone, *History of American Pediatrics*; Victor C. Vaughare, R. James McKay, and Waldo E. Nelson, *Textbook of Pediatrics*, pp. 1–12.

3. Cone, *History of American Pediatrics*.

4. Smith and Vidyasagar, *Historical Review and Recent Advances in Neonatal and Prenatal Medicine*; Cone, "Perspectives in Neonatology," *Historical Review and Recent Advances in Neonatal and Prenatal Medicine*, vol. 1, pp. 9–34.

5. For a detailed study of the historical background, origin and development of pediatric medicine in traditional China, see Hsiung, "Ch'ing-tai chung-kuo êrh-k'o i-hsüeh chih ch'ü-yü-hsing ch'u-t'an" (A preliminary study on the regional characteristics of Chinese pediatrics under the Ch'ing), pp. 17–38; Hsiung, "Ming-tai tê yu-k'o i-hsüeh" (Pediatric medicine in the Ming period), pp. 53–69.

6. In modern medicine, newborn care, or neonatal medicine, is defined as a subspecialty dealing with the infant in its first twenty-eight days of life. Here, however, a newborn is defined in terms of traditional Chinese pediatrics: an infant in its first day or first few days of life as it was seen through the initial survival crises.

7. A different and more detailed treatment of this issue was published earlier in Chinese. See Hsiung, "Chung-kuo chin-shih tê hsin-shêng-êrh chao-hu" (The evolution of newborn care in early modern China), pp. 387–428. Although in China there was the separate field of obstetrics, which was closely associated with gynecology and developed at roughly the same period as pediatrics, its care was focused solely on maternal health. In the event of delivery, therefore, Chinese obstetric medicine concerned itself with the prenatal aspect, as well as a smooth childbirth, but look-

ing primarily after the women's well-being and physical needs. All that was required to receive the newborn infant, from the moment it emerged out of the birth canal and including the cutting of the cord, was considered to belong to the provision of the *yu-k'o* (pediatrics), or child medicine specialists. For a monographic treatment on the historical development of traditional Chinese gynecology, see Charlotte Furth, *A Flourishing Yin: Gender in China's Medical History, 960–1665.*

8. For a fuller discussion of the social and cultural backgrounds of the emergence of Chinese pediatrics and the influence of Confucian philosophy, see Hsiung, "Ming-tai tê yu-k'o i-hsüeh" (Pediatric medicine in the Ming period), pp. 53–69.

9. A well-known medical text of the seventh century, *Wai-t'ai mi-yao fang* (Medical secrets of a frontier official) by Wang T'ao contains two sections devoted exclusively to the care of infants: "Seventeen Notes on the Care of the Newborn" and "Two Observations on Looking after Newborn Infants." The much-revered eighth-century medical text *Ch'ien-chin fang* (Prescriptions worth a thousand) by Sun Ssû-miao also has a separate chapter called "A Discourse on Newborn Infants." See Wang, *Wai-t'ai mi-yao fang, chuan* 35, pp. 421–29; Sun, "Discussion on Newborn Infants" (Ch'u-shêng ch'u-fu lun), *Ch'ien-chin fang,* in KCTSCC, *chuan* 422, pp. 30–31.

10. See Ch'ên, *Chung-kuo i-hsüeh shih,* p. 81; Ming-wên shu-chü, ed., *Chung-kuo i-yao hsüeh-chia shih-hua,* pp. 67–69, 97–99.

11. "Hsiao-êrh ch'u-shêng wei-han" (Newborn infants are afraid of cold) in Chang Kao's *I-shuo* (On medicine) of the Sung era, and "Newborn" (Ch'u-shêng) in Wei I-lin's *Shih-i tê-hsiao fang* (Effective recipes of experienced physicians) are good examples of this. See Chang, *I-shuo,* "Hsiao-êrh ch'u-shêng wei-han," *chuan* 10, p. 746; Wei, "Ch'u-shêng," and "Hu-yang fa," *Shih-i tê-hsiao fang, chuan* 11, pp. 359–60, 363. The best example can be found in "Ch'u-shêng lun" (On the newborns) from *Hsiao-êrh wei-shêng tsung-wei lun-fang* (A thorough discussion of infant hygiene), *chuan* 1, p. 52.

12. See, for instance, *Pao-ch'an yü-ying yang-shêng lu* (Advice for safe birth, infant rearing and maintaining health).

13. K'ou, "Hu-yang chih fa," "Ch'u-shêng chiang-hu fa," "Chiang-hu fa t'ang-shih wei hu-yang," and "Fa-chi," *Ch'üan-yu hsin-chien, chuan* 1, 2; Lu, "Hu-yang fa," *Ying-t'ung pai-wên, chuan* 1, pp. 18–21; Wang, "Hu-yang lun" and "Hsiao-êrh ch'u-shêng tsung-lun," *Yu-k'o lei-ts'ui,* pp. 7–9, 55–56; Hsüeh, "Ch'u-tan fa" and "Hu-yang fa," *Pao-ying ch'üan-shu,* pp. 1–3, 5–8.

14. "Hsiao-êrh ch'u-shêng hu-yang mên," *Ku-chin t'u-shu chi-ch'êng, chuan* 422, p. 306.

15. See, for instance, "Ch'u-tan chiu-hu" (Newborn emergency care) (pp. 25–26), in *Yu-yu chi-ch'êng* (Complete works on the care of children), by the prestigious Ch'ing pediatric author Ch'ên Fu-chêng.

16. Lu, "Ch'u-tan," *Ying-t'ung pai-wên, chuan* 1, p. 15.

17. Ibid., pp. 15–16.

18. Hsü, "Hsiao-êrh ch'u-shêng tsung-lun" and "Ch'u-shêng yü-fa," *Ku-chin i-t'ung ta-ch'üan, chuan* 10, pp. 5635–36, 5639; Ch'ên, *Fu-jên ta-ch'üan liang-fang* (All-inclusive good prescriptions for women), *chuan* 24, p. 800; K'ou, "Ch'u-shêng yü-fa," *Ch'üan-yu hsin-chien, chuan* 2; Wang, "Yü-êrh fa" (Methods of bathing in-

fants), *Yu-k'o chun-shêng* (Standards of treatments in pediatrics), *chuan* 1, p. 10; Wang, "Hsi-yü," *Ying-t'ung lei-ts'ui* (Essentials in looking after infants and children), p. 4; Wu, "Yü-êrh," *Yu-k'o tsa-ping hsin-fa yao-chüeh*, p. 15.

19. See "Tuan-ch'i lun," *Hsiao-êrh wei-shêng tsung-wei lun-fang*, *chuan* 1, pp. 53–55; K'ou, "Tuan-ch'i fa," *Ch'üan-yu hsin-chien*, *chuan* 2; Sun, "Tuan-ch'i fa," *Ch'ih-shui yüan-chu*, *chuan* 25, p. 843; Kung, "Tuan-ch'i fa," *Shou-shih pao-yüan* *(Preserving the original principle in order to obtain longevity)*, *chuan* 8, p. 568.

20. Wei, "Chiu-fa lun," *Shih-i tê-hsiao fang*, in KCTSCC, *chuan* 422, p. 31b; Wan, "Hsiao-êrh pu-i wang-chên-chiu," *Yü-ying chia-mi*, in KCTSCC, *chuan* 422, p. 32a; K'ou, "Hsin-shêng-êrh chieh-chiu," *Ch'üan-yu hsin-chien*, *chuan* 2; Wang, *Yu-k'o lei-ts'ui*, pp. 14–15; Sun, "Chieh-chiu," *Ch'ih-shui yüan-chu*, *chuan* 25, p. 843.

21. Sun, "Ch'u-shêng ch'u-fu ti-êrh," *Shao-hsiao ying-ju fang*, pp. 7–13.

22. Chang, "Kuo-ai hsiao-êrh fan-hai hsiao-êrh shuo," *Ju-mên shih-ch'in*, pp. 5935–41; Kung, "Hsiao-êrh ch'u-shêng," *Shou-shih pao-yüan*, *chuan* 8, pp. 567–68.

23. Sun, "Discussion on Newborn Infants" (Ch'u-shêng ch'u-fu lun), *Shao-hsiao ying-ju fang*, pp. 7–13; Chu, "Ch'u-shêng," *Tan-hsi hsien-shêng chih-fa hsin-yao*, *chuan* 8, pp. 826–30; Fang, "Ch'u-shêng tsung-shuo," *Ch'i-hsiao liang-fang*, *chuan* 64, pp. 75–79; Lu, "Ch'u-shêng," *Ying-t'ung pai-wên*, pp. 15–18; Wang, "Ch'u-shêng," *Yu-k'o chun-shêng*, *chuan* 1, p. 10; Wang, "Ch'u-tan lun," *Ying-t'ung lei-ts'ui*, pp. 61–65; Kung, "Hsiao-êrh ch'u-shêng," *Hsin-k'an chi-shih ch'üan-shu*, pp. 751–53.

24. K'ou, "Hsia t'ai-tu," *Ch'üan-yu hsin-chien*, *chuan* 2; Wang, "Hsia t'ai-tu lun," *Yu-k'o lei-ts'ui*, *chuan* 1, pp. 11–12; Hsü, "Hsia t'ai-tu lun," *Ku-chin i-t'ung ta-ch'üan*, *chuan* 10, p. 5639; Wang, "Hsia t'ai-tu fa," *Chêng-chih chun-shêng*, pp. 46–48; Sun, "Ch'u t'ai-tu," *Ch'ih-shui yüan-chu*, *chuan* 25, pp. 1–2.

25. Chu, "Ch'u-shêng," *Tan-hsi hsien-shêng chih-fa hsin-yao*, pp. 826–30.

26. For instance, some pediatric texts were known to advise people first to lift the newborn infant immediately and "wrap him with cotton padding and hold him against the warm chest of an adult." Only later should one wipe his mouth, clean the body, and so on. This advice represents that special concern for body warmth: "When the infant suddenly emerges from the mother's womb, he must not be allowed to be exposed to coldness." See "Ch'u-shêng lun," *Hsiao-êrh wei-shêng tsung-wei lun-fang*, p. 52.

27. Some pediatric authors held, for instance, that besides the wiping of the mouth and tongue, the fluids and blood around the eyes should also be cleaned. The method for expelling the meconium was used throughout history and among the social classes. Cinnabar with honey and licorice were preferred during the T'ang and Sung periods whereas *coptis japonica* and ox bezoar were used in the Ming. Peasant households adopted the coarse but convenient recipe for fermented bean or chive juice instead of the classically recommended cinnabar and honey. See Sun, *Shao-hsiao ying-ju fang*; Lu, "Ch'u-tan," *Ying-t'ung pai-wên*, *chuan* 1, pp. 15–18; Fang, "Ch'u-shêng tsung-shuo," *Ch'i-hsiao liang-fang*, *chuan* 64, pp. 75–79; Hsüeh, "Ch'u-tan fa" and "Hu-yang fa," *Pao-ying ch'üan-shu*, pp. 1–3, 5–8.

28. Richer families were known to administer medicinal drinks to calm the child or give pig's milk or other nutrients when first born. In addition, families in north

China were accustomed to practice moxabustion on the infant as a preventive measure against such diseases as "lock jaw" (*chin-k'o*) or "umbilical wind" (*ch'i-fêng*), although as a regional practice it was opposed by pediatricians from the south. Villagers, furthermore, tended to combine mouth wiping and cleansing of the meconium into one procedure, or to trim the whole process down to the bare necessities of breaking the cord, swaddling, and feeding. See Sun, "Ch'u-shêng ch'u-fu lun," *Shao-hsiao ying-ju fang*, pp. 30b–31a; Chu, "Tz'u-yu lun," *Kê-chih yü-lun*, pp. 9324–28; idem, "Ch'u-shêng," *Tan-hsi hsien-shêng chih-fa hsin-yao*, pp. 826–30; Ch'êng, *I-shu*, chuan 14, p. 919; see also note 22.

29. Sun, "Ch'u-shêng ch'u-fu lun" (Discussion on newborn infants), *Shao-hsiao ying-ju fang*, pp. 30b–31a; "Tuan-ch'i lun," *Hsiao-êrh wei-shêng tsung-wei lun-fang*, chuan 1; K'ou, "Tuan-ch'i fa," *Ch'üan-yu hsin-chien*, chuan 2; Hsü, "Tuan-ch'i fa," *Ku-chin i-t'ung ta-ch'üan*, pp. 5640–41.

30. See Kao, "Tuan-ch'i fa," *Ku-tai êrh-k'o chi-ping hsin-lun*, pp. 2–3.

31. *Chia-i-ching*, published in 282. For information on ancient Chinese ideas concerning umbilical tetanus, see Kao, "Tuan-ch'i fa," *Ku-tai êrh-k'o chi-ping hsin-lun*, pp. 14–16.

32. Sun, "Ch'u-shêng ch'u-fu lun," *Shao-hsiao ying-ju fang*, pp. 30b–31a.

33. Wang, *Wai-t'ai mi-yao fang*, chuan 35, pp. 421–30.

34. For a long time, medieval medical authors made no clear distinction between "umbilical wind," on the one hand, and such infections as "umbilical swelling" (*ch'i chung*) or "umbilical boils" (*ch'i-ch'uang*). In addition, references continued to be made regarding such symptoms of what appeared to be neonatal tetanus as "fetal fits" (*t'ai-chin*) and "fetal wind" (*t'ai-fêng*), which alluded to fits or seizures inherited from the fetal period. See Hsiung, "Chung-kuo chin-shih tê hsin-shêng-êrh chao-hu" (The evolution of newborn care in early modern China), pp. 402–7.

35. Due to Sun's personal fame and the influence of his text, his method was often cited and widely adopted. The discussion on breaking the cord in Wang T'ao's "Seventeen Notes on the Care of the Newborn" (Hsiao-êrh chiang-hu fa i-shih-ch'i shou) from the second half of the eighth century is nearly identical. See Wang, *Wai-t'ai mi-yao fang*, chuan 35, pp. 421–29.

36. "Ch'u-shêng lun," *Hsiao-êrh wei-shêng tsung-wei lun-fang*, chuan 1, p. 52.

37. Upon investigation of the possible cause of the "umbilical wind," the author pointed out that "when the infant had just been born and as the umbilical cord was being cut, a certain harm [*shang*] had occurred. It thus suffered wind and dampness [*fêng-shih so-ch'êng*]." This statement, made against the background of the mainstream of medicine's assumption of the prenatal origin and inherited nature of umbilical tetanus, was a bold notion. See "Ch'i-fêng ts'o-k'ou," *Hsiao-êrh wei-shêng tsung-wei lun-fang*, chuan 1, pp. 56–58.

38. At the time, there was already a notion of adult tetanus in Chinese medicine. To this day, in fact, modern medicine has inherited the classical terminology of tetanus (*p'o-shang-fêng*) in Chinese medical and daily language; "Ch'i-fêng ts'o-k'ou," *Hsiao-êrh wei-shêng tsung-wei lun-fang*, chuan 1, pp. 56–58.

39. The original text reads: "As soon as the cord is broken, one should place an umbilical branding cake on the cord stump and burn it three times. The wick of the flames should be of the size of the ears of wheat. If the infant does not cry, use moxa

to burn it up to five or seven times." The umbilical branding cake was made of "fermented soy beans and yellow wax, one portion each, and a small amount of musk. Grind the fermented soybeans into a powder and mix in the musk. Melt the wax and add it to the mixture. Mold the mixture into cakes." See "Tuan-ch'i lun," *Hsiao-êrh wei-shêng tsung-wei lun-fang, chuan* 1, pp. 53–55.

40. For a detailed discussion of the process, see Hsiung, "Chung-kuo chin-shih tê hsin-shêng-êrh chao-hu" (The evolution of newborn care in early modern China)," pp. 398–412.

41. Wu, "Tuan-ch'i," *Yu-k'o tsa-ping hsin-fa yao-chüeh*, pp. 14–15.

42. Wan's original treatise had it that: "If one does not understand protection before disease strikes nor understands treating the onset of the disease, after its seeds [*p'ao-tzû*] upon the belly, it will develop into three problems: mouth grabbing [*ts'o-k'ou*], lock-jaw [*chin-fêng*], and confined stomach [*so-tu*]. Though these are separate symptoms, they are all part of umbilical wind. Infants with mouth grabbing cry often, repeatedly grabbing at the mouth. . . . Those who stop sucking cannot be saved." See Wan, *Yu-k'o fa-hui*, pp. 11–12.

43. In explaining the contamination process preceding it, Ch'in asserted that "inappropriate moves in cutting and tying off the cord when a child was newly born, . . . or the use of a cold blade [*leng-tao*] to cut the cord," could cause "a foreign air (*k'o-fêng*)." See Ch'in, "Ch'i-fêng ts'o-k'ou," *Yu-k'o chin-chên*, pp. 5–7.

44. Hence derived the name "four-six wind" (*ssû-liu fêng*) or "four-seven wind" (*ssû-ch'i fêng*), which was known to the rural Chinese population from at least medieval times until well into the twentieth century. See Kao, "Tuan-ch'i fa," *Ku-tai êrh-k'o chi-ping hsin-lun*, pp. 2–3. Modern literary works such as Chên's *The White Deer Praire (Pai-lu Yüan)* still refer vividly to the rage of this four-seven wind over rural north China supposedly earlier in this century.

45. Although there was recognition of common umbilical infections from at least the eighth century, the relationship between this mildly irritating infection and the deadly umbilical tetanus was not understood. Wang Tao's eighth-century *Medical Secrets of a Frontier Official* contained a section called "Eleven Notes on the remedies for Umbilical Stump Excretion, Swelling and Boils of Infants" (Hsiao-êrh ch'i chih-ch'u ping ch'uang-chung fang i-shih-i shou). But it was not until the twelfth century, with the publication of *A Thorough Discussion*, that the relative harmlessness of these infections and their difference from the tetanus of a lethal kind was clarified. See Wang, *Wai-t'ai mi-yao fang, chuan* 36, pp. 57–60; "Ch'i-fêng ts'o-k'ou," *Hsiao-êrh wei-shêng tsung-wei lun-fang, chuan* 1, pp. 56–58.

46. *Advice for Safe Birth, Infant Rearing, and Maintaining Health (Pao-ch'an yü-ying yang-shêng lu)*, a popular health manual written during the Ming period, had meticulous instruction for the refined procedure. It had it that: "When wrapping an umbilical stump, one should prepare a four-*ts'un* [inch] square piece of soft white silk, folded with half-a-*ch'un* thickness of new cotton and additional silk fabric. It should be tied neither too tight nor too loose. . . . Twenty days after birth, unwrap the umbilical stump and examine it. In the event that it appears too dry or irritating to the infant's abdomen, causing him to hurt or cry, it should be unwrapped. Change the bandage and wrap it up again. When unwrapping the umbilical stump, be sure the doors are shut and the curtains drawn. During winter, keep it warm by

putting it near a fire. And apply some mild powder [*wên-fên*] upon it." See "Kuo-ch'i fa," *Pao-ch'an yü-ying yang-shêng lu, chuan* 1.

47. Li, *I-hsüeh ju-mên*, in KCTSCC, *chuan* 422, p. 346; There are many kinds of desiccant medical powders to be applied when wrapping the umbilical stump mentioned in traditional medical texts. Some of the more common ones are the mild powder in *Pao-ch'an yü-ying yang-shêng lu, chuan* 1, or the so-called dried alum powder in *Tan-hsi hsien-shêng chih-fa hsin-yao*, pp. 909–10; Kao, *Ku-tai êrh-k'o chi-ping hsin-lun*, pp. 3–4.

48. Lu, *Ying-t'ung pai-wên, chuan* 1, pp. 21–34; Wan, *Yü-ying chia-mi*, pp. 59–60; K'ou, *Ch'üan-yu hsin-chien, chuan* 2; Ch'in, "Ch'i-fêng ts'o-k'ou," *Yu-k'o chin-chên*, pp. 5–7; Wu, *Yu-k'o tsa-ping hsin-fa yao-chüeh*, pp. 25–30.

49. At least as early as the T'ang dynasty, Sun Ssû-miao's works attested to the popular custom of mouth wiping. The opening lines of Sun's "Discussion on Newborn Infants" (Ch'u-shêng ch'u-fu lun) said, "As the infant is just born, first wrap cotton around the figure and wipe the bluish tar and foul blood from his mouth and tongue. This is called 'jade hold' [*yü-hêng*]. If one does not wipe this off quickly, once the infant starts crying, it will enter into his stomach and cause countless illnesses." See Sun, *Shao-hsiao ying-ju fang*, pp. 30b–31a.

50. K'ou, "Shih-k'ou fa," *Ch'üan-yu hsin-chien, chuan* 2; Wei, "Chiu-fa lun," *Shih-i tê-hsiao fang, chuan* 422, p. 31b; *Pao-ch'an yü-ying yang-shêng lu, chuan* 1; Hsü, *Ku-chin i-t'ung ta-ch'üan*, pp. 5736–39.

51. K'ou, "Shih-k'ou fa," *Ch'üan-yu hsin-chien, chuan* 2.

52. Chang, "Ch'u-tan fa," *Ching-yüeh ch'üan-shu, chuan* 40, pp. 75–76.

53. Kao, "Hsin-shêng-êrh chi-ping lei" (Diseases of the newborn), *Ku-tai êrh-k'o chi-ping hsin-lun*, pp. 11–13.

54. Cloherty and Stark, *Manual of Neonatal Care*, pp. 203–206.

55. Chang, "Ch'u-tan fa," *Ching-yüeh ch'üan-shu, chuan* 40, pp. 75–76.

56. Hsüeh, *Pao-ying ch'üan-shu, chuan* 1, pp. 3–5.

57. Chang, "Ch'u-tan fa," *Ching-yüeh ch'üan-shu, chuan* 40, pp. 75–76; Ch'êng, "Shih-k'ou," *I-shu*, pp. 917–18; Wu, "Shih-k'ou," *Yu-k'o tsa-ping hsin-fa yao-chüeh*, pp. 12–14.

58. Ch'êng suggested that "when the infant is just born and has not yet cried, use a finger to wipe his mouth lightly and remove dirty blood. Then wrap a finger with silk soaked in licorice juice to wipe off the saliva in the mouth" or "use salt water on silk to wash its mouth and remove sticky saliva." This was intended to clean the fluids in the infant's mouth and guard against such diseases as those traditionally called "horse tooth, goose mouth, heavy tongue, and wooden tongue." Ch'êng also agreed with physicians, such as Ch'ên Fei-hsia, that in caring for infants one should consider extending "mouth wiping," whether with salt water or mild ginger soup. Wipe the infant's mouth and tongue three to six times a day all the way up until his first birthday. As long as one "wipes and cleans every day, malice will be removed along with the saliva. From where then can disease arise?" See Ch'êng, "K'ai-k'ou," *I-shu*, pp. 918–19.

59. Chang, "Ch'u-tan fa," *Ching-yüeh ch'üan-shu, chuan* 40, pp. 75–76.

60. Sun, "Discussion on Newborn Infants" (Ch'u-shêng ch'u-fu lun), *Shao-hsiao ying-ju fang*, pp. 30b–31a.

61. Wang, *Wai-t'ai mi-yao fang*, chuan 35, pp. 442–43.

62. "On Washing and Bathing" (Hsi-yü lun), from *A Thorough Discussion*, the Sung dynasty author explained in detail as to the proper preparation of the bathing water: "When boiling the water, for every deciliter (*tou*), add the medicinal ingredients and boil it down to seven liters (*shêng*). Remove any sediment. Feel the temperature and then use it. It should neither be too hot in the winter, nor too cold during the summer. It must be adjusted to the right [temperature] before use." See "Hsi-yü lun," *Hsiao-êrh wei-shêng tsung-wei lun-fang*, chuan 1, pp. 52–53.

63. *A Thorough Discussion* serves as a good example of these Sung pediatric instructions. It states: "When an infant is just born, it must first be bathed to remove the filth. After that, the umbilical cord may be broken. If one breaks the umbilical cord first, the bathing water will enter the umbilical stump and cause such ailments as umbilical boils. As for the bath water, medicinal ingredients ought to be added. One should prepare it in advance, store it in a bottle, and warm it for use as the time arrives. It is best not to touch any unboiled water [*pu-fan shêng-shui*]." See "Hsi-yü lun," *Hsiao-êrh wei-shêng tsung-wei lun-fang*, chuan 1, pp. 52–53.

64. An article called "Methods of Bathing Infants" (Yü-êrh fa) from the Ming text *Advice for Safe Birth*, for instance, thought that maintaining the warmth of the newborn before and after the first washing was of grave importance. It advised wrapping the infant in cotton while waiting to bathe him and keeping him warm after the bath. See *Pao-ch'an yü-ying yang-shêng lu*, chuan 1.

65. Wang, "Ch'u-tan lun," *Ying-t'ung lei-ts'ui*, pp. 61–65.

66. Kao, "Yü-êrh fa," *Ku-tai êrh-k'o chi-ping hsin-lun*, pp. 4–5.

67. K'ou, "Ch'u-shêng yü-fa," *Ch'üan-yu hsin-chien*, chuan 2; Sun, "Yü-êrh fa," *Ch'ih-shui yüan-chu*, chuan 25, pp. 843–44; Wang, "Yü-êrh fa," *Yu-k'o chun-shêng*, chuan 1, p. 10; Wu, "Tuan-ch'i," *Yu-k'o tsa-ping hsin-fa yao-chüeh*, pp. 14–15.

68. For instance, in the famous novel *Chin-p'ing-mei*, Hsi-men Ching paid for the occasion of "washing on the third" for Li P'ing-êrh's new baby. See Hsiao-hsiao-shêng, *Chin-p'ing-mei*, chap. 31, p. 459.

69. Of these, the five-root soup was the most popular. Its recipe is as follows: "When washing the infant on the third day, I always use five-root soup and find it nice. What constitutes five-root soup are [roots from] mulberry [*sang*], locust [*huai*], elm [*yü*], peach [*t'ao*], and willow [*liu*]. Pick twenty to thirty-three-*ch'un* [inch] tender lengths of each, to cook into a soup. Adjust its temperature, add the juice of two pig's gallbladders and bathe in it. This will prevent the baby from developing scabies within the first year, also keep him from evil influences [*pi hsieh-o*]." See Sun, *Ch'ih-shui yüan-chu*. Other medicinal plants such as the leaves and blanches of *coix agrestis* (*i-i*) were also used.

70. *Ch'ih-shui yüan-chu* stated that: "Bathing the infant on the third day is thus only a ritual. If the infant is born weak, delaying it for over ten days or half a month will cause no harm. Choose a clear and good day, and bathe him in a room with no draft." See Sun, "Yü-êrh fa," *Ch'ih-shui yüan-chu*, chuan 25, pp. 843–44.

71. From earlier medical texts, we know that it was believed in ancient China that during pregnancy the fetus could receive a sort of "heat poison" (*jê-tu*) from the conception that later became the source of disease. For this reason, texts advised using cooling laxatives on the infant after birth to clear this "fetal poison" before

beginning to nurse. The earliest method used was the "cinnabar and honey method" (*chu-mi fa*). Medical scholars of the Sui and T'ang eras began promoting the use of the more gentle "licorice method" (*kan-ts'ao fa*). Such T'ang medical texts as *Prescriptions Worth a Thousand* and *Medical Secrets of a Frontier Official* prescribed cleaning the "foul liquids in the chest" (*hsiung-chung o-chih*). Paste or juice made with licorice, with cinnabar and honey, or with ox bezoar was often used for this purpose. Either through vomiting or bowel movement, the infant was to be rid of the meconium before he started nursing. *Prescriptions Worth a Thousand* also mentioned that if no effect was produced after administering the prepared licorice juice, one should not press any further for fear of harming the child. See Sun, "Ch'u-shêng ch'u-fu lun," *Shao-hsiao ying-ju fang*, pp. 30b–31a; Wang, *Wai-t'ai mi-yao fang*, *chuan* 35, pp. 421–29.

72. In the article K'ou noted that: "Ancient medical texts claimed that when an infant is first born, one should administer cinnabar powder, white honey, or *coptis japonica* to bring down the fetal poison. The better physicians all know this quite well. My opinion, however, is that when comparing people today with those of ancient times, the way they handled their daily living, eating, and care was quite different. Those old recipes contain drugs that can harm one's spleen and hurt one's strength. When administered to infants, they are bound to make them ill. . . . In general, humans are the same as everything else; their growth begins at the root. If the root is solid and strong, it will endure wind and chill. . . . To bring down the fetal poison, one may simply boil some lightly fermented soybeans into a thick juice and administer it three to five times. The poison will be naturally expelled. This can also aid him [the infant] in the cultivation of the *ch'i* of the spleen and in the digestion of milk and food. The lightly fermented soybeans used are without salt." See K'ou, "Hsia t'ai-tu," *Ch'üan-yu hsin-chien*, *chuan* 2.

73. Wang, "Hsia t'ai-tu lun," *Yu-k'o lei-ts'ui*, *chuan* 1, pp. 11–12; Hsü, "Hsia t'ai-tu fa," *Ku-chin i-t'ung ta-ch'üan*, *chuan* 10, p. 5639; Wang, "Fu-yao hsia t'ai-tu fa," *Yu-k'o chun-shêng*, pp. 10–11. These pediatric works stressed that the differences in "everyday living, eating and care" of the past and of the present were the bases for their revision. Whereas in fact continuous advancements in pediatric knowledge and medical thinking were probably a more powerful factor for the more considerate and sophisticated approach.

74. Kao, "Hsieh-tu fa," *Ku-tai êrh-k'o chi-ping hsin-lun*, pp. 6–7.

75. Ch'ên, "T'iao-hsieh," *Yu-yu chi-ch'êng*, *chuan* 1, pp. 26–27.

76. Chang, "Hsiao-êrh ch'u-shêng wei-han," *I-shuo*, *chuan* 10, p. 746.

77. The late Ming pediatrician Wang Ta-lun, in "Discussion on Newborns" (Ch'u-tan lun) from his *Essentials in Looking After Infants and Children* (*Ying-t'ung lei-ts'ui*) (pp. 61–65), also advised people that "when first out of the womb, it [the infant] ought to be [kept] warm."

78. "Hui-ch'i lun," *Hsiao-êrh wei-shêng tsung-wei lun-fang*, *chuan* 1, p. 52.

79. Ch'ên, *San-yin chi-i ping-chêng fang-lun*, *chuan* 18, pp. 426–27; Chang, *I-shuo*, *chuan* 1; Wei, *Shih-i tê-hsiao fang*, p. 359; K'ou, *Ch'üan-yu hsin-chien*, *chuan* 2; Hsü, *Ku-chin i-t'ung ta-ch'üan*, pp. 5636–37; Sun, *Ch'ih-shui yüan-chu*, *chuan* 25, p. 3; Wang, *Ying-t'ung lei-ts'ui*, pp. 61–65.

80. "Hui-ch'i lun," *Hsiao-êrh wei-shêng tsung-wei lun-fang*, *chuan* 1, p. 52.

81. K'ou, "Hu-yang fa," "Ch'u-shêng chiang-hu fa," and "Chiang-hu fa t'ang-shih wei hu-yang," *Ch'üan-yu hsin-chien, chuan* 2.

82. Wang, "Ch'u-tan," *Ying-t'ung lei-ts'ui*, pp. 61–65.

83. Ch'ên, "Ch'u-tan chiu-hu," *Yu-yu chi-ch'êng, chuan* 1, pp. 25–26.

84. Thomas E. Cone Jr., *History of American Pediatrics*; idem, *History of the Care and Feeding of the Premature Infant*; George F. Smith and Dharmapuri Vidyasagar, eds., *Historical Review and Recent Advances in Neonatal and Perinatal Medicine*, vol. 1, *Neonatal Medicine*.

85. For discussions on the general trend of popularization in pediatric medicine, as well as the evolution of this area of the state, of Confucian scholars together with medical scholars, see Hsiung, "Pediatric Medicine in the Ming Period" (Ming-tai tê yu-k'o i-hsüeh), pp. 53–69.

86. Wu, "Tuan-ch'i," *Yu-k'o tsa-ping hsin-fa yao-chüeh*, p. 14.

87. Lu, *Ying-t'ung pai-wên*, pp. 21–34; Wan, *Yu-k'o fa-hui*, pp. 59–60; K'ou, *Ch'üan-yu hsin-chien, chuan* 2; Ch'in, "Ch'i-fêng ts'o-k'ou," *Yu-k'o chin-chên*, pp. 5–7; Wu, *Yu-k'o tsa-ping hsin-fa yao-chüeh*, pp. 25–30.

88. K'ou, *Ch'üan-yu hsin-chien, chuan* 2.

89. Wu "Tuan-ch'i," *Yu-k'o tsa-ping hsin-fa yao-chüeh*, p. 12.

90. Liu, "The Demographic Dynamics of Some Clans in the Lower Yangtze Area, ca. 1400–1900," pp. 115–60; idem, "The Demography of Two Chinese Clans in Hsiao-shan, Chekiang, 1650–1850," pp. 13–61; Yüan, "Life Tables for a Southern Chinese Family from 1365–1849," pp. 157–79.

91. For a monographic treatment of the subject, see Hsiung, *Yu-yu: Ch'uan-t'ung chung-kuo tê ch'iang-pao chih tao*.

CHAPTER 3

This chapter has been adapted from chapter 5 of *Yu-yu: Ch'uan-t'ung chung-kuo tê ch'iang-pao chih tao* (To nurse the young: Infant care in traditional China) (Taipei: Lien-ching, 1995).

1. Yen, *Tso Wên-hsiang-kung nien-p'u*, p. 5.

2. Yao, *Ch'ing Shao Nien-lu hsien-shêng T'ing-ts'ai nien-p'u*, p. 9.

3. Chao, *Ch'ing Ts'ên Hsiang-ch'in-kung Yü-ying nien-p'u*, pp. 7–8.

4. Chien, "Chi-yü-ju pu-nêng-shih," *Hsiao-êrh yao-chêng chih-chüeh*, p. 18.

5. Wan, *Yu-k'o fa-hui, chuan* 3, pp. 66–69.

6. See World Health Organization, *Contemporary Patterns of Breastfeeding*.

7. See Whitehead, *Maternal Diet, Breast-Feeding Capacity, and Lactational Infertility*; Dobbing, *Maternal Nutrition and Lactational Infertility*.

8. According to Valerie Fildes, notions on breast-feeding from Western medical and advice literature remained mostly unchanged from around 700 to 1860. See Fildes, *Wet Nursing: A History from Antiquity to the Present*.

9. See Sun, *Shao-hsiao ying-ju fang*, p. 6; Wang, *Wai-t'ai mi-yao fang, chuan* 35, pp. 444–46; Lee Jen-der has discussed reproduction and women's health in pre-T'ang China, see Lee Jen-der, "Han-t'ang chih-chien i-shu chung tê shêng-ch'an chih tao" (Childbirth in the medical writings of late antiquity and early medieval China), Chung-yang yen-chiu-yüan li-shih yü-yen yen-chiu-so chi k'an (*Bulletin of the insti-*

tute of history and philogy, Academia Sinica), 67 (3): 533–654; idem, "Han-t'ang chih chien chiu-tzû i-fang shih-t'an: Chien-lun fu-k'o lan-shang yü hsing-pieh lun-shu" (Reproductive medicine in late antiquity and early medieval China: Gender discourse and the birth of gynecology), *Chung-yang yen-chiu-yüan li-shih yü-yen yen-chiu-so chi-k'an (Bulletin of the institute of history and philogy, Academia Sinica),* 68 (2): 283– 367.

10. The text is not clear whether it is the mother or the child who is not to eat too much. There may have been textual corruption.

11. "Ju-mu lun," *Hsiao-êrh wei-shêng tsung-wei lun-fang, chuan* 2, pp. 10–11. In rendering this and other texts in this essay into English, I have benefited from discussions with Lawrence Gartner and Charles Stone.

12. Ch'ên, "Ch'an-ju chi," *Fu-jên ta-ch'üan liang-fang, chuan* 24, p. 8.

13. Tsêng, "I ju-shih-shih pu-pu-chieh," *Huo-yu k'ou-i, chuan* 5, pp. 79–80.

14. "Ju-êrh fa," *Pao-ch'an yü-ying yang-shêng lu, chuan* 1.

15. K'ou, "Ju-êrh fa," *Ch'üan-yu hsin-chien, chuan* 2; Wang, "Ju-pu lun," *Yu-k'o lei-ts'ui, chuan* 1, pp. 9–10; Hsü, "Ju-pu," *Ku-chin i-t'ung ta-ch'üan, chuan* 10, p. 5633.

16. K'ou, "Ju-êrh fa," *Ch'üan-yu hsin-chien, chuan* 2.

17. Wang, "Ju-pu lun," *Yu-k'o lei-ts'ui, chuan* 1, p. 10.

18. Ch'ên, "Ch'an-ju chi," *Fu-jên ta-ch'üan liang-fang, chuan* 24, p. 9.

19. Wei, "Ju-pu fa," *Shih-i tê-hsiao fang, chuan* 11, p. 17; K'ou, "Ju-êrh fa," *Ch'üan-yu hsin-chien, chuan* 2.

20. Ch'ên, "Ch'an-ju chi," *Fu-jên ta-ch'üan liang-fang, chuan* 24, p. 9.

21. K'ou, "Ju-êrh fa," *Ch'üan-yu hsin-chien, chuan* 2.

22. Wei, "Ju-pu fa," *Shih-i tê-hsiao fang, chuan* 11, p. 17.

23. K'ou, "Ju-êrh fa," *Ch'üan-yu hsin-chien, chuan* 2.

24. Kao, *Ku-tai êrh-k'o chi-ping hsin-lun,* pp. 24–28; Houlbrooke, *English Family Life, 1576–1716,* pp. 103–4.

25. "Ju-êrh fa," *Pao-ch'an yü-ying yang-shêng lu, chuan* 1; K'ou, "Ju-êrh fa," *Ch'üan-yu hsin-chien, chuan* 2.

26. Ch'ên, "Ch'an-ju chi," *Fu-jên ta-ch'üan liang-fang, chuan* 24, p. 10.

27. "Ju-êrh fa," *Pao-ch'an yü-ying yang-shêng lu, chuan* 1.

28. Chu, "Ju-êrh fa," *Tz'u-yu hsin-ch'uan,* p. 3.

29. K'ou, "Ju ling-êrh-ping chêng," *Ch'üan-yu hsin-chien, chuan* 2.

30. Wang, "Ju-pu lun," *Yu-k'o lei-ts'ui, chuan* 1, p. 9.

31. European references from the twelfth to the fifteenth centuries such as *Practica Puerorum* mentioned folkloric practices like the "nail test" to check on the quality of the human milk. It also recommended looking into a crystal or placing drops of human milk "upon a rock or polished sword" to tell its character. As quoted in Fildes, *Wet Nursing,* pp. 32–33.

32. See Fildes *Wet Nursing,* chaps. 2 and 3, pp. 26–35.

33. "Ju-mu lun," *Hsiao-êrh wei-shêng tsung-wei lun-fang, chuan* 2, p. 9.

34. Concerning the matter of hired milk, doctors and scholars of the Sung, Yüan, Ming, and Ch'ing did not have serious disagreements. Ch'êng Hao's suggestion was the only deliberation on the subject. See "Chia-fan tien chih-chia p'ien," in *Ku-chin t'u-shu chi-ch'êng,* vol. 321, *chuan* 2, p. 10a. This traditional Chinese humanitar-

ianism is different from the Western attitude toward hiring wet nurses. The Western consideration was on the importance of the nutrition of the mother's own milk and concern that the low quality of the hired milk could cause the child to die prematurely.

35. Stone, *The Family, Sex, and Marriage in England, 1500–1800*, pp. 55, 65, 269–73; Mitterauer and Sieder, *The European Family*, p. 42.

36. Valerie Fildes discusses changing patterns of what she calls "professional breastfeeding" in Western history and speaks of the beginning of the modern reforms. See Fildes, *Wet Nursing*, chap. 8, pp. 111–26.

37. Sun, "Tsê-ju-mu fa," *Shao-hsiao ying-ju fang*, p. 6.

38. Wang, "Tsê-ju-mu fa," *Wai-t'ai mi-yao fang, chuan* 35, p. 446.

39. Ch'ên, "Chiang-hu ying-êrh fang-lun," *Fu-jên ta-ch'üan liang-fang, chuan* 24, pp. 9–10.

40. "Tsê-ju-mu fa," *Pao-ch'an yü-ying yang-shêng lu, chuan* 1.

41. K'ou, "Ju ling-êrh-ping chêng," *Ch'üan-yu hsin-chien, chuan* 2.

42. Chu, "Tsê-ju-mu," *Tz'u-yu hsin-ch'uan*, p. 4.

43. Wang, "Tsê-ju-mu lun," *Ying-t'ung lei-ts'ui*, pp. 7–8.

44. Ibid.

45. Wang, "Pu êrh fa," *Wai-tai mi-yao fang, chuan* 35, p. 444.

46. Tsêng, "I ju-shih-shih pu-pu-chieh," *Huo-yu k'ou-i, chuan* 35, pp. 79–80.

47. Wei, "Ju-pu fa," *Shih-i tê-hsiao fang, chuan* 11, p. 17.

48. "Pu êrh fa," *Pao-ch'an yü-ying yang-shêng lu, chuan* 1; K'ou, "Ju ling-êrh-ping chêng," *Ch'üan-yu hsin-chien, chuan* 2.

49. "Pu êrh fa," *Pao-ch'an yü-ying yang-shêng lu, chuan* 1.

50. Another paragraph from the same text had it that "three days after a child is born, he should be given a little food. One may cook millet into a congee-like drink, grind it into a milk-like form, and give him a half shell every day. This is to help with digestion and to get his stomach and intestines moving." See "Pu êrh fa," *Pao-ch'an yü-ying yang-shêng lu, chuan* 1.

51. "Pu-êrh fa," *Pao-ch'an yü-ying yang-shêng lu, chuan* 1.

52. Ibid.

53. Ibid.

54. K'ou, "Ju ling-êrh-ping chêng," *Ch'üan-yu hsin-chien, chuan* 2.

55. *Ku-chin t'u-shu chi-ch'êng, chuan* 422, p. 34a.

56. Ibid.

57. Ibid.

58. Wang, "Ju-pu," *Yu-k'o chun-shêng, chuan* 1, p. 9.

59. Ch'êng, *I-shu*, pp. 915–16.

60. *Ku-chin t'u-shu chi-ch'êng, chuan* 422, p. 34a. Although cited as from Ch'ien I, this passage does not appear on the text of *Proven Formula* as existent today.

61. K'ou, "Pu êrh," *Ch'üan-yu hsin-chien, chuan* 2.

62. Ch'ien, "Chi-yü-ju pu-nêng-shih," *Hsiao-êrh yao-chêng chih-chüeh*, p. 18.

63. Chang, "Pu-ju," *I-shuo, chuan* 10, p. 12; Wei, "Pu-ju," *Shih-i tê-hsiao fang, chuan* 11, pp. 14–15; Wang, *Yu-k'o lei-ts'ui, chuan* 3, pp. 61–62, 74–75.

64. "Ch'u-shêng pu-ju pu-hsiao-pien," *Hsiao-êrh wei-shêng tsung-wei lun-fang, chuan* 1, p. 56; Wang, "Pu-ju," *Yu-k'o chun-shêng, chuan* 1, p. 12; Kung, "Pu-ju," *Shou-shih pao-yüan, chuan* 8, pp. 572–73; Ch'êng, "Pu-ju," *I-shu, chuan* 14, p. 920.

65. Wu, "Pu-ju," *Yu-k'o tsa-ping hsin-fa yao-chüeh*, p. 18.

66. See discussions in Ch'ên, "Pu-ju," *Chung-i êrh-k'o hsüeh*, p. 24.

67. Ch'ien, "Shêng-hsia t'u" and "T'u-ju," *Hsiao-êrh yao-chêng chih-chüeh*, pp. 14–15; Chang, *I-shuo, chuan* 10, p. 6.

68. Tsêng, *Huo-yu k'ou-i, chuan* 5, pp. 73–74; Lu, *Ying-t'ung pai-wên, chuan* 5, pp. 338–45.

69. Wan, "Ou-t'u," *Yu-k'o fa-hui, chuan* 1, p. 66.

70. Ibid.

71. Ibid.

72. Ibid.

73. Hsüeh, "Ou t'u ju," *Pao-ying ch'üan-shu, chuan* 5, pp. 661–73; Wang, "Pu-ju" and "T'u pu-chih," *Yu-k'o chun-shêng, chuan* 1, pp. 12–13; Chang, "T'u-ju," *Ching-yüeh ch'üan-shu, chuan* 41, pp. 101–2; Sun, "Shang-ju," *Ch'ih-shui yüan-chu*, p. 25; Wu, *Yu-k'o tsa-ping hsin-fa yao-chüeh*, pp. 39–41; Ch'êng, *I-shu*, pp. 954–55.

74. K'ou, "Ju-êrh fa," *Ch'üan-yu hsin-chien, chuan* 2.

75. K'ou P'ing and Wang K'ên-t'ang both expressed concern over children not weaned by the age of four or five years. Kung T'ing-hsien, however, said that children at the age of five or six should be weaned. K'ou, "Tuan-ju fa," *Ch'üan-yu hsin-chien, chuan* 2; Wang, "Tuan-ju fa," *Yu-k'o chun-shêng, chuan* 1, p. 6; Kung, "Tuan-ju," *Shou-shih pao-yüan, chuan* 7, p. 518.

76. Chu, "Tuan-ju fang," *Tan-hsi hsien-shêng chih-fa hsin-yao, chuan* 8, p. 913.

77. K'ou, "Tuan-ju fa," *Ch'üan-yu hsin-chien, chuan* 2.

78. Chu, "Tuan-ju fang," *Tan-hsi hsien-shêng chih-fa hsin-yao, chuan* 8, p. 913, had specific instructions for weaning difficulties.

79. K'ou, "Tuan-ju fa," *Ch'üan-yu hsin-chien, chuan* 2.

80. Kung, "Tuan-ju," *Shou-shih pao-yüan, chuan* 7, p. 518.

81. Wan, "Ou-t'u," *Yu-k'o fa-hui, chuan* 1, pp. 66–67.

82. Ibid., p. 67.

83. Ibid., pp. 67–68.

84. Ibid., pp. 68–69.

85. Ibid., p. 69.

86. Wei, "Hsiao-êrh ju-ping," *Hsü ming-i lei-an*, pp. 82–84.

87. Ibid., pp. 82–84.

88. Ibid.

89. Kao, *Ku-tai êrh-k'o chi-ping hsin-lun*, p. 25.

90. Wei, "Hsiao-êrh ju-ping," *Hsü ming-i lei-an*, p. 84.

91. Ibid., p. 84.

92. Ch'ên, *Hou-kuan Ch'ên Shih-i nien-p'u*, p. 11.

93. P'i, *Ch'ing P'i Lu-mên hsien-shêng Hsi-jui nien-p'u*, pp. 4–5.

94. Yen, *Tso Wên-hsiang-kung nien-p'u*, p. 5.

95. Chao, *Ch'ing Ts'ên Hsiang-ch'in-kung Yü-ying nien-p'u*, pp. 7–8.

96. Nien, *Ch'ung-tê lao-jên tzû-ting nien-p'u*, p. 9.

97. Hsü, *Min-kuo Ch'ên Ying-shih hsien-shêng Ch'i-mei nien-p'u*, p. 4.

98. Yao, *Ch'ing Shao Nien-lu hsien-shêng T'ing-ts'ai nien-p'u*, p. 9.

99. Hsü, *Ch'ing P'i Lu-mên hsien-shêng Hsi-jui nien-p'u*, pp. 3–4.

100. Wang, *Wang Jang-ch'ing hsien-shêng chuan-chi*, p. 10.

CHAPTER 4

1. See, for instance, the essays in Ebrey and Watson, *Kinship Organization in Late Imperial China, 1000–1940.*

2. Sun, *Mêng-tzû chu-shu, chuan* 13, p. 291.

3. Wang, *San-tzû Ching*, p. 1.

4. Ibid.

5. Extant *nien-p'u* of the Ming-Ch'ing period number more than eight hundred. Those of the Ch'ing dynasty represent the majority and are the richest and most informative. *Nien-p'u* recorded lives of merchants, peasants, artisans, artists, the military, as well as minority and religious figures in addition to the usual gentry-official figures. However, only about half of the *nien-p'u* contain meaningful accounts of childhood years, three to four hundred cases with vivid depictions of growing up experienced in this period. See Lai, *Chin San-pai-nien jên-wu nien-p'u chih-chien lu.*

6. Cheng Hsüan, Li-chi chêng-chu, chuan 8, pp. 28–29.

7. Ssû-ma, *Chü-chia tsa-i*, pp. 5–6; Hu Kuang, ed., *Hsing-li ta-ch'üan, chuan* 45, p. 41; Chu, *Chin-ssû Lu, chuan* 11, p. 1b.

8. Ssû-ma Kuang laid out development programs for boys and girls to age eight. See Ssû-ma, "Chiao-nan-nü" (Instructing boys and girls), *Chü-chia tsa-i, chuan* 19, p. 333.

9. Ibid.

10. In middle- and upper-class families, the wet nurse, maids, and other women in the household staff could play a vital role in shaping a child's experience. These various female helpers were unrelated to the family and had the low status of servants, yet their duty of daily care for the physical and emotional needs of the child helped to build a strong bond between them and the children they raised. Appreciating the importance of their role, contemporary medical texts as well as pedagogical literature recommended that special attention be paid to choosing appropriate wet nurses or nannies. See Yao, *Ch'ing Shao Nien-lu hsien-shêng T'ing-ts'ai nien-p'u*, p. 9; Miu, *I-fêng lao-jên nien-p'u*, p. 2; Wung, *Wung T'ieh-an nien-p'u*, p. 2.

11. Wang, *Ping-t'a mêng-hên lu*, pp. 5–8.

12. Sometimes, the feelings among different wives of the same man were not cordial and thus created a distressful emotional environment and destructive living condition for their young. Children born of a first wife were not guaranteed attention and affection either. See Yang, *T'an Ssû-t'ung nien-p'u, pp.* 24–26.

13. See Chiang, *Niu K'ung-shan hsien-shêng nien-p'u*, p. 2.

14. Pao, *Lü Liu-liang nien-p'u*, p. 7.

15. Wang, *Ping-t'a mêng-hên lu*, p. 5.

16. Chang, "Shu-sao wu-fu, ch'ing ho i-k'an? Ch'ing-tai li-chih yü jên-ch'ing chih ch'ung-t'u i-li" (The Conflict between Classic Ritual and Human Desire in Late Imperial China: A Case Study of Mourning Garments), in Hsiung and Lu, ed., *Li-chiao yü ch'ing-yü: Ch'ien-chin-tai chung-kuo wên-hua chung-tê hou/hsien-tai hsing* (Neo-Confucian orthodoxy and human desires: Post/Modernity in pre-modern Chinese culture), pp. 125–78.

17. My study on changing patterns and contents of early education explains some of these developments. See Hsiung, "Hao-tê-k'ai-shih: Chung-kuo chin-shih shih-jên tzû-ti tê yu-nien chiao-yü" (Getting off with a good start: Early childhood

education of elite families in late imperial China), pp. 203–38; Hsiung, "Shei-jên chih-tzû? Chung-kuo chia-t'ing yü li-shih mai-lo-chung tê êrh-t'ung ting-i wên-t'i" (Whose Children are They? Reflections on the Status of Children in the Context of Chinese Family and History), pp. 259–94.

18. For discussions on activities related to children's literature, see Hsiung, "êrh-t'ung wên-hsüeh" (Children's literature), pp. 31–38.

19. For detailed discussions on the role of mothers and female relatives on a child's initial education, see Hsiung, "Hao-tê-k'ai-shih: Chung-kuo chin-shih shih-jên tzû-ti tê yu-nien chiao-yü," pp. 203–38.

20. In his essay "Famous Chinese Childhoods," Kenneth J. Dewoskin talks about the records of usually brilliant childhoods in early imperial China and the built-in cultural bias in official biographies.

21. Wung, *Wung T'ieh-an nien-p'u*, pp. 2–3.

22. Fêng, *Li Shu-ku hsien-shêng nien-p'u, chuan* 1, p. 3.

23. Chao, *Ch'ing Hsia Êrh-ming hsien-shêng Ching-ch'ü nien-p'u*, p. 14.

24. Hu, *Pao Shên-po hsien-shêng nien-p'u*, pp. 11–12.

25. Liu, *Wang-shih fu-tzû nien-p'u*, pp. 4–5.

26. T'ang, "T'ang Chieh-t'ai mu-piao," in *Ch'ien Shu*, pp. 213–15.

27. Liang, *T'ui-an tzû-ting nien-p'u*, p. 4.

28. Wei, *Lin Wên-chung-kung nien-p'u*, p. 6.

29. Liu, *Wang-shih fu-tzû nien-p'u*, pp. 5–6.

30. Chiang, *Ch'üan Hsieh-shan hsien-shêng nien-p'u*, p. 68.

31. Yao, *Ts'ui Tung-pi nien-p'u*, p. 1.

32. Ibid., p. 2.

33. Ibid., p. 3.

34. Ibid.

35. Ibid., pp. 4–5.

36. See Chu, *T'ung-mêng hsü-chih*.

37. Tung, *Kung Chih-lu nien-p'u*, pp. 2–6.

38. Huang, *Wang Hsi-chuang hsieh-shêng nien-p'u*, pp. 2–3.

39. Huang, *Shao Êrh-yün hsien-shêng nien-p'u*, pp. 11–12.

40. Liu, *Tuan Yü-ts'ai nien-p'u*, pp. 3–4.

41. Liang, *T'ui-an tzû-ting nien-p'u*, pp. 3–4.

42. Chang, *Ku T'ing-lin hsien-shêng nien-p'u*, pp. 5–8.

43. Huang, *Huang Chung-tsê nien-p'u*, pp. 1–2.

44. Ni, *Ming Ni Wên-chêng-kung (Yüan-lu) nien-p'u*, pp. 2–6.

45. Yeh, *Yao Shih-fu chuan*, p. 105; Hu, *Chang Shih-chai hsien-shêng nien-p'u*, pp. 1–5; Fang, *Hsü Sung-k'an hsien-shêng nien-p'u*, p. 2.

46. T'ang, *Sun Hsia-fêng hsien-shêng nien-p'u*, p. 7.

47. Ch'ien, "Hsi-chih hsien-shêng mu-chih-ming," *Ch'ien-yen-t'ang wên-chi, chuan* 48, pp. 5–7.

48. Ting, *Hsü Hsia-k'o hsien-shêng nien-p'u*, p. 6.

49. Tung, *Kung Chih-lu nien-p'u*, p. 2.

50. Pao, *Lü Liu-liang nien-p'u*, p. 9.

51. T'ang, *Sun Hsia-fêng hsien-shêng nien-p'u*, p. 2.

52. Chang, *Yen Ch'ien-chiu hsien-shêng nien-p'u*, pp. 17–18.

53. Chiang, *Niu K'ung-shan hsien-shêng nien-p'u*, p. 3.
54. Huang, *Huang Chung-tsê nien-p'u*, pp. 1–2.
55. Chien, *Chu chiu-chiang hsien-shêng nien-p'u*, p. 3.
56. Wên, *Wei Shu-tzû nien-p'u*, p. 3.
57. Yao, *Ch'ing Shao Nien-lu hsien-shêng T'ing-ts'ai nien-p'u*, pp. 9–22.
58. Chiang, *Ch'üan Hsieh-shan hsien-shêng nien-p'u*, pp. 9–10.
59. Ma, *Ma Tuan-min-kung nien-p'u*, pp. 11–13.
60. Dewoskin, "Famous Chinese Childhoods," pp. 57–78.
61. Pei-yi Wu's book, *The Confucian's Progress: Autobiographical Writings in Traditional China*, gives a good account of the historical evolution of China's auto-biographical writing in the larger context and the longer tradition of the literary genre of biographies.
62. Li, *Li Wên-chên-kung nien-p'u*, pp. 3–4.
63. Ch'ên, *Ch'ing K'ung Tung-t'ang hsien-shêng Shang-jên nien-p'u*, pp. 16–17.
64. Wang, *Wei Yüan nien-p'u*, pp. 1–4.
65. Wu, "Yü-ting-chih hsü," pp. 4–5.
66. Yin, *Yin P'u-ching shih-lang nien-p'u*, p. 4.
67. See Chapters 5 and 7.
68. Ch'ên, *Ch'ing K'ung Tung-t'ang hsien-shêng Shang-jên nien-p'u*, pp. 12–17.

CHAPTER 5

1. See, for instance, the observation of Johnson, "Women and Childbearing in Kwan Mun Hau Village: A Study of Social Change," pp. 215–42.
2. Margery Wolf has explained the particular value of mother-son bonds (clearly more so than the father-son relations on a personal level) in the context of uterine family. See Margery Wolf, *Women and the Family in Rural Taiwan*, pp. 32–41, 156–64.
3. See T'ang, *Ch'ien Shu*, pp. 79–80; see also Hsiung, "The Works in Obscurity: Life and Thought of a Provincial Intellectual in Seventeenth Century China."
4. Liu, *Tuan Yü-ts'ai hsien-shêng nien-p'u*, pp. 3–4.
5. Huang, *Wang Hsi-chuang hsien-shêng nien-p'u*, p. 3.
6. Wang, *Ping-t'a mêng-hên lu*, pp. 5–8.
7. Ch'ên, *Ming Ch'ên Pai-sha hsien-shêng nien-p'u*, p. 6.
8. Hsü, *Pi-chou-chai chu-jên nien-p'u*, pp. 3–4; Ch'ên, *Hou-kuan Ch'ên Shih-i nien-p'u*, p. 11; Hsü, *Min-kuo Ch'ên Ying-shih hsien-shêng Ch'i-mei nien-p'u*, p. 4.
9. Nieh, *Ch'ung-tê lao-jên tzû-ting nien-p'u*, p. 9.
10. Kuei, "The Life of My Deceased Mother" (Hsien-pi shih-lüeh), in *Chên-ch'uan wên-chi*, pp. 10–12.
11. P'i, *Ch'ing P'i Lu-mên hsien-shêng Hsi-jui nien-p'u*, pp. 4–5.
12. Yen, *Tso Wên-hsiang-kung nien-p'u*, pp. 4–5.
13. Ma, *Wu Mei-ts'un nien-p'u*, p. 18.
14. Shên, *Shên Wên-chung-kung tzû-ting nien-p'u*, p. 2.
15. Chang, "Pai-shih lao-jên tzû-shu," *Chuan-chi wên-hsüeh* 3, no. 1, p. 41.
16. Chao, *P'u-sa hsin-ch'ang tê ko-ming chia—Chü Chêng chuan*, p. 4.

17. Wung, *Wung T'ieh-an nien-p'u*, p. 4.

18. Chang, *Sun Yüan-ju hsien-shêng nien-p'u*, pp. 1–2.

19. Wang, *K'uei-yüan tzû-ting nien-p'u*, p. 4.

20. Miu, *I-fêng lao-jên nien-p'u*, p. 2.

21. In addition to the cases mentioned in this article, the following historical figures all lost their fathers at a young age and were said to have owed their upbringing entirely to the works of their widowed mothers: for the late-imperial period, Chu Shun-shui (1600–1682); Chang P'u (1602–1641); Chang Lü-hsiang (1611–1674); Wu Li (1631–1681); Hu Wei (1633–1714); Wung Shu-yüan (1633–1701); Yen Hsi-chai (1635–1704); Wang Fu (1677–1732); Yin Hui-i (1691–1748); Li Fan-hsieh (1692–1752); Hsia Ching-ch'ü (1705–1787); Wang Nien-sun (1744–1832); Huang Ching-jên (1749–1783); Ling T'ing-K'an (1757–1812); Ku Kuang-ch'i (1766–1835); Yang Fang (1770–1846) as well as, for the modern era, K'ang Yu-wei (1858–1927); Chiang Kai-shek (1887–1975); Hu Shih (1891–1962); Ch'ên Tu-hsiu (1879–1942); Ch'ü Ch'iu-pai (1899–1935); Yü Ta-fu (1896–1945); Fu Ssû-nien (1896–1946); Chêng Yen-fên (1902–1990); Wang Ch'ung-chih (1896–1970); Wang Juo-fei (1896–1946); Chêng Chên-wên (1891–1969); Chu Ching-nung (1887–1951); Lu Ti-p'ing (1887–1935); Kao Pu-ying (1873–1940); Li Shu-sên (1898–1964); Wang P'ing (1896–1982); Chang Yün (1896–1958); Chang Ching-yü (1895–1984); Wang Kuang-ch'i (1892–1963); Liu Shih-i (1886–1982); Hung Hsü-tung (1883–1945); Hu K'ang-min (1880–1953); Hsü Fu-lin (1879–1958); Wang T'ung-chao (1900–1958); and Chang Ch'ung (1904–1941).

22. Yao, *Liu Tsung-chou nien-p'u*, p. 2.

23. The biographical record said that the father contracted a disease and passed away. At the time, Yü-ching was six. He had two elder sisters, one younger sister (at nine, eight, and three, respectively), and two younger brothers (then at three and two). See Lü, *Chao K'o-t'ing nien-p'u chi-lüeh*, pp. 18–19.

24. Liu, *Pao-ying Liu Ch'u-chên hsien-shêng nien-p'u*, p. 6.

25. Corporal punishment is often part of the child-training practices in China, and the mother is usually the main disciplinarian on the scene. See Wolf, *Women and the Family in Rural Taiwan*, pp. 69–72. Liu, *Pao-ying Liu Ch'u-chên hsien-shêng nien-p'u*, pp. 5–6.

26. Shên, *Hsü Shih-ch'ang p'ing-chuan*, p. 6.

27. Kao, *Ts'ai Yüan-p'ei nien-p'u*, p. 2.

28. Lü, *Hung Pei-chiang hsien-shêng nien-p'u*, p. 4.

29. Chang, "Wu-shih Liu I-mou hsien-shêng," p. 39.

30. Huang Fu had three elder brothers, one elder sister, and a younger sister; all six of them were then young dependents of the family. See Shên, *Huang Ying-pai hsien-shêng nien-p'u*, p. 8; idem, "Huang Ying-pai hsien-shêng pai-ling tan-ch'ên chi-nien," p. 11.

31. Mann, "Widows in the Kinship, Class, and Community Structures of Qing Dynasty China," pp. 37–56.

32. Wang, *Wei Yüan nien-p'u*, p. 4.

33. See Hsiung, "Hao-tê k'ai-shih: chung-kuo chin-shih shih-jên tzû-ti tê yu-nien chiao-yü," pp. 203–38.

34. Yang, *Liu-chou fu-chün nien-p'u*, p. 3.

35. Liu, *Pao-ying Liu Ch'u-chên hsien-shêng nien-p'u*, pp. 5–6.

36. Wang, *Ping-t'a mêng-hên lu*, pp. 10–11.

37. Liang and Liang, *Kuei-lin Liang hsien-shêng nien-p'u*, pp. 7–8.

38. Wei, *Lin Wên-chung-kung nien-p'u*, pp. 3–4.

39. Chao, *Chao Wên-k'o-kung tzû-ting nien-p'u*, pp. 8–9.

40. Kuo, *Lo Chung-chieh-kung nien-p'u*, pp. 5–6.

41. Wolf, "Child Training and the Chinese Family," pp. 37–62.

42. Yen, *Tso Wên-hsiang-kung nien-p'u*, pp. 4–5.

43. Ch'ên, "Shih-an tzû-chuan," p. 56.

44. Wung, *Wung T'ieh-an nien-p'u*, p. 5.

45. Tung, *Huan-tu-wo-shu-shih lao-jên shou-ting nien-p'u*, p. 2.

46. Lo, *Hsien-k'ao Yu-shan fu-chün nien-p'u*, pp. 562–63.

47. Chang, *Ku T'ing-lin hsien-shêng nien-p'u*, pp. 1–4; Li, *Chung-kuo ku-tai chu-ming chê-hsüeh-chia p'ing-chuan*, pp. 2–4.

48. Liang and Liang, *Kuei-lin Liang hsien-shêng nien-p'u*, pp. 2–3.

49. Shên, *Huang Ying-pai hsien-shêng nien-p'u*, p. 8; idem, "Huang Ying-pai hsien-shêng pai-ling tan-ch'ên chi-nien," p. 11.

50. Wang, *Kuo Mo-juo nien-p'u*, pp. 2–3.

51. Chiang, "Pao-kuo yü ssû-ch'in," pp. 68–72.

52. Yüan, "Chang Kung-ch'üan hsien-shêng t'an-wang lu," pp. 13–19.

53. Mo, *Mo Liu-ch'ên hsien-shêng Tê-hui tzu-ting nien-p'u*, pp. 1–2.

54. Chao, "Tsao-nien hui-i," p. 23.

55. Other than the sons cited above, P'i Hsi-juei, Sun Hsing-yen, Liang Chi, and Tai Ch'uan-hsien also recorded similar accounts.

56. Chêng, *Ch'ing Yü Ch'ü-yüan hsien-shêng Yüeh nien-p'u*, p. 5.

57. Ch'ên, *Hou-kuan Ch'ên Shih-i nien-p'u*, p. 11.

58. Jung, *Li Chuo-wu hsien-shêng Chih nien-p'u*, p. 1.

59. Yao, *Ch'ing Shao Nien-lu hsien-shêng T'ing-ts'ai nien-p'u*, p. 8.

60. Ku, *Huang K'un-p'u hsien-shêng nien-p'u*, p. 2–3; Lo, *Lo Chuang-yung-kung tzû-ting nien-p'u*, pp. 13–14.

61. Liang, *T'ui-an tzû-ting nien-p'u*, p. 5.

62. Yüan, *Hsü Han nien-p'u*, pp. 7–8.

63. Lo, *Chu Ssû-ho hsien-shêng nien-p'u*, p. 6.

64. Fang, *T'an-chê hsüan tzû-ting nien-p'u*, pp. 2–3.

65. See "On Chaste Women" (Chên-nü lun), in Kuei, *Kuei Chên-ch'uan hsien-shêng wên-chi*, pp. 312–13; Kuei, "The Life of My Deceased Mother" (Hsien-pi shih-luêh), in Kuei, *Kuei Chên-ch'uan hsien-shêng wên-chi*, pp. 31–32; Hsiung, "The Relationship between Women and Children in Early Modern China," paper presented at AAWS, Seattle, 1985.

66. Chou, *Ch'ü Ch'iu-pai nien-p'u*, pp. 8–9.

67. Ch'ên, "Shih-an tzû-chuan," p. 55.

CHAPTER 6

1. Wang, *Ping-t'a mêng-hên lu*, pp. 5–8.

2. Anthony, Lee, and Suen, "Adult Mortality in Rural Liaoning, 1795 to 1820";

Ts'ui-jung Liu, "The Demographic Dynamics of Some Clans in the Lower Yangtze Area, ca. 1400–1900," pp.115–60; idem, "The Demography of Two Chinese Clans in Hsiao-shan, Chekiang, 1650–1850," pp.13–61.

3. Laslett, *Family Life and Illicit Love in Earlier Generations*, p. 13.

4. Yang, *A Chinese Village, Taitou, Shantung Province*, p.13.

5. In terms of nuptial patterns, Western Europe and China seem to represent two different extremes in the early modern era. It is estimated that in Western Europe, women on average did not get married until they reached twenty-three or twenty-six. Men, too, only entered into marriage in their late twenties or early thirties. The average age of first marriage for women in late imperial China ranged between eighteen and twenty, and the average age at first marriage for men was twenty-one to twenty-three. See Hanjal, "European Marriage Patterns in Perspective," pp. 101–43.

6. Wolf, *Women and the Family in Rural China*, chap. 4.

7. Kuo, *Lo-chung-chieh nien-p'u*, pp. 2–3.

8. Hu, *Chang Shih-chai hsien-shêng nien-p'u*, p. 4.

9. Huang, *Huang Chung-tsê nien p'u*, pp. 1–2.

10. Chang, *Chang Hui-su-kung nien-p'u*, p. 143.

11. Mei, *Hu Wên-chung-kung nien-p'u*, v. 1, p. 12.

12. Hsiung, "The Domestic, the Personal and the Intimate: Father-Daughter Bond in Late Imperial China."

13. Lo, *Lo Chuang-yung-kung tzû-ting nien-p'u*, p. 11.

14. Chiang, *Shêng-i-chai nien-p'u*, vol. 1, pp. 3–4.

15. Wolf, *Women and the Family in Rural China*, chap. 3, pp. 32–52.

16. Yang, *A Chinese Village, Taitou, Shantung Province*, pp. 59, 127.

17. Chiang, *Niu Kung-shan hsien-shêng nien-p'u*, p. 2.

18. Chiang, *Chang P'u nien-p'u*, p. 6.

19. T'an, "Hsien-pi Hsü-fu-jên i-shih-chuang," quoted in Yang, *T'an Ssû-t'ung nien-p'u*, p. 25.

20. Wang, *Ping-t'a mêng-hên lu*, p. 5.

21. Pao, *Lü Liu-liang nien-p'u*, p. 7.

22. On traditional Chinese concerns for selecting wet nurses, see discussions in Hsiung, "The Nurturing Women: Idea and Practices of Breastfeeding in Late Imperial China."

23. Yao, *Ch'ing Shao Nien-lu hsien-shêng T'ing-ts'ai nien-p'u*, p. 9.

24. Miu, *I-fêng lao-jên nien-p'u*, p. 2.

25. Wung, *Wung T'ieh-an nien-p'u*, p. 92.

26. Wei, *Hsü Ming-i lei-an*, pp. 82–84. For a more detailed analysis on the event, see Hsiung, "The Nurturing Women: Idea and Practices of Breastfeeding in Late Imperial China."

27. Fêng, *Li Shu-ku hsien-shêng nien-p'u*, p. 3.

28. Wung, *Wung T'ieh-an nien-p'u*, pp. 2–3.

29. Chao, *Ch'ing Hsia Êrh-ming hsien-shêng Ching-ch'ü nien-p'u*, p. 14.

30. Liang, *T'ui-an tzû-ting nien-p'u*, p. 4.

31. Wei, *Lin Wên-chung-kung nien-p'u*, p. 6.

32. Laslett, "Parental Deprivation in the Past," *Family Life and Illicit Love in*

Earlier Generations, pp. 160–72. See also Watkins and de Walle, "Nutrition, Mortality and Population Size: Malthus' Court of Last Resort," pp. 205–26.

33. Yao, *Ch'ing Shao Nien-lu hsien-shêng T'ing-ts'ai nien-p'u*, pp. 10–21.

34. Yüan, *Hsü Han nien-p'u*, pp. 7–8.

35. Huang, *Huang Chung-tsê nien p'u*, p. 2.

36. Wang, *Wang T'ai-ch'ang nien-p'u*, p. 5.

37. Lu, *Chao K'o-t'ing nien-p'u chi-lüeh*, pp. 18–19.

38. Lu, *Hung Pei-chiang hsien-shêng nien-p'u*, pp. 4–7.

39. Wang, *Ku Ch'ien-li hsien-shêng nien-p'u*, p. 2.

40. Yao, *Ch'ing Shao Nien-lu hsien-shêng T'ing-ts'ai nien-p'u*, p. 29.

41. Ku, *Huang K'un-p'u hsien-shêng nien-p'u*, pp. 1.

42. Chao, *Chao Wên-k'o-kung tzû-ting nien-p'u*, pp. 25–28.

43. Li, *Chu-hsien tao-jên tzû-shu nien-p'u*, p. 3.

44. Yang, "Fu Chiao-shan yü Ying-wei Ying-chi Liang-êrh," *Yang Chung-min-kung i-pi*, pp. 2629–31.

45. Tung, *Huan-tu-wo-shu-shih lao-jên shou-ting nien-p'u*, pp. 11–12.

46. Kuei, "Chia-p'u," *Kuei Chên-ch'uan chi*, pp. 231–32.

47. Wung, *Wung T'ieh-an nien-p'u*, pp. 2–3.

48. T'êng, *Chiang Chien-jên hsien-shêng nien-p'u*, pp. 4–5. For a discussion on the religious practices and spiritual sentiment of young children, consult Coles, *The Spiritual Life of Children*.

49. Yin, *Yin P'u-ching shih-lang tzû-ting nien-p'u*, p. 10.

50. Chien, *Chu Chiu-chiang hsien-shêng nien-p'u*, p. 4.

51. Li, *Li Wên-chên-kung nien-p'u*, pp. 12–13.

52. Wung, *Wung Tieh-an nien-p'u*, p. 5.

53. Fang, *T'an-chê hsüan tzû-ting nien-p'u*, pp. 3, 8–10.

54. Yao, *Ch'ing Shao Nien-lu hsien-shêng T'ing-ts'ai nien-p'u*, pp. 9–22; Ch'ên, *Sung Ssû-ma Wên-chêng-kung Kuang nien-p'u*, p. 2.

55. Chao, *Chao Wên-k'o-kung tzû-ting nien-p'u*, p. 13.

56. Ch'ên, *Sung Ssû-ma Wên-chêng-kung Kuang nien-p'u*, pp. 2–3.

57. Wang, *Ping-t'a mêng-hên lu*, p. 8.

58. Chang, *Sung Chou Lien-hsi hsien-shêng Tun-i nien-p'u*, p. 112; Liang, *Hsü Kuang-ch'i nien-p'u*, p. 37.

59. The National Palace Museum in Taipei has a painting dating from the Sung period entitled "Date Picking." For painting depicting children, see also Wei, *Chung-kuo ku-tai êrh-t'ung t'i-ts'ai hui-hua*.

60. Su, *Wu Ch'êng-ên nien p'u*, p. 3.

61. When Hsü P'u was young, he once heard his maternal uncle (who was visiting with the family) speak fondly of a certain child "who could sing beautifully." Fu responded precociously by saying, "But uncle, uncle, can singing bring a big name to one's parents?" See Hsü, *Ming-tai ta chêng-chih-chia Hsü P'u nien-p'u*, p. 9.

62. Chao, *Kung An-chieh hsien-shêng nien-p'u*, p. 2.

63. See Lu Shih-i, "Fu-shê chi-luêh," quoted in Chiang, *Chang P'u nien-p'u*, pp. 6–8.

64. T'an, *T'an Ssû-t'ung ch'üan-chi*, pp. 197–200.

65. T'êng, *Chiang Chien-jên hsien-shêng nien-p'u*, pp. 4–5.

66. Ibid.

67. Historians of early modern Europe and colonial America seemed to present a picture of fairly prevalent and severe physical punishment in the tradition of child rearing and training practices. Philip Greven Jr. has written extensively on the American tradition. See Greven, *The Protestant Temperament: Patterns of Child-Rearing, Religious Experience, and the Self in Early America*; idem, *Spare the Child: The Religious Roots of Punishment and the Psychological Impact of Physical Abuse*.

68. Liu, *Pao-ying Liu Ch'u-chên hsien-shêng nien-p'u*, pp. 5–6.

69. See Hu shih, "Wo-tê mu-ch'in," *Ssû-shih tzû-shu*, pp. 56–59; Chiang, "Pao-kuo yû ssû-ch'in," in *Chiang tsung-t'ung yen-lun hui-chi*, vol. 24.

70. Hsü, *Pi-chou-chai chu-jên nien-p'u*, pp. 5–6.

71. Wang, *Ping-t'a mêng-hên lu*, pp. 7–8.

72. Ch'ên, *Shih-an tzû-chuan*, pp. 55–58.

73. Hu, *Chang Chih-chai hsien-shêng nien-p'u*, pp. 5–6.

CHAPTER 7

1. See Confucius, "Wei-chêng" (Government), *Lun Yü, chuan* 2, p. 4.

2. Many child specialists acknowledge that present understandings of children and childhood are largely based on studies of boys and that by comparison girls and girlhood remain subjects little studied. The few historical studies on children and childhood either did not make any gender distinctions or really speak only of boys. Sommerville's *The Rise and Fall of Childhood*; Mause's *The History of Childhood*; Pollock's *Forgotten Children, Parent-Child Relations from 1500 to 1900*; and Wiedemann's *Adults and Children in the Roman Empire* are examples of the former case. Whereas Ariès's *Centuries of Childhood*; Hunt's *Parents and Children in History*; and Shahar's *Childhood in the Middle Ages* represent the latter case. Golden, in his study on *Children and Childhood in Classical Athens*, does have a chapter entitled "The Child and His or Her Peers" (pp. 51–79), which addresses the social life of boys and that of girls separately, but the long younger life of girls and boys is not further differentiated.

3. Jon Saari's *Legacies of Childhood: Growing Up Chinese in a Time of Crisis, 1890–1920* is as much a study about social upheaval and cultural change at the turn of the century as it is about the experience of growing up in such an environment. The samples he cites, however, are mostly boys and older boys. A number of essays in Ann B. Kinney's edited volume *Chinese Views of Childhood* are relevant to the question of girlhood. Pei-yi Wu's pathbreaking study, "Childhood Remembered: Parents and Children in China, 800–1700," examines the special feature and inadequacies in traditional biographical materials for a realistic grasp of the subject. He introduces, in addition, parents' writing about children, especially what he called the necrological literature, as a source of rich information about the world of young lives in traditional China. He includes famous men's memorial essays for their daughters as well as their sons, making it clear that girls were not excluded from the parents' memories, not unanimously in the inscriptions, at least. The gender difference, however, was not at the core of Wu's concerns to elicit any explicit compari-

son of remembering girls as opposed to boys in the genre. Ann Waltner's imaginative exploration, "Infanticide and Dowry in Ming and Early Ch'ing China," and Lucien Miller's essay, "The Adolescent World in Ts'ao Hsüeh-chin's *Hung-lou Mêng*," both speak of the issue of gender. Infanticide, dowry, and adolescent sentiments relative as they are to a consideration of the gender factor in the development of the life cycle, considered in precise terms, fall outside of the boundary of childhood, thus making a specific investigation of early girlhood all the more necessary and meaningful for a composite picture.

4. Ko, Mann, and Widmer and Chang's recent works on literary women to a large extent coincide with the elite girls that are mostly considered here. Their studies assumed, however, an intellectually oriented and culturally sophisticated world that their subjects emerge from without delving into the details of such an experience of growing up. Ebrey, Furth, and Bray's investigations touch on the general domestic life and physical aspect of female existence after the Sung that share many of the basic experiential concerns of the present chapter. The earliest phase of that experience is the focus of this study, which should complement well with these other related explorations of female existence in China's past. See Ko, *Teachers of the Inner Chambers: Women and Culture in Seventeenth-century China*; Mann, *The Precious Record: Women's Culture in China's Long Eighteenth Century*; Widmer and Sun, eds., *Writing Women in Late Imperial China*.

5. Chêng Hsüan, "Nei-tsê" (Domestic rules), *chuan* 8, p. 28.

6. Ibid., p. 29.

7. Chêng Hsüan, "Ch'ü-li" (The rites of Ch'ü), *chuan* 1, p. 3; Chêng Hsüan, "Nei-tsê," *chuan* 8, p. 28.

8. See *Pu-chu huang-ti nei-ching su-wên*, *chuan* 1, pp. 29–33.

9. Hsiung, *Yu-yu: Ch'uan-t'ung chung kuo tê ch'iang-pao chih tao*, pp. 137–56.

10. Ibid., pp. 103–36.

11. Lü Tê-shêng, *Hsiao-êrh Yü*, pp. 2–3. The exact authorship of Lü Tê-shêng for both *Words for Little Children* (*Hsiao-êrh Yü*) and *Words for Little Girls* (*Nü hsiao-êrh yü*) can only be assumed, according to the words of his son Lü K'un (1536–1618). Almost nothing can be found out about the actual life or date of this senior Lü, except through the general eulogical remarks from his son in the brief preface. See Handlin, *Action in Late Ming Thought*, pp. 144–45.

12. See Chang and Mu-chih, *Chung-kuo ku-tai mêng-shu chi-chin*.

13. Lü, *Hsiao-êrh Yü*.

14. Lü, *Nu hsiao-êrh Yü*.

15. Lü, *T'ung-mêng hsün*; also see Han, *Chung-hua Mêng-hsüeh Chi-ch'êng*; Hsü and Wang, *Mêng-hsüeh hsü-chih*.

16. See for example the oral history account of Kao Tzû prepared for publication in *Chuan-chi wên-hsüeh* for active physical activities of girls with boys in late-nineteenth-century China in the south. Many personal interviews concur about people's childhood experience as it occurred in the early twentieth century, from different regions of China, when the social scenes remained largely "traditional." See Chiang, *A-ma tê ku-shih*.

17. Kuei, "Hsiang-chi-hsüan chi" (A note of the Hutchback Hall), in Kuei, *Chên-ch'uan wên-chi*, *chuan* 17, pp. 4–5.

18. Li, *Ch'ing Tsêng Wên-chêng-kung Kuo-fan nien-p'u*, p. 5.

19. *Wang, Wei Yüan nien-p'u, pp. 2–3.*

20. Ts'ai, *Ts'ai T'ing-k'ai tzû-chuan*, pp. 9–10.

21. See for instance, Wang, *Ming-yüan shih-wei ch'u-pien*; see also Lin, "Wang Tuan-shu T'ao-lun chih P'ing-hsi—Chien-lun ch'i hsüan-shih piao-chün" (An analysis of deliberations on Wang Tuan-shu: Also as related to her selection of poetry), pp. 45–62; Kao and Shên, *Chung-hua ku-chin nü-chieh p'u*, pp. 32–33.

22. Kuei, *Chên-ch'uan wên-chi, chuan* 17, pp. 1, 4–5; *chuan* 22, pp. 5–7.

23. Hsü, *Ming-tai ta chêng-chih-chia Hsü P'u nien-p'u*, pp. 25–26, 39–40, 54–55.

24. Wên, *Wei Shu-tzû nien-p'u*, pp. 101–2.

25. Recent works by Dorothy Ko, Susan Mann, Ellen Widmer, and Kang-i Sun Chang have brought much new light and added emphasis on this perspective. See Ko, *Teachers of the Inner Chambers: Women and Culture in Seventeenth-century China*; Mann, *The Precious Record, Women's Culture in China's Long Eighteenth Century*; Widmer and Sun, *Writing Women in Late Imperial China*.

26. Waltner, "Infanticide and Dowry in Ming and Early Ch'ing China," in Kinney, *Chinese Views of Childhood*, p. 193.

27. Here many oral history records may be used to supplement the sketchy information gained from conventional textual evidence. For the present study, the entire oral history series published by the Institute of Modern History of Academia Sinica, including the monographs and journals as well as the set of *Chuan-chi wên-hsüeh*, was perused for relevant sources. Correlation studies on cultural values, social practices, and vital historical demographic changes (such as mortality and average life expectancy) also bring valuable insights. See Lee and Saito, *Abortion, Infanticide and Neglect in Asian Historical Populations*.

28. See for instance the autobiography of General Ts'ai for a vivid and terse account of a poor peasant boyhood in south China at the turn of the nineteenth century. Ts'ai, *Ts'ai T'ing-k'ai tzû-chuan*, pp. 9–10.

29. Infanticide is the extreme case, though not an issue of concern here. Studies indicate that social and economic conditions or class background and famine management could be decisive in such affairs. See Waltner, "Infanticide and Dowry in Ming and Early Qing China," pp. 193–218.

30. Hsiung, "Chung-kuo chin-shih shih-jên pi-hsia tê *êrh*-t'ung chien-k'ang wên-t'i" (Children's health as noted by the educated elite in the late imperial China), pp. 1–29.

31. Hsiung, "Narrative or Story? Case Records in Chinese pediatrics," paper presented at the international conference on "Thinking with Cases," Center of Far Eastern Languages and Civilizations, University of Chicago, Oct. 2001; Hsiung, "An-chü ch'üeh-tsao: I-an chih ch'uan-ch'êng yü ch'uan-ch'i," pp. 201–54.

32. These generalizations are made based on my own studies on Chinese pediatric medicine and children's diseases. See Hsiung, "Ching-fêng: chung-kuo chin-shih êrh-t'ung tê chi-ping yü chien-k'ang yen-chiu chih-i" (Ching-fêng: A study of the disease and health of young children in late imperial China [I])," pp. 169–203; Hsiung, "Kan: Chung-kuo chin-shih êrh-t'ung chi-ping yü chien-k'ang yen-chiu chih-êrh" (Kan: A study on the disease and health of young children in late imperial

China [II]), pp. 263–94; Hsiung, "Hsiao-êrh chih t'u: I-ko chung-kuo i-liao fa-chan shih ho êrh-t'ung chien-k'ang shih shang tê k'ao-ch'a" (The problem of throwing up: A historical observation in Chinese pediatric medicine and children's health), pp. 1–51; Hsiung, "Hsieh yü Li: Chien-lun chin-shih chung-kuo êrh-t'ung hsiao-hua-tao tê ping-pien yü chien-k'ang" (Hsieh and Li: A discussion on children's digestive illnesses and health in late imperial China), pp. 129–70; Hsiung, *An-yang: Chung-kuo chin-shih erh-t'ung tê chi-ping yü chien-k'ang* (Ill or well: Diseases and health of young children in late imperial china).

33. Wung, *Wung T'ieh-an nien-p'u*, p. 4.

34. Lee and Wang, *One Quarter of the Humanity*, pp. 42–62.

35. Wu, "Private Love and Public Duty: Images of Children in Early Chinese Art," pp. 129–56.

36. Kuei, "Ju-lan k'uang-chih" (Burial inscription for Ju-lan), *chuan* 22, pp. 6–7.

37. Ibid.

38. Kuei, "Êrh-êrh k'uang-chih" (Burial inscription for Êrh-êrh), chuan 22, p. 7.

39. Huang, *Wang Hsi-chuang hsien-shêng Ming-shêng nien-p'u*, pp. 30–32.

40. Ibid., pp. 30–32.

41. Ibid., p. 33.

42. Wang, "Yü-ku p'ien" (The selling of an orphan), *Ping-t'a mêng-hên lu*, p. 124.

43. Ch'êng Hao and Ch'êng I, *Êrh-ch'êng wên-chi*, p. 35.

44. Waltner, *Getting an Heir: Adoption and the Construction of Kinship in Late Imperial China*, p. 30.

45. Most editions of the *Twenty-Four Stories of Filial Piety* contain only one to three items depicting filial acts of a female character. The common one is that not of a young daughter but of an adult daughter-in-law breast-feeding her mother-in-law. Others include stories of Han physician Ch'un-yü-I's daughter petitioning the throne for the pardoning of her father, and the legendary Hua Mu-lan's effort to substitute for her father in the military draft. See *Sung-k'o Hsiao-ching êrh-shih-ssû-hsiao t'u-shuo*, p. 2; Hu, *Êrh-shih-ssû-hsiao t'u-shuo*, p. 4.

46. T'ang, "Fu-fu" (On husband and wife), *Ch'ien-shu*, pp. 78–79. See also Hsiung, "T'ang Chên and the Works in Obscurity: Life and Thought of a Provincial Intellectual in Seventeenth Century China," p. 78.

47. T'ang, *Ch'ien-shu*, p. 79.

48. Shên, *Shên Wên-chung-kung tzû-ting nien-p'u*, p. 6.

49. Hsiung, "Children and Childhood in Late-Imperial China: The Notions vs. the Realities."

50. Nieh, *Ch'ung-tê lao-jên tzû-ting nien-p'u*, pp. 10, 20.

51. Ch'ên, *Hou-kuan Ch'ên Shih-i nien-p'u*, p. 145.

52. Wên, *Wei Yüan nien-p'u*, p. 101.

53. Ch'ên, *Chiao-nü i-kuei* (Collected instructions for girls), pp. 1–24.

54. Wang, *Yüan Mei chuan-chi*, vol. 15, pp. 291–92.

55. Lin, *Ch'ing chien-hu nü-hsia Chiu Chin nien p'u*, pp. 6–7, 15–16, 21–35.

56. Waltner, "The Moral Status of the Child in Late Imperial China: Childhood in Ritual and in Law," pp. 667–87; See also Ko, "Pursuing Talent and Virtue: Edu-

cation and Women's Culture in Seventeenth- and Eighteenth-Century China," pp. 9–39.

57. Rawski, *Education and Popular Literacy in Ch'ing China*, pp. 24–53.

58. A number of essays collected in Ellen Widmer and Kang-i Sun Chang, ed., *Writing Women in Late Imperial China*, document the manifestation of this development. Kang-i Sun Chang also reminded people of the 3,500 published female authors from the Ming-Ch'ing era. See "Ming and Qing Anthologies of Women's Poetry and Their Selection Strategies," in Widmer and Sun, *Writing Women in Late Imperial China*, pp. 147–70.

59. Hsiung, "Hao-tê-k'ai-shih: Chung-kuo chin-shih shih-jên tzû-ti tê yu-nien chiao-yü" (Getting off with a good start: Early childhood education of elite families in late imperial China), pp. 203–38.

60. Huang, *Ch'ing Shao Êrh-yün hsien-shêng Chin-han nien p'u*, pp. 10–11.

61. Yao, *Ch'ing Shao Nien-lu hsien-shêng T'ing-ts'ai nien-p'u*, p. 48.

62. Yao, *Liu Tsung-chou nien-p'u*, p. 42.

63. Yang, *Min-kuo K'ang Ch'ang-ssû hsien-shêng Yu-wei Liang Jên-kung hsien-shêng Ch'i-ch'ao shih-shêng ho-p'u*, p. 15.

64. Li, *Chu-hsien tao-jên tzû-shu nien-p'u*, p. 2.

65. Kung-Sun, *Fêng Kuo-chang nien-p'u*, p. 188.

66. Nieh, *Ch'ung-tê lao-jen tzû-ting nien-p'u*, p. 11.

67. Fong, "Boudoir World and Professional Life—Contrasting Self-Representations by Two Women Poets of the Mid and Late-Ching," paper delivered at the Institute of Chinese Literature and Philosophy, Taipei, 1996.

68. Ko, "Pursuing Talent and Virtue: Education and Women's Culture in Eighteenth-century China," p. 21; Lin, *Ch'ing chien-hu nü-hsia Ch'iu Chin nien-p'u*, pp. 14–16.

69. Liang and Liang, *Ch'ing Liang Chü-ch'uan hsien-shêng Chi nien-p'u*, p. 10.

70. Yen, *Yen Hsiu hsien-shêng nien-p'u*, p. 144.

71. P'i, *Ch'ing P'i Lu-mên hsien-shêng Hsi-jui nien-p'u*, p. 5.

72. Nieh, *Ch'ung-tê lao-jên tzû-ting nien-p'u*, pp. 21–22.

73. Liu, *Ch'ing Liu Ch'u-chên hsien-shêng Pao-nan nien-p'u*, p. 4.

74. Wang, *Ch'ing Wang Hsiang-chi hsien-shêng K'ai-yün nien-p'u*, p. 20.

75. At the time Yü noted this, he was forty-three. His daughter passed away at thirty-four from "lack of care after childbirth," leaving behind two daughters and six sons. Saddened by the tragedy, Yü appended her poetry and lyrics to his own published work. See Chêng, *Ch'ing Yü Ch'ü-yüan hsien-shêng Yüeh nien-p'u*, pp. 60–61.

76. Tsêng Chi-fên, for example, preserved a complete training curriculum that her family used to train older girls and young women in "womanly work." See Nieh, *Ch'ung-tê lao-jên tzû-ting nien-p'u*, pp. 15–16. See also Hsiung, "Fathers and Daughters in Late Imperial China: Culture, Cultivation and Gender in the Family Setting."

77. The training of songstresses, actresses, entertainers, and courtesans, though numerically insignificant, probably constituted a known exception to the rule, with that of the even fewer skilled female practitioners, women merchants, and female martial artists, following suit. For a glimpse of the cultivating process of late impe-

rial Chinese courtesans' occupational skills, see Ropp, "Ambiguous Images of Courtesan Culture in Late Imperial China," in Widmer and Sun, *Writing Women in Late Imperial China*, pp. 20–25. Angela Leung's contribution speaks of possible training paths for female healers in this period. See Angela Ki Che Leung, "Women practicing medicine in Pre-modern China," in Harriet T. Zurndorfer, ed., *Chinese Women in the Imperial Past: New Perspectives*, pp. 101–34.

78. I, "Ts'ung san-ku liu-p'ou k'an ming-tai fu-nü yû shê-hui."

79. Angela Ki Che Leung, in "Elementary Education in the Lower Yongtze Region in the Seventeenth and Eighteenth Centuries," gives a good picture of the institutional setup and a brief description of the learning activities for boys as beginners in school. See Elman and Woodside, *Education and Society in Late Imperial China, 1600–1900*, pp. 381–96.

80. Li, *Chu-hsien tao-jên tzû-shu nien-p'u*, p. 3.

81. P'i, *Ch'ing P'i Lu-mên hsien-shêng Hsi-jui nien-p'u*, p. 5.

82. Hsiung, "Hao-tê-k'ai-shih: Chung-kuo chin-shih shih-jên tzû-ti tê yu-nien chiao-yü," pp. 232–36.

83. Chang Ch'uan-yüan and Yü Mei-nien, *Ming Kuei Chên-ch'uan hsien-shêng Yu-kuang nien-p'u*, p. 37; Ni, *Ming Ni Wên-chêng-kung (Yüan-lu) nien-p'u*, p. 14.

84. Kuo, *Kung Tzû-chên nien-p'u*, p. 12.

85. For Ellen Johnston Laing's study in the edited volume of female paintings see Ellen Johnston Laing, "Wives, Daughters, and Lovers: Three Ming Dynasty Women Painters," in Marsha Weidner, et al., *Views from Jade Terrace: Chinese Women Artists, 1300-1912*, pp. 31–39; idem, "Women Painters in Traditional China," in Marsha Weidner, ed., *Flowering in the Shadows: Women in the History of Chinese and Japanese Painting*, pp. 81–101.

86. Li, *Chu-hsien tao-jên tzû-shu nien-p'u*, p. 21.

87. Sun, *Min-kuo Ts'ai Chüeh-min hsien-shêng Yüan-p'ei chien-yao nien-p'u*, p. 4.

88. Li, *Chang Ta-ch'ien nien-p'u*, p. 6.

89. Fong, "Boudoir World and Professional Life—Contrasting Self-representations by Two Women Poets of the Mid- and Late-Ch'ing."

90. Mann, "The Education of Daughters in the Mid-Ch'ing Period," in Elman and Woodside *Education and Society in Late Imperial China, 1600–1900*, pp. 35–36.

91. Susan Mann calls Chang Hsüeh-ch'êng's argument with Yüan Mei on this point as the beginning of China's "querelle des femmes." See Mann, "Classical Revival and the Gender Question: China's First Querelle des Femmes," pp. 377–411.

92. Li, *Chu-hsien tao-jên tzû-shu nien-p'u*, p. 4.

93. Wang, *Ch'ing Wang Hsiang-ch'i hsien-shêng K'ai-yün nien-p'u*, p. 20.

94. Sun, *Min-kuo Ts'ai Chüeh-min hsien-shêng Yüan-p'ei chien-yao nien-p'u*, p. 4.

95. Nieh, *Ch'ung-tê lao-jên tzû-ting nien-p'u*, p. 16.

96. Chu, *Wung T'ung-ho hsien-shêng nien-p'u*.

97. Kuei Yu-kuang, "Hsiang-chi-hsüan chi," "Wang-ju-jên ling-piao" (Memorial inscription for my wife Madame Wang), "Hsien-pi *Chou-ju-jên* ling-piao" (Memorial inscription for my mother Madame Chou), in Kuei, *Chên-ch'uan wên-chi, chuan* 17, p. 4b.

98. Hsiung, "Hao-tê-k'ai-shih: Chung-kuo chin-shih shih-jên tzû-ti tê yu-nien chiao-yü," pp. 215–29.

99. Mann, in her study "The Education of Daughters in the Mid-Ch'ing Period," gives a vivid presentation of the training of women through "the world of signs and symbols." See Elman and Woodside (eds.), *Education and Society in Late Imperial China, 1600–1900*, pp. 27–35; see also Pollert, *Girls, Wives, Factory Lives*; and Mann, "Grooming a Daughter for Marriage: Brides and Wives in the Mid-Ch'ing Period," pp. 204–30.

100. See Ko, *Teachers of the Inner Chambers: Women and Culture in Seventeenth-Century China*; Ko, *Every Step A Lotus: Shoes for Bound Feet*; Bray, *Technology and Gender: Fabrics of Power in Late Imperial China*; Fong, *Wu Wenying and the Art of Southern Song Ci Poetry*.

101. Dorothy Ko terms the written word and the bound foot as "two faces of civility." See Ko, "The Written Word and the Bound Foot: A History of the Courtesan's Aura," in Widmer and Sun (eds), *Writing Women in Late Imperial China*, pp. 74–100.

CHAPTER 8

1. Ariès, *Centuries of Childhood*, pp. 25–49. Some experienced scholars like Lawrence Stone and Peter Laslett have noticed that modern social sciences (sociology and psychology) may not be very helpful on research such as family history, domestic affairs, and affective ties.

2. See Chêng, *Li-chi chêng-chu, chuan* 28, p. 243.

3. Like the *Li-chi*, the *Chü-chia tsa-i* draws a plan of the ideal upbringing from infancy to adulthood but adds still further programs concerning specified activities. See Ssû-ma, *Chü-chia tsa-i* (Miscellaneous rites for the family). Also see Hsiung, "Hao-tê-k'ai-shih: Chung-kuo chin-shih shih-jên tzû-ti tê yu-nien chiao-yü" (Getting off with a good start: Early childhood education of elite families in late imperial China), pp. 204–6.

4. Chuang, *Ti-tzû chih chi-chieh*, p. 1.

5. Ibid., p. 1.

6. Ssû-ma, "Chiao nan-nü" (Teaching boys and girls), in Hu Kuang, *Hsing-li ta-ch'üan, chuan* 19, p. 333.

7. Ssû-ma, "Chiao nan-nü," in Hu Kuang, *Hsing-li ta-ch'üan, chuan* 19, p. 334.

8. Wang, "Hsün-mêng ta-i," *Yang-ming ch'uan-hsi-lu*, pp. 276–77.

9. Here Li could presumably be speaking of human beings across gender lines, so it can be a "she" as well as a "he." Although like all philosophical exercises before him, when translated into practical social terms, such idealistic ponderings often had mostly the males in mind.

10. Li, "T'ung-hsin shuo," *Li-shih Fên-shu, chuan* 3, pp. 22–24.

11. See Hsiung, "Shih-k'uei Chung-kuo chin-shih êrh-t'ung tê jên-shih huan-ching yü ch'ing-kan shih-chieh" (A preliminary investigation of the human environment and the emotional world of children in Ming-Ch'ing China), pp. 251–306.

12. Elsewhere I have explained the advantages and limitation of biographical and autobiographical sources to recreate childhood experience, as well as the

methodological problems in approaching them. See Hsiung, "Constructed Emotions: The Bond Between Mothers and Sons in Late Imperial China," pp. 88, 104–7.

13. See Hsiung, "Ching-fêng: chung-kuo chin-shih êrh-t'ung tê chi-ping yü chien-k'ang yen-chiu chih-i" (Ching-fêng: A study of the disease and health of young children in late imperial China [I]), pp. 169–203.

14. Ibid.

15. Shao Hsing-chung, "Wu-shih hsing lüeh" (Family history of five generations), in Yao, Ch'ing Shao Nien-lu hsien-shêng T'ing-ts'ai nien-p'u, p. 9.

16. Hsü, Pi-chou-chai chu-jên nien-p'u, pp. 3–4.

17. Chao, Ch'ing Ts'ên Hsiang-kung Yü-ying nien-p'u, pp. 7–8.

18. See Hsiung, "To Raise the Young: Nursing and Infant-feeding in Late Imperial China," pp. 217–38.

19. Ch'ên, Sung Ssû-ma Wên-chêng-kung Kuang nien-p'u, pp. 2–3.

20. Chang, Sung Chou Lien-hsi hsien-shêng Tun-i nien-p'u, pp. 4.

21. Liang, Hsü Kuang-ch'i nien-p'u, p. 37.

22. Ch'ên, Ch'ing K'ung Tung-t'ang hsien-shêng Shang-jên nien-p'u, p. 16.

23. Wang, Ch'ên Tung-shu hsien-shêng nien-p'u, pp. 3–5.

24. Ku-chin t'u-shu chi-ch'êng, vol. 324, chuan 39, p. 12.

25. Tz'ui, Yu Hsün, vol. 2, chuan 8, p. 4.

26. Hsü, Ming-tai ta chêng-chih-chia Hsü P'u nien-p'u, p. 9.

27. Su, Wu Ch'êng-ên nien-p'u, p. 3.

28. Chao, Chang Chung-lieh-kung nien-p'u, p. 8.

29. Yao, Ching Shao Nien-lu hsien-shêng T'ing-ts'ai nien-p'u, p. 14.

30. Su, Fang Wang-hsi hsien-shêng nien p'u, p. 42.

31. Yin, Yin P'u-ching shih-lang tzû-ting nien p'u, pp. 9–10.

32. Wang, Ch'ing Wang Hsiang-ch'i hsien-shêng K'ai- yün nien-p'u, pp. 9–10.

33. Lo, Lo Chuang-yüng-kung tzû-ting nien-p'u, pp. 12–14.

34. Hsü, Pi-chou-chai chu-jên nien-p'u, pp. 5–6.

35. Wang, Ping-t'a mêng-hên lu, p. 8.

36. Ku-chin t'u-shu chi-ch'êng, vol. 324, chuan 39, p. 12.

37. Lü, Hsiao-êrh yü, p. 2.

38. Li, Ti-tzû kuei, pp. 4–5.

39. Ts'ui, Yu Hsün, vol. 2, chuan 8, p. 5.

40. Ch'ên, Sung Ssû-ma wên-chêng-kung Kuang nien-p'u, p. 2.

41. Yao, Ch'ing Shao Nien-lu Hsien shêng T'ing-ts'ai nien-p'u, pp. 13–14.

42. Chiang, Niu Kung-shan hsien-shêng nien-p'u, pp. 3–4.

43. Ch'ên, Ming-mo Lu Chung-chieh-kung Shan-chi nien-p'u, p. 2.

44. Yeh, Huang Tao-chou chuan, pp. 29–30.

45. Lü, Yin Chien-yü hsien-shêng nien-p'u, p. 22.

46. Ma, Ma Tuan-min-kung nien-p'u, p. 12.

47. Lo, Wang Chuang-wu-kung nien-p'u, p. 6.

48. Yao, Tz'ui Tung-pi nien-p'u, p. 2.

49. Wang, Wei Yüan nien-p'u, pp. 2–3.

50. Li, Ch'ing Tsêng Wên-chêng-kung Kuo-fan nien-p'u, chuan 1, p. 6.

51. Hsieh, Ch'i Chi-Kuang, pp. 6–7.

52. Wu, Ho Hui-kao nien-p'u, p. 4.

53. Wang, *Ping-t'a mêng-hên lu*, pp. 10-11.

54. Tuan, "Wo-tê fu-ch'in," p. 26.

55. Ts'ai, *Ts'ai T'ing-k'ai tzû-chuan*, p. 12; P'u, "Chi Ho Lien hsiung shêng-p'ing," p. 27.

56. Hsüeh, "K'un-hsing i-wang," p. 46.

57. Hsiung, "Shih-k'uei Chung-kuo chin-shih êrh-t'ung tê jên-shih huan-ching yü ch'ing-kan shih-chieh" (A preliminary investigation of the human environment and the emotional world of children in Ming-Ch'ing China), pp. 261-62.

58. Kuei, "Hsien-pi Chou-ju-jên ling-piao," *Chên-ch'uan wên-chi, chuan* 17, p. 1.

59. Wung, *Wung T'ieh-an nien-p'u*, pp. 2-3.

60. Chao, *Hsia Êrh-ming hsien-shêng Ching-ch'ü nien-p'u*, pp. 14-15.

61. Liu, *Pao-ying Liu Ch'u-ch'ên hsien-shêng nien-p'u*, pp. 5-6.

62. Wu, *Li Yung*, pp. 2-3.

63. Li, *Li Wên-chên-kung nien-p'u*, pp. 12-13.

64. Yin, *Yin P'u-ching shih-lang tzû-ting nien p'u*, p. 10.

65. Chien, *Chu Chiu-chiang hsien-shêng nien-p'u*, p. 4.

66. Ku, *Huang K'un-p'u hsien-shêng nien-p'u*, pp. 2-3.

67. T'êng, *Chiang Chien-jên hsien-shêng nien-p'u*, pp. 4-5.

68. Chiang, *Chang P'u nien-p'u*, pp. 6-8.

69. T'an, "Hseng-pi Hsü fu-jên i-shih-chuang" in *T'an Ssû-t'ung ch'üan-chi*, pp. 197-200.

70. Wang, *Ping-t'a mêng-hên lu*, pp. 7-10.

71. Lü, *Chao K'o-t'ing nien-p'u chi-lüeh*, pp. 18-19.

72. Li, *Li Hung-tsao hsien-shêng nien-p'u*, p. 2.

73. Wang, *Wang Jang-ch'ing hsien-shêng chuan-chi*, p. 10.

74. Lo, *Chu Ssû-ho hsien-shêng nien-p'u*, p. 6.

75. Lü, *Chao Ko-t'ing nien-p'u chi-lüeh*, p. 19.

76. Wang, *Ping-t'a mêng-hên lu*, p. 11.

77. Hsüeh, "K'un-hsing i-wang," p. 46.

78. Hu, *Chang Shih-chai hsien-shêng nien-p'u*, pp. 4-6.

79. Chien, *Chu Chiu-chiang hsien-shêng nien-p'u*, p. 3.

80. Liang, *Kuei-lin Liang hsien-shêng nien-p'u*, pp. 7-8.

81. Ma, *Wu Mei-ts'un nien-p'u*, p. 15.

82. Huang, *Huang Chung-tsê nien-p'u*, p. 2

83. Hu, *Pao Shên-po hsien-shêng nien-p'u*, p. 12.

84. Lo, *Wang Chuang-wu-kung nien-p'u*, p. 5.

85. Ma, *Ma Tuan-min-kung nien-p'u*, pp. 12-13.

86. Chang, *Ku T'ing-lin hsien-shêng nien-p'u*, pp. 17-19.

87. Chao, *Hsia Êrh-ming hsien-shêng Ching-ch'ü nien-p'u*, p. 14.

88. Liu, *Pao-ying Liu Ch'u-ch'ên hsien-shêng nien-p'u*, pp. 5-6.

89. Yen, *Tso Wên-hsiang-kung nien-p'u*, pp. 4-5.

90. Ts'ên, *Hsü-yün ho-shang nien p'u*, p. 1.

91. Liu, "Min-kuo jên-wu hsiao-chuan," p. 141.

92. Mo, *Mo Liu-chên hsien-shêng Tê-hui tzû-ting nien-p'u*, p. 1.

93. Hsü, *Huang Tsung-hsi nien-p'u*, pp. 16-18.

94. Chao, "Wo-tê tsu-fu," p. 17.

95. Chiang, *Hu Han-min hsien-shêng nien p'u*, p. 14.

96. Kuo, *Yen Hsi-chai nien p'u*, pp. 6–7.

97. Hsüeh, "K'un-hsing i-wang," p. 47.

98. Ts'ai, *Ts'ai T'ing-k'ai tzû-chuan*, pp. 19–20.

99. Fang, *Fu Ch'ing-chu hsien-shêng nien-p'u*, p. 259.

100. Chien, "Fêng Yü-hsiang Chuan," p. 36.

101. Hsü, "Hsü Yung-ch'ang Ch'iu-chi-chai hui-i-lu," pp. 13–14.

102. Chien, "Ko-ming hua-chia Kao Chien-fu," p. 83.

103. Hu, *Chang Wên-hsiang-kung nien-p'u*, pp. 11–12.

104. Ch'ên, "Wo yu-shih ch'iu-hsüeh tê ching-kuo," p. 87.

AFTERWORD

1. Hsiung, "The Other Side of Filial Piety: Reflections on Compassion versus Loyalty in Late Imperial Chinese Family Relations," pp. 313–59.

2. Elsewhere I have attempted further exploration of the world of children using material evidence. See Hsiung, "Hsi-shuai shih-tien: Ying-hsiung pu-lun ch'u-shên ti" (The Epistomology of a Children's Game: Cricket Fight in China's Cultural Lexicon), pp. 55–96.

3. Golden, *Children and Childhood in Classical Athens*; Wiedemann, *Adults and Children in the Roman Empire*.

4. Stone, *The Family, Sex, and Marriage in England, 1500–1800*.

5. Ariès, *Centuries of Childhood*.

6. Hsiung, "Introduction," *T'ung-nien i-wang: Chung-kuo hai-tzû tê li-shih*.

Works Cited

Anthony, Lawrence, James Lee, and Alice Suen. "Adult Mortality in Rural Liaoning, 1795 to 1820." Paper presented at a workshop on Qing Population History, California Institute of Technology, Pasadena, Calif., Aug. 1985.

Ariès, Philippe. *Centuries of Childhood: A Social History of Family Life*. Trans. R. Baldick. New York: Vintage, 1962.

Bodde, Derk. "Age, Youth, and Infirmity in the Law of Ch'ing China." In Jerome Alan Cohen, R. Randle Edwards, and Fu-mei Chang Chen, eds., *Essays on China's Legal Tradition*, pp. 137–69. Princeton: Princeton University Press, 1980.

Bowell, John. *The Kindness of Strangers: The Abandonment of Children in Western Europe from Late Antiquity to the Renaissance*. New York: Pantheon Books, 1988.

Bradley, Keith R. *Discovering the Roman Family: Studies in Roman Social History*. Oxford: Oxford University Press, 1991.

Bray, Francesca. *Technology and Gender: Fabrics of Power in Late Imperial China*. Berkeley: University of California Press, 1997.

Carlitz, Katherine. "The Social Uses of Female Virtue in Late Ming Editions of Lienü Zhuan." *Late Imperial China* 12, no. 2 (1991): 117–48.

Catalog of the Clifford G. Grulee Collection on Pediatrics. Chicago: The John Crerar Library, 1959.

Chang Ch'i-yün 張其昀. "Wu-shih Liu I-mou hsien-shêng" 吾師柳翼謀先生. *Chuan-chi wên-hsüeh* 傳記文學 12, no. 2 (1968): 39–41.

Chang Chieh-pin 張介賓. *Ching-yüeh ch'üan-shu* (The complete works of Chang Chieh-pin) 景岳全書. In *Ying-yin wên-yüan-ko ssû-k'u ch'üan-shu* 景印文淵閣四庫全書, vol. 778. Taipei: Shang-wu, 1986.

Chang Ch'uan-yüan 張傳元 and Yü Mei-nien 余梅年. *Ming Kuei Chên-ch'uan hsien-shêng Yu-kuang nien-p'u* 明歸震川先生有光年譜. 1935. Reprint, Taipei: Shang-wu, 1980.

Chang Ho 張河 and Mu-chih 牧之, eds. *Chung-kuo ku-tai mêng-shu chi-chin* (A collection of traditional Chinese children's primers) 中國古代蒙書集錦. Chi-nan: Shantung yu-i, 1990.

Chang Hsüeh-ch'êng 章學誠. *Chang-shih i-shu* 章氏遺書. Taipei: Shang-wu, n.d.

Chang Kao 張杲. *I-shuo* (On medicine) 醫説. Taipei: Hsin-wên-fêng, 1981.

Chang Mu 張穆. *Ku T'ing-lin hsien-shêng nien-p'u* 顧亭林先生年譜. N.d. Reprint from Ch'ing Yüeh-ya-t'ang ts'ung-shu 清粵雅堂叢書. Taipei: Kuang-wên, 1971.

———. *Yen Ch'ien-ch'iu hsien-shêng nien-p'u* 閻潛邱先生年譜. N.d. Reprint, Taipei: Kuang-wên, 1971.

Chang Po-hsing 張伯行. *Sung Chou Lien-hsi hsien-shêng Tun-i nien-p'u* 宋周濂溪先

生敦頤年譜. N.d. Reprint from Ch'ing chêng-i-t'ang edition 清正誼堂. Taipei: Shang-wu, 1978.

Chang Shao-nan 張紹南. *Sun Yüan-ju hsien-shêng nien-p'u* 孫淵如先生年譜. Reprinted from *O-hsiang lin-shih tz'ung-shu* 藉香零拾叢書. Taipei: Hsin-wên-fêng, 1989.

Chang So-an 張壽安. "Shu-shao wu-fu, ch'ing ho i-k'an? Ch'ing-tai li-chih yü jên-ch'ing chih ch'ung-t'u i-li"(The conflict between classic ritual and human desire in late imperial China: A case study of mourning garments) 叔嫂無服，情何以堪？清代禮制與人情之衝突議例. In Hsiung Ping-chen and Lu Miaw-fen, eds. *Li-chiao yü ch'ing-yü: Ch'ien-chin-tai chung-kuo wên-hua chung-tê hou/hsien-tai hsing* (Neo-Confucian orthodoxy and human desires: Post/Modernity in pre-modern Chinese culture) 禮教與情慾：前近代中國文化中的後/現代性, pp. 125–78. Taipei: Institute of Modern History, Academia Sinica, 1999.

Chang Tsu-yu 張祖佑. *Chang Hui-su-kung nien-p'u* 張惠肅公年譜. 1936. Reprint, Taipei: Kuang-wên, 1971.

Chang Tz'u-hsi 張次溪. "Pai-shih lao-jên tzû-shu 白石老人自述." *Chuan-chi wên-hsüeh* 傳記文學 3, no. 1 (1963): 39–51.

Chang Ts'ung-chêng 張從正. *Ju-mên shih-ch'in* 儒門事親. In *Ku-chin t'u-shu chi-ch'êng* 古今圖書集成. 1931. Reprint, Taipei: Ting-wên, 1976.

Chao Chih-ch'ien 趙之謙. *Chang chung-lieh-kung nien-p'u* 張忠烈公年譜. 1776. Reprint, Taipei: Kuang-wên, 1971.

Chao Ching-shên 趙景深. *Ch'ing Hsia Êrh-ming hsien-shêng Ching-ch'ü nien-p'u* 清夏二銘先生敬渠年譜. 1932. Reprint, Taipei: Shang-wu, 1980.

Chao Fan 趙藩. *Ch'ing Ts'ên Hsiang-ch'in-kung Yü-ying nien-p'u* 清岑襄勤公毓英年譜. 1892. Reprint, Taipei: Shang-wu, 1978.

Chao I-i 趙詒翼. *Kung An-chieh hsien-shêng nien-p'u* 龔安節先生年譜. 1925. Reprint, Taipei: Kuang-wên, 1971.

Chao Kuang 趙光. *Chao Wên-k'o-kung tzû-ting nien-p'u* 趙文恪公自訂年譜. 1890. Reprint, Taipei: Kuang-wên, 1971.

Chao P'u-shan 趙璞珊. *Chung-kuo ku-tai i-hsüeh* (Traditional Chinese medicine) 中國古代醫學. Beijing: Chung-hua, 1983.

Chao Yang Pu-wei 趙楊步偉. "Wo-tê tsu-fu" (My grandfather) 我的祖父. *Chuan-chi wên-hsüeh* 傳記文學 3, no. 3 (1963): 17–21.

Chao Yü-ming 趙玉明. *P'u-sa hsin-ch'ang tê ko-ming chia—Chü Chêng chuan* 菩薩心腸的革命家—居正傳. Taipei: Chin-tai chung-kuo, 1982.

Chao Yüan-jên 趙元任. "Tsao-nien hui-i" (Recollection on my early years) 早年回憶. *Chuan-chi wên-hsüeh* 傳記文學 15, no. 5 (1969): 19–24.

Ch'ao Yüan-fang 巢元方. *Chu-ping yüan-hou lun* (On the origins and symptoms of diseases) 諸病源候論. Nan-ching chung-i hsüeh-yüan edition. Beijing: Jên-min wei-shêng, 1985.

Ch'ên Chi-ju 陳繼儒. *Pao-yen-t'ang mi-chi* 寶顏堂祕笈. Shanghai: Wên-ming, 1922.

Ch'ên Fu-chêng 陳復正. *Yu-yu chi-ch'êng* (Complete works on the care of children) 幼幼集成. Shanghai: K'o-chi, 1978.

Ch'ên Hêng-chê 陳衡哲. "Wo yu-shih ch'iu-hsüeh tê ching-kuo" 我幼時求學的經過. *Chuan-chi wên-hsüeh* 傳記文學 26, no. 4 (1975): 84–88.

Ch'ên Hung 陳鋐. *Ming-mo Lu Chung-chieh-kung Shan-chi nien-p'u* 明末鹿忠節公

善繼年譜. N.d. Reprint from Ch'ing Chi fu ts'ung shu 清畿輔叢書. Taipei: Shang-wu, 1978.

Ch'ên Hung-mou 陳宏謀. *Chiao-nü i-kuei* (Collected instructions for girls) 教女遺規. In *Wu-chung i-kui* 五種遺規, collected in *Ssû-pu pei-yao* 四部備要, vol. 146. Taipei: Chung-hua, 1965.

———. *Sung Ssû-ma Wên-chêng-kung Kuang nien-p'u* 宋司馬文正公光年譜. 1741. Reprint, Taipei: Shang-wu, 1978.

Ch'ên Mêng-lei 陳夢雷. *Ku-chin t'u-shu chi-ch'êng* (The complete classics collection of ancient China) 古今圖書集成. 1931. Reprint, Taipei: Ting-wên, 1976.

Ch'ên Pang-hsien 陳邦賢. *Chung-kuo i-hsüeh shih* (History of Chinese medicine) 中國醫學史. Shanghai: Shang-wu, 1937.

Ch'ên Shêng-chi 陳聲暨. *Hou-kuan Ch'ên Shih-i nien-p'u* 侯官陳石遺年譜. N.d. Reprint, Taipei: Kuang-wên, 1971.

Ch'ên Ting-hsiang 陳定祥. *Ch'ing Huang T'ao-lou hsien-shêng P'êng-nien nien-p'u* 清黃陶樓先生彭年年譜. N.d. Reprint, Taipei: Shang-wu, 1978.

Ch'ên Ts'ung-jung 陳聰榮. *Chung-i êrh-k'o hsüeh* (Chinese pediatrics) 中醫兒科學. Taipei: Chêng-chung, 1987.

Ch'ên Tu-hsiu 陳獨秀. "Shih-an tzû-chuan" (My autobiography) 實庵自傳. *Chuan-chi wên-hsüeh* 傳記文學 5, no. 3 (1964): 55–58.

Ch'ên Tzû-ming 陳自明. *Fu-jên ta-ch'üan liang-fang* (All-inclusive good prescriptions for women) 婦人大全良方. In *Ying-yin wên-yüan-ko ssû-k'u ch'üan-shu* 景印文淵閣四庫全書, vol. 742. Taipei: Shang-wu, 1986.

Ch'ên Wan-nai 陳萬鼐. *Ch'ing K'ung Tung-t'ang hsien-shêng Shang-jên nien-p'u* 清孔東塘先生尚任年譜. N.d. Reprint. Taipei: Shang-wu, 1980.

Ch'ên Yen 陳言. *San-yin chi-i ping-chêng fang-lun* (Prescriptions elucidated on the premise that all pathological symptoms have only three primary causes) 三因極一病證方論. In *Ying-yin wên-yüan-ko ssû-k'u ch'üan-shu* 景印文淵閣四庫全書, vol. 743. Taipei: Shang-wu, 1986.

Ch'ên Yü-fu 陳郁夫. *Ming Ch'ên Pai-sha hsien-shêng Hsien-chang nien-p'u* 明陳白沙先生獻章年譜. N.d. Reprint, Taipei: Shang-wu, 1980.

Chêng Chên-mo 鄭振模. *Ch'ing Yü Ch'ü-yüan hsien-shêng Yüeh nien-p'u* 清俞曲園先生樾年譜. N.d. Reprint, Taipei: Shang-wu, 1987.

Chêng Hsüan 鄭玄. "Ch'ü-li" (The rites of Ch'ü) 曲禮. *Li-chi chêng-chu* 禮記鄭注, *chuan* 1, p. 31. Taipei: Chung-hua, 1965.

———. "Nei-tsê" (Domestic rules) 內則. *Li-chi chêng-chu* 禮記鄭注, *chuan* 8, pp. 28–29. Taipei: Chung-hua, 1965.

Ch'êng Hao 程顥 and Ch'êng I 程頤. *Êrh-ch'êng wên-chi* 二程文集. Reprint from Ch'ing Chêng-i-t'ang ch'üan-shu 清正誼堂全書. Shanghai: Shang-wu, 1937.

Ch'êng Hsing-hsüan 程杏軒. *I-shu* (Medical deliberations) 醫述. Hofei: An-hui k'o-chi, 1983.

Chêng P'ei-k'ai 鄭培凱. "T'ien-ti chêng-i chin chien yü fu-nü—Ming-Ch'ing tê ch'ing-sê-i-shih yü chên-ying wên-t'i" 天地正義僅見於婦女—明清的情色意識與貞淫問題. In Pao Chia-lin 鮑家麟, ed., *Chung-kuo-fu-nu-shih-lun-chi III* (Anthology of Chinese women's history, vol. 3) 中國婦女史論集三集, p. 97–119. Taipei: Tao-hsiang, 1993.

"Chia-fan tien chih-chia pien" 家範典·治家篇. In *Ku-chin t'u-shu chi-ch'êng* (The complete classics collection of ancient China) 古今圖書集成, vol. 321. 1931. Reprint, Taipei: Ting-wên, 1976.

Chiang Chih-chung 蔣致中. *Niu K'ung-shan hsien-shêng nien-p'u* 牛空山先生年譜. Shanghai: Shang-wu, 1935.

Chiang I-hsüeh 蔣逸雪. *Chang P'u nien-p'u* 張溥年譜. Shanghai: Shang-wu, 1946.

Chiang Kai-shek 蔣介石. "Pao-kuo yü ssû-ch'in" (Serving my country and remembering my mother) 報國與思親. In *Chiang tsung-t'ung yen-lun hui-chi* 蔣總統言論彙集, vol. 24. Taipei: Chêng-chung, 1956.

Chiang T'ien-shu 蔣天樞. *Ch'üan Hsieh-shan hsien-shêng nien-p'u* 全謝山先生年譜. Shanghai: Shang-wu, 1933.

Chiang Wên-yü 江文瑜, ed. *A-ma tê ku-shih* (Grandma's stories) 阿媽的故事. Taipei: Yü-shan-shê, 1995.

Chiang Yung-ching 蔣永敬. *Hu Han-min hsien-shêng nien-p'u* 胡漢民先生年譜. Taipei: Chung-yang wên-wu, 1978.

Chiang Yu-tien 蔣攸恬. *Shêng-i-chai nien-p'u* 繩枻齋年譜. 1835. Reprint, Taipei: Kuang-wên, 1971.

Chien Ch'ao-liang 簡朝亮. *Chu Chiu-chiang hsien-shêng nien-p'u* 朱九江先生年譜. 1897. Reprint, Taipei: Kuang-wên, 1971.

Ch'ien I 錢乙. *Hsiao-êrh yao-chêng chih-chüeh* (Proven formulae of pediatric medicine) 小兒藥證直訣. 1930. Reprint, Taipei: Hsin-wên-fêng, 1985.

Ch'ien I-chi 錢儀吉. *Ch'ing Ch'ien Wên-tuan-kung Ch'ên-Ch'ün nien-p'u* 清錢文端公陳群年譜. 1894. Reprint, Taipei: Shang-wu, 1980.

Ch'ien Ta-hsin 錢大昕. "Hsi-chih hsien-shêng mu-chih-ming" 西沚先生墓誌銘. *Ch'ien-yen-t'ang wên-chi* 潛研堂文集, *chüan* 48, collected in *Ssû-pu ts'ung-k'an* 四部叢刊初編, vols. 301–3, pp. 5–7. Shanghai: Shanghai Shu-t'ien, 1989.

Chien Yu-wên 簡又文. "Fêng Yü-hsiang Chuan" 馮玉祥傳. *Chuan-chi wên-hsüeh* 傳記文學 35, no. 6 (1979): 30–36.

———. "Ko-ming hua-chia Kao Chien-fu" 革命畫家高劍父. *Chuan-chi wên-hsüeh* 傳記文學 22, no. 2 (1973): 83–91.

Ch'in Ching-ming 秦景明. *Yu-k'o chin-chên* (The golden needle of pediatrics) 幼科金鍼. Taipei: Hsin-wên-fêng, 1977.

Chou Yung-hsiang 周永祥. *Ch'ü Ch'iu-pai nien-p'u* 瞿秋白年譜. Kwangtung: Jênmin, 1983.

Chu Chên-hêng 朱震亨. *Kê-chih yü-lun* 格致餘論. Reprinted from *Ku chin i-t'ung chêng-mai ch'üan-shu* 古今醫統正脈全書. Taipei: Hsin-wên-fêng, 1985.

———. *Tan-hsi hsien-shêng chih-fa hsin-yao* 丹溪先生治法心要. Reprinted from *Ku chin i-t'ung chêng-mai ch'üan-shu* 古今醫統正脈全書. Taipei: Hsin-wên-fêng, 1985.

Chu Hsi 朱熹. *Chin-ssû lu* 近思錄. Ed. Chiang Yung. Kiangsu: Kiangsu shu-tien, 1869.

———. *T'ung-mêng hsü-chih* (Essential knowledge for school children) 童蒙須知. In *Ku-chin t'u-shu chi-ch'êng* 古今圖書集成, vol. 324, *chuan* 39., p. 12. 1931. Reprinted, Taipei: Ting-wên, 1976.

Chu Hui-min 朱惠民. *Tz'û-yu hsin-ch'uan* (The true method of caring for the young) 慈幼心傳. 1603, microfilm. Taipei: National Central Library.

Chu Shang-wên 朱尚文. *Wung T'ung-ho hsien-shêng nien-p'u* 翁同龢先生年譜. N.d. Reprint, Taipei: Shang-wu, 1971.

Chuang Shu-tsu 莊述祖. *Ti-tzû chih chi-chieh* 弟子職集解. Shanghai: Shang-wu, 1937.

Cloherty, John P., and Ann R. Stark. *Manual of Neonatal Care*. Boston: Little, Brown and Co., 1985.

Cogan, Frances B. *All-American Girl*. Athens and London: University of Georgia Press, 1989.

Cohen, Samuel K., Jr. *Women in the Streets: Essays on Sex and Power in Renaissance Italy*. Baltimore: Johns Hopkins University Press, 1996.

Coles, Robert. *The Spiritual Life of Children*. Boston: Houghton Mifflin, 1990.

Cone, Thomas E., Jr. *History of American Pediatrics*. Boston: Little, Brown and Co., 1979.

———. *History of the Care and Feeding of the Premature Infant*. Boston: Little, Brown and Co., 1985.

———. "Perspectives in Neonatology." In George F. Smith and Dharmapuri Vidyasagar, eds., *Historical Review and Recent Advances in Neonatal and Prenatal Medicine*, vol. 1, pp. 9–34. Toronto: Mead Johnson Nutritional.

Confucius 孔子. *Lun Yü* 論語. Taipei: Chung-hua, 1965.

———. "Wei-chêng" (Government) 為政. In *Lun Yü* 論語, *chuan* 2, p. 4. Taipei: Chung-hua, 1965.

Cunningham, Hugh. *Children and Childhood in Western Society Since 1500*. New York: Longman, 1995.

Davis, Glenn. *Childhood and History in America*. New York: The Psychohistory Press, 1976.

De Bary, Wm. Theodore, and John W. Chaffee, eds. *Neo-Confucian Education: The Formative Stage*. Berkeley: University of California Press, 1989.

De Bary, Wm. Theodore, and the Conference on Ming Thought. *Self and Society in Ming Thought*. New York: Columbia University Press, 1970.

Demos, John. *A Little Commonwealth: Family Life in Plymouth Colony*. London: Oxford University Press, 1970.

Dewoskin, Kenneth J. "Famous Chinese Childhoods." In Anne Behnke Kinney, ed., *Chinese Views of Childhood*, pp. 57–78. Honolulu: University of Hawaii Press, 1995.

Dobbing, John, ed. *Maternal Nutrition and Lactational Infertility*. New York: Raven Press, 1985.

Duhouse, Carol. *Girls Growing Up in Late Victorian and Edwardian England*. London: Routledge and Kegan Paul, 1981.

Ebrey, Patricia, and James Watson, eds. *Kinship Organization in Late Imperial China, 1000–1940*. Berkeley: University of California Press, 1986.

Elman, Benjamin A., and Alexander Woodside, eds. *Education and Society in Late Imperial China, 1600–1900*. Berkeley: University of California Press, 1994.

Fang Hsien 方賢. *Ch'i-hsiao liang-fang* 奇效良方. Taipei: Hsin-wên-fêng, 1989.

Fang Shih-kan 方士淦. *Tan-chê-hsüan tzû-ting nien-p'u* 淡蕉軒自訂年譜. N.d. Reprint, Taipei: Kuang-wên, 1971.

Fang Wên 方聞. *Fu Ch'ing-chu hsien-shêng ta-chuan nien-p'u* 傅青主先生大傳年譜. Taipei: Chung-hua, 1970.

———. *Hsü Sung-k'an hsien-shêng nien-p'u* 徐松龕先生年譜. Taipei: Kuang-wên, 1971.

Fêng Ch'ên 馮辰. *Li Shu-ku hsien-shêng nien-p'u* 李恕谷先生年譜. Reprint from Ch'ing chi-fu ts'ung-shu 清畿輔叢書. Taipei: Kuang-wên, 1971.

Fildes, Valerie A. *Wet Nursing: A History from Antiquity to the Present.* New York: Basil Blackwell, 1988.

Fong, S. Grace. "Boudoir World and Professional Life—Contrasting Self-Representations by Two Women Poets of the Mid- and Late- Ching." Paper delivered at the Institute of Chinese Literature and Philosophy, Academia Sinica, Taipei, 1996.

———. *Wu Wenying and the Art of Southern Song Ci Poetry.* Princeton: Princeton University Press, 1987.

Freedman, Maurice. *Family and Kinship in Chinese Society.* Stanford: Stanford University Press, 1970.

Fuch, Rachel. *Abandoned Children.* Albany: State University of New York Press, 1984.

Furth, Charlotte. *A Flourishing Yin: Gender in China's Medical History, 960–1665.* Berkeley: University of California Press, 1999.

———. "From Birth to Birth: The Growing Body in Chinese Medicine." In Anne Behnke Kinney, ed., *Chinese Views of Childhood,* pp. 157–92. Honolulu: University of Hawaii Press, 1995.

———. "The Patriarch's Legacy: Household Instructions and the Transmission of Orthodox Values." In Kwang-ching Liu, ed., *Orthodoxy in Late Imperial China,* pp. 187–211. Berkeley: University of California Press, 1990.

Glenn, Davis. *Childhood and History in America.* New York: The Psychohistory Press, 1976.

Golden, Mark. *Children and Childhood in Classical Athens.* Baltimore: Johns Hopkins University Press, 1990.

Goodenough, Elizabeth, Mark A. Heberle, and Naomi Sokoloff, eds. *Infant Tongues: The Voice of the Child in Literature.* Detroit: Wayne State University Press, 1994.

Gottlieb, Beatrice. *The Family in the Western World from the Black Death to the Industrial Age.* New York: Oxford University Press, 1992.

Grendler, Paul F. *Schooling in Renaissance Italy: Literacy and Learning, 1300–1600.* Baltimore: Johns Hopkins University Press, 1959.

Greven, Philip J., Jr. *Four Generations: Population, Land, and Family in Colonial Andover, Massachussetts.* Ithaca: Cornell University Press, 1970.

———. *The Protestant Temperament: Patterns of Child-Rearing, Religious Experience, and the Self in Early America.* Chicago: The University of Chicago Press, 1977.

———. *Spare the Child: The Religious Roots of Punishment and the Psychological Impact of Physical Abuse.* New York: Vintage Books, 1990.

Grew, Raymond, and Patrick J. Harrigan. *School, State and Society: The Growth of Elementary Schooling in Nineteenth-Century France. A Quantitative Analysis.* Ann Arbor: The University of Michigan Press, 1991.

Han Hsi-tuo 韓錫鐸. *Chung-hua mêng-hsüeh chi-ch'êng* 中華蒙學集成. Shên-yang: Liao-ning chiao-yü, 1993.

Handlin, Joanne F. *Action in Late Ming Thought: The Reorientation of Lu K'un and Other Scholar Officials.* Berkeley: University of California Press, 1983.

Hanjal, John. "European Marriage Patterns in Perspective." In D. V. Glass and D. E. C. Eversley, eds., *Population in History: Essays in Historical Demography*, pp. 101–46. London: Edward Arnold, 1965.

Hanley, Susan, and Arthur Wolf, eds. *Family and Population in East Asian History.* Stanford: Stanford University Press, 1985.

Hareven, Tamara K., and Andrejs Plakans, eds. *Family History at the Crossroads: Journal of Family History Reader.* Princeton: Princeton University Press, 1987.

Herlihy, David. *Medieval Households.* Cambridge: Harvard University Press, 1985.

Hoffer, Peter C., and N. E. H. Hull. *Murdering Mothers: Infanticide in England and New England, 1558–1803.* New York: New York University Press, 1984.

Houlbrooke, Ralph. *The English Family, 1450–1700.* New York: Longman, 1984.

———. *English Family Life, 1576–1716: An Anthology from Diaries.* New York: Basil Blackwell, 1988.

Hsiao-êrh wei-shêng tsung-wei lun-fang (A thorough discussion of infant hygiene) 小兒衛生總微論方. In *Ying-yin wên-yüan-ko ssû-k'u ch'üan-shu* 景印文淵閣四庫全書, vol. 741. Taipei: Shang-wu, 1986.

Hsiao-hsiao-shêng 笑笑生. *Chin-p'ing-mei* 金瓶梅. Shantung: Ch'i-lu, 1991.

Hsieh Ch'êng-jên 謝承仁. *Ch'i Chi-kuang* 戚繼光. Shanghai: Jên-min, 1978.

Hsiung Ping-chen. "An-chü ch'üeh-tsao: I-an chih ch'uan-ch'êng yü ch'uan-ch'i" 案據確鑿: 醫案之傳承與傳奇. In Hsiung Ping-chen, ed., *Jang-chêng-chü shuo-hua*: chung-kuo p'ien (Allows evidence to speak: The case of China) 讓證據說話: 中國篇, pp. 201–54. Taipei: Mai-t'ien, 2001.

———. *An-yang: Chung-kuo chin-shih êrh-t'ung tê chi-ping yü chien-k'ang* (Ill or well: Diseases and health of young children in late imperial China) 安恙: 中國近世兒童的疾病與健康. Taipei: Lien-ching, 1999.

———. "Case Histories of Chinese Pediatrics and their Bio-medical Value." Paper presented at the conference on the Case History in Chinese Medicine: History, Science, and Narrative, UCLA, Jan. 1998.

———. "Children and Childhood in Late-imperial China: The Notions vs. the Realities." Lecture given at the East Asian Seminar, Free University of Berlin, Nov. 1995.

———. "Ching-fêng: Chung-kuo chin-shih êrh-t'ung tê chi-ping yü chien-k'ang yen-chiu chih-i" (Ching-fêng: A study of the disease and health of young children in late imperial China [II]) 驚風: 中國近世兒童疾病研究之一. *Chinese Studies* 13, no. 1 (1995): 169–203.

———. "Ch'ing-tai chung-kuo êrh-k'o i-hsüeh tê ch'ü-yü-hsing ch'u-t'an" (A preliminary study on the regional characteristics of Chinese pediatrics under the Ch'ing) 清代中國兒科醫學的區域性初探. In Institute of Modern History, Academia Sinica, ed., *Ch'ing-tai chung-kuo ch'ü-yü-shih yen-t'ao-hui lun-wên-chi* 近代中國區域史研討會論文集, vol. 1, pp. 17–39. Taipei: Institute of Modern History, Academia Sinica, 1987.

———. "Chung-kuo chin-shih êrh-t'ung lun-shu tê fu-hsien" (The emergence of the discourse on children in late imperial China) 中國近世兒童論述的浮現. In Hao Yen-p'ing 郝延平 and Wei Hsiu-mei 魏秀梅, eds., *Chin-shih Chung-kuo chih ch'uan-t'ung yü pien-ch'ien: Liu Kwang-ching hsien-shêng ch'i-shih-wu sui chu-*

shou lun-wên chi (Tradition and metamorphosis in modern Chinese history: Essays in honor of professor Kwang-ching Liu's seventy-fifth birthday) 近世中國之傳統與蛻變:劉廣京先生七十五歲祝壽論文集, vol. 1, pp. 139–70. Taipei: Institute of Modern History, Academia Sinica, 1998.

———. "Chung-kuo chin-shih shih-jên pi-hsia tê êrh-t'ung chien-k'ang wên-t'i" (Children's health as noted by the educated elite in the late imperial China) 中國近世士人筆下的兒童健康問題. *Bulletin of the Institute of Modern History* 23 (1994): 1–29.

———. "Chung-kuo Chin-shih tê hsin-shêng-êrh chao-hu" (The evolution of newborn care in early modern China) 中國近世的新生兒照護. In Institute of History and Philology, Academia Sinica, ed., *Society and Culture of Early Modern China*, pp. 387–428. Taipei: Institute of History and Philology, Academia Sinica, 1990.

———. "Constructed Emotions: The Bond Between Mothers and Sons in Late Imperial China." *Late Imperial China* 15, no. 1 (1994): 87–117.

———. "The Domestic, the Personal and the Intimate: Father-Daughter Bonds in Late Imperial China." Paper presented at the Privacy Conference, project of "Crossing Borders: Revitalizing Area Studies," Center for Japanese Studies, University of Michigan, Ann Arbor, Oct. 3, 1998.

———. "Êrh-t'ung wên-hsüeh" (Children's literature) 兒童文學. In William Nienhauser, ed., *Indiana Companion to Traditional Chinese Literature*, vol. 2, pp. 31–38. Bloomington: Indiana University Press, 1998.

———. "Fathers and Daughters in Late Imperial China: Culture, Cultivation and Gender in the Family Setting." Paper presented at the International Congress of Asian and North African Studies, Budapest, 1997.

———. "Hao-tê k'ai-shih: Chung-kuo chin-shih shih-jên tzû-ti tê yu-nien chiao-yü" (Getting off to a good start: Early childhood education of elite families in late imperial China) 好的開始—中國近世士人子弟的幼年教育. In Institute of Modern History, Academia Sinica, ed., *Family Process and Political Process in Modern Chinese History*, pp. 203–38. Taipei: Institute of Modern History, Academia Sinica, 1992.

———. "Hsi-shuai shih-tien: Ying-hsiung pu-lun ch'u-shên ti" (The epistomology of a children's game: Cricket fight in China's cultural lexicon) 蟋蟀釋典:英雄不論出身低. In Hsiung Ping-chen, ed., *Tu-wu ssû-jên* (Viewing the humanity through things) 睹物思人, pp. 55–96. Taipei: Mai-t'ien 2003.

———. "Hsiao-êrh chih t'u: I-ko chung-kuo i-liao fa-chan shih ho êrh-t'ung chien-k'an shih shang tê k'ao-ch'a" (The problem of throwing up: A historical observation in Chinese pediatric medicine and children's health) 小兒之吐:一個中國醫療發展史和兒童健康史上的考察. *Bulletin of the Institute of Modern History* 25 (1996): 1–51.

———. "Hsieh yü Li: Chien-lun chin-shih chung-kuo êrh-t'ung hsiao-hua-tao tê ping-pien yü chien-k'ang" (Hsieh and Li: A discussion on children's digestive illnesses and health in late imperial China) 瀉與痢:兼論近世中國兒童消化道的病變與健康. *Journal of the Institute of Chinese Studies of The Chinese University of Hong Kong*, new series 6 (1997): 129–70.

———. "Ju-li ju-ch'ing: Ming-ch'ing yu-hsüeh fa-chan yü êrh-t'ung kuan-huai chih liang-mien hsing" (To be rational and to be sensible: The contradiction in the early education development and concerns for children in the Ming-Ch'ing period) 入理入情:明清幼學發展與兒童關懷之兩面性. In Hsiung Ping-chen and Lü Miaw-fen 呂妙芬, eds., *Li-chiao yü ch'ing-yü: Ch'ien-chin-tai chung-kuo wên-hua chung-tê hou/hsien-tai hsing* (Neo-Confucian orthodoxy and human desires: Post/Modernity in pre-modern Chinese culture) 禮教與情慾:前近代中國文化中的後/現代性, pp. 313–26. Taipei: Institute of Modern History, Academia Sinica, 1999.

———. "Kan: Chung-kuo chin-shih êrh-t'ung chi-ping yü chien-k'ang yen-chiu chih-êrh" (Kan: A study on the disease and health of young children in late imperial China [II]) 疳:中國近世兒童疾病與健康研究之二. *Bulletin of the Institute of Modern History* 24 (1995): 263–94.

———. "Konzepte von Kindheit im traditionellen China." In Heike Frick, Mechthild Leutner, and Nicola Spakowski (Hrsg.), *Die Befreiung der Kinder: Konzepte von Kindheit im China der Republikzeit*, pp. 21–34. Hamburg: Lit Verlag, 1999.

———. "Ming-tai tê yu-k'o i-hsüeh" (Pediatric medicine in the Ming period) 明代的幼科醫學. *Chinese Studies* 9, no. 1(June 1991): 53–69.

———. "More or Less: Cultural and Medical Factors Behind Marital Fertility in Late Imperial China." Paper presented at the International Union on the Scientific Study of Population's (IUSSP) workshop on "Abortion, Infanticide and Neglect in Historical Populations," Kyoto, Oct. 1994.

———. "Narrative or Story? Case Records in Chinese Pediatrics." Paper presented at the international conference on "Thinking with Cases," Center of Far Eastern Languages and Civilizations, University of Chicago, Oct. 2001.

———. "The Nurturing Women: Idea and Practices of Breastfeeding in Late Imperial China." Paper presented at the Yale Conference on Women and Literature in Ming-Qing China, New Haven, June 22–26, 1993.

———. "The Relationship between Women and Children in Early Modern China." Paper presented at American Association of Women's Studies, Seattle, Washington, 1985.

———. "Shei-jên chih-tzû: chung-kuo chia-t'ing yü li-shih mai-lo chung tê êrh-t'ung ting-i wên-t'i" (Whose children are they? Reflections on the status of children in the context of Chinese family and history) 誰人之子? 中國家庭與歷史脈絡中的兒童定義問題. In Center for Chinese Studies, ed., *Essays on Chinese Family and Ethics*, pp. 259–94. Taipei: Center for Chinese Studies, 2000.

———. "Shih-k'uei Chung-kuo chin-shih êrh-t'ung tê jên-shih huan-ching yü ch'ing-kan shih-chieh" (A preliminary investigation of the human environment and the emotional world of children in Ming-Ch'ing China) 試窺明清幼兒的人事環境與情感世界. *Pen-t'u hsin-li-hsüeh yen-chiu* (Indigenous psychological research in Chinese societies) 本土心理學研究 2(Dec. 1993): 251–306.

———. "T'ang Chên and the Works in Obscurity: Life and Thought of a Provincial Intellectual in Seventeenth Century China." Ph. D. diss., Brown University, 1983.

———. "To Raise the Young: Nursing and Infant-feeding in Late Imperial China." *Journal of Family History* 20, no. 7 (1995): 217–38.

———. "Treatment of Children in Traditional China." *Berliner China-Hefte* 10 (Mar. 1996): 73–79.

————. *T'ung-nien i-wang: Chung-kuo hai-tzû tê li-shih* (Childhood in the past: A history of Chinese children) 童年憶往—中國孩子的歷史. Taipei: Mai-t'ien, 2000.

————. *Yu-yu: Ch'uan-t'ung chung-kuo tê ch'iang-pao chih tao* (To nurse the young: Infant care in traditional China) 幼幼：傳統中國的襁褓之道. Taipei: Lien-ching, 1995.

Hsiung Ping-chen and Lü Miaw-fen 呂妙芬, eds. *Li-chiao Yü ch'ing-yü: Ch'ien-chin-tai chung-kuo wên-hua chung-tê hou/hsien-tai hsing* (Neo-Confucian orthodoxy and human desires: Post/Modernity in pre-modern Chinese culture) 禮教與情慾：前近代中國文化中的後/現代性. Taipei: Institute of Modern History, Academia Sinica, 1999.

Hsü Chao 徐照. *Ming-tai ta chêng-chih-chia Hsü P'u nien-p'u* 明代大政治家徐溥年譜. Taipei: Shih-ta, 1963.

Hsü Ch'un-fu 徐春甫. *Ku-chin i-t'ung ta-ch'üan* (Complete collection of medicine past and present) 古今醫統大全. Reprinted from Ming edition. Taipei: Hsin-wên-fêng, 1978.

Hsü Hung 徐泓. "Ming-tai chia-t'ing tê ch'üan-li-chieh-kou chi ch'i ch'êng-yüan chien tê kuan-hsi" 明代家庭的權力結構及其成員的關係. *Fu-jen Historical Journal*. 5 (1993): 167–202.

————. "Ming-tai tê hun-yin-chih-tu" 明代的婚姻制度. *Ta-lu tsa-chih* 大陸雜誌. 78, nos. 1–2 (1989): 68–82.

Hsü Nai 徐鼐. *Pi-chou-chai chu-jên nien-p'u* 敝帚齋主人年譜. 1874. Reprint, Taipei: Kuang-wên, 1971.

Hsü Ting-pao 徐定寶. *Huang tsung-hsi nien-p'u* 黃宗羲年譜. Shanghai: Hua-tung Shih-fan, 1995.

Hsü Tzû 徐梓 and Wang Hsüeh-mei 王雪梅. *Mêng-hsüeh hsü-chih* 蒙學須知. T'ai-yüan: Shang-hsi Chiao-yü, 1991.

Hsü Yung-ch'ang 徐永昌. "Hsü Yung-ch'ang Ch'iu-chi-chai hui-i-lu" 徐永昌「求已齋回憶錄」. *Chuan-chi wên-hsüeh* 傳記文學 48, no. 5 (1986): 10–15.

Hsü Yüng-p'ing 徐詠平. *Min-kuo Ch'ên Ying-shih hsien-shêng Ch'i-mei nien-p'u* 民國陳英士先生其美年譜. 1930. Reprint, Taipei: Shang-wu, 1980.

Hsüeh K'ai 薛鎧. *Pao-ying ch'üan-shu* (Complete writings on infant protection) 保嬰全書. 1637. Reprint, Taipei: Hsin-wên-fêng, 1978.

Hsüeh Kuang-ch'ien 薛光前. "K'un-hsing i-wang" 困行憶往. *Chuan-chi wên-hsüeh* 傳記文學 32, no. 5 (1978): 45–50.

Hu Ch'i-kuang 胡奇光. *Chung-kuo hsiao-hsüeh shih* 中國小學史. Shanghai: Jên-min, 1987.

Hu Chün 胡鈞. *Chang Wên-hsiang-kung nien-p'u* 張文襄公年譜. 1939. Reprint. Taipei: Kuang-wên, 1971.

Hu Huai-ch'ên 胡懷琛. *Erh-shih-ssû-hsiao t'u-shuo* (Illustrations of the twenty-four stories of filial piety) 二十四孝圖說. Shanghai: Ta-tung, 1925.

Hu Kuang 胡廣, ed. *Hsin-li ta-ch'üan* 性理大全. In *Ying-yin wên-yüan-ko ssû-k'u ch'üan-shu* 景印文淵閣四庫全書, vol. 710–11. Taipei: Shang-wu, 1986.

Hu Shih 胡適. *Chang Shih-chai hsien-shêng nien-p'u* 章實齋先生年譜. Shanghai: Shang-wu, 1933.

————. "Tz'u-yu te wên-t'i 慈幼的問題." In *Hu Shih wên-ts'un* 胡適文存, p. 39. Taipei: Yüan-tung, 1968.

———. "Wo-tê mu-ch'in" 我的母親. In *Ssû-shih tzû-shu* 四十自述, pp.56–59. Taipei: Wên-hai, 1983.

Hu Wên-k'ai 胡文楷. *Li-tai fu-nü chu-tso k'ao* 歷代婦女著作考. Shanghai: Ku-chi, 1985.

Hu Yün-yü 胡韞玉. *Pao Shên-po hsien-shêng nien-p'u* 包慎伯先生年譜. 1923. Reprint, Taipei: Kuang-wên, 1971.

Huang I-chih 黃逸之. *Huang Chung-tsê nien-p'u* 黃仲則年譜. Shanghai: Shang-wu, 1933.

Huang Wên-hsiang 黃文相. *Wang Hsi-chuang hsien-shêng nien-p'u* 王西莊先生年譜. 1942. Reprint, Taipei: Kuang-wên, 1971.

Huang Yün-mei 黃雲眉. *Ch'ing Shao Êrh-yün hsien-shêng Chin-han nien-p'u* 清邵二雲先生晉涵年譜. 1931. Reprint, Taipei: Shang-wu, 1982.

———. *Shao Êrh-yün hsien-shêng nien-p'u* 邵二雲先生年譜. 1931. Reprint, Taipei: Kuang-wên, 1971.

Hunt, David. *Parents and Children in History: The Psychology of Family Life in Modern France.* New York: Harper and Row, 1970.

I Jo-lan 衣若蘭. "Ts'ung san-ku liu-p'uo k'an ming-tai fu-nü yü shê-hui" 從三姑六婆看明代婦女與社會. Master's thesis, National Taiwan Normal University, 1997.

Johnson, Elizabeth. "Women and Childbearing in Kwan Mun Hau Village: A Study of Social Change." in Margery Wolf and Roxane Witke, eds., *Women in Chinese Society*, pp. 215–42. Stanford: Stanford University Press, 1975.

Jung Chao-tsu 容肇祖. *Li Chuo-wu hsien-shêng Chih nien-p'u* 李卓吾先生贄年譜. N.d. Reprint, Taipei: Shang-wu, 1982.

Kao Ching-lang 高鏡朗. *Ku-tai êrh-k'o chi-ping hsin-lun* 古代兒科疾病新論. Shanghai: Shanghai k'o-hsüeh chi-shu, 1983.

Kao K'uei-hsiang 高魁祥 and Shên Chien-kuo 申建國. *Chung-hua ku-chin nü-chieh p'u* 中華古今女杰譜. Beijing: Chung-kuo she-hui chu-pan-she, 1991.

Kao P'ing-shu 高平叔. *Ts'ai Yüan-p'ei nien-p'u* 蔡元培年譜. Beijing: Chung-hua, 1980.

King, Margaret L. *The Death of the Child Valerio Marcello.* Chicago: University of Chicago Press, 1994.

Kinney, Anne Behnke, ed. *Chinese Views of Childhood.* Honolulu: University of Hawaii Press, 1995.

———. "Dyed Silk: Han Notions of the Moral Development of Children." in idem, ed., *Chinese Views of Childhood*, pp. 17–56. Honolulu: University of Hawaii Press, 1995.

Ko, Dorothy. *Every Step a Lotus: Shoes for Bound Feet.* Berkeley: University of California Press, 2001.

———. "Pursuing Talent and Virtue: Education and Women's Culture in Seventeenth- and Eighteenth-Century China." *Late Imperial China* 13, no. 1 (1992): 9–39.

———. *Teachers of the Inner Chambers: Women and Culture in Seventeenth-Century China.* Stanford: Stanford University Press, 1994.

———. "The Written Word and The Bound Foot: A History of the Courtesan's Aura." in Ellen Widmer and Kang-i Sun Chang, eds., *Writing Women in Late Imperial China.* Stanford: Stanford University Press, 1997.

————. Ku Chên 顧鎮. *Huang K'un-p'u hsien-shêng nien-p'u* 黃昆圃先生年譜. N.d. Reprint from Ch'ing chi-fu ts'ung-shu 清畿輔叢書. Taipei: Kuang-wên, 1971.

K'ou P'ing 寇平. *Ch'üan-yu hsin-chien* (Precious guide for saving the young) 全幼心鑑. 1468 edition, microfilm from National Central Library.

Kuei Yu-kuang 歸有光. *Chên-ch'üan wên-chi* 震川文集. In *Ssû-pu pei-yao* 四部備要, vol. 187. Taipei: Chung-hua, 1965.

————. *Kuei chên-chúan chi* 歸雲川集. Taipei: shih-chieh, 1970.

Kung-sun Hung 公孫訇. *Fêng Kuo-chang nien-p'u* 馮國璋年譜. Ho-pei: Jên-min, 1989.

Kung T'ing-hsien 龔廷賢. *Hsin-k'an chi-shih ch'üan-shu* 新刊濟世全書. Taipei: Hsin-wên-fêng, 1987.

————. *Shou-shih pao-yüan* (Preserving the original principle in order to obtain longevity) 壽世保元. Shanghai: Shanghai k'o-hsüeh chi-shu, 1989.

Kuo Ai-ch'un 郭靄春. *Yen Hsi-chai nien-p'u* 顏習齋年譜. Hong Kong: Ch'ung-wên, 1971.

Kuo Sung-t'ao 郭嵩燾. *Lo Chung-chieh-kung nien-p'u* 羅忠節公年譜. 1859. Reprint, Taipei: Kuang-wên, 1971.

Kuo Yen-li 郭延禮. *Kung Tzû-chên nien-p'u* 龔自珍年譜. Chi-nan: Ch'i-lu, 1987.

Lai Hsin-hsia 來新夏. *Chin San-pai-nien jên-wu nien-p'u chih-chien lu* 近三百年人物年譜知見錄. Shanghai: Jên-min, 1983.

Laing, Ellen Johnston. "Wives, Daughters, and Lovers: Three Ming Dynasty Women Painters," in Marsha Weidner, et al., *Views from Jade Terrace: Chinese Women Artists, 1300–1912*, pp. 31–39. Indianapolis, Ind.: Indianapolis Museum of Art, 1988.

————. "Women Painters in Traditional China," in Marsha Weidner, ed., *Flowering in the Shadows: Women in the History of Chinese and Japanese Painting*, pp. 81–101. Honolulu: University of Hawaii Press, 1990.

Laslett, Peter. *Family Life and Illicit Love in Earlier Generations*. Cambridge: Cambridge University Press, 1979.

————. *The World We Have Lost*. London: Methuen, 1965.

Laslett, Peter, and Richard Wall, eds. *Household and Family in Past Times*. Cambridge: Cambridge University Press, 1972.

Lee, James, and Cameron Campbell. *Fate and Fortune in Rural China: Social Organization and Population Behavior in Liaoning, 1774–1873*. Cambridge: Cambridge University Press, 1997.

Lee, James, and Osamu Saito, eds. *Abortion, Infanticide and Neglect in Asian Historical Populations*. Oxford: Oxford University Press, forthcoming.

Lee, James Z., and Wang Feng. *One Quarter of the Humanity*. Cambridge, Mass.: Harvard University Press, 1999.

Lee Jen-der 李貞德. "Han-t'ang chih-chien chiu-tzû i-fang shih-t'an: Chien-lun fu-k'o lan-shang yü hsing-pieh lun-shu (Reproductive medicine in late antiquity and early medieval China: Gender discourse and the birth of gynecology) 漢唐之間求子醫方試探：兼論婦科濫觴與性別論述. *Chung-yang yen-chiu-yüan li-shih yü-yen yen-chiu-so chi-k'an* (Bulletin of the Institute of History and Philology, Academia Sinica) 中央研究院歷史語言研究所集刊68, no. 2: 283–367.

————. "Han-t'ang chih-chien i-shu chung tê shêng-ch'an chih tao" (Childbirth in the medical writings of late antiquity and early medieval China) 漢唐之間醫書中的生產之道. *Chung-yang yen-chiu-yüan li-shih yü-yen yen-chiu-so chi-k'an* (Bulletin of the institute of history and philogy, Academia Sinica) 中央研究院歷史語言研究所集刊67, no. 3: 533–654.

Lee, Ronald Demos, et al. *Population Patterns in the Past*. New York: Academic Press, 1977.

Legge, James. *The Chinese Classics*. Taipei: Southern Materials Center, 1985.

Leung, Angela Ki Che. "Elementary Education in the Lower Youngtze Region in the Seventeenth and Eighteenth Centuries." In Benjamin A. Elman and Alexander Woodside, eds., *Education and Society in Late Imperial China, 1600–1900*, pp. 381–96. Berkeley: University of California Press, 1994.

———. "Organized Medicine in Ming-Qing China: State and Private Medical Institutions in the Lower Yangzi Region." *Late Imperial China* 8, no. 1 (1987): 134–66.

———. "Relief Institution for Children in Nineteenth-century China." In Anne Behnke Kinney, ed., *Chinese Views of Childhood*, pp. 251–78. Honolulu: University of Hawaii Press, 1995.

———. 梁其姿. *Shih-shan yü chiao-hua: Ming-ch'ing tê tz'u-shan tsu-chih* (Philanthropy and inculation: Charity organizations in the Ming-Ch'ing period) 施善與教化:明清的慈善組織. Taipei: Lien-ching, 1997.

———. "Women practicing medicine in Pre-modern China." In Harriet T. Zurndorfer, ed., *Chinese Women in the Imperial Past: New Perspectives*, pp. 101–34. Leiden: Brill Academic Publishers, 1999.

Li Ch'êng-li 黎承禮. *Chu-hsien tao-jên tzû-shu nien-p'u* 竹閒道人自述年譜. 1891. Reprint, Taipei: Kuang-wên, 1971.

Li Chih 李贄. "T'ung-hsin shuo" (On the heart of the child) 童心説. *Li-shih Fên-shu* 李氏焚書, *chuan* 3, pp. 22–24. N.d. Reprint from Ming edition. Shanhsi: Chiao-yü t'u-shu ch'u-pan-shê, n.d.

Li Ch'ing-chih 李清植. *Li Wên-chên-kung nien-p'u* 李文貞公年譜. 1849. Reprint, Taipei: Kuang-wên, 1971.

Li Hsi 李曦. *Chung-kuo ku-tai chu-ming chê-hsüeh-chia p'ing-chuan* 中國古代著名哲學家評傳, vol. 3. Shantung: Ch'i-lu, 1980.

Li Shu-ch'ang 黎庶昌. *Ch'ing Tsêng Wên-chêng-kung Kuo-fan nien-p'u* 清曾文正公國藩年譜. 1876. Reprint, Taipei: Shang-wu, 1978.

Li T'ing 李梴, *I-hsüeh ju-mên* 醫學入門. In *Ku-chin t'u-shu chi-ch'êng* (KCTSCC) 古今圖書集成, vol. 456, *chuan* 422. 1931. Reprint, Taipei: Ting-wên, 1976.

Li Tsung-t'ung 李宗侗. *Li Hung-tsao hsien-shêng nien-p'u* 李鴻藻先生年譜. Taipei: Shang-wu, 1971.

Li Yü-hsiu 李毓秀. *Ti-tzû kuei* 弟子規. 1881. Ch'ing kuang-hsü ch'i-nien chin-ho kuang-jên-t'ang k'an-pên from Fu Ssû-nien Library, Taiwan.

Li Yung-ch'iao 李永翹. *Chang Ta-ch'ien nien-p'u* 張大千年譜. Ch'êng-tu: Ssû-ch'uan shê-hui k'o-hsüeh yüan, 1987.

Liang Chang-chü 梁章鉅. *T'ui-an tzû-ting nien-p'u* 退庵自訂年譜. 1845. Reprint, Taipei: Kuang-wên, 1971.

Liang Ch'i-ch'ao 梁啓超. *Chu Shun-shui hsien-shêng nien-p'u* 朱舜水先生年譜. Taipei: Kuang-wên, 1971.

Liang Chia-mien 梁家勉. *Hsü Kuang-ch'i nien p'u* 徐光啓年譜. Shanghai: Shanghai Ku-chi, 1981.

Liang Huan-nai 梁煥鼎 and Liang Huan-ting 梁煥鼎. *Ch'ing Liang Chü-ch'uan hsien-shêng Chi nien-p'u* 清梁巨川先生濟年譜. 1925. Reprint, Taipei: Shang-wu, 1980.

———. *Kuei-lin Liang hsien-shêng nien-p'u* 桂林梁先生年譜. 1925. Reprint, Taipei: Kuang-wên, 1971.

Liang I-chên 梁乙真. *Chung-kuo fu-nü wên-hsüeh-shih kang* 中國婦女文學史綱. Shanghai: Shanghai shu-tien, 1990.

Lin I 林逸. *Ch'ing chien-hu nü-hsia Ch'iu Chin nien-p'u* 清鑑湖女俠秋瑾年譜. Taipei: Shang-wu, 1985.

———. *Ch'ing Hung Pei-chiang hsien-shêng Liang-chi nian-p'u* 清洪北江先生亮吉年譜. Taipei: Shang-wu, 1981.

Lin Mei-i 林玫儀. "Wang Tuan-shu T'ao-lun chih P'ing-hsi—Chien-lun ch'i hsüan-shih piao-chün" (An analysis of deliberations on Wang Tuan-shu: Also as related to her selection of poetry) 王端淑討論之評析—兼論其選詩標準. *Chiu-chou Hsüeh-k'an* 九州學刊 6, no. 2 (1994): 45–86.

Liu Ch'i 劉跂. *Ch'ien Chung-yang chuan* 錢仲陽傳. In Ch'ien I 錢乙, *Hsiao-êrh yao-cheng chih-chüeh* (Proven formulae of pediatric medicine) 小兒藥證直訣. 1930. Reprint, Taipei: Hsin-wên-fêng, 1985.

Liu, Hui-chen Wang. *The Traditional Chinese Clan Rules*. Association for Asian Studies Monographs, no. 7. Locust Vally, N.J.: J. J. August, 1959.

Liu, Kwang-Ching, ed. *Orthodoxy in Late Imperial China*. Berkeley: University of California Press, 1990.

Liu P'an-sui 劉盼遂. *Tuan Yü-ta'si hsien-shêng nien-p'u* 段玉裁先生年譜. Taipei: Ch'ung-wên, 1971.

———. *Wang-shih fu-tzû nien-p'u* 王氏父子年譜. Taipei: Ch'ung-wên, 1971.

Liu Shao-t'ang 劉紹唐. "Min-kuo jên-wu hsiao-chuan" 民國人物小傳. *Chuan-chi wên-hsüeh* 傳記文學 32, no. 6 (1978): 141.

Liu Ts'ui-jung 劉翠溶. "The Demographic Dynamics of Some Clans in the Lower Yangtze Area. ca. 1400–1900." *Academia Economic Papers* 9, no. 1 (1981): 115–60.

———. "The Demography of Two Chinese Clans in Hsiao-shan, Chekiang, 1650–1850." In Susan Hanley and Arthur Wolf, eds., *Family and Population in East Asian History*, pp. 13–61. Stanford: Stanford University Press, 1985.

———. *Ming-ch'ing shih-ch'i chia-tsu jên-k'ou yü shê-hui ching-chi pien-ch'ien* (Lineage population and socioeconomic changes in the Ming-Ch'ing period) 明清時期家族人口與社會經濟變遷, 2 vols. Taipei: Institute of Economics, Academic Sinica, 1992.

Liu Wên-hsin 劉文興. *Pao-ying Liu Ch'u-chên hsien-shêng nien-p'u* 寶應劉楚楨先生年譜. 1933. Reprint, Taipei: Kuang-wên, 1971.

Lo Chêng-chün 羅正鈞. *Wang Chuang-wu-kung nien-p'u* 王壯武公年譜. 1897. Reprint, Taipei: Kuang-wên, 1971.

Lo Chi-tsu 羅繼祖. *Chu Ssû-ho hsien-shêng nien-p'u* 朱筍河先生年譜. 1931. Reprint, Taipei: Kuang-wên, 1971.

Lo Hsiang-lin 羅香林. *Hsien-k'ao Yu-shan fu-chün nien-p'u* 先考幼山府君年譜. 1936. Reprint, Beijing: Beijing Library, 1998.

Lo Ssû-chü 羅思舉. *Lo Chuang-yung-kung tzû-ting nien-p'u* 羅壯勇公自訂年譜. N.d. Reprint from Ch'ing edition. Taipei: Kuang-wên, 1971.

Lü Chih 呂熾. *Yin Chien-yü hsien-shêng nien-p'u* 尹健餘先生年譜. 1749. Reprint, Taipei: Kuang-wên, 1971.

Lü K'un 呂坤. *Hsü hsiao-êrh yü* (A sequel to words for little children) 續小兒語. 1881. Reprint, Shanghai: Shang-wu, 1936.

————. *Nü hsiao-êrh yü* (Words for little girls) 女小兒語. 1881. Kuang-jên-t'ang kuang-hsü ch'i-nien pên.

Lü P'ei 呂培. *Hung Pei-chiang hsien-shêng nien-p'u* 洪北江先生年譜. N.d. Reprint from Ch'ing edition. Taipei: Kuang-wên, 1971.

Lü Pên-chung 呂本中. *T'ung-mêng hsün* 童蒙訓. In *Ying-yin wên-yüan-ko ssû-k'u ch'üan-shu* 景印文淵閣四庫全書. Taipei: Shang-wu, 1983.

Lü Tê-shêng 呂得勝. *Hsiao-êrh yü* (Words for little children) 小兒語. 1881. Reprint, Shanghai: Shang-wu, 1936.

Lü Yuan-liang 呂元亮. *Chao K'o-t'ing nien-p'u chi-lüeh* 趙客亭年譜紀略. 1744. Reprint, Taipei: Kuang-wên, 1971.

Lu Po-ssû 魯伯嗣. *Ying-t'ung pai-wên* (One hundred questions on infants and children) 嬰童百問. 1539. Reprint, Taipei: Hsin-wên-fêng, 1987.

Lupher, Mark. "Revolutionary Little Red Devils: The Social Psychology of Rebel Youth, 1966–1967." In Anne Behnke Kinney, ed., *Chinese Views of Childhood*. Honolulu: University of Hawaii Press, 1995.

Ma Hsin-yu 馬新祐. *Ma Tuan-min-kung nien-p'u* 馬端敏公年譜. 1877. Reprint, Taipei: Kuang-wên, 1971.

Ma Tao-yüan 馬導源. *Wu Mei-ts'un nien-p'u* 吳梅村年譜. Shanghai: Shang-wu, 1935.

Mann, Susan. "Classical Revival and the Gender Question: China's First Querelle des Femmes." in Institute of Modern History, Academia Sinica, ed., *Family Process and Political Process in Modern Chinese History* 近世家庭與政治比較歷史論文集., pp. 377–412. Taipei: Institute of Modern History, Academia Sinica, 1992.

————. "The Education of Daughters in the Mid-Ch'ing Period." in Benjamin A. Elman and Alexander Woodside, eds., *Education and Society in Late Imperial China, 1600–1900*, pp. 19–49. Berkeley: University of California Press, 1994.

————. "Grooming a Daughter for Marriage: Brides and Wives in the Mid-Ch'ing Period." In Rubie S. Watson and Patricia Buckley Ebrey, eds., *Marriage and Inequality in Chinese Society*, pp. 204–30. Berkeley: University of California Press, 1991.

————. *The Precious Record: Women's Culture in China's Long Eighteenth Century*. Stanford: Stanford University Press, 1997.

————. "Widows in the Kinship, Class, and Community Structures of Qing Dynasty China." *The Journal of Asian Studies* 46, no. 1 (Feb. 1987): 37–56.

Mause, Lloyd, ed. *The History of Childhood*. New York: Harper and Row, 1974.

McCarthy, Mary. *Memories of a Catholic Girlhood*. San Diego: A Harvest/HBJ Book, 1981.

McClure, Ruth. *Coran's Children*. New Haven: Yale University Press, 1981.

Mei Ying-chieh 梅英杰. *Hu Wên-chung-kung nien-p'u* 胡文忠公年譜. 1867. Reprint, Taipei: Kuang-wên, 1971.

Miller, Lucien. "Children of the Dream: The Adolescent World in Cao Xuequin's Honglou Meng." In Anne Behnke Kinney, ed., *Chinese Views of Childhood*, pp. 219–50. Honolulu: University of Hawaii Press, 1995.

Ming Jên-hsiao Huang-hou 明仁孝皇后. *Nei-hsün* 內訓. In *Ying-yin wên-yüan-ko ssû-k'u ch'üan-shu* 景印文淵閣四庫全書. Taipei: Shang-wu, 1983.

Ming-shih 明史. Beijing: Chung-hua, 1960.

Ming-wên shu-chü 明文書局, ed. *Chung-kuo i-yao hsüeh-chia shih-hua* 中國醫藥學家史話. Taipei: Ming-wên shu-chü, 1983.

Mitterauer, Michael, and Reinard Sieder. *The European Family: Patriarchy to Partnership from the Middle Ages to the Present.* Trans. Karla Oosterveen and Manfred Horzinger. Chicago: The University of Chicago Press, 1982.

Miu Ch'üan-sun 繆荃孫. *I-fêng lao-jên nien-p'u* 藝風老人年譜. 1936. Reprint, Taipei: Kuang-wên, 1971.

Mo Tê-hui 莫德惠. *Mo Liu-ch'ên hsien-shêng Tê-hui tzû-ting nien-p'u* 莫柳忱先生德惠自訂年譜. 1968. Reprint, Taipei: Shung-wu, 1981.

National Palace Museum, ed. *Ying-hsi t'u* 嬰戲圖. Taipei: National Palace Museum, 1990.

Needham, Joseph. *Clerks and Craftsmen in China and the West.* Cambridge: University of Cambridge Press, 1970.

Ni Hui-ting 倪會鼎. *Ming Ni Wên-chêng-kung (Yüan-lu) nien-p'u* 明倪文正公(元璐)年譜. N.d. Reprint from Ch'ing Yüeh-ya-t'ang ts'ung-shu 清粵雅堂叢書. Taipei: Shang-wu, 1978.

Nieh Ch'i-chieh 聶其杰. *Ch'ung-tê lao-jên tzû-ting nien-p'u* 崇德老年人自訂年譜. 1931. Reprint, Taipei: Kuang-wên, 1971.

Nieh Shang-hêng 聶尚恆. *Tou-k'o tz'u-hang* 痘科慈航, microfilm. Beijing: China Central Academic Library, 1998.

Nienhauser, William, ed. *Indiana Companion to Traditional Chinese Literature.* Bloomington: University of Indiana Press, 1998.

Ozment, Steven. *When Fathers Ruled: Family Life in Reformation Europe.* Cambridge: Harvard University Press, 1983.

Pao-ch'an yü-ying yang-shêng lu (Advice for safe birth, infant rearing, and maintaining health) 保產育嬰養生錄. Microfilm from Ming edition. Taipei: National Central Library.

Pao Chia-lin 鮑家麟, ed. *Chung-kuo fu-nü-shih lun-chi III* 中國婦女史論集三集. Taipei: Tao-hsiang, 1993.

Pao Lai 包賚. *Lü Liu-liang nien-p'u* 呂留良年譜. 1936. Reprint, Taipei: Kuang-wên, 1971.

Parry, Joy, ed. *Childhood and Family in Canadian History.* Toronto: McClelland Stewart, 1982.

P'i Ming-chên 皮名振. *Ch'ing P'i Lu-mên hsien-shêng Hsi-jui nien-p'u* 清皮鹿門先生錫瑞年譜. 1932. Reprint, Taipei: Shang-wu, 1981.

Pindbeck, Ivy, and Margaret Hewitt. *Children in English Society*, vol. 2, *From the Eighteenth Century to the Children's Act, 1948.* London: Routledge and Kegan Paul, 1973.

Pollert, Anna. *Girls, Wives, Factory Lives.* London: The Macmillan Press, 1981.

Pollock, Linda A. *Forgotten Children: Parent-Child Relations from 1500 to 1900.* Cambridge: Cambridge University Press, 1983.

Pu-chu huang-ti nei-ching su-wên (Commentary to Yellow Emperor's Inner Cannon) 補注黃帝內經素問. N.d. Reprint from *Ku-chin i- t'ung chêng-mai ch'üan-shu* 古今醫統正脈全書. Beijing: Chung-hua, 1985.

P'u Hsüeh-fêng 浦薛鳳. "Chi Ho Lien hsiung shêng-p'ing" 記何廉兄生平. *Chuan-chi wên-hsüeh* 傳記文學 27, no. 4 (Oct. 1976): 27–38.

Ransel, David L. *Mothers of Misery.* Princeton: Princeton University Press, 1988.

Rawski, Evelyn Sakakida. *Education and Popular Literacy in Ch'ing China.* Ann Arbor: The University of Michigan Press, 1979.

Rawski, Thomas G., and Lillian M. Li. *Chinese History in Economic Perspective.* Los Angeles: University of California Press, 1992.

Robins, Joseph. *The Lost Children.* Dublin: Institute of Public Administration, 1980.

Ropp, Paul S. "Ambiguous Images of Courtesan Culture in Late Imperial China." in Ellen Widmer and Kang-i Sun Chang, eds., *Writing Women in Late Imperial China.* Stanford: Stanford University Press, 1997.

Ropp, Paul 羅溥洛, and Angela Leung Ki Che 梁其姿. "Ming-ch'ing fu-nü yen-chiu: p'ing-chieh tsui-chin yu-kuan chih ying-wên chu-tsuo" (Ming-Ch'ing women's studies: Comments on recent works in English) 明清婦女研究:評介最近有關之英文著作. *Hsin-shih-hsüeh* 新史學 2, no. 4 (Dec. 1991): 77–116.

Rothman, David J. "Documents in Search of a Historian: Toward a History of Childhood and Youth in America." *Journal of Interdisciplinary History* 2 (1971): 367–77.

Saari, Jon L. *Legacies of Childhood: Growing up Chinese in a Time of Crisis, 1890–1920.* Cambridge and London: Council on East Asian Studies, Harvard University, 1990.

Shahar, Shulamith. *Childhood in the Middle Ages.* New York: Routledge, 1990.

Shên Chao-lin 沈兆霖. *Shên Wên-chung-kung tzû-ting nien-p'u* 沈文忠公自訂年譜. N.d. Reprint from Ch'ing edition. Taipei: Kuang-wên, 1971.

Shên Yün-lung 沈雲龍. *Hsü Shih-ch'ang p'ing-chuan* 徐世昌評傳. Taipei: Chuan-chi wên-hsüeh, 1979.

———. *Huang Ying-pai hsien-shêng nien-p'u* 黃膺白先生年譜. Taipei: Lien-ching, 1976.

———. "Huang Ying-pai hsien-shêng pai-ling tan-ch'ên chi-nien" 黃膺白先生百齡誕辰紀念. *Chuan-chi wên-hsüeh* 傳記文學 36, no. 3 (1980): 11–19.

Shih Chung-hsü 史仲序. *Chung-kuo i-hsüeh shih* 中國醫學史. Taipei: Chêng-chung, 1984.

Shih Shu-I 施淑儀. *Ch'ing-tai kui-ko shih-jên chêng-lüeh* 清代閨閣詩人徵略. Shanghai: Shanghai, 1987.

Smith, George F., and Dharmapuri Vidyasagar, eds. *Historical Review and Recent Advances in Neonatal and Perinatal Medicine.* Printed and distributed by Mead Johnson Nutritional Division, n.d.

Sommerville, John C. Foreword to Anne Behnke Kinney, ed., *Chinese Views of Childhood,* pp. xi–xiii. Honolulu: University of Hawaii Press, 1995.

————. *The Rise and Fall of Childhood*. Beverly Hills: Sage, 1982.

Ssû-ma Kuang 司馬光. "Chiao-nan-nü" (Instructing boys and girls) 教男女. *Chü-chia tsa-i* (Miscellaneous rites for the family) 居家雜儀. In Hu Kuang 胡廣, ed., *Hsing-li ta-ch'üan* 性理大全, *chuan* 19. 1443. Reprint, Ching-tu: Chung-wên, 1981.

Stone, Lawrence. *The Family, Sex, and Marriage in England, 1500–1800*. New York: Harper and Row, 1979.

Su Ch'un-yüan 蘇惇元. *Fang Wang-hsi hsien-shêng nien p'u* 方望溪先生年譜. 1911. Reprint, Taipei: Kuang-wên, 1971.

Su-chou-fu chih 蘇州府志. 1883. Reprint, Taipei: Ch'êng-wên, 1970.

Su Hsing 蘇興. *Wu Ch'êng-ên nien-p'u* 吳承恩年譜. Beijing: Jên-min wên-hsüeh, 1980.

Sun I-k'uei 孫一奎. *Ch'ih-shui yüan-chu* 赤水元珠. In *Ying-yin wên-yüan-ko ssû-k'u ch'üan-shu* 景印文淵閣四庫全書. Taipei: Shang-wu, 1983.

Sun Shih 孫奭, ed. *Mêng-tzû chu-shu* 孟子注疏. In *Ying-yin wên-yüan-ko ssû-k'u ch'üan-shu* 景印文淵閣四庫全書, vol. 195, *chuan* 13. Taipei: Shang-wu, 1983.

Sun Ssû-miao 孫思邈. *Ch'ien-chin fang* (Prescriptions worth a thousand) 千金方. In *Ku-chin t'u-shu chi-ch'êng* 古今圖書集成, *chuan* 422. Taipei: Ting-wên, 1977.

————. *Shao-hsiao ying-ju fang* (Recipes for infants and children) 少小嬰孺方. Microfilm from Japan. Taipei: National Palace Museum.

Sun Tê-chung 孫德中. *Min-kuo Ts'ai Chüeh-min hsien-shêng Yüan-p'ei chien-yao nien-p'u* 民國蔡孑民先生元培簡要年譜. Taipei: Shang-wu, 1981.

Sung-k'o Hsiao-ching êrh-shih-ssû-hsiao-t'u-shuo 宋刻孝經二十四孝圖説. N.d. Reprint from Sung edition, as collected by Ch'ing Ch'ien-lung nei-fu 清乾隆內府. Tien-chin: Ku-chi, 1987.

T'an Ssû-t'ung 譚嗣同. *T'an Ssû-t'ung ch'üan-chi* 譚嗣同全集. Beijing: San-lien, 1954.

T'ang Chên 唐甄. *Ch'ien-shu* 潛書. Beijing: Chung-hua, 1963.

T'ang Pin 湯斌. *Sun hsia-fêng hsien-shêng nien-p'u* 孫夏峰先生年譜. N.d. Reprint from Ch'ing chi-fu ts'ung-shu 清畿輔叢書. Taipei: Kuang-wên, 1971.

T'êng Ku 滕固. *Chiang Chien-jên hsien-shêng nien-p'u* 蔣劍人先生年譜. 1933. Reprint, Taipei: Kuang-wên, 1971.

Ting Wên-chiang 丁文江. *Hsü Hsia-k'o hsien-shêng nien-p'u* 徐霞客先生年譜. 1933. Reprint, Taipei: Shang-wu, 1978.

Trumbach, Randolph. *The Rise of the Egalitarian Family: Aristocratic Kinship and Domestic Relations in Eighteenth-Century England*. New York: Academic Press, 1978.

Ts'ai T'ing-k'ai 蔡廷鍇. *Ts'ai T'ing-k'ai tzû-chuan* 蔡廷鍇自傳. 1946. Reprint, Taipei: Lung-wên, 1989.

Ts'ao Hsüeh-ch'in 曹雪芹. *Hung-lou Mêng* (Dream of the Red Chamber) 紅樓夢. Taipei: San-min, 1990.

Ts'ên Hsüeh-lü 岑學呂. *Hsü-yün ho-shang nien-p'u* 虛雲和尚年譜. Hong Kong: Fo-ching liu-t'ung-ch'u, 1977.

Tsêng Shih-jung 曾世榮. *Huo-yu k'ou-i* (Daily deliberation on saving the young) 活幼口議. Beijing: Chung-i ku-chi, 1985.

Ts'ui Hsüeh-ku 崔學古. *Yu Hsün* 幼訓. Hsin-an Chang-shih Hsia-chü-t'ang 新安張氏霞舉堂. 1685 edition, rare book collection, Taipei: National Central Library.

Ts'ui Shu 崔述. *K'ao-hsin fu-lu* 考信附錄, Reprint from Ch'ing Wang Hao 王灝, ed., Kuang-hsü Ting-chou Wang-shih Ch'ien-tê-t'ang edition 光緒定州王氏謙德堂. Taipei: Shih-chieh, 1989.

Tu Shu-hwa 杜書華. "Ku-hua chung tê êrh-t'ung shih-chieh" (The world of children as seen in old paintings) 古畫中的兒童世界 *Ku-kung wên-wu yüeh-k'an* 故宮文物月刊 4, no. 1 (Apr. 1986): 4–15.

Tuan Yung-lan 段永蘭. "Wo-tê fu-ch'in" 我的父親. *Chuan-chi wên-hsüeh* 傳記文學 3, no. 4 (1963): 26–27.

Tung Chi 董汲. *Hsiao-êrh pan-chên pei-chi fang-lun* (Emergency treatments of rashes and measles of small children) 小兒班疹備急方論. Sung edition from Japan, collected by National Palace Museum, Taipei.

Tung Ch'ien 董遷. *Kung Chih-lu nien-p'u* 龔芝麓年譜. 1935. Reprint, Taipei: Kuang-wên, 1971.

Tung Hsün 董恂. *Huan-tu-wo-shu-shih lao-jên shou-ting nien-p'u* 還讀我書室老人手訂年譜. 1894. Reprint, Taipei: Kuang-wên, 1971.

Unschuld, Paul. *Medical Ethics in Imperial China.* Baltimore: Johns Hopkins University Press, 1979.

———. *Medicine in China.* Berkeley: University of California Press, 1986.

Vaughare, Victor C., R. James Mckay, and Waldo E. Nelson. *Textbook of Pediatrics.* Philadelphia: W. B. Saunders, 1975.

Waltner, Ann. *Getting an Heir: Adoption and the Construction of Kinship in Late Imperial China.* Honolulu: University of Hawaii Press, 1990.

———. "Infanticide and Dowry in Ming and Early Ch'ing China." In Anne Behnke Kinney, ed., *Chinese Views of Childhood.* Honolulu: University of Hawaii Press, 1995.

———. "The Moral Status of the Child in Late Imperial China: Childhood in Ritual and in Law." *Social Research* 53, no. 4 (1986): 667–87.

Wan Ch'üan 萬全. *Yu-k'o fa-hui* (Elaboration on pediatrics) 幼科發揮. Beijing: Jênmin wei-shêng, 1986.

———. *Yü-ying chia-mi* (Family secrets on infant-care) 育嬰家秘. N.d. Reprint from Ming Chia-ching 明嘉靖 edition. Hubei: K'o-hsüeh chi-shu, 1984.

Wang Chi-ch'üan 王繼權. *Kuo Mo-juo nien-p'u* 郭沫若年譜. Kiangsu: Jên-min, 1983.

Wang Chia-chien 王家儉. *Wei Yüan nien-p'u* 魏源年譜. Taipei: Institute of Modern History, Academia Sinica, 1967.

Wang Fu 王符. *Wang T'ai-ch'ang nien-p'u* 王太常年譜. N.d. Reprint, Taipei: Shangwu, 1978.

Wang Hsien-ch'ien 王先謙. *K'uei-yüan tzû-ting nien-p'u* 葵園自訂年譜. N.d. Reprint from Ch'ing edition. Taipei: Kuang-wên, 1971.

Wang Hui-tsu 汪輝祖. *Ping-t'a mêng-hên lu* (A dream like record by the sick bed) 病榻夢痕錄. 1796. Reprint, Taipei: Kuang-wên, 1971.

Wang K'ang-nien 汪康年. *Wang Jang-ch'ing hsien-shêng chuan-chi* 汪穰卿先生傳記. Taipei: Kuang-wên, 1971.

Wang K'ên-t'ang 王肯堂. *Chêng-chih chun-shêng* (Standards of treatments in medicine) 證治準繩. 1607. Reprint from Ming Wan-li edition. Taipei: Hsin-wên-fêng, 1983.

———. *Yu-k'o chun-shêng* (Standards of treatments in pediatrics) 幼科準繩. As part of *Chêng-chih chun-shêng* (Standards of treatments in medicine) 證治準繩. 1607. Reprint from Ming Wan-li edition. Taipei: Hsin-wên-fêng, 1983.

Wang Luan 王鑾. *Yu-k'o lei-ts'ui* (The essence of pediatric medicine) 幼科類萃. Reprint, Beijing: Chung-i ku-chi, 1984.

Wang Po-yüeh 汪伯岳 and Chiang Yü-jên 江育仁, eds. *Chung-i êrh-k'o-hsüeh* 中醫兒科學. Beijing: Jên-min, 1987.

Wang Ta-lun 王大綸. *Ying-t'ung lei-ts'ui* (Essentials in looking after infants and children) 嬰童類萃. Reprint from Ming T'ien-ch'i edition. Beijing: Jên-min, 1983.

Wang Tai-kung 王代功. *Ch'ing Wang Hsiang-ch'i hsien-shêng K'ai-yün nien-p'u* 清王湘綺先生闓運年譜. N.d. Reprint from Ch'ing edition. Taipei: Shang-wu, 1978.

Wang T'ao 王燾. *Wai-t'ai mi-yao fang* (Medical secrets of a frontier official) 外台秘要方. N.d. Reprint from Ming Ch'ung-chên edition. Taipei: Hsin-wên-fêng, 1987.

Wang Tsung-yen 汪宗衍. *Ch'ên Tung-shu hsien-shêng nien-p'u* 陳東塾先生年譜. Macao: Yü-chin shu-wu, 1970.

———. *Ku Ch'ien-li hsien-shêng nien-p'u* 顧千里先生年譜. N.d. Copy from Ch'ing edition. Taipei: Kuang-wên, 1971.

Wang Tuan-shu 王端淑. *Ming-yüan shih-wei ch'u-pien* 名媛詩緯初編. N.d. Reprint from Ch'ing K'ang-hsi edition. Taipei: National Central library.

Wang Yang-ming 王陽明. "Hsün-mêng ta-i" (The principles in child education) 訓蒙大意. *Yang-ming ch'uan-hsi-lu* 陽明傳習錄, *chuan* 2, pp. 57–58. Taipei: Hsüeh-shêng, 1983.

Wang Ying-chih 王英志, ed. *Yüan Mei chüan-chi* 袁枚全集. Nanching: Kiangsu ku-chi, 1993.

Wang Ying-lin 王應麟, ed. *San-tzû-ching* (The three-character classic) 三字經. Ch'eng-tu: n.p., 1928.

Watkins, Susan C., and Etienne Van de Walle. "Nutrition, Mortality and Population Size: Malthus' Court of Last Resort." *Journal of Interdisciplinary History* 13, no. 2(1983): 205–26.

Watson, Rubie S., and Patricia Buckley Ebrey, eds. *Marriage and Inequality in Chinese Society*. Berkeley: University of California Press, 1991.

Wei Chih-hsiu 魏之琇. *Hsü ming-i lei-an* (More cases from famous doctors) 續名醫類案. In *Ying-yin wên-yüan-ko ssû-k'u ch'üan-shu* 景印文淵閣四庫全書, vol. 785. Taipei: Shang-wu, 1986.

Wei I-lin 危亦林. *Shih-i tê-hsiao fang* (Effective recipes of experienced physicians) 世醫得效方. In *Ying-yin wên-yüan-ko ssû-k'u ch'üan-shu* 景印文淵閣四庫全書, vol. 746. Taipei: Shang-wu, 1986.

Wei Tung 畏冬. *Chung-kuo ku-tai êrh-t'ung t'i-ts'ai hui-hua* 中國古代兒童題材繪畫. Beijing: Tzû-chin-ch'êng, 1988.

Wei Ying-ch'i 魏應麒. *Lin Wên-chung-kung nien-p'u* 林文忠公年譜. N.d. Reprint from Ch'ing edition. Taipei: Kuang-wên, 1971.

Wên Chü-min 溫聚民. *Wei Shu-tzû nien-p'u* 魏叔子年譜. N.d. Reprint, Taipei: Shang-wu, 1980.

Whitehead, R. G., ed. *Maternal Diet, Breast-Feeding Capacity, and Lactational Infertility*. Tokyo: The United Nations University, 1983.

Widmer, Ellen, and Kang-i Sun Chang, eds. *Writing Women in Late Imperial China.* Stanford: Stanford University Press, 1997.

Wiedemann, Thomas. *Adults and Children in the Roman Empire.* New Haven: Yale University Press, 1989.

Wolf, Margery. "Child Training and the Chinese Family." In Maurice Freedman, ed., *Family and Kinship in Chinese Society*, pp. 37–62. Stanford: Stanford University Press, 1970.

———. *Women and the Family in Rural Taiwan.* Stanford: Stanford University Press, 1972.

Wolf, Margery, and Roxane Witke, eds. *Women in Chinese Society.* Stanford: Stanford University Press, 1975.

World Health Organization. *Contemporary Patterns of Breastfeeding. Report on the WHO Collaborative Study on Breast-Feeding.* Geneva: World Health Organization, 1981.

Wrigley, E. A. *Population and History.* New York: McGraw-Hill, World University Library, 1969.

Wrigley, E. A., and R. S. Schofield. *The Population History of England, 1541–1871: A Reconstruction.* London: Edward Arnold, 1981.

Wu Ch'ien 吳謙. *Yu-k'o tsa-ping hsin-fa yao-chüeh* (Key methods for various diseases in pediatrics) 幼科雜病心法要訣. In *I-tsung chin-chien* (The golden mirror for medicine) 醫宗金鑑, *chuan* 50. Taipei: Hsin-wên-fêng, 1981.

Wu Ch'êng-ên 吳承恩. "Yü-ting-chih hsü" (禹鼎志序). In Su Hsin 蘇興, *Wu Ch'êng-ên nien-pu* 吳承恩年譜. Beijing: Jên-ming wên-hsüeh, 1980.

Wu Fang 巫妨. *Lu-hsin Ching* (The classic on the soft skull) 顱囟經. In *Ying-yin wên-yüan-ko ssû-k'uch'üan-shu* 景印文淵閣四庫全書, vol. 738. Taipei: Shang-wu, 1983.

Wu, Hung. "Private Love and Public Duty: Images of Children in Early Chinese Art." In Anne Behnke Kinney, ed., *Chinese Views of Childhood*, pp. 77–110. Honolulu: University of Hawaii Press, 1995.

Wu, Pei-yi. "Childhood Remembered: Parents and Children in China, 800 to 1700." In Anne Behnke Kinney, ed., *Chinese Views of Childhood*, pp. 129–56. Honolulu: University of Hawaii Press, 1995.

———. *The Confucian's Progress: Autobiographical Writings in Traditional China.* Princeton: Princeton University Press, 1990.

———. "Education of Children During the Sung." In Wm. Theodere de Bary and John Chaffee, eds., *Neo-Confucian Education: The Formative Stage*, pp. 307–24. Berkeley: University of California Press, 1989.

Wu K'ai-liu 吳開流. *Li Yung* 李顒. Shantung: Ch'i-lu, 1982.

Wu T'ien-jên 吳天任. *Ho Hui-kao nien-p'u* 何翽高年譜. N.d. Reprint, Taipei: Shang-wu, 1981.

Wung Shu-yüan 翁叔元. *Wung T'ieh-an nien-p'u* 翁鐵庵年譜. 1920. Reprint, Taipei: Kuang-wên, 1971.

Yang Chi-shêng 楊繼盛. *Yang Chung-min-kung i-pi* 楊忠愍公遺筆. N.d. Reprint, Taipei: Hsin-hsing, 1989.

Yang K'o-chi 楊克己. *Min-kuo K'ang Ch'ang-ssû hsien-shêng Yu-wei Liang Jên-kung hsien-shêng Ch'i-ch'ao shih-shêng ho-p'u* 民國康長素先生有為梁任公先生啓超師生合譜. N.d. Reprint, Taipei: Shang-wu, 1982.

Yang, Martin C. *A Chinese Village: Taitou, Shantung Province*. New York: University of Columbia Press, 1945.

Yang T'ing-fu 楊廷福. *T'an Ssû-t'ung nien-p'u* 譚嗣同年譜. Beijing: Jên-min, 1957.

Yang Tsêng-hsü 楊增勗. *Liu-chou fu-chün nien-p'u* 柳州府君年譜. N.d. Reprint, Taipei: Kuang-wên, 1971.

Yao Ming-ta 姚名達. *Ch'ing Shao Nien-lu hsien-shêng T'ing-ts'ai nien-p'u* 清邵念魯先生廷采年譜. N.d. Reprinted from Ch'ing edition. Taipei: Shang-Wu, 1982.

———. *Liu Tsung-chou nien-p'u* 劉宗周年譜. N.d. Reprint from Ch'ing edition. Shanghai: Shanghai shu-tien Press, 1992.

Yao Shao-hua 姚紹華. *Ts'ui Tung-pi nien-p'u* 崔東壁年譜. Shanghai: Shang-wu, 1931.

Yeh Ying 葉英. *Huang Tao-chou chuan* 黃道周傳. Tainan: Yeh Ying, 1959.

———. *Yao Shih-fu chuan* 姚石甫傳. Tainan: Yeh Ying, 1977.

Yen Chêng-chün 嚴正鈞. *Tso Wên-hsiang-kung nien-p'u* 左文襄公年譜. N.d. Reprint from Ch'ing edition. Taipei: Kuang-wên, 1971.

Yen Hsiu 嚴修. *Yen Hsiu hsien-shêng nien-p'u* 嚴修先生年譜. N.d. Reprint from Ch'ing edition. Chi-nan: Ch'i-lu, 1990.

Yin Chao-yung 殷兆鏞. *Yin P'u-ching shih-lang tzû-ting nien-p'u* 殷譜經侍郎自定年譜. N.d. Reprint from Ch'ing edition. Taipei: Kuang-wên, 1971

Yüan Hsing-yün 袁行雲. *Hsü Han nien-p'u* 許瀚年譜. Shantung: Chi-lu shu-shê, 1983.

Yüan, I-chin. "Life Tables for a Southern Chinese Family from 1365–1849." *Human Biology* 3, no. 2 (1981): 157–79.

Yüan Tao-fêng 袁道豐. "Chang Kung-ch'üan hsien-shêng t'an-wang lu" 張公權先生談往錄. *Chuan-chi wên-hsüeh* 傳記文學 16, no. 1 (1970): 1–4.

Character List

A-ma tê ku-shih　阿媽的故事
ai　愛
an　案
Anhwei　安徽

Ch'an-ju chi　產乳集
Chang-an　長安
chang-hsiung ju-fu, chang-shao ju-mu
　長兄如父，長嫂如母
Chang Chieh-pin　張介賓
Chang Chih-tung　張之洞
Chang Ching-yü　張靜愚
Chang Ch'i-yün　張其昀
Chang Ch'ung　張沖
Chang Ho　張河
Chang Hsüeh-ch'êng　章學誠
Chang Huang-yen　張煌言
Chang Kao　張杲
Chang Kung-ch'üan　張公權
Chang Liang-chi　張亮基
Chang Lü-hsiang　張履祥
Chang Mu　張穆
Chang P'u　張溥
Chang Ta-ch'ien　張大千
Chang Ts'ung-chêng　張從正
Chang Tzû-ho　張子和
Chang Yü　章鈺
Chang Yün　張雲
Ch'ang-lo　長樂
Changsha　長沙
Chao, Duke of　趙公
Chao Kuang　趙光
Chao Yang Pu-wei　趙楊步偉
Chao Yü-ching　趙于京
Chao Yüan-jên　趙元任
Ch'ao Yüan-fang　巢元方
Chê-p'u　蔗圃

Chekiang　浙江
Chên-hsiao　貞孝
chên-hsin　真心
chên-jên　真人
Chên-nü lun　貞女論
chên-nü shou-chieh　貞女守節
Ch'ên Ch'i-mei　陳其美
Ch'ên Chin-lin　陳金陵
Ch'ên Fei-hsia　陳飛霞
Ch'ên Fu-chêng　陳復正
Ch'ên Hêng-chê　陳衡哲
Ch'ên Hsiang　陳相
Ch'ên Hsien-chang　陳獻章
Ch'ên Hung-mou　陳宏謀
Ch'ên Shih-i　陳石遺
Ch'ên Ting-hsiang　陳定祥
Ch'ên Tu-hsiu　陳獨秀
Ch'ên Tung-shu　陳東塾
Ch'ên Tzû-ming　陳自明
Ch'ên Wên-chung　陳文中
Ch'ên Yen　陳衍
Ch'ên Ying-shih　陳英士
Chêng-chih chun-shêng　證治準繩
Chêng Chên-wên　鄭貞文
Chêng Hsüan　鄭玄
Chêng Yen-fên　鄭彥棻
Ch'êng　程
ch'êng (sincerity)　誠
Ch'êng-Chu　程朱
ch'êng-huan (please)　承歡
ch'êng-huang (city god)　城隍
ch'êng-jên　成人
ch'êng-jên chih-shih　成人之事
Ch'êng-wu　城武
Ch'êng Hao　程顥
Ch'êng Hsing-hsüan　程杏軒
Ch'êng I　程頤

chi 積

chi 笄

chi-mu 繼母

chi-yü-ju pu-nêng-shih 急欲乳不能食

ch'i (energy/spirit) 氣

ch'i (strange) 奇

ch'i (a wife) 妻

ch'i-ch'uang 臍瘡

Ch'i Chi-kuang 戚繼光

ch'i-chung 臍腫

ch'i-fêng 臍風

ch'i-fêng ts'o-k'ou 臍風撮口

Ch'i Huang 齊璜

ch'i-shih 臍濕

ch'i-ying (special talent) 奇穎

chia chang 家長

chia-chi-wên 家祭文

Chia-ching 嘉靖

Chia-fan tien 家範典

chia-hsün 家訓

Chia-i-ching 甲乙經

chia-jên 假人

chia-li 家禮

chia-p'u 家譜

Chiang Kai-shek 蔣介石

Chiang Tun-fu 蔣敦復

Chiang Yu-tien 蔣攸恬

Ch'iang-shih ju-shih ling-êrh-ping 強施乳食令兒病

chiao 教

chiao-nan-nü 教男女

Chiao-nü i-kuei 教女遺規

ch'iao 巧

chieh-chiu 戒灸

ch'ieh (a concubine) 妾

chien-tzû 毽子

Ch'ien-chin fang 千金方

Ch'ien I 錢乙

Ch'ien-lung 乾隆

Ch'ien shu 潛書

Ch'ien-t'ang 錢塘

Ch'ien-tzû wên 千字文

chih-chih wei chih-chih, pu-chih wei pu-chih, shih chih yeh 知之為知之，不知為不知，是知也

chih-ch'ing chih-ch'ü 稚情稚趣

Chih-li 直隸

chih-shu chieh-wên 知書解文

Ch'ih-shui yüan-chu 赤水元珠

Chin-chen (Golden Needles) 金針

chin-fêng 噤風

Chin-p'ing-mei 金瓶梅

chin-shih 進士

Chin-ssû lu 近思錄

Chin-t'an 金壇

Ch'in Ching-ming 秦景明

ch'in-k'o 親課

ching 經

ching (respect) 敬

ching (quietness) 靜

Ching 涇

Ch'ing 清

ch'ing-nien 青年

Chiu-fa lun 灸法論

Ch'iu Chin 秋瑾

Chou 周

Chou Ch'ên 周臣

Chou-hou fang 肘後方

Chou Tun-i 周敦頤

Chu-ping yüan-hou lun 諸病源候論

Chu Chên-hêng 朱震亨

Chu Ching-nung 朱經農

Chu Hsi 朱熹

Chu Hui-min 朱惠民

chu-mi fa 硃蜜法

chu-mu 諸母

Chu Shang-wên 朱尚文

Chu Shun-shui 朱舜水

chu-tan chih 豬膽汁

Chu Tz'u-ch'i 朱次琦

Chu Yün 朱筠

chü 句

Chü Chêng 居正

Chü-chia tsa-i 居家雜儀

chü-hsuan 菊軒

ch'u-pu 初哺

ch'u-shêng 初生

Ch'u-shêng chiang-hu fa 初生將護法

Ch'u-shêng ch'u-fu lun 初生出腹論

Ch'u-shêng lun (On Newborns)
初生論

Ch'u-shêng pu-ju pu-hsiao-pien 初生
不乳不小便

Ch'u-shêng shuo 初生説

ch'u-shêng yang-hu 初生養護

ch'u-shêng yü-fa 初生浴法

ch'u-shih 出仕

ch'u-tan 初誕

ch'u-tan chiu-hu 初誕救護

ch'u-tan fa 初誕法

ch'u-tan lun 初誕論

ch'u t'ai-tu 除胎毒

Ch'u tz'u 楚辭

ch'u-yü (first wash) 初浴

Ch'ü Ch'iu-pai 瞿秋白

ch'ü ch'ung 曲從

Ch'ü-yang 曲陽

chuan 卷

Chuan-chi wên-hsüeh 傳記文學

Ch'üan Hsieh-shan 全謝山

Ch'üan Tsu-wang 全祖望

chuang 壯

chun-pei chang-yu 尊卑長幼

ch'un-shih t'u 春市圖

Ch'un-yü I 淳于意

chung-nan ch'ing-nü 重男輕女

chung-o 重顎

Chung Yung 中庸

Êrh-êrh 二二

Êrh-êrh k'uang-chih 二二壙誌

Êrh-shih-ssû hsiao 二十四孝

Êrh-shih-ssû hsiao t'u-shuo 二十四孝
圖説

êrh-t'ung 兒童

Êrh-t'ung wên-hsüeh 兒童文學

Êrh-ya 爾雅

fa-chi 髮際

fang 方

fang-chi 方伎

Fang Pao 方苞

Fang Shih-kan 方士淦

fei ju chih shu 非儒之書

fên 粉

Fêng Kuo-chang 馮國璋

fêng-shih so-ch'êng 風濕所乘

Fêng Yü-hsiang 馮玉祥

fu 婦

Fu Chiao-shan Yü Ying-wei Ying-chi
Liang-Êrh 父椒山喻應尾應箕兩兒

Fu-jên ta-ch'üan liang-fang 婦人大全
良方

fu-k'o 婦科

fu-kung 婦工

fu-mu tsai, pu yüan-yu 父母在不遠遊

Fu Shan 傅山

Fu-shê chi-lüeh 復社紀略

Fu Ssû-nien 傅斯年

Fukien 福建

Hai-chou 海州

Han 漢

han-ju 寒乳

Hang-chou 杭州

ho-fa t'ung-yen 鶴髮童顏

Ho Hui-kao 何翽高

Ho Lien 何廉

Honan 河南

Hopei 河北

Hsi-mêng Ch'ing 西門慶

hsi-san 洗三

Hsi-yu chi 西遊記

hsi-yü 洗浴

Hsi-yü lun 洗浴論

Hsia Ching-ch'ü 夏敬渠

hsia t'ai-fên 下胎糞

hsia t'ai-tu 下胎毒

Hsiang-chi-hsüan chi 項脊軒記

hsiao (young) 小

hsiao (filiality) 孝

Hsiao ching 孝經

Hsiao-êrh ch'u-shêng 小兒初生

Hsiao-êrh ch'u-shêng hu-yang mên
小兒初生養護門

hsiao-êrh ch'u-shêng hui-ch'i fa 小兒
初生回氣法

hsiao-êrh ch'u-shêng wei-han 小兒初
生畏寒

Hsiao-êrh ju-ping 小兒乳病

Hsiao-êrh pan-chên pei-chi fang-lun
小兒斑疹備急方論

Hsiao-êrh pu-i wang-chên-chiu 小兒
不宜妄針灸

Hsiao-êrh tou-chên fang-lun 小兒痘
疹方論

Hsiao-êrh wei-shêng tsung-wei lun-
fang 小兒衛生總微論方

Hsiao-êrh yao-chêng chih-chüeh
小兒藥證直訣

Hsiao-êrh yü 小兒語

hsiao-fang mai 小方脈

Hsiao-hsiao-shêng 笑笑生

Hsiao-hsüeh 小學

Hsiao-shan 蕭山

hsiao-tsu-tsung 小祖宗

hsiao-wo 小我

Hsieh-tu fa 瀉毒法

Hsien-p'i shih-lüeh 先妣事略

hsin-hsüeh 心學

Hsing-ch'êng 杏城

Hsing-li ta-ch'üan 性理大全

Hsing-ning-ssû 興寧司

hsü 恤

Hsü Chi-yü 徐繼畬

Hsü Ch'un-fu 徐春甫

Hsü Fu-lin 徐傅霖

Hsü Han 許瀚

Hsü hsiao-êrh yü 續小兒語

Hsü Hung-tsu 徐宏祖

Hsü Kuang-ch'i 徐光啓

Hsü ming-i lei-an 續名醫類案

Hsü Nai 徐鼐

Hsü P'u 徐溥

Hsü Shih-ch'ang 徐世昌

Hsü Tsan 許讚

Hsü Tzû 徐鼒

Hsü Yün 盧雲

Hsü Yung-ch'ang 徐永昌

hsüeh 學

hsüeh-ch'i 血氣

Hsüeh Chi 薛己

Hsüeh K'ai 薛鎧

Hsüeh Kuang-ch'ien 薛光前

Hsüeh Li-chai 薛立齋

hsüeh tso jên 學作人

Hsün-mêng ta-i 訓蒙大意

Hu Han-min 胡漢民

Hu K'ang-min 胡康民

Hu Kuang 胡廣

Hu Lin-i 胡林翼

Hu Shih 胡適

Hu Wei 胡渭

Hu-yang chih fa 護養之法

Hu-yang fa 護養法

Hu-yang lun 護養論

Hua Hsien-k'an êrh-t'ung cho liu-hua
畫閒看兒童捉柳花

Hua Mu-lan 花木蘭

huai 槐

Huang Ching-jên 黃景仁

Huang Fu 黃郛

Huang-fu Mi 皇甫謐

Huang Shu-lin 黃叔琳

Huang Tao-chou 黃道周

Huang-ti nei-ching 黃帝內經

Huang Tsung-hsi 黃宗羲

Huang Ying-pai 黃膺白

hui 穢

Hui-ch'i lun 回氣論

hui-shêng ch'i-ssû 回生起死

Hunan 湖南

Hung Hsü-tung 洪旭東

Hung Liang-chi 洪亮吉

Hung-lou Mêng 紅樓夢

huo-lang t'u 貨郎圖

Huo-yu k'ou-i 活幼口議

Hupei 湖北

i 異

i-an 醫案

I ching 易經

i-fang 醫方

i-fu-tzû 遺腹子

I-hsüeh ju-mên 醫學入門

i-i 薏苡

i-ju 溢乳

i-lun 醫論
I-shu 醫述
I-shuo 醫說
i-tzû êrh chiao 易子而教
I-tsung chin-chien 醫宗金鑑

jê-ju 熱乳
jê-tu 熱毒
jên 人
jên 仁
jên-hsin (human heart) 人心
jên-hsing (human nature) 人性
Jih-chao 日照
ju 乳
Ju-êrh fa 乳兒法
ju-i 儒醫
Ju-lang 如蘭
Ju-lan k'uang-chih 如蘭壙誌
Ju-lin êrh-ping chêng 乳令兒病證
Ju-mên shih-ch'in 儒門事親
Ju-mu lun 乳母論
Ju-pu 乳哺
Ju-pu fa 乳哺法
Ju-pu lun 乳哺論
ju shih-shih 乳失時
Jung-hsing mi-hao 榮興米號
juo 弱

k'ai-k'ou 開口
K'ai-k'ou fa 開口法
K'ai-yüan-t'ou 開源頭
kan 疳
kan-ts'ao fa 甘草法
Kang-chien chêng-shih yüeh 網鑑正
史約
K'ang-hsi 康熙
K'ang Yu-wei 康有為
Kao-ch'un 高淳
Kao Chien-fu 高劍夫
Kao Pu-ying 高步瀛
Kao Tzû 高梓
Kê-chih yü-lun 格致餘論
kêng-chih t'u 耕織圖
Kiangnan 江南

Kiangsi 江西
Kiangsu 江蘇
Ko Hung 葛洪
K'ou P'ing 寇平
k'ou-shou 口授
Ku-chin i-t'ung ta-ch'üan 古今醫統
大全
Ku-chin t'u-shu chi-ch'êng 古今圖書
集成
ku-êrh chih chih 孤兒之志
ku-êrh kua-mu 孤兒寡母
Ku Juo-p'u 顧若璞
Ku Kuang-ch'i 顧廣圻
Ku Yen-wu 顧炎武
k'u-hai 苦海
kuan 冠
Kuan Tzû 管子
K'un-hsing i-wang 困行憶往
Kuei-fan 閨範
Kuei-lin 桂林
Kuei Yu-kuang 歸有光
Kung An-chieh 龔安節
kung-fu 功夫
kung-hsien 弓繊
Kung Hsin 龔信
Kung-sun Hung 公孫弘
Kung Ting-tzû 龔鼎孳
Kung T'ing-hsien 龔廷賢
Kung Tzû-chên 龔自珍
K'ung Shang-jên 孔尚任
K'ung Tung-t'ang 孔東塘
Kuo-ai hsiao-êrh fan-hai hsiao-êrh
shuo 過愛小兒反害小兒說
kuo-ch'i 裹臍
kuo-ch'i fa 裹臍法
kuo-êrh 裹兒
Kuo Mo-juo 郭沫若
Kuo Sung-t'ao 郭嵩燾
Kwangtung 廣東

Lan-t'ien 蘭田
Lê-sê 垃圾
Li-chi 禮記
Li-chi chu-shu 禮記注疏

Li Chih 李贄
Li-ch'üan-t'ang 麗泉堂
Li Fan-hsieh 厲樊榭
Li Hung-tsao 李鴻藻
Li Kuang-ti 李光地
Li Kung 李塨
Li P'ei-ching 黎培敬
Li P'ing-êrh 李瓶兒
Li-shih Fên-shu 李氏焚書
Li Shu-sên 李樹森
Li Tsung-t'ung 李宗侗
Li Yung 李顒
Liang Chang-chü 梁章鉅
Liang Chi 梁濟
Liang Ch'i-ch'ao 梁啓超
Liang Shu-ming 梁漱溟
Lieh-nü-chuan 列女傳
Lin I 林逸
Lin Tsê-hsü 林則徐
ling-i 鈴醫
Ling T'ing-k'an 凌廷堪
liu 柳
Liu-an (tea) 六安(茶)
Liu-ch'ên 柳忱
Liu Ch'i 劉跂
Liu Fang 劉昉
Liu I-chêng 柳詒徵
Liu-k'o chun-shêng 六科準繩
Liu Pao-nan 劉寶楠
Liu Shih-i 劉士毅
Liu Tsung-chou 劉宗周
Liu Tsung-yüan 柳宗元
lo 烙
Lo Chi-tsu 羅繼祖
lo-ch'i ping-tzû 烙臍餅子
Lo Hsiang-lin 羅香林
Lo Shih-yang 羅師揚
Lo Ssû-chü 羅思舉
Lo-t'ien 羅田
Lo Tsê-nan 羅澤南
Lu Hsiang-shan 陸象山
Lu-hsin ching 顱囟經
Lu Pao-chung 陸寶忠
Lu Po-ssû 魯伯嗣

Lu Shan-chi 鹿善繼
Lu Ti-p'ing 魯滌平
Lü K'un 呂坤
Lü Liu-liang 呂留良
Lü Pên-chung 呂本中
Lü Tê-shêng 呂得勝
Lü Yüan-liang 呂元亮
lun 論
Lun yü 論語
Lung-shan 龍山

Ma Hsin-i 馬新貽
Mao-shih 毛詩
Mencius 孟子
mêng-hsüeh 蒙學
Mêng-hsüeh hsü-chih 蒙學須知
mêng-hsün 蒙訓
Mêng-tzû chu-shu 孟子注疏
mêng-yang 蒙養
mi-chih 米汁
mien-shang chêng 面上症
Ming 明
Ming-Ch'ing 明清
Ming-Ch'ing Kiangnan 明清江南
Ming-shih 明史
ming yu pu k'o hsing 命有不可行
Ming-yüan shih-wei ch'u-pien 名媛詩
  緯初編
Miu Ch'üan-sun 繆荃孫
Mo Tê-hui 莫德惠
mu 母
Mu-lien 目蓮
Mu-lien ch'iu-mu 目蓮救母
mu-nei chêng 目內症

Nan-ch'ang 南昌
Nanking 南京
nan-nü yu-pieh 男女有別
nao-hsüeh t'u 鬧學圖
nei 內
nei-hsün 內訓
Nei-ko ta-hsüeh-shih 內閣大學士
Nei-tsê 內則
Ni Yüan-lu 倪元璐

nien-p'u 年譜

Niu Yün-chên 牛運震

nü-chiao 女教

nü chiao-shih 女教師

Nü-chieh 女誡

Nü Hsiao-ching 女孝經

Nü Hsiao-êrh yü 女小兒語

nü hsien-shêng 女先生

nü-hsüeh 女學

nü-hung 女紅

nü-kung 女工

Nü Lun-yü 女論語

nü-shu 女塾

nü shu-shêng 女書生

nü shu-shih 女塾師

nü-tzû wu-ts'ai pien-shih tê 女子無才
便是德

Nuo Cha 哪吒

Nuo Cha nao-hai 哪吒鬧海

o-chih 惡汁

o-k'ou-ch'uang 鵝口瘡

ou-ju 嘔乳

Ou-t'u 嘔吐

Pai-chia hsing 百家姓

pai-tzû t'u 百子圖

Pan Chao 班昭

pang-t'ou ch'u hsiao-tzû 棒頭出孝子

Pao-kuo yü ssû-ch'in 報國與思親

pao nei 暴內

Pao Shih-ch'ên 包世臣

p'ao-tzû 泡子

Pao-ying ch'üan-shu 保嬰全書

pao-ying hui 保嬰會

Pao-ying ts'o-yao 保嬰撮要

pei (a child) 卑

pei (inferior) 卑

Pei-chi ch'ien-chin yao-fang 備急千金
要方

Pei-ching-lou 北井樓

pei-yu (junior) 卑幼

Peking 北京

Pên-ch'ao chi-shih 本朝記事

pên-t'u hsin-li hsüeh 本土心理學

P'êng 彭

p'i 癖

P'i Hsi-jui 皮錫瑞

pi hsieh-o 避邪惡

p'i wei 脾胃

pien-chêng 變蒸

Ping-t'a mêng-hên lu 病榻夢痕錄

Po Chü-i 白居易

p'o-shang-fêng 破傷風

pu 哺

pu-fan shêng-shui 不犯生水

pu-ju (refusing to nurse) 不乳

pu-ju (nursing and infant feeding)
哺乳

pu êrh 哺兒

pu êrh fa 哺兒法

pu hui 不慧

pu-p'ing 不平

pu pu-chieh 哺不節

pu ssû huang ching 不死黃精

P'u-chi fang 普濟方

p'u-chu 譜主

P'u Hsüeh-fêng 浦薛鳳

san-chao hsi-êrh 三朝洗兒

San-kuo yen-i 三國演義

San-pai-ch'ien 三百千

San-tzû ching 三字經

sang 桑

se 色

Shang (dynasty) 商

shang (prematurely deceased) 殤

Shangtung 山西

Shansi 山東

shao chê chih shih 少者之事

Shao Chin-han 邵晉涵

shao-hsiao k'o 少小科

Shao-hsiao ying-ju fang 少小嬰孺方

Shao Hsing-chung 邵行中

shao-nien 少年

Shao Nien-lu 邵念魯

shên 神

Shên Chao-lin 沈兆霖

shên-ch'i shêng　腎氣盛

Shên Ts'ai　沈彩

shên-t'ung　神童

Shên Yu-lung　沈猶龍

shêng　升

Shêng-chi ching　聖濟經

Shêng-chi tsung-lu　聖濟總錄

shêng-hsia t'u　生下吐

shêng ju ch'êng-jên　生如成人

shêng-mu　生母

shêng pu-ju ssû　生不如死

shêng-shui　生水

Shensi　陝西

shih　詩

Shih chi　史記

Shih ching　詩經

shih-k'ou　拭口

Shih-k'ou fa　拭口法

shin-lin chia-hsün　石林家訓

shih wu ta-hai　事無大害

shou-man　手慢

Shou-shih pao-yüan　壽世保元

shou-t'ang　熟湯

Shu　書

Shu ching　書經

shu-mu　庶母

shu-shih　塾師

Shü-p'u　須浦

Shuang-chieh-t'ang yung-hsün　雙節
　堂庸訓

shui-ching　睡驚

so-tu　鎖肚

Ssû-k'u ch'üan-shu　四庫全書

ssû-liu fêng　四六風

Ssû-ma Kuang　司馬光

Ssû-shih tzû-shu　四十自述

Ssû shu　四書

Su-chou　蘇州

Su Hsing　蘇興

su-ju　宿乳

Su-pei　蘇北

Sui　隋

sui　歲

Sui-T'ang　隋唐

Sun (family name)　孫

Sun Ch'i-fêng　孫奇逢

Sun Hsing-yen　孫星衍

Sun Ssû-miao　孫思邈

Sun wu k'ung　孫悟空

Sung　宋

Szechwan　四川

Ta-i (village)　大義

ta-i　大意

ta-wo　大我

Ta hsüeh　大學

t'ai-ching　胎癥

Tai Ch'uan-hsien　戴傳賢

t'ai-fêng　胎風

t'ai-i chü　太醫局

t'ai-i shu　太醫署

t'ai-i yüan　太醫院

t'ai-i yüan-shih　太醫院士

T'ai-p'ing shêng-hui fang　太平聖惠方

t'ai-tu　胎毒

T'aiping　太平

Tan-t'u　丹徒

tan tou-shih chih　淡豆豉汁

t'an-chi　痰疾

T'an Ssû-t'ung　譚嗣同

T'ang　唐

t'ang (soup)　湯

T'ang Chên　唐甄

T'ang Chieh-t'ai　唐階泰

t'ang-t'ou ko-chüeh　湯頭歌訣

T'ao (family name)　陶

t'ao (peach)　桃

T'êng-wang-ko　滕王閣

ti-mu　嫡母

ti-tzû　弟子

Ti-tzû chih　弟子職

Ti-tzû kuei　弟子規

T'iao-hsieh　調燮

t'ien　天

t'ien-chên　天真

t'ien-k'uei　天癸

Ting Wên-chiang　丁文江

ting-yu　丁憂

tou 斗
tou-fu 豆腐
tsa 雜
tsa-shui 雜水
Ts'ai T'ing-k'ai 蔡廷鍇
Ts'ai Yüan-p'ei 蔡元培
tsao 竈
tsao-hui 早慧
tsao-nien hui-i 早年回憶
Ts'ao Hsüeh-ch'in 曹雪芹
Tsê-ju-mu 擇乳母
Ts'ên Yü-ying 岑毓英
Tsêng Chi-fên 曾紀芬
Tsêng Chi-tsê 曾紀澤
Tsêng Kuo-fan 曾國藩
Tsêng Shih-jung 曾世榮
Tso Tsung-t'ang 左宗棠
tso-tui 作對
tso wan 作頑
ts'o-k'ou 撮口
tsu-p'u 族譜
ts'u-hsin 粗心
Ts'ui Hsüeh-ku 崔學古
Ts'ui Shu 崔述
ts'un 寸
tsun-chang 尊長
ts'ung-pien fa 蔥鞭法
Tu 杜
tu-shu 讀書
t'u-ju 吐乳
tuan-ch'i 斷臍
Tuan-ch'i fa 斷臍法
Tuan-ch'i lun 斷臍論
Tuan Hsi-p'êng 段錫朋
tuan-ju 斷乳
tuan-ju fa 斷乳法
tuan-ju fang 斷乳方
Tuan Yü-ts'ai 段玉裁
Tung Chi 董汲
Tung Hsün 董恂
t'ung 童
T'ung chien 通鑑
t'ung-hsin 童心
T'ung-hsin shuo 童心說

t'ung-hsin wei-min 童心未泯
T'ung-mêng hsün 童蒙訓
T'ung-mêng hsü-chih 童蒙須知
t'ung-nien 童年
t'ung-pien fa 通便法
t'ung-tzû 童子
t'ung-yao 童謠
tzû 子
Tzû-chih t'ung-chien 資治通鑒
Tzû-fu tsê-shan tsei ên chih ta-chê
　　子父責善，賊恩之大者
tzú-k'o 自課
tzú-p'an 字盤
tzú-shu 自述
tzû-sun wan-tai yung pao-yung 子孫
　　萬代永保用
tzû-ting 自訂
tz'u (lyrics) 詞
tz'u (compassion) 慈
tz'u-hang 慈航
Tz'u-yu hsin-ch'uan 慈幼心傳
Tz'u-yu lun 慈幼論

wai 外
Wai-t'ai mi-yao fang 外台秘要方
Wan Ch'üan 萬全
Wan-li 萬曆
Wang Ch'i 王緝
Wang Ch'ung-chih 王崇植
Wang Fu 王符
Wang Hsien-ch'ien 王先謙
Wang Hsin 王鑫
Wang Hui-tsu 汪輝祖
Wang Juo-fei 王若飛
Wang K'ai-yün 王闓運
Wang K'ang-nien 汪康年
Wang K'ên-t'ang 王肯堂
Wang Kuang-ch'i 王光圻
Wang Li-ming 王立明
Wang Luan 王鑾
Wang Ming-shêng 王鳴盛
Wang Nien-sun 王念孫
Wang P'ing 王平
Wang San-fêng 王三峰

Wang Ta-lun　王大綸
Wang T'ao　王燾
Wang T'ung-chao　王統照
Wang Tuan-shu　王端淑
Wang Tz'u-fêng　王次峰
Wang Yang-ming　王陽明
Wang Yin-chih　王引之
Wang Ying-lin　王應麟
Wei (rivers)　渭
wei　唯
Wei Chih-hsiu　魏之琇
Wei Hsi　魏禧
Wei I-lin　危亦林
Wei Yüan　魏源
Wên-hsien t'ung-k'ao　文獻通考
Wu Ch'êng-ên　吳承恩
Wu Ch'ien　吳謙
Wu-chiang　吳江
Wu-chin　武進
Wu ching　五經
Wu-chung i-kuei　五種遺規
Wu Fang　巫妨
wu-hou　無後
wu-hsü　戊戌
wu-i chih-shih　無益之事
wu-i wei-jên　無以為人
wu-kên t'ang　五根湯
Wu Li　吳歷
Wu-shih hsing lüeh　五世行略
wu-tsang chêng-chih　五臟證治
Wu Wei-yeh　吳偉業
wu-wu　戊午
Wung Shu-yüan　翁叔元
Wung T'ung-ho　翁同龢

yang　陽
Yang Chi-shêng　楊繼盛
Yang Fang　楊芳
Yang Jên-shan　楊仁山
yang-k'o　瘍科
Yang Kuei-fei　楊貴妃
Yang Tao-lin　楊道霖
Yao Ming-shui　姚明水
Yao Ying　姚瑩

yeh-yen pai-shih　野言稗史
yen-chih fa　燕脂法
Yen Hsi-chai　顏習齋
Yen Hsiu　嚴修
Yen Juo-chü　閻若璩
Yen-shih chia-hsün　顏氏家訓
yen-shih ch'u kao-t'u　嚴師出高徒
Yen Sung　嚴嵩
Yen Yüan　顏元
yin　陰
Yin Chao-yung　殷兆鏞
Ying-chi　應箕
ying-hsi t'u　嬰戲圖
Yin Hui-i　尹會一
Yin Kung　尹公
Ying-t'ung lei-ts'ui　嬰童類萃
Ying-t'ung pai-wên　嬰童百問
Ying-wei　應尾
yin-yang　陰陽
yin-yang yu-pieh　陰陽有別
yin-yu p'o-shang êrh kan-fêng　因有
　　破傷而感風
Yu　幼
yu-hsüeh　幼學
Yu-hsüeh ku-shih ch'iung-lin　幼學故
　　事瓊林
Yu hsün　幼訓
yu-i　幼醫
yu-k'o　幼科
Yu-k'o chin-chên　幼科金鍼
Yu-k'o chun-shêng　幼科準繩
Yu-k'o fa-hui　幼科發揮
Yu-k'o fa-hui hsü　幼科發揮序
Yu-k'o lei-ts'ui　幼科類萃
Yu-k'o tsa-ping hsin-fa yao-chüeh
　　幼科雜病心法要訣
yu-kuo　有過
yu-mêng　幼蒙
yu ts'ung-huei　幼聰慧
yu-tzû　幼子
Yu-yu chi-ch'êng　幼幼集成
Yu-yu hsin-shu　幼幼新書
yü (elm)　榆
yü　俞

Yü-êrh 浴兒
Yü-êrh fa 浴兒法
Yü-fu hsing 鬻婦行
yü-hêng 玉衡
Yü Hsiao-ming 余嘯溟
Yü-ku p'ien 鬻孤篇
Yü Kung 庾公

Yü Ta-fu 郁達夫
Yü-ying chia-mi 育嬰家秘
Yü Yüeh 俞樾
Yüan 元
Yüan Mei 袁枚
yün-hsieh 蘊邪
Yung-lo ta-tien 永樂大典

Index

Note: Page references in italics refer to illustrations. Page references followed by the letter *n* refer to notes.